# The Early Childhood Curriculum

D1379180

Based on research that demonstrates the powerful advantages of ....  he curriculum while providing inquiry opportunities, *The Early Childhood Curriculum* shows how to make such an approach work for all children, preschool through the primary grades. The text demonstrates how to confidently teach using inquiry-based methods that address the whole child, while also meeting and exceeding academic standards. Offering a foundation in early childhood theory, philosophy, research, and development, the second edition of this unique textbook helps future teachers, as well as current educators, understand the "why" of curriculum in early childhood and invests them with the skills they need to move from simply following a script to knowledgeably creating curricula on their own.

Since each curricular subject has its own integrity, there is a chapter for each discipline, grounding the reader in the essentials of the subject in order to foster knowledgeable and effective integration. The second edition of *The Early Childhood Curriculum* includes information on the most recent trends in national curriculum standards, particularly in regard to the Common Core State Standards Initiative and the Next Generation Science Standards. Coupled with this information are practical suggestions for meeting standards while still providing young learners with a truly child-centered educational experience. Chapters contain real-life vignettes that demonstrate inquiry and integration in practice. The entire text reflects the philosophy that the use of inquiry to seek and obtain information is one of the most valuable and powerful tools children can acquire along the way to becoming lifelong learners.

**Suzanne L. Krogh** is Professor Emerita of Elementary and Early Childhood Education at Western Washington University.

**Pamela Morehouse** is a retired Washington state elementary school teacher. She is an active trainer of teachers, recently returning from Pakistan where she volunteered to train teachers and administrators for The Citizens Foundation, a non-profit NGO. The text she used for the class was the first edition of the proposed book. She is currently developing a teacher-training program for Guatemala, centering on early literacy.

# The Early Childhood Curriculum

## Inquiry Learning Through Integration

### Second Edition

Suzanne L. Krogh

Pamela Morehouse

Routledge
Taylor & Francis Group

NEW YORK AND LONDON

First published 2014
by Routledge
711 Third Avenue, New York, NY 10017

and by Routledge
2 Park Square, Milton Park, Abingdon, Oxon OX14 4RN

*Routledge is an imprint of the Taylor & Francis Group, an informa business*

*Library of Congress Cataloging-in-Publication Data*
Krogh, Suzanne.
  The early childhood curriculum : inquiry learning through integration / by Suzanne L. Krogh, Pamela Morehouse.—Second edition.
    pages cm
  Includes bibliographical references and index.
  1. Early childhood education—Curricula—United States.   2. Curriculum planning—United States.
I. Morehouse, Pam.   II. Title.
  LB1139.4.K734   2014
  372.21—dc23        2013031748

ISBN: 978-0-415-82822-2 (pbk)
ISBN: 978-0-203-52162-5 (ebk)

Typeset in Minion
by Apex CoVantage, LLC

For Hayley, Connor, Decker, and Brenner, whose demonstrations of curiosity
and love of learning can be found throughout the pages of this book.
—Suzanne Krogh

To Megan and Andy, who continue to embrace wonder.
And to Welles, my forever support and teacher.
—Pam Morehouse

# CONTENTS

# PREFACE

In recent years, schooling in the United States has become increasingly prescriptive and regimented, with assessment issues taking center stage. As a result, the child as a whole often seems to be forgotten. This has become as true for early childhood education as for the elementary and secondary years. Yet compelling research argues for a child-centered approach to teaching young children, an approach that respects their inherent curiosity by devoting learning time to inquiry experiences, and an approach that replaces rigidly divided subject matter with cross-curricular study.

The purpose of this book is not only to share the research that demonstrates the efficacy of inquiry and integration, but to show how such an approach to early education can work. This book also provides a foundation in theory, philosophy, research, and child development. This foundation is essential, because it is only when teachers know *why* they teach as they do that they can move from simply following a script to knowledgeably creating curricula on their own. And when teachers become skilled in creating curriculum on their own, they can more aptly make it child centered and child relevant and meaningful.

This second edition of *The Early Childhood Curriculum: Inquiry Learning Through Integration* presents the newest curriculum standards, such as the Common Core Curriculum Standards in Math and English Language Arts, as well as the Next Generation Science Standards. As in the first edition, there are suggestions for meeting such standards while still providing extensive inquiry learning opportunities to curious young learners. The textbook has been divided into three sections. Part One provides an overview of inquiry-based learning and curriculum integration. The section's five chapters cover background history and theory; environment and management; assessment issues; and themes, units, and investigative projects. Part Two's seven chapters cover each subject of the curriculum individually and discuss practical ways they can be integrated with each other. Finally, a single chapter provides the focus of Part Three. Essentially, this chapter is our own passionate position statement in which we share our hopes and dreams with our readers.

The authors of this curriculum text have extensive experience related to early childhood teaching, writing, and research. Suzanne, a professor emerita at Western Washington University, has taught young children and adults in five states and Washington, DC, as well as in Japan, Spain, Bosnia, and most recently, South Korea. Currently, she is on the governing board of a childcare and learning center, volunteering her teaching assistance in its two-year-old classroom. She has written extensively on integrating the curriculum for preschool and primary grades.

Pam, a retired elementary school teacher, studied at Lilian Katz and Sylvia Chard's institute on the Project Approach and has given workshops and presentations nationally on inquiry-based learning. She recently went to Karachi, Pakistan to train teachers of a non-profit group on ways to integrate the curriculum using no-cost, low-cost materials. She is currently developing teacher-training and basic literacy programs for non-profits in Guatemala, while also taking on the role of a "student" as she challenges herself to become fluent in Spanish.

As you read through our last chapter and reflect on the magnitude of inquiry-based learning, you will see why we so devoutly believe in Nelson Mandela's words: "Education is the most powerful weapon which you can use to change the world."

# Part One

## Inquiry-Based Learning and Curriculum Integration: An Overview

Learning through inquiry begins at birth as infants explore their new environment and the people in it. Children learn more in their first few years of life than they will in any other development phase. They learn through continual inquiry and observation using all their senses, coupled with encouragement and modeling of adults. Would it be worthwhile to adapt this model of education to the school setting? Indeed, early childhood educators have traditionally held this view and provided their young charges with guided exploration using a curriculum that integrates subject areas. Despite the evidence that inquiry-based, integrated learning leads to maximum growth, there are often forces that work against such an approach. We are now living in such a time with an accountability movement that has led to widespread standardized testing and formulaic approaches to teaching even very young children. For most early childhood teachers, it is a struggle to maintain the kind of teaching they believe, observe, and know works most effectively.

The primary purpose of this textbook is to demonstrate that such teaching can still be done. It is grounded philosophically in your authors' belief that inquiry-based learning throughout the integrated curriculum is essential to preparing young children to live safely, productively, and harmoniously in a global community on a planet whose very survival is at stake. In the final chapter, we delve into this topic at some length, and you are invited to read the last chapter first if you like. (It won't ruin the plot. We promise.)

In the first chapter of Part One, you will be provided with background information about inquiry learning and curriculum integration: current views and the history behind them. Chapter 2 discusses the importance of the classroom environment, not only the physical surroundings but also the social-emotional aspects of it, along with implications for teaching methods and classroom management. Assessment and evaluation are the topics of Chapter 3. Assessments—before, during, and after teaching—are critical to good curriculum development, but in today's climate of high stakes testing, these activities take on new and often stressful importance. Chapter 4 describes how themes and units can connect curricular subjects, and the pros and cons of doing so. And finally, Chapter 5 discusses why student questions are vital to student learning and how such questions can facilitate learning connections. This chapter also provides the framework of an inquiry-based learning project along with the rationale for using inquiry learning throughout the integrated curriculum.

# 1

## AN INTRODUCTION TO CURRICULUM INTEGRATION AND INQUIRY LEARNING

*The object of education is to prepare the young to educate themselves throughout their lives.*
—Robert Maynard Hutchins

After reading this chapter you should be able to:

- Describe the historical events and people behind today's early childhood education;
- Explain the various theories of child development and their sources;
- Define the concepts of integrated curriculum and inquiry learning.

Take a moment to visualize a very small boy and an equally small girl playing happily in a sandbox. Watch the boy as he places several empty containers on the side of the sandbox and then realizes for the first time in his life that he can line them up from smallest to largest. "Look!" he exclaims with excitement. "Look what I did!" His friend, however, ignores him because she is busy with her own realization: If she picks up a handful of sand it will stay put unless she opens her fingers. Furthermore, how fast the sand drains out is dependent on the spread of the fingers.

Through this playful experience, two young children have each learned something, although it might be difficult to categorize into which school subjects their learning would fit. It would also be difficult to plan in advance the precise form their sandbox activity should take or the specific learning goals appropriate to the experience. This is frequently the case with young children's learning. It doesn't fit into neat categories of subject matter; neither is it planned from start to finish by a teacher or curriculum design team; nor is it generated from a commercially "canned" program; and it may be advanced most effectively through what adults might dismiss as "just child's play." Yet this kind of learning can be the most powerful for young children and it is the primary focus of this book.

For an example of what this kind of learning looks like, on a much grander scale, in a first-grade classroom, take a moment to enter room 4's Pet Shop. The Pet Shop was developed by young learners under the direction of a teacher well versed in teaching in a manner that embraces learning through inquisitiveness.

Room 4's classroom menagerie of worms, turtles, fish, frogs, and a rabbit was a continual source of wonder and amusement. These animals were also the catalyst for animated chats and questions students had about pets in their own homes or in homes of friends and relatives. The teacher observed the children's interest in pets. After making a mental note of the various academic subject skills that could be integrated in a study of pets, the teacher proposed to the students that perhaps "pets" would be a good topic to pursue.

The young investigators enthusiastically embraced the idea of discovering more about pets. However, after doing sufficient research on pets—after they ascertained, from various resources, the care pets need, what and how much they eat, pets' different heights and weights, their degrees of friendliness, and so on—the students enthusiastically declared that they were prepared to research pet shops as well. Through the course of the next week the students, with guidance from the teacher, constructed a "What We Know About Pet Shops" chart followed by a "What We Want To Find Out About Pet Shops" chart and

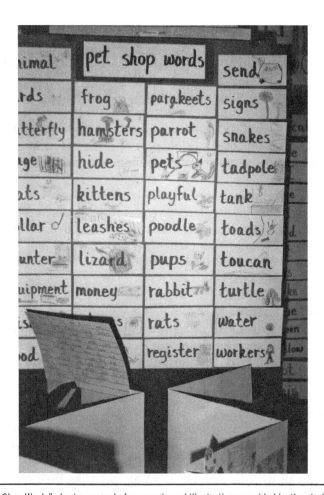

**Figure 1.1** This "Pet Shop Words" chart was made from words and illustrations provided by the students.

a "Pet Shop Words" chart to use in their writings in conjunction with their "Pet Verbs" and "Pet Adjectives" charts.

Following a trip to the local pet store, where many of the student-generated questions and wonders about pets and pet stores were answered and addressed, the now pet-shop-savvy young learners constructed the "Room 4 Pet Shop" in a corner of their classroom. It took weeks to fine-tune the pet shop to be as realistic as possible. The completed shop included several sections: animal care products alongside student-produced brochures titled "How to Keep Your Pet Healthy and Happy"; animal food in varying sizes and weights in student-made cans and bags; "guaranteed-to-make-your-pet-happy" student-designed pet toys and supplies; and an area with a cash register and a wipe-off schedule board for the pet shop workers.

Once the "Room 4 Pet Shop" was officially opened, the room 4 students, as well as students from other classes, parents, the principal, and other school district personnel would occasionally come to shop, peruse the merchandise, or seek information. Everyone—even some very happy pets—benefited from the kind of learning the room 4 investigators used in order to find out more about pets and pet shops.

**Figure 1.2** A partial glimpse into the "Room 4 Pet Shop."

Young children are, by nature, curious about the world around them. Providing opportunities for them to inquire and explore will, therefore, generally engage their interest. It should be noted that the world around does not frequently divide itself into curriculum segments such as math or science or social studies. More frequently, it is an integrated combination of society's definition of subject matter. This indicates that, for young children (and for many older ones and adults as well), the most effective approach to truly successful learning is one of using inquiry through an integrated curriculum.

When children are provided meaningful opportunities to use their curiosity and to pose questions in order to gain in-depth knowledge of a topic, it is termed *investigative learning, inquiry-based learning,* or simply *inquiry learning.* When skills from more than one curricular subject area are drawn together and connected in purposeful ways it is called *curriculum integration.* This text emphasizes the ways that children's natural curiosity, the backbone of inquiry, can be infused throughout the integrated academic subjects.

Research in recent years has demonstrated the powerful advantages of integrating the curriculum while providing inquiry opportunities (Audet, 2005; Copple & Bredekamp, 2009; Etim, 2005; Helm, 2012; Hyson, 2008; Vars & Beane, 2000). At the same time, however, state and national requirements have moved schools, and even early childhood centers, in the opposite direction, all in the name of making sure that no child is left behind. In other words, as described above, programs are canned, come from a curriculum design team, or follow teacher-made plans that offer no room for child direction or creativity.

Does any caring teacher—or parent, caregiver, legislator, governor, president— intentionally set out to leave children behind? Most assuredly, those who care about and for children have the best intentions when they make decisions about their education. However, the best route to ensuring children's school success is the subject of longstanding, and sometimes intense, debate. The debates are always a reflection of the times and people's responses to them. For example, when in the 1950s the Soviets began to win the race into space, American education became much more structured and "basic," even in early childhood settings. Later, the counterculture movement of the 1960s and 1970s led to a view of early education that was more focused on the young child's social and psychological needs. It is easy to forget, when we are in the middle of developing a new and seemingly progressive view of early education, that theory, research, and practice are all influenced to a degree by the politics of the time.

Thus, as we, in the early years of the 21st century, labor to leave no child behind, even labeling national legislation after this sentiment, the ways in which policy makers choose to accomplish this feat are most certainly influenced by today's societal expectations and current politics—just as the case was in previous decades and centuries. For the early 21st century, the national No Child Left Behind (NCLB) legislation of the George W. Bush administration has meant a move toward more structured education accompanied by continual testing to ensure progress. The Barack Obama administration's adaptation of NCLB, known as Race to the Top (RTT), continues to focus on structure and testing. Meanwhile, the most recent work of early childhood educators and researchers has shown that most young children thrive best when their learning is at least somewhat less structured and more personalized, and testing is kept to a minimum. It is the tension between these two views of how best to leave no child behind that this book addresses. Accountability is here to stay—at least for the foreseeable future—but it is possible to provide young children with an education that is engaging, exciting, and meaningful to their lives while ensuring that they do well on the necessary assessments.

In the following section, we give a brief history of the development of this most recent view of the way young children learn best.

## A BRIEF HISTORY

In writing about the history of curriculum integration in American schools, Daniel Tanner (1989) referred to its development and acceptance as a *struggle*. Indeed, despite the awareness on the part of many educators that this is the way in which children of all ages learn most naturally, such integration disappears from the curriculum more often than it appears.

At the beginning of the 20th century, public schools focused primarily on providing children with the basic skills they needed to join the workforce brought about by the Industrial Revolution. The rise of laboratory schools connected with universities, particularly the one begun by John Dewey at the University of Chicago, brought about a major shift that had nationwide implications. Dewey's view of providing basic public education for the workforce was that it fostered an elite, privately educated class and an underclass of the undereducated and uninformed masses. This situation, he argued, was untenable for a democratic society. The progressive and experimental education he introduced included an integrated curriculum that was related to real life, and it gained widespread popularity (Mayhew & Edwards, 1966; Tanner, 1989).

Various interpretations of Dewey's views eventually led to a watering down of a curriculum that should have been challenging and exciting. By the end of World War II, the desire for lower-tax support for the schools soon linked with Soviet leadership in space to return the curriculum to fragmented basics. It was argued that Dewey's progressive curriculum had been responsible for American education falling behind that of the Soviets, who were thus able, in 1957, to soar first into space. Therefore, the argument continued, it was apparent that a much more basic elementary education was needed along with specifically defined subject areas in secondary schools.

For about a decade, university scholars in mathematics and science focused on developing updated materials and curricula for children of all ages. There was little or no intent to integrate math and science curricula or to relate content to the real world. "The nature of the learner was recast in the form of a budding scholar-specialist, while the relevance of the curriculum to the life of the learner and the life of a free society was shunted aside" (Tanner, 1989, p. 9). In the 1960s, it became obvious that this approach was not working. For younger children, the British primary schools seemed appealing. There in large classrooms, children of varying ages would work together on projects that crossed the curriculum. Without regard for the many years that had gone into developing this model, or for the training that should be invested in teachers unfamiliar with it, American schools quickly tore down walls and attempted to replicate the British program. Again, success was elusive and backlash inevitable.

The result was that much of the 1970s and 1980s was a time of "back to basics" in which children spent most of their days plodding through worksheets and workbooks. Gone were all but the most basic of manipulative materials; toys often disappeared altogether. Accountability was important, so teachers, even of very young children, found themselves teaching to the test. The financial price for such a pared down and basic education was right, but the cost was high in terms of competitiveness. International comparisons showed that American children, despite the U.S. focus on testing and preparations for it, did not do as well academically as most other nations. Particularly galling was the leadership of the Japanese, whom Americans had once defeated in war and helped bring back from wartime devastation and poverty. Observation of the Japanese curriculum, however, showed that Japan's view of how young children learn had much more in common with the American John Dewey than with the American perception that young Japanese children simply worked harder at their drills and worksheets. The Japanese, along with the British, had national expectations but flexible approaches to young children's learning.

At the same time as the back to basics movement was taking place in K–12 public education, however, something quite different was happening in federally funded preschool education. In 1964, as part of his War on Poverty, President Lyndon Johnson (1908–1973) helped initiate a federally funded summer program for children of poverty headed to kindergarten that September. It quickly became apparent that, while this new "Project Head Start" program held promise, it needed to be extended to a full year. In the years since then, Head Start has grown to include several programs related to early education as well as parent education programs.

The resulting success of the original Head Start programs has been studied from their beginnings and into the 21st century. Of some importance has been the fact that, because federal funding was given to varying models of early education, it was possible to compare the models' approaches to education on children's progress. In the early years, it was demonstrated that children's progress in any of the programs was initially worth the investment in Head Start, no matter the model. By the third grade, however, the academic advantages began to fade. Funding has been in peril ever since, with some federal budget years more problematic than others.

However, more in-depth research has continued over the years with some surprising and positive results, particularly in the 1990s, as we shall see. It is these longitudinal studies, particularly as applied to one of the original Head Start models, which are most important to this textbook. This model, Perry Preschool program, in Ypsilanti, Michigan, was already in place when President Johnson took office and found itself uniquely positioned to become part of the nationwide funding of early learning. The focus of preschools in Ypsilanti, as well as nationally, was on preschool-age children living in poverty. As ongoing research demonstrated the benefits of the Perry program, its curriculum and teaching methodology became widely known until by the 1990s, more than a third of all Head Start programs were using what is now known as the High/Scope curriculum (Schweinhart, Barnes, & Weikart, 1993).

Based in part on the constructivist theories of Jean Piaget (1948) as well as on the philosophy of Developmentally Appropriate Practices put forth by the National Association for the Education of Young Children (NAEYC) (Copple & Bredekamp, 2009), the High/Scope program advocates for children's self-initiated learning. As stated by the High/Scope Educational Research Foundation, "Effective programs use explicitly stated, developmentally appropriate active-learning curricula that support children's self-initiated learning activities" (Schweinhart, Barnes, & Weikart, 1993). This position from High/Scope was based on the results of a longitudinal study from the early 1990s, when the original Perry Preschool children had been followed to age 27. As compared to the control group that had also been in place from the 1960s, Perry preschool graduates were more likely to have significantly higher monthly earnings, more likely to have completed more years of schooling, less likely to have been placed in special education, less likely to have children out of wedlock, and found to have significantly fewer arrests.

To explain the long-term effects of the High/Scope approach, the study's authors argued that, "Realizing they have the ability to achieve classroom success, children believe and act accordingly, thereby developing a stronger commitment to schooling" (Schweinhart, Barnes, & Weikart, 1993, p. 18). They went on to say that when teachers recognize children's proficiency, they have higher expectations and the children rise to meet them. Self-initiated, active, and developmentally appropriate learning is at the base of the inquiry learning model proposed by this textbook.

In the 1980s, two developments of importance to American early education presented themselves: (1) the introduction, by Lilian Katz and Sylvia Chard, of a model of inquiry learning that integrates the curriculum called the Project Approach and (2) the discovery that, for more than 50 years, the Reggio Emilia region in northern Italy had been developing an approach to early education that incorporated both inquiry learning and curriculum integration. Each of these developments is important enough to be treated in some detail and you will read about them in upcoming sections. First, however, the most recent developments in federal education will be summarized.

In 2001, the federal No Child Left Behind Act (NCLB) was passed, referred to by its supporters as "a landmark educational reform initiative designed to improve student achievement and change the culture of schools in America" (Essex, 2006, p. 1). The act was created to raise expectations and standards in all school systems across the country, particularly in regard to reading and math. For K–3 teachers, this meant requiring that all their children learn to read, learning to assess children's progress, and knowing how to alter their teaching methods if sufficient progress was not being made. Grant money was provided, through competition, to districts with low-scoring children in poverty. This "Reading First" program required schools to use "scientifically based instructional programs" (p. 32). On the surface, this would seem to be a reasonable requirement. However, controversy arose regarding the research that created the definition of *scientific*, with some reading experts concerned that the focus on technical aspects of reading left out any concern for understanding or enjoyment of reading.

Then, a new president was elected and new Department of Education leadership installed. Under President Barack Obama, states were provided opportunities to retain their funding while not engaging in all the requirements of NCLB. For early childhood, a new program under the Obama education initiative, Race to the Top, provided a competition for grant money that included far more than reading instruction. It was expected that recipients would be states "that are leading the way with ambitious yet achievable plans for implementing coherent, compelling, and comprehensive early learning education reform" (U.S. Department of Education, 2012, n.p.). The Race to the Top—Early Learning Challenge made its first awards in late 2011. Just nine states were the recipients of funding designed to increase the number of low-income infants, toddlers, and preschool-aged children in high quality programs. As this is written, planning for the nine states is getting underway.

With the federal government supportive of flexibility and innovation, and state early childhood reformers supportive of developmentally appropriate practices, Race to the Top programs may emerge that truly lead early education forward in positive ways. Most certainly, one aspect of this will include curriculum integration.

### The Rediscovery of Curriculum Integration

Curriculum integration has existed in a number of forms, moving in and out of fashion, most notably in the 1890s, 1920s, and again in the 1930s and 40s (Beane, 1995). It has been applied at many levels, from preschool through university, thus leading to a variety of models. Here, in table form, is a collection of the models. Included are those that might be considered by educators of young children; not included are others that would only apply to high school and college (adapted and expanded from Fogarty, 1991).

In this text, Chapters 4 and 5 will expand on these descriptions and examples, and provide explanations of ways to try some of the ideas yourself. Although a number of curriculum integration models have been used at various levels of education, and in a variety of countries, it has been to Italy that we have turned in recent years for early childhood inspiration. The model that has evolved there over more than half a century is most closely related to "Immersed" in Table 1.1.

### Reggio Emilia Schools and Their Influence

In 1945, just days after the end of World War II, a young Italian middle school teacher by the name of Loris Malaguzzi went out for an exploratory bike ride near his home in the northern Italy province of Reggio Emilia. He had not gone far when he came upon a group of women washing the bricks of a bombed-out building. They explained to him that they planned to use the bricks to build a preschool for their young children and that the equipment and horses left behind by the fleeing Germans would fund the rest of the building. As yet they had no idea how to pay for a teacher, but they were confident that something would turn up. Malaguzzi was impressed with the women's zeal and creativity and returned many times to check on their progress. Eventually, other such schools were built and, by the 1960s, had become funded by municipal taxes that emerged from local, grassroots efforts by parents and interested others (Katz, 1993).

**Table 1.1** Models of Curriculum Integration

| Method of Integration | Description | Example for Early Childhood |
|---|---|---|
| Fragmented | Focus is on only one academic subject. | Children recite addition tables. |
| Nested | Skills are inserted within an academic subject. | A social studies project is designed to promote group work skills. |
| Themed | Several learning experiences are taught around a single theme. They may, or may not, include integration of curriculum areas. | A preschool class spends a week focusing on a specific color or animal. |
| Webbed | A single theme or topic is integrated throughout a number of academic subjects. | A scientific study of butterflies is expanded to include experiences in art, music, literature, etc. |
| Immersed | A class, group, or single child focuses on a topic of inquiry that incorporates several academic subjects. | Three or four children expand their study of a topic that the rest of the class has completed. The teacher provides support, but children self-direct as possible. |

While the act of building preschools out of the rubble of war is an impressive feat on its own, it is the approach to education within those schools that has been the focus of international attention. Malaguzzi retained his interest in and connection to the Reggio Emilia preschools (named for the place of origin) up until his death in 1994. He provided, in fact, the intellectual base on which were built the curriculum and teaching methodology. Not only he, but the teachers as well, continually looked to theory and research for their ideas. In the early years, they became especially influenced by John Dewey's ideas related to inquiry learning and integrated curriculum. These included inquiry projects based on children's real life interests. Another early influence was Jean Piaget and his theories of child development as well as his work with mathematics teaching. To Piaget, children did not learn mathematics best by drilling and memorizing, but by inquiring, discovering, and applying their findings to problems important to them. He even promoted a teaching methodology in which real-life problems were solved by young children before they were exposed to written numbers and predetermined mathematical processes (Piaget, 1948).

Making practical the abstract concepts of inquiry learning and integrated curriculum became the challenge, one that resulted in a project-based model. From the early days until the present, Reggio Emilia children have spent much of their time (but certainly not all of it) engaging in projects of their own creation. One of the best known, primarily because its whimsical attractiveness led to a video (Forman & Gandini, 1994), was an amusement park for birds. The children constructed models of various carnival attractions out of readily available materials. Although they had teacher assistance, the project was of their own design and creativity and of a size that made playing with the products manageable. That actual birds never showed up to ride the Ferris wheel or engage in other park activities bothered the children not at all.

At the end of the 1980s, the Reggio Emilia schools were recognized by like-minded educators from North America such as Lilian Katz and Sylvia Chard (2000), creators of the project approach to learning in the primary grades. Eventually, Katz, Chard, and other North Americans joined with representatives from the Reggio Emilia schools to introduce the Reggio model to the United States and Canada. It is highly important to realize that this did not mean the introduction of a patented, structured, replicable model. Reggio Emilia teachers have continued to study new theories and research, realizing that there is always something new to learn. In addition, what works for them in their society and culture might not be successfully transported to the United States. For example, a study of neighborhood shops and park areas would likely be quite different from one country to the next, or even from one area to another within a single country.

There are several important points to remember in considering the adoption of Reggio Emilia ideas for American early childhood learning: Much learning occurs through inquiry projects of children's creation; a curriculum should integrate subject matter to make learning meaningful; attention should be paid to local culture when adapting another country's or area's ideas; and there should be continual self-education on the part of teachers.

## DEEPER INTO THE THEORIES

At this point, we encourage our readers to emulate the scholarliness of the Reggio Emilia teachers by thinking more deeply about why so many early childhood educators believe that inquiry learning through curriculum integration is the most effective way to teach young children. The following overview of theories explicates the bases on which this book's ideas are built.

### The Emergence of Constructivism: Piaget

Any theory begins with the father or mother who originates it or most clearly or forcefully espouses it. Thus, the story of constructivism appropriately begins with the man who, in most educators' minds, is most closely tied to its origins. *Constructivism*, in this "father's" version, can be defined briefly as a theory of learning in which humans actively construct their own meaning of the world around them.

Jean Piaget (1896–1980) did not intend to spend his life studying children. As a child, a young man, and finally a briefly retired octogenarian, his interests lay in the mollusks that inhabited the lakes of western Switzerland. At the same time, his varied interests and broadly based intelligence led him to the exploration of other scientific fields.

After receiving his doctorate in biology, he studied and worked in France, standardizing IQ tests and interviewing children in an attempt to learn why similar ages gave similar wrong answers.

Returning to Switzerland, Piaget became director of studies at the Institut J. J. Rousseau in Geneva. His research there focused on various aspects of intellectual growth such as the concepts of space, time, number, language, logic, reasoning, and even morality. As each study evolved, so did Piaget's understanding of his early findings in Paris. There were, indeed, patterns of intellectual growth that were age related. Further, they could be divided into several stages that were found to hold true across races and cultures. Only the ages at which a stage was acquired might differ somewhat, depending on intelligence or the environment, while the sequence of the stages never varied.

Let's take a brief look at each of the four major periods, or stages, of child development according to Piaget. Within each of the four major stages there are sub-stages, some of which are also described. Some knowledge of Piaget's developmental theory is essential for teachers who wish to make competent decisions about curriculum and teaching methodology.

### Sensorimotor Period

Motor activities and the physical senses provide the primary means of learning in this first period. Its duration covers the first two years of life and begins with repetition of reflex actions such as sucking. Children then move on to coordinate some behavioral schemes to create intentional behaviors. When the period ends, they have enough understanding of the world that deliberate imitative behavior and true make-believe are possible.

During this period, children take their first steps in *decentering*, or moving out of their total focus on self. As very young infants they cannot distinguish themselves from others, but by the end of the period they have no trouble comprehending this kind of separation.

### Preoperational Period

As children enter preschool, they also enter the preoperational period. A major development is a new ability known as *symbolic functioning*. Children can now, with no difficulty, use one thing to symbolize another. In practical terms that means they can pretend a mud pie is really for lunch or a tricycle is their father's car. It is partly because of this ability that children's language now develops at such a rapid rate. Words are abstract utterances that symbolize objects, actions, and so on that may not be present.

Of course, there is still much that the child cannot do, and it is important for teachers to be aware of these limitations. For example, when sorting objects with varying attributes, the child can focus on only one variable at a time. This inability to focus more broadly Piaget called *centration*, or centering attention on just one attribute at a time. If sorting buttons, the child may put all the red ones together and all the white in a separate pile. She will not notice, however, that they could also have been divided into a pile of large and small buttons. This same limitation keeps her from successfully ordering objects from smallest to largest or relating parts to wholes.

Appearances can be deceiving, even to adults. For the preoperational child the problem is much more pronounced. If we were to take the piles of buttons the child had made and spread them into two rows of five buttons each, she would agree that the rows were equivalent—as long as they were equally spaced. But if we then spread out the red row to cover more territory, she would believe that now there were more red buttons.

Variations of the same lack of understanding occur if the child considers liquid or mass: Pouring from one shape container into another shape may make him think the amount of liquid has changed; changing the shape of a ball of clay may make him think that one has more clay in it than another of equal amount.

In language development, children center on their own need to communicate and assume that those around them know exactly what they mean, and they may respond with frustration when someone does not. Although their understanding of the rules of grammar is growing, they will not yet have a grasp of the exceptions that are a common part of the most everyday speech.

While the preoperational child is advancing impressively in making sense of the world, it is obvious that much is still not understood. Her intellectual perceptions are still bound by the most salient physical attributes of the objects she manipulates, and so far she is aware only of her own view of the world, assuming that everyone sees it as she does.

### Concrete Operational Period

As children move out of the preprimary years and into elementary school, they become adept at performing intellectual skills that were previously beyond their reach. They become more able to classify according to more than one variable, to rank order items in logical series, to understand that amounts of mass or liquid do not change just because their shape does, and to intellectually manipulate new and more complex relationships. Linguistic communication improves as children complete their basic understanding of grammar.

Again, it is important to mention what children cannot do. Although they have a much more mature understanding of many processes and relationships, it is still based on concrete reality. True abstraction is not yet possible, and learning takes place most successfully when concrete objects are present.

Although Piaget suggested that concrete operations emerge at about seven years of age, teachers can expect to see the first signs of development toward the end of kindergarten and sometimes before then. (In different cultures at different historical times, ages have varied, sometimes widely.)

### Formal Operational Period

The term *formal operations* signifies the ability to form abstract ideas, to formulate and test hypotheses, and to think reflectively. The period can begin as early as 11 years and continues into adulthood.

### Constructivist Theory: Vygotsky

Compatible with Piaget's view of development, but approaching it from a more social and less individualistic angle is another theory that can be called *constructivist*. Its origins are in the early days of the Soviet Union and emerged from the efforts of Lev Vygotsky (1896–1934) to create an approach to psychology that would complement the quickly evolving socialist culture. (Note that Piaget's views of development did incorporate social elements and Vygotsky's included individualism. Their differences in this regard were more a matter of emphasis.)

If he had been permitted to follow his early interests into adulthood, Lev Vygotsky would have studied literature, history, or philosophy at university. But he had been born a Jew in czarist Russia and teaching, the only career generally open to graduates of those programs, was closed to Jews. Instead, Vygotsky chose first to study medicine and, later, law. Nevertheless, he was eventually able to take classes in the subjects he loved by attending two universities at once. The restless intellectual received his law degree from Moscow University and, at the same time, graduated from Shaniavsky People's University where anticzarist professors taught and Jews were permitted to study what they chose.

The year of Vygotsky's graduation, 1917, was an important one in that it also encompassed the revolution that overthrew the czarist royalty and led to a Communist government throughout the emerging Soviet Union. With new laws permitting Jews many more freedoms, Vygotsky was able to join the faculty of the Psychological Institute in Moscow where he took the lead in developing a new theory of psychology compatible with emerging socialist views. Although he would agree with Piaget that children aid in constructing their own intelligence, Vyotsky emphasized more the influence of other children and adults. It is the social world that would provide children much input and guidance as they interacted with others. Referring to this world using socialist terminology, Vygotsky (1934) spoke of the child's *collective* (family, school, or peer group) as being critical to his or her development. Primarily when more knowledgeable others (parents, teachers, older children) provided teaching or other assistance, the child could then construct meaning of his or her own.

Sadly, Vygotsky developed tuberculosis while in his 20s. Despite his ill health, he continued to write and teach until his death at 38. Vygotsky's best known work, *Thought and Language* (1934) was, in fact, completed on his deathbed. Vygotsky's following ideas about child development and education have stood the test of time.

### Language Development

For Vygotsky, language emerges in infancy as a means of communication; in the preschool years, purposeful communicating with the self is added. Frequently, preschoolers can be observed talking out loud to themselves, a phenomenon that disappears with time. Vygotsky explained such development by saying that, as children observe older children and adults not talking to themselves, they learn to talk to themselves silently. Piaget, it should be noted, disagreed, saying that the phenomenon of *private speech* could be explained by young children's egocentrism.

### The Role of Instruction

Vygotsky's view of instruction differed greatly from Piaget's. While Piaget believed that the influential teacher should act merely as a facilitator, asking well-timed and appropriate questions to encourage children to continue learning on their own, Vygotsky thought otherwise. Teachers, in his view, should take a more proactive role and are essential to children's progress. Learning through inquiry was, however, valued by both men.

### The Zone of Proximal Development (ZPD)

This "zone" is where the teacher must lead children for the most effective learning. It is that space between what is already known and what would be over the children's heads. If the teacher understands each child sufficiently, it is possible to provide learning experiences that will take each one to that challenging but not frustrating place.

### Scaffolding

*Scaffolding* is not a term ever used by Vygotsky, but it is a concept he would recognize immediately because it describes for later followers a primary activity of teachers who aspire to help their students toward their ZPDs. Teachers provide the framework—scaffold—that children need by skillfully guiding, instructing, and supplying appropriate materials.

After his death, Vygotsky's work was repressed by a Stalinist government and the Cold War that ensured a lack of communication with the United States. Thus, while Piaget's ideas became widely known and accepted in America, Vygotsky's writings were not translated into English until the mid-1970s. Then, it was still more years before psychologists and educators began to see wisdom in a model of child development once based in a highly unpopular political system.

### Ego Development: Erikson

A third developmental theorist important to the views of teaching and learning contained in this book was Erik Erikson (1902–1994). Although he based his research and conclusions on the theories of Sigmund Freud, Erikson (1963) shifted emphasis from Freud's ideas of neurotic conflict to his own observations of ego development. He then placed the concept of ego development within a societal framework. He postulated that the ego goes through eight stages on its way from birth to full maturity. The first four of these are completed by the end of elementary school. At each stage there is a central crisis that must be resolved in some way before the next stage can be approached. This crisis consists of antagonistic social-emotional forces pulling the infant, child, or adult in opposing directions. One direction is affectively positive, the other negative. If the person resolves the conflicts in a positive way, his emotional and social life will be more successful. In the description of the first four stages that follows, the ages that are given are approximate.

### Stage 1: 0–12 Months

*Crisis: Trust versus Mistrust.* It is the mother's responsibility to provide the infant with sufficient sensitive care so that the infant feels secure in trusting her. An indication that this stage is developing positively is the baby's ability to let its mother leave the room, confident that she will come back.

### Stage 2: 12 Months–3 Years

*Crisis: Autonomy versus Shame and Doubt.* As the child becomes autonomous he learns to control his use of the toilet. He needs both assurance and guidance to "protect him against meaningless and arbitrary experience of shame and of early doubt" (Erikson, 1963, p. 252).

### Stage 3: 3–5 Years

*Crisis: Initiative versus Guilt.* The child has much energy and easily forgets failures. Tasks are taken on "for the sake of being active and on the move" (Erikson, 1963, p. 255). The child may feel guilt about some of the tasks he has in mind, particularly the desire to take the place of the same-sex parent.

### Stage 4: 6–12 Years

*Crisis: Industry versus Inferiority.* Children become industrious as they increase their skills, learn diligence, and apply themselves to their tasks. These capabilities, plus the ability and willingness to work with others, are necessary for success in school. With failure, a sense of inadequacy and inferiority may emerge.

## Motor Development and Physical Growth

In recent years, the emphasis in education has been primarily on cognitive growth and, to a lesser extent, on psychological and social elements. In addition, there has been a general decline in physical experiences, recess times, and availability of proper nutrition in American society and its schools and childcare centers. The physical dimension has been often neglected, although it is critical to the development of infants and young children. Therefore, in this text we devote significant attention to physical and motor development, as well as to incorporating kinesthetic aspects of learning throughout the book. Since young children learn so much through their kinesthetic experiences, and because they have difficulty concentrating on their learning without them, this focus must be an integral part of the curriculum.

Although there is agreement among theorists on the existence of motor development stages, there are slightly differing models. We use the one presented by David Gallahue (1982) and expanded on by Carl Gabbard (1992), which indicates four general phases that begin before the baby is born and end in the teen years.

### Reflexive Movement Phase

The fetus or the newborn infant learns during this stage by involuntary reactions to stimuli. These reactions are called *reflexes*, and by the time the infant is about four months old they are becoming more intentional. Sucking and rooting, both important for early survival, are examples. Others that have lifelong utility are sneezing, blinking, yawning, and coughing.

### Rudimentary Movement Phase

With the development of the brain, it is possible for the child to reject reflexes in favor of voluntary movement, although at first this skill is primitive and rudimentary. With practice, more body control, and stability, the infant gains the ability to lift head and chest, roll over, sit, stand, crawl, creep, and eventually take those first exciting steps alone.

*Fundamental Movement Phase*

This is the phase that concerns us most as early childhood educators, for it describes the motor development of children from the time they are two years old until they are seven. The movements that characterize the fundamental movement phase are fundamental for two reasons: They are basic rather than complex, and they form the necessary foundation for future development.

*Initial Stage.* In this initial stage of the fundamental movement phase, children make their "first goal-oriented attempts at performing a fundamental skill" (Gallahue, 1982, p. 46). These attempts are uncoordinated, badly sequenced, and off the proper rhythm. Generally, the observer can expect to see success in the development of simple skills such as walking up and down stairs, throwing a ball overhand, kicking a ball or rolling it, walking on tiptoe, building a tower of blocks, jumping in place or from a bottom step, running, and riding a tricycle (Skinner, 1979).

*Elementary Stage.* The elementary stage of the fundamental movement phase "involves greater control and better rhythmical coordination of fundamental movements" (Gallahue, 1982, p. 46). Achieving this stage depends largely on proper maturation. Advancing beyond it often requires some instruction, practice, or at least motivation. (Yes, without one or more of these, many adults never develop some skills beyond this stage.)

Children of four and five years are typically at this stage, although some skills may be achieved earlier. The observer may note skills developing such as doing somersaults, using scissors, dressing self (tying shoes may remain a problem), catching a ball with two hands, hopping easily on one foot, roller skating, riding a junior bicycle, possibly hitting a swinging ball, and a smoother control of body activity in general (Skinner, 1979).

*Mature Stage.* Achieving this stage means that children, ordinarily by the age of five, six, or seven, can produce "mechanically efficient, coordinated, and controlled performances" (Gallahue, 1982, p. 46). Over the years, general development takes place in three areas: manipulation (both gross and fine motor), stability (both while the body is still and during movement), and locomotion (moving through space). Within the acceptable range of accomplishment there is still room for differences.

Some mature skills that children should be expected to achieve include walking and running with total ease and control; jumping, hopping, galloping, sliding, leaping, and skipping with fluid motion and correct landings; climbing (ladders and so on) with good balance and body control; and correct throwing, catching, kicking, striking, rolling, trapping, volleying, and dribbling of balls.

*Sports-Related Movement Phase.* This final phase in the development of motor abilities begins at about age seven and continues through the high school years. "It is a period when basic locomotor, manipulation, and stability skills are progressively refined, combined, and elaborated upon in order that they may be used in increasingly demanding activities" (Gallahue, 1982, p. 46). At its most advanced stage athletes develop their most complex and specialized skills and demonstrate most strongly their preferences for specific types of sports.

The teacher of young children will, at the most, be exposed to children in the first of this phase's three stages; for that reason, it is the only stage we will discuss further.

*General (or transitional) stage.* This subsection initiates the Sports-Related Phase. It begins at age seven or eight and continues through the rest of elementary school. It is built on the preceding stage in that children bring to it the skills they have been perfecting and are now ready to incorporate into a variety of play activities and games. For example, the many ways children learned to jump in kindergarten can now be transferred to jumping rope; kicking a ball just for the fun of it carries over into the game of kickball; the act of running applies to relay races and other games.

It is important during the early years of this sports-related phase to ensure that the many skills learned in the previous phase are not lost through too much specialization too soon. If children are exposed to a large variety of games and activities, they will know the joy of performing competently and will build a base from which they can make later decisions about competitive sports or recreational activities.

It is important that teachers of young children be aware of the motor development stages of their students and the ways that are most appropriate to support their progress.

## HOW THEORY AND PHILOSOPHY INFLUENCE THE PROFESSION

The history of the Italian Reggio Emilia Schools demonstrates how theory and philosophy can provide the groundwork for an entire system of early childhood programs. In the United States, the impact of theory and philosophy is perhaps best demonstrated in the evolution of *developmentally appropriate practice* as defined and explicated by the National Association for the Education of Young Children (NAEYC).

In the mid-1980s, many leaders in early childhood education became increasingly concerned about the growing tendency to place "undue emphasis on rote learning and whole-group instruction of narrowly defined academic skills at the expense of more active learning approaches based on a broader interpretation of children's educational needs and abilities" (Bredekamp & Copple, 1997, p. v). In response, NAEYC published a series of position papers that, by 1987, had been expanded into book form as *Developmentally Appropriate Practice in Early Childhood Programs* (described in Copple & Bredekamp, 2009). Wide distribution of the book ensured that, to at least a degree, programs for children were revised, new research studies took place, and advocates for children were provided with ammunition to use in presentations to legislators, school officials, and others in authority.

To understand why the NAEYC position statements could have a nationwide positive impact, it is important to realize that the organization did not simply decide on its own what would be developmentally appropriate. Those involved in creating the statements were, themselves, active researchers, theorists, and practitioners, and many of their views were influenced by the people you have read about in this chapter. For example, the theories of human development suggested by Piaget, Vygotsky, Erikson, and Gallahue are all presented as viable. Here are a few quotations from the most recent edition of *Developmentally Appropriate Practice* (Copple & Bredekamp, 2009). Note that their sources are in the theories you have just read about.

- "Children develop best when they have secure, consistent relationships with responsive adults and opportunities for positive relationships with peers" (p. 13). (Piaget, Erikson, Vygotsky)
- "Development and learning occur in and are influenced by multiple social and cultural contexts . . . Every culture structures and interprets children's behavior and development in its own way" (p. 13). (Vygotsky; Edwards & Gandini, 1989, for Reggio Emilia)

- "Learning and development are most likely to occur when new experiences build on what a child already knows and is able to do and when those learning experiences also entail the child stretching a reasonable amount in acquiring new skills" (p. 10). (Piaget, Erikson, Vygotsky)

Based on such views as these, NAEYC has presented further positions regarding curriculum development. Here are a few that relate directly to this text.

- "Teachers consider what children should know, understand, and be able to do across the domains of physical, social, emotional, and cognitive development and across the disciplines . . ." (p. 20).
- "Teachers plan curriculum experiences that integrate children's learning *within* and *across* the domains (physical, social, emotional, cognitive) and the disciplines (including literacy, mathematics, social studies, science, art, music, physical education, and health" (p. 21).
- ". . . curriculum experiences . . . do not skim lightly over a great many content areas, but instead allow children to spend sustained time with a more select set" (p. 21).

*Developmentally Appropriate Practice in Early Childhood Programs* (2009) offers many more such positions as well as specific suggestions for teaching. Readers are encouraged to make use of this valuable resource in their work with young children.

## INTEGRATING THE CURRICULUM AND LEARNING THROUGH INQUIRY: THE ADVANTAGES

Advantages of curriculum integration and inquiry learning have been touched on above, but there are others as well. Here is a brief overview of the best arguments from the point of view of most early childhood specialists, including those who have contributed to NAEYC's ongoing research and writing.

- *Individual children and their own personal development are a focus.* As children inquire into topics of new or continuing interest to them, they grow in many unexpected ways, ways that no amount of legislation or prefabricated curriculum could suggest or predict. For example, materials designed for one set of skills might inspire children to create something that adults never dreamed of. Thus, inquiry learning benefits advanced learners by not tying them down to curriculum they have already outgrown and, at the same time, provides more reluctant learners with materials that are far more engaging than (frequently boring) catch-up drills.
- *Individual and group interests are also a focus.* Frequently, learning experiences in this approach are created at the direction of small or large groups of children as well as individuals. Young children may have interests that are somewhat unformed, or there may be learning opportunities that fit their interests but that they are unaware of. In either case, the teacher's role is to introduce the options and then help direct new learning explorations. Excitement for learning is generally the result.
- *Children are permitted to learn in their own natural way rather than through segmented, adult-derived subject matter.* Yes, there are times when an individual

curriculum subject is the focus of learning, even for very young children. It is also the case, however, that ordinarily the world is not so segmented. The natural state of young children is one of unbridled curiosity about everything they experience, and they will remain most enthusiastic about new experiences if adults don't insist on creating an academic overlay that stifles enthusiasm.

• *Children learn to take risks, make choices, be independent, and prepare to live in a democracy.* These four advantages have been placed in one category because they are all traditionally valued in our society, although we tend not to trust children to engage in them. Perhaps it is because they all require a bit—sometimes a lot—of courage and we hope to shield children from fear, failure, and even from just the fear of failure. But providing children with such opportunities in a safe environment gives them courage, while overcoming failure and watching themselves grow enhances self-esteem, far more than activities designed to promote self-esteem could ever do.

• *There are opportunities to learn through play while standards are still met.* Inquiry learning incorporates many playful activities, particularly when the curriculum is not devoted to single-subject learning. Teachers who plan for this kind of learning are alert to the standards that must be met and informally introduce them into the many kinds of activities the children engage in.

• *Antibias opportunities are expanded.* When children engage in inquiry learning through small and large groups, they often group themselves according to interests rather than by culturally or academically defined differences. Alert teachers can encourage regroupings that promote varieties of interactions, as well as highlight the individual talents and successes of every child in the class.

• *Technology can be easily incorporated as a learning tool when appropriate.* With good reason, early childhood educators have historically been skeptical of the use of technology in their classrooms. But when children are engaged in investigative learning, technology can be introduced so that it enhances that learning. It thus becomes a useful tool, rather than a subject in itself.

## INTEGRATING THE CURRICULUM AND LEARNING THROUGH INQUIRY: POTENTIAL CONCERNS

Although we extol the virtues of teaching and learning through the use of integration and inquiry, these approaches are not without possible drawbacks and concerns. As with most methods, they must be done right to be successful. Critics have long suggested that there are pitfalls teachers must avoid, and we believe it is important to share these with our readers so that integration and inquiry are not entered into naively.

• *The importance and integrity of individual subjects may be lost.* This is probably not an issue until the primary grades or, perhaps, in kindergarten and above. Once it becomes important for standards to be met, report cards written, and budgets justified, those who provide funding and other support for schools generally want to know how subjects are being covered. Primary interest usually centers on literacy, followed closely by mathematics. Other stakeholders include subject specialists at all levels, from the district curriculum coordinator to the university researcher. They are more aware than most of the contributions made by each subject area and have a vested interest in promoting the inclusion of each one at all levels of education.

- *Surface study, rather than in-depth understanding, may result.* This argument has been particularly strong when curriculum has been integrated according to themes (for example, colors, holidays) or because the teacher finds them cute (teddy bears, cartoon characters). It has also been a concern when study experiences are turned over to the children's direction. There is a fear on the part of the same stakeholders mentioned above, that both teachers and children will skate across the surface of real learning if the focus is too strongly on the integrating topic and insufficiently on the subject matter that needs emphasizing, and that giving power to children automatically translates into low-level learning.
- *Integrating curriculum and providing for inquiry learning may be overwhelming for many teachers.* This concern is principally directed toward beginning teachers who are just learning to plan and toward long-term veterans who have taught so many years in a more traditional fashion that integration and inquiry would require a difficult shift in philosophy and practice.

We, too, share these concerns. Thus, we have been careful, in writing this book, to address them throughout. Here are a few of the ways.

- *Each subject is addressed individually before it is incorporated into the various integrated topics.* You have, no doubt, already noticed that this book includes a chapter for each of the traditional subject areas. Within each of those chapters you will find reference to the position statements of the subject's curriculum agency (for example, The National Council of Teachers of Mathematics and The National Council for the Social Studies). The positions are then taken into account as ideas are provided for integration and inquiry.
- *Ways to meet standards are included.* Teachers who choose to incorporate integrated curriculum and inquiry learning have always had to demonstrate that their students can and do meet whatever the current standards might be. We will share with you a variety of ways these teachers have found to incorporate the excitement of this approach while always remembering the expectations of the standards.
- *Ways of achieving depth, as well as breadth, of learning are provided throughout.* We once attended an early childhood conference at which a spirited argument about "cuteness" arose. One teacher fairly snarled, "We don't do cutesy. It's demeaning and insulting to children who take their learning very seriously." Many teachers feel conflicted about this topic, perhaps feeling different ways at different times. One good approach might be to first realize that young children do look at their learning as very important and so take their interests seriously, while realizing that, when all is said and done, they will at times be cute to us (although not usually to themselves). An article on this topic concludes with the following powerful food for thought:

Young children naturally have inquiring minds. If we take their questions seriously, we can develop authentic experiences and avoid the cute curriculum. There is no need to sugarcoat a study unit if we allow children to actively seek answers to their own questions. Learn to re-examine what we do with children. When we hear ourselves saying, "Isn't that cute?" try to remember that "cute" is a four-letter word and that children deserve much more. (Kirkland & Aldridge, 1999, p. 3)

- *While there are ideas for giving children some control over their own learning, there are also ideas for the teacher, who also plays an important role in children's learning.* Completely turning power over to young children can be overwhelming, confusing, and frightening for them. They need to know that, ultimately, the teacher is in charge and is there for them. In Chapter 2 we define the teacher's role whenever teaching, learning, and management are discussed. In addition, we demonstrate the appropriate steps for moving from teacher as authority to teacher as guide. At times it is necessary to move in the opposite direction as well, and we describe when and how to do this.
- *We recommend that integration and inquiry be introduced gradually into the classroom.* Just about no one, including the authors, has found it possible, or even desirable, to engage in curriculum integration and inquiry learning at all times. And just about everyone, including the authors, learns that it is most effective to begin by introducing elements of such teaching a bit at a time, increasing such practices as teacher and children are comfortable doing so. At the end of each chapter, as is seen in the two upcoming sections, there are suggested activities to help our readers on their way.

## IN SUMMARY

Curriculum integration has existed in various forms during the last century with varying degrees of visibility. At its roots, curriculum integration is dedicated to making learning meaningful, taking into account that the world around children does not frequently divide itself into curriculum segments. The immersed method of integration supports and encourages children's natural curiosity and provides opportunities for them to inquire and explore topics, thus naturally incorporating several academic subjects.

The theories of Piaget, Vygotsky, and Erikson support the belief that inquiry learning, infused through curriculum integration, is the most effective way to teach young children. The influence of these theories and philosophies is demonstrated in the evolution of developmentally appropriate practice as defined and explicated by the National Association for the Education of Young Children (NAEYC). Upcoming chapters will further demonstrate ways to make the theories and philosophies practical in the early childhood classroom and center.

## TO DISCUSS

1. In what ways will your understanding of the nature and development of young children influence your teaching?
2. Which ideas that have influenced early childhood education do you think will affect you the most? Why?
3. This chapter laid out benefits and potential drawbacks and concerns related to integrating the curriculum and learning through inquiry. Can you think of others?
4. Why is inquiry learning important in the early childhood classroom? Relate your answer to what you know about child development.

# TO DO

1. Observe a young child at play for 30 or more minutes. Try to categorize the school subjects that the child's playful learning might fit into.
2. Observe one boy and one girl in an early childhood play setting. Write a running commentary of their social behaviors over at least 30 minutes. Then compare and contrast your findings with those of the social/affective theorists featured in this chapter.
3. Interview a teacher of young children who incorporates integrated curriculum and/or inquiry learning into the classroom learning activities. Ask about the benefits and possible concerns. Do they match those suggested in this chapter?

# REFERENCES

Audet, R. (2005). Curriculum integration: Capitalizing on student inquiry. In Audet, R. & Jordan, L. (Eds.), *Integrating inquiry across the curriculum.* Thousand Oaks, CA: Corwin Press.

Beane, J. (1995). Curriculum definitions. In *What's all this talk about curriculum integration?* Third Annual National Conference on Curriculum Integration, Scottsdale, AZ.

Bredekamp, S. & Copple, C. (Eds.). (1997). *Developmentally appropriate practice in early childhood programs.* Washington, DC: NAEYC.

Copple, C. & Bredekamp, S. (2009). *Developmentally appropriate practice in early childhood programs serving children from birth through age 8.* Washington, DC: NAEYC.

Edwards, C. & Gandini, L. (1989). Teachers' expectations about the timing of developmental skills: A cross-cultural study. *Young Children,* 44 (4), 15–19.

Erikson, E. (1963). *Childhood and society.* New York, NY: W.W. Norton.

Essex, N. (2006). *What every teacher should know about No Child Left Behind.* Boston, MA: Pearson.

Etim, J. (2005). Curriculum integration: The why and how. In Etim, J. (Ed.), *Curriculum integration K–12: Theory and practice* (pp. 3–11). Lanham, MD: University Press of America.

Fogarty, R. (1991). *How to integrate the curricula.* Palatine, IL: IRI/Skylight.

Forman, G. & Gandini, L. (1994). *The amusement park for birds* [a video]. Amherst, MA: Performanetics Press.

Gabbard, C. (1992). *Lifelong motor development.* Dubuque, IA: Brown.

Gallahue, D. (1982). *Understanding motor development in children.* New York, NY: Wiley.

Helm, J. (2012). From theory to curriculum. In File, N., Mueller, J., & Wisneski, D. (Eds.), *Curriculum in early childhood education.* New York, NY: Routledge.

Hyson, M. (2008). *Enthusiastic and engaged learners: Approaches to learning in the early childhood classroom.* New York, NY: Teachers College Press.

Katz, L. (1993). What can we learn from Reggio Emilia? In Edwards, C., Gandini, L., & Forman, G. (Eds.), *The hundred languages of children.* Norwood, NJ: Ablex.

Katz, L. & Chard, S. (2000). *Engaging children's minds: The project approach* (2nd ed.). Norwood, NJ: Ablex.

Kirkland, L. & Aldridge, J. (1999). Isn't that cute? Transforming the cute curriculum into authentic learning. *ACEI: Focus on Pre-K & K,* 12 (1), 1–3.

Mayhew, K. & Edwards, A. (1966). *The Dewey school.* New York, NY: Atherton Press.

Piaget, J. (1973/1948). *To understand is to invent: The future of education.* New York, NY: Viking Books.

Schweinhart, L., Barnes, H., & Weikart, D. (1993). *Significant benefits: The High/Scope Perry preschool study through age 27.* Ypsilanti, MI: The High/Scope Press.

Skinner, L. (1979). *Motor development in the preschool years.* Springfield, IL: Charles C. Thomas.

Tanner, D. (1989). A brief historical perspective of the struggle for an integrative curriculum. *Educational Horizons,* 65 (1), 7–11.

U.S. Department of Education. (2012). *Race to the Top—Early learning challenge.* Retrieved from www2.ed.gov/programs/racetothetop-earlylearningchallenge.

Vars, G. & Beane, J. (2000). *Integrative curriculum in a standards-based world.* Champaign, IL: ED441618, ERIC Clearinghouse on Elementary and Early Childhood Education.

Vygotsky, L. (1962/1934). *Thought and language.* Cambridge, MA: MIT Press.

# 2

## THE CHILD-CENTERED LEARNING ENVIRONMENT

*The ideal environment would support children's desire to find
out about things, facilitate the process of discovery, and,
in general, meet children's needs.*
—Alfie Kohn

After reading this chapter you should be able to:

- Explain the importance of indoor and outdoor learning environments and the effect they have on young investigators;
- Describe ideas to prepare environments for integrated, inquiry-based learning;
- Identify ways teachers influence child-centered classrooms;
- Identify ways children influence the environment of a child-centered classroom;
- Describe approaches to establishing a harmonious, caring community of learners;
- Outline the preparation guidelines for the critical first days of school.

Think back, as best you can, to the classrooms or centers you knew as a small child. Try to recall the sounds and smells that greeted you as you entered the rooms. Do you remember the look and feel of the sun coming through the windows? What hung on the walls? What elements of your classrooms called out to you? Do you remember how the desks, tables, and other furniture were placed in any of those early classrooms and where you fit, or didn't fit, into the overall design? Think about your teachers. Were they approachable and kind? As a young child did you feel welcomed, safe, and important? Do you remember your classmates as being friendly, helpful, and supportive? What emotions are elicited from these memories?

Just as we remember, however vaguely, the people and environments of our early school experiences, so too will the children that we ourselves teach. And with good reason. The environment and the people working within it provide a powerful influence on how children feel about learning, on how well they learn, and on what they learn.

# ENVIRONMENTAL EXTREMES

Let's look at two examples of what the environment can do to and for children. In the first, a teacher's thoughtlessness deprived children of both enjoyment and learning. In the second, a teacher was well aware of the importance of the environment and continually experimented with it.

## Example I

*The class of 24 second graders spent most of the day seated around three long, rectangular tables. One Friday afternoon their teacher decided to reward the class for a week of good behavior by showing a video of a favorite movie. The children were, as usual, seated at the three large tables. The video monitor was in its stationary place: about 7 feet above the floor, in a corner, with the screen angled down toward the classroom. Obviously, this meant that the children who were seated with their backs to the monitor would have to turn around to see the film. But as the film started, the teacher began to pass around a patterned art project (which required glue) for everyone to do while the movie was on. The children who had their backs to the screen thus had to remain that way in order to use the tables for the art project. The teacher made no comments that would give the children any solution to their dilemma, and the children all stayed the way they were originally seated.*

*Within a short time, the children facing the screen became involved in the video and lost interest in the art project. The other children finished the project and then began to play games with the glue. Soon the classroom became a combination of two types of behavior: passive movie watching and out-of-control mischief. The teacher loudly reprimanded the more troublesome children, snatching glue containers away in obvious anger. Quiet was restored. Half the children continued to watch the video and half stared into space, occasionally peering over their shoulders at the movie but without interest in a plot that was, by now, lost on them. The teacher still made no suggestions for turning chairs around. None of the children offered solutions to the quandary either.*

## Example II

*The large variety of blocks in the kindergarten block corner made it a popular place. Its popularity was enhanced further when the teacher combined it with the housekeeping corner. Once the two were intermingled in one large corner, the boys became more interested in interacting with dolls and housekeeping equipment while the girls participated in constructing airplanes and trucks, which became vehicles for the dolls.*

*The teacher still saw room for improvement. On the opposite side of the room was a cabinet with a dozen containers filled with assorted math-based manipulatives, pattern blocks, Unifix cubes, fraction circles, two-sided counters, and so on. The children rarely chose these materials during free play and instead mass migrated to the block/housekeeping area. At first the teacher tried to visualize a way to move the entire cabinet of manipulatives over to this corner, but dismissed the idea as too unwieldy. She then began moving a couple of containers at a time, placing one with the blocks and one with the housekeeping equipment. She did this for several days, choosing containers randomly.*

*The children never questioned the presence of mysteriously placed containers in their environment; they simply began to use them in their construction and role-play. The Unifix cubes and pattern blocks often became part of vehicles' instrument panels, the fraction pieces and two-sided counters represented various portions of food, and so on. Before too many days, some containers of manipulatives began to prove more useful than others, and if those containers weren't already placed in the center, the children fetched them from the cabinet. At the end of free-play time, without any suggestion from the teacher, the children returned the materials to their rightful containers and then to the cabinet, even when it was the teacher who had removed them.*

In reading about these two environments, it is easy to ascertain that Example II is more conducive to children's learning and constructive behavior. And as the first example revealed, the teacher's lack of attention to the environment and the young learners in it not only impeded learning but also raised barriers against child-initiated input. It is not as easy to define a good learning environment or to identify one that has problems when in the midst of trying to work with children. This is particularly true in the beginning years of teaching. For that reason, it is important to enter the classroom with as much understanding as possible of the effects of the environment on children's learning behavior.

Attitude is as important as knowledge. In our first example, the teacher immediately blamed inappropriate behavior on the children even though she had offered them no alternatives to an uncomfortable situation. In the second example, the teacher considered the environment something that was always ripe for improvement. She experimented with it continually throughout the year, taking leads from her students, hoping always to find more ways to augment their learning. Even a beginning teacher can expect a good measure of success when his or her attitude is as open and as observant as the teacher's in Example II.

Of importance in planning a successful environment is to keep in mind one's educational goals. In the second example, the teacher apparently wanted to avoid gender stereotyping in the children's choices of materials, and she hoped to have them work more with math-based educational materials. This teacher valued the children's initiative to construct meaning for themselves and honored their need for independence. It is difficult to try and define the first teacher's goals. She rewarded the children for good behavior by providing them with a movie and then made it impossible for fully half the class to continue to behave well. In addition, she gave the children a second activity that made it difficult to fully enjoy the first.

The word *environment* can be defined as the surroundings, conditions, and influences in which people live, learn, and work. The purpose of this chapter is to show you how thoughtfully created classroom environments promote child-directed, inquiry-based learning as well as enabling and supporting success for all. We will discuss the physical and social-emotional environments and how they affect children in the classroom setting, along with the paramount influence the teacher has on young learners. You will see how educators can create the much desired classroom environment necessary for establishing a harmonious, caring community of learners. You will gain knowledge about how to establish a learning community that operates democratically under an umbrella of clear and fair expectations, all with the goal of helping every student succeed.

Historical background begins our discussion of both the physical and the social-emotional environments. Each section concludes with ways in which the environment should be considered for inquiry learning through curriculum integration.

## THE PHYSICAL ENVIRONMENT

Both indoor and outdoor environments influence the learning of young children. Some historical figures, as we see below, have been even more focused on what the outdoors has to offer children than on what the more traditional indoors might provide.

### A History of Learning Environments for Preprimary Children

Educator Friedrich Froebel, known as the "father of kindergarten," introduced the concept of kindergarten to Germany in the first half of the 19th century. He believed that children needed to have playtime in order to learn and thus was well aware of the influence of the physical environment on children's learning. Although Froebel's schools often had to make do with the space available to them, an important part of his philosophy was to make kindergarten a pleasant place to be. He advocated that the classroom be sunny, the walls brightly painted, and that a garden adjoin the building. There would be plants, animals, and pictures throughout. Froebel has been credited, too, with being the first to design that most logical and humane of classroom equipment: child-size furniture.

Maria Montessori, Italy's first female doctor and a champion of early education, studied Froebel's ideas, and then created her own version of the kindergarten. In addition to child-size furniture, shelving and materials were now placed within children's reach. This helped to move the curriculum from a teacher-directed one to a more child-directed approach. Respect for children's capabilities was also demonstrated by the inclusion of materials that were real tools for real work. For example, brooms, polishing cloths, and cleaning lotions were all those that adults might use, although smaller in size. Materials, such as peg-to-corresponding-hole games and academic puzzles that matched up when correctly put together, were still quite structured with built in "correction of error" so that children could see for themselves if they had done something correctly or not. Youngsters could work at low tables or on the floor, placing their work on small rugs.

Radically different from any plan seen before was the outdoor nursery school designed by Rachel and Margaret McMillan in the early 1900s. Responding to the general ill health of England's children, they were determined to found a school that would not only educate the very young but nurture their health as well. Hence, the concept of nurturing children led to the name "nursery" school, with the first coming into being in 1913. Designed by Rachel, the school resembled a lean-to with only three sides enclosed. It was the sisters' belief that fresh air and proper diet would cure most, if not all, of the children's diseases. And, indeed, many successes were reported over a number of years. In 1927, for example, the Open-Air Nursery School reported that just 7% of its children were diseased in any way. The national average of diseased children that year for children entering elementary school was 30% to 40%. The school also reported dramatic decreases in cases of rickets (caused by a deficiency in vitamin D), measles, and skin diseases in their children (Nursery School Association of Great Britain, n.d.).

Clearly, these three designs for preschool learning environments—Froebel's and Montessori's pleasant classroom with child-size amenities and the McMillan sisters' health-promoting lean-to—reflected their creators' goals for young children's well-being. The designs also demonstrated their educational goals. Froebel envisioned children learning through directed but active play and through interaction with carefully designed materials. To support his philosophy, the environment contained a combination of open space for games and large muscle activities and small, child-friendly tables and chairs for working with the materials he designed. Montessori had a similar vision, but she regarded the children's activities as *work*, because of her respect for the ways in which her young learners thought about what they did. The McMillans included in their learning materials a number of Froebel-like pieces of equipment but focused more on the importance of outdoor, health-promoting activities. In their case, as in Froebel's and Montessori's, the rooms were designed as places where children could move about freely, thus reflecting a view of the teacher as facilitator rather than as authority figure.

### A History of Learning Environments for Primary Grade Children

Like the environments for early learning introduced by Froebel, Montessori, and the McMillans, primary classrooms have undergone change over time as well. In medieval Europe, the plan, if it really can be called a plan, generally consisted of a large room broken up in ever-varying designs as different masters spoke on different topics while their students, all ages including primary, gathered around.

During the centuries of the Early Modern Era, primary education was many things in different places. In the American colonies, for example, the only available space might be in a storefront or someone's home. When schools were built purposely, it was usually for older children.

Joseph Lancaster's plan for English children in the early 19th century was one of the first to break away from the medieval tradition. The Industrial Revolution brought with it the need for new kinds of education, including the need for mass literacy. Lancaster designed a room 70 by 32 feet in which 320 children were thus provided 7 square feet each. Long desks and benches ensured a student body devoted to receiving knowledge from the authority figures in front of them (Seaborne, 1971).

In the United States several changes in elementary classroom designs took place over the 20th century. Jacob Getzels (1974) suggested that, in reference to the placement of furniture within a classroom, there had been four basic general designs during that time: rectangular, then square, then circular, and finally open. Your authors include the following room arrangement descriptions to encourage readers to reflect on the philosophical attitudes and expectations of teaching and learning that coincide with the different classroom configurations.

The *rectangular* room arrangement of a century ago contained desks bolted to the floor in orderly rows with the teacher's desk in front. Since learner and teacher at that time were viewed as receptacle and fount of knowledge, respectively, this design made sense. It also had much in common with the earlier Lancaster plan in England.

As research in learning evolved over the first three decades of the 20th century, the view of children as receptacles of knowledge gave way to the concept that they, too, brought something to the teaching-learning experience. Leaders in psychology began to talk about children's affective needs in the learning process. The philosophy of John Dewey—that children learn much from democratic social interaction—began to take hold. These changes in view produced primary classrooms that started to have the freer look of nurseries and kindergartens. Desks were unbolted, and the teacher's desk was moved to an out-of-the-way corner. Interaction with materials and with one another became more common as it became physically more possible. Thus, the classroom configuration resembled a flexible *square*.

The third classroom configuration identified by Getzels was *circular*. This shape was less important in the primary grades than in upper elementary and secondary classes.

Students were encouraged to learn through social interaction by the placement of desks in a large circular shape.

The square and circular classroom arrangements, with remaining vestiges of the rectangular, carried us through World War II and beyond. Once the Piagetian view of children as interactive with their environment, contributing to the creation of their own intelligence, took hold, a new kind of design was needed. Learners were not seen as simply responding to stimuli; they sought them out. This meant that the early rectangular classroom configuration with its rows of bolted desks, would be totally inappropriate. Even the squarish classroom configuration with its movable desks could be improved upon. Desks might now be removed entirely, to be replaced by tables of varying sizes. Interest centers would beckon the young learners to come try new activities. Children would naturally seek out new learning experiences, and it was the teacher's obligation to provide the tools and materials for new learning to open up. To provide optimal interaction with materials and with one another, rooms were made larger or walls were torn down. In this fourth classroom configuration, labeled an *open* classroom configuration, teachers were encouraged, sometimes mandated, to work in teams. Often times, team teaching resulted in having an unduly large number of learners in one large teaching area.

This wide open classroom configuration did not stay in vogue for long. As described in Chapter 1, in the mid-1970s a move was already underway to return to an educational focus on "the basics." No longer did the large, open classroom, with an abundance of seemingly free-roaming children, fit most educators' vision of what a classroom in action should look like. Walls that had opened were now replaced, or sturdy dividers were installed. Teachers who had worked in teams returned to self-contained classrooms.

No doubt there have been times in history when classroom design did not mesh with the goals of that period's education. For the most part, however, the examples we have just shown of preschool and primary environments demonstrate that a consciousness of one's educational goals will generally lead naturally to the appropriate shape and size of classroom configuration.

By the 1980s, it was understood that a balance of open and closed space within a classroom or center is the ideal in learning settings that encourage child-directed, inquiry-based learning. David Day (1983) cautioned that large, open rooms could only partially provide children the setting that is best for their well-being and education. If a room is simply large and open, the noise from the block corner or noise-producing activity areas can be disturbing in the library area and a large open space in the center of a classroom begs young children to run across the area. Further, children have little or no opportunity to engage in solitary play or to work without interruption from others. In a totally open room privacy is virtually impossible, although everyone, even a small child, needs it occasionally. Day gave two suggested solutions for different types of activities: separate rooms or inexpensive barricades. Your authors, in their experience, have found that smaller areas for privacy can also be formed by deliberate placement of furniture such as cupboards, shelves, screens, tables, and so on.

Day believed that the same considerations can be given for open and closed space whether the classroom is inadequately small or overly large. In either type of room, children can be provided with the open space that gives them freedom to move and the closed space that provides them with a feeling of security or privacy.

Ingenuity on the part of the teacher is needed to accommodate children's needs in child centers and classrooms of challenging size. In a *small room*, a table placed on its side draped with a bedspread over it makes an inviting, intimate space; covering the back side of a shelf or cupboard with felt or a wipe-off board encourages it to be used in a variety of ways; furniture fitted with easy-rolling castor wheels provides needed flexibility in the creation of learning spaces; opportunities to take learning outside should be utilized. In an *overly spacious room* (we should all be so fortunate), a teacher still needs to be attentive to furniture placement. Individual rugs can help to define activity areas; furniture can be strategically placed to minimize a cavernous effect and to create intimate areas; large cardboard boxes, filled with imagination, can readily transform large spaces into smaller, intimate, child-centered domains.

In work that mirrored and extended Day's, Elizabeth Prescott (2008, originally 1994) presented "five key dimensions of environment that impact on the experiences of children" (p. 34). Both sides of each pairing are important to include in young children's environment.

- *Softness/Hardness.* Providing materials at both ends of the tactile range makes the environment most welcoming. Sand and clay are examples of soft; tile floors and wooden furniture are examples of hard.
- *Open/Closed.* Prescott defines these differently than Day. Here she speaks of materials with just one right way of using them as closed, and those with a variety of possibilities as being open. Dress-up clothes would be open, while a jigsaw puzzle with its single right solution would be closed.
- *Simple/Complex.* Complex materials have more than one feature or element to their use. A sandbox with only sand in it would be simple. Adding shovels and toys would make it complex.
- *High mobility/Low mobility.* Materials such as trikes and balls provide opportunities for mobility, while coloring or pencil and paper activities are low mobility.
- *Intrusion/Seclusion.* Seclusion areas of the environment give children possibilities for privacy; areas of intrusion are closely supervised by adults. Both, according to Prescott, are important for children.

Young learners themselves have excellent insight and suggestions on how to best utilize space for learning and welcome opportunities to contribute to the enhancement of their environment. At the younger ages, the decisions and input from the learners will probably be modest. But even the very youngest children enjoy making their room truly theirs by contributing to the beauty of their classroom's physical environment as they decide where their artwork could be displayed or where child-arranged bouquets of flowers might be placed.

When Pam's kindergarten class was housed in a tiny, storage-challenged room, she asked her kindergarteners for advice on how they could make their small classroom environment more effectual. A wise student suggested that Pam cover her "ugly" (but necessary) storage totes with a blanket. This then became a backdrop for the children's art. Another child suggested that a large cardboard box be brought in, and, after beautification by the students, it made a cozy, quiet spot for enjoying books. Pam asked and received the children's permission to use one of the sides of the box to affix an engaging alphabet chart and some beginning reading words such as: *I, you, can, are, am, see, have, big, little, Mom, Dad,* and so on.

Much has been learned in recent years about the importance of the teaching and learning environment. In the next section, we see how today's brain research demonstrates the effects of the environment on young children's learning.

### What Brain Research Shows

Research supports the fact that the physical environment profoundly impacts not only adult worker performance but student performance as well. Neuroscientists are taking this issue very seriously as they appeal to architects to consider the effect environments have on our brains as they design new buildings. Thus, neuroscience is being linked with the design and building industries (Jensen, 2005).

Of importance to educators is the neuroscience research about the effect the physical classroom environment has on student learning. In this research three points stand out:

- "Physical environments influence how we feel, hear, and see. Those factors, in turn, influence cognitive and affective performance.
- Some variables exert a much greater influence on student achievement than others.
- Better awareness, smarter planning, and simple changes can be made in every environment to improve learning." (Jensen, 2005, p. 82)

Most educators usually have little input into the architecture and design of the center or school where they teach. They can, however, enhance the settings in which they teach and do what they can to make it most favorable to learning. Classroom and center environments do matter, and they must be given attention in order for children to learn, behave, and perform optimally. Environmental variables impact teachers as well as their young learners.

Erik Jensen (2005), in support of his brain-based approach to teaching and learning, suggests variables in the classroom physical environment that have the greatest effect on academic success: seating, temperature, lighting, and noise.

*Seating* affects learners' stress levels as well their physical well-being. Who they sit next to as well as where they sit influences their stress level and hence their cognitive development. Are students sitting by classmates who hinder their progress or by those who complement their learning style and temperament? Does a child need to be near the teacher's desk area or close to a bathroom? Do specific children work more comfortably when sitting in small group arrangements or do they benefit by sitting solo at times at individual desks? What is considered a stressful seating placement for one child may or may not be for another.

Chairs should provide good, posture-friendly support to encourage optimal blood flow to the nervous system and reduce musculoskeletal symptoms. A chair should allow the child to sit *in* it rather than merely *on* it (Jensen, 2005). Surprisingly, a large percentage of weight is supported by only a few square inches of bone in the buttocks. No wonder stress, fatigue, and discomfort set in for some people when sitting upright on a hard surface for long times. A soft pillow or carpet can be much more inviting and allows for needed variety in seating.

*Temperature* is a factor that notably affects the acquisition of knowledge as well as our behavior, thoughts, and emotions. Studies in temperate climates show that classroom temperatures kept between 68° and 72° are most conducive for learning intellectual and physical tasks. Of course, in warmer or colder climates, adjustments for comfort must be made. In general, because bodies adapt more easily to slightly cooler environments, a cooler (but not cold) learning environment is better than warmer or hot (Jensen, 2005). Keep in mind that the most supportive inside temperatures will be relative to the extremes of the temperatures outside. Research also shows that higher temperatures affect chemicals in the brain associated with moods that can evoke anxiety and aggressiveness as well as lethargy, all of which obstruct learning. Children with panic disorder or attention-deficit hyperactivity disorder may be adversely affected by very warm classroom temperatures (Jensen, 2005). Your authors advocate encouraging young learners to become aware of their own temperature preferences and supporting their efforts to dress accordingly. Temperature preferences can be vastly different, and most children find it difficult to concentrate when they are either too cool or too warm.

*Lighting* and lack of lighting are contributors to learners' academic attainments as well as to issues of health. Experts are concerned with the decline of outdoor light that children are exposed to. Outdoor light includes ultraviolet light, which activates vitamin D needed to aid absorption of essential minerals, including calcium, that bodies need to grow strong. Many children simply do not get enough exposure to sunlight and outdoor light. Some students spend six or more hours in school facilities with artificial light being their main source of illumination. Studies show dramatic results from both inadequate lighting and abundant natural lighting in classrooms. A study conducted in 1951, which evaluated 160,000 school children, reported "more than 50 percent of children developed academic or health deficiencies as a result of insufficient light at school" (Jensen, 2005, p. 85). More recently, a 1999 study of 21,000 children from three states, found that, "students with the most sunlight in their classrooms progressed 20 percent faster on math tests and 26 percent faster on reading tests compared with students exposed to the least lighting" (p. 85).

*Noise*—including inside and outside environmental noise, reverberation, and acoustical difficulties—can compromise student focus. Noise interference also boosts off-task behaviors and discipline problems, all of which result in negative impacts on learning. Children for whom English is a second language have an especially difficult time discriminating verbal messages in noisy classrooms. Because young children are still learning language and need to clearly hear new speech sounds, noise interference can hinder not only language acquisition but reading ability as well.

When addressing the negative impact of loud noise, Jensen states, "Beyond causing an immediate stress response in the nervous system and the voluntary muscular reflex system, loud noise also increases heart rate, grimacing and sudden muscle flexion. Together, these stress responses impair learning over time" (2005, p. 89).

For teaching with the brain in mind, the following suggestions, as adapted from Jensen (2005), are offered to make the most of the classroom physical environment:

- *Promote feelings of safety:* Do the learners feel physically and emotionally secure?
- *Incorporate kinesthetics:* Are seating and classroom arrangements flexible and do they encourage student movement?
- *Monitor room temperature:* Is the room temperature in the optimal local range for peak occupant performance?

- *Monitor visual environment and lighting:* Are learners visually stimulated appropriately and is the lighting most favorable for learning?
- *Monitor acoustics:* Can learners hear the teachers and other learners and is there no interference from obtrusive noise?

### Classroom Environments for the Integrated, Inquiry-Based Curriculum

What of the environment that supports the integrated, inquiry-based curriculum espoused by this book? This curriculum is based on the view that children take an active part in constructing their own learning, that interacting with the environment is a vital way of learning, and that inquiry and curiosity are key to making learning relevant and connected.

Unfortunately, to some people unfamiliar with child-initiated curricula and inquiry or investigative learning, there is an assumption that child-centered learning necessitates young learners running willy-nilly—without limits, direction, or goals as they partake in whatever suits their young whims and desires. Nothing could be further from the truth, although it is certainly true that any classroom, no matter what its presumed philosophy is, could be chaotic if the teacher does not plan and prepare thoughtfully. To support an integrated, inquiry-based, and child-centered curriculum, much attention and deliberation go into not only curriculum planning and preparation but into the planning and use of the environment as well. Such care is essential to promote as well as sustain a high level of learning.

For this kind of learning, it should be apparent that children need room to move about. Ideally they should be given the opportunity to combine the indoors and outdoors in a natural way. The classroom configuration needs to be an open, flexible one. It goes without saying that desks should not be bolted to the floor, and even at the primary level tables might best replace them. In this setting the teacher would be a facilitator rather than an authority figure, so his or her desk would be of inconsequential size and be well out of the way, or perhaps not visible at all. Once furniture is in place, it would probably not remain the same throughout the school year but would be altered as needs and interests dictated.

A balance of both large and small classroom space is needed. For presentation of projects, creative movement, and class meetings, open areas are needed; committee work, individual research, and reflection require smaller, cozier areas.

Equipment and supplies required for child-initiated work need to be well organized, visible, and easily accessible for all. Containers that house materials and tools needed for investigations and other classroom endeavors should be labeled. Making a one-to-one correspondence between a container and a spot on its shelf helps even further. For instance a "3" on a container can be matched to the "3" on a corresponding shelf space. Labeling not only reinforces emerging reading skills, but also encourages young learners to put items away in an organized fashion, thus aiding the tidiness of the room.

As was noted earlier in this chapter, educators often do not have much input into the physical learning spaces in which they teach. And, in many cases, they are expected to make do with the furnishings that have been placed already in the classroom or center. However, an aware teacher can make the best of the furnishings afforded to him or her if the environment is set up with the focus on the children's well-being.

Importantly, the concepts of freedom of movement, of interaction between children, and of environments designed with children's welfare in mind are all a natural part of planning for an integrated, child-centered curriculum. Learning environments where teachers prefer to facilitate rather than direct children's learning, where young learners are encouraged to have a say in what their learning environment looks like, and that are arranged to encourage and assist inquiry-based learning through integration take the following criteria into account:

- The environment should be used to communicate what behavior is expected and appropriate.
- Children should be able to move easily from area to area without interrupting work spaces.
- Incompatible areas (blocks and library, for example) should have distance between them.
- Places should be made for children to be alone, to work in small groups, and to gather in a total class group.
- All materials that young learners use should be within children's reach, with a policy of free access for all.
- Shelved materials should be labeled to encourage reading and independence and indicate that everything has its place.
- Areas for displayed projects and artwork should be at the children's viewing level.
- Environments that are most favorable to child-centered learning should be flexible and encourage as well as honor input from their young occupants.

### The Outdoor Environment

The McMillan sisters began their outdoor nursery, in great part, for the purpose of improving children's health. They did not have access to the medical technology we do today, but the statistics showing the bettered health of their students gave strength to their argument that exercise and being outdoors were beneficial. Although today we have better medicine and a better understanding of nutrition, the health-giving properties of exercising and being outdoors remain the same. In support of exercise and movement, multiple research studies now support connections between physical activity and increases in academic performance and intellectual growth (Jensen, 2005). Thus, the environment outside of the classroom is rich with potential and becomes a valuable, multi-use learning arena.

In the 1950s, Sweden, Denmark, and Germany, although known for their chilly winter weather, began experimenting with an outdoor approach to education. *Forest schools* were developed, backed by efforts of enthusiastic parents. The basic concept of a forest school is that youngsters learn and play in outdoor environments, under most weather conditions, over large periods of time throughout their school day and use the materials at hand in the natural settings to implement their learning.

At the beginning of the 21st century, England began to create forest kindergartens in rural areas, and now they are appearing in large cities such as London with supporters arguing that

Children who have played in natural spaces are far more likely to develop a deep desire to protect the natural living systems, which provide us with fuel, health, richness and other essential services. Forest School is an effective way to develop children's pro-environmental values and behaviours. (Milchem, 2011, p. 20)

In the United States, more than 100 Waldorf programs have embraced the forest model with their focus on nature and natural learning materials (Leyden, 2009). Elements of a forest school model—exploration and learning in a forest or other natural environment—could be included in any curriculum.

Another approach to outdoor education in recent years provides opportunities for school children to be involved in growing produce to be used in their school lunch and snack programs. Known as the *Farm to School* program, schools and communities work together to encourage the appreciation and healthy benefits of growing and eating nutritious foods (Farm to School, n.d.). In this way, school gardens can become living learning laboratories while supplementing schools' food supplies, aiding in the development of healthy food-related curriculum, and providing experiential learning opportunities in the outdoor environment. At its core, Farm to School is about establishing relationships between local foods and school children, and these come in many shapes and sizes unique to the communities and schools that build them.

Most recently, the program has expanded to include the Farm to Preschool approach to gardening. According to the program:

Preschool gardening engages children by providing an interactive environment to observe, discover, experiment, nurture and learn. School and child care gardens are living laboratories where interdisciplinary lessons are drawn from real life experiences, encouraging children to become active participants in the learning process. (Farm to Preschool, n.d.)

Children of all ages need opportunities to reap the healthy benefits of the outdoors. In the traditional view, the area outside the classroom is a playground, a place where children can run, shout, climb, and swing to blow off steam, as a break from the rigors of classroom learning. However, if the atmosphere of the classroom is more like those we are prescribing in this textbook, where children are allowed and encouraged to move around and interact with each other, then there are fewer times when letting off steam is a critical need. Still, the playground concept should not be forgotten. Even in classrooms where much mobility is permitted, children need opportunities to be outside to engage in large motor play as loudly as necessary, to partake in active social play if they so choose, to re-energize by being alone. As a society we have become sedentary, and we are often more comfortable indoors than out. For some children it is easy to fall into this pattern of life, but for others, probably most, it is frustrating. Some teachers also feel frustrated by sedentary, indoor living and are naturally alert to children's requirements; others have to make a mental leap into their children's shoes to keep alert to their young learners' physical needs.

First Lady Michelle Obama's focus on moving America to be more active offers challenge and encouragement for creating healthier school environments for schoolchildren. The Internet website dedicated to the Let's Move initiative offers helpful tips and step-by-step strategies for families, schools, and communities to help children be more active, eat better, and grow up healthy. Included in this website are engaging age-appropriate activities designed to help integrate physical education, as well as nutrition education, into the school day.

*Activities for the Outdoor Environment*

Another way of looking at the area outside the classroom is to use it to enhance children's learning. Many times academic activities done inside can be undertaken outside, thus incorporating the pleasantness and benefits of being out-of-doors. Even if the outdoor area is a relatively confined space, there are learning opportunities to be had. Merely using an outdoor setting to read a story to a class of youngsters provides a welcome breath of fresh air. The natural elements in the outdoors are objects of wonder, cost nothing, and are always engaging. The following list shows some examples of academic activities that incorporate the out-of-doors. See if you can add to the list with ideas of your own, keeping in mind that the geographic area where you teach will have an impact on your choices:

- The possibilities for counting are numerous: rocks, trees, bugs, sticks, and so on.
- Articles in nature are very engaging to sort and classify according to size, shape, color, and weight.
- Measuring has great potential: length of distances between objects, circumference of trees, lengths of fields, widths of sidewalks, height of fences, and so on.
- An area of dirt or sand (make mud, if you dare) is a welcoming slate on which to practice forming numerals, letters, words, and shapes, or play tic-tac-toe.
- Containers of water and large paintbrushes encourage "painting and writing" on almost everything.
- Sounds heard in the outdoors provide opportunities for identification and recording in words or pictures.
- The ever-changing cloud shapes stimulate creative visualization.
- Nature provides a wide variety of collage materials for imaginative artwork.
- Any kind of movement or dance is, of course, more open and free outdoors, especially when the sun produces shadows and the wind joins in.

*Inquiry-Based Learning and the Outdoors*

Inquiry-based learning to integrate the curriculum also calls on the learning potential of the outside environment. The outdoor classroom holds a wealth of data and possibilities for investigations that beckon even the youngest of researchers. When teachers encourage children to use and incorporate wonder and curiosity in their exploration of elements outside of the classroom they are instilling a gift, of sorts, that will last a lifetime—a gift of thoughtful observation of nature. How many times have you, an adult reader, watched an ant and wondered about the how and why of its industriousness? Have you ever pondered where and how that tricolored pebble came to be? And just where *do* butterflies go when it rains?

The outdoors is a primary, firsthand resource for children to utilize when collecting data for their research. Observational drawings, documentation of cause and effect, and experimentation, as well as other gathered information, provide answers to questions surrounding child-centered research topics. For example, an in-depth, inquiry-based study of leaves might call on young investigators to:

- Make observational drawings of individual leaves and trees;
- Record how long it takes for leaves to begin to fall;

**Figure 2.1** The outdoor classroom holds great potential for learning.

- Experiment with the textures and colors of leaves that have fallen;
- Note what happens when the weather turns cooler or warmer;
- Estimate how many leaves are on a small tree and strive to find the exact answer;
- Record changes over time.

Many times, teachers find that the field research trip needed for their young investigators' in-depth study is right outside their classroom.

### Meeting the Needs and Interests of All Children

The physical environment plays an integral and vital part in supporting practices that encourage high levels of child-initiated engagement and exploration. Young investigators need ready access to appropriate materials and equipment. Children's curiosity should be stimulated and reinforced with an engaging, dynamic, user-friendly environment. And at all times issues of safety—of the furniture, toys, equipment, and supplies, and of the intangible properties of the classroom or center, both inside and outside—should be the primary and ongoing concern of the educators in charge.

Much of what children need in their environment is related to their level of development. In an important position statement, The National Association for the Education of Young Children (NAEYC) addressed environmental needs of children of various ages (Copple & Bredekamp, 2009). The position statement advocates environments that allow for large muscles to be exercised and physical skills to be expanded both indoors and out. Learning environments should be planned to promote children's initiative and active interaction with a variety of materials. Children also need times for sustained engagement with other children. The NAEYC position statement asks that "teachers foster a learning environment that encourages exploration, initiative, positive peer interaction, and cognitive growth" (p. 221).

Increasingly, young children with identified disabilities or special learning requirements are being included in preschool and public school programs. Young learners with disabilities have needs in common with all youngsters who come together in group settings. When discussing environmental issues for children, including those with special needs, Kristine Slentz and Suzanne Krogh (2001) explain that children "need safe and comfortable spaces that promote curiosity and exploration and an order to the day that supports a variety of age-appropriate opportunities for learning and development" (p. 135). Slentz and Krogh offer reassurance to teachers who fret about the ability of the physical environment to ensure safe social interactions for children with special needs when they state, "Increased mindfulness to the immediate surroundings may be inspired by children with disabilities, with positive outcomes for everyone" (p. 135). With this in mind, your authors offer the following points to consider when arranging a center or classroom that will accommodate the needs of *all* learners:

- Is there sufficient space to move among all areas?
- Is the environment safe while still allowing for children's increasing independence and responsibility?
- Is there a variety of flexible work areas—large group, creative play, as well as smaller, more intimate spaces—and are incompatible activity areas separated?
- Is the furniture appropriately child sized and does it allow for flexible room arrangement?
- Are messy areas located close to a sink?
- Are learning materials varied, conducive to active engagement, and chosen with children's developmental levels in mind?
- Is the environment equitable for all with no gender, cultural, or special need biases?
- Are there opportunities to take learning outside whenever possible?
- Does the outside environment provide interesting challenges while still remaining safe for every child who will use it?

Today's inclusion of all children in a classroom, no matter their motor, sensory, social, or cognitive needs, calls for an increased mindfulness about the room decor, not only for students with special needs, but for all of the occupants of the classroom or center.

For example, it is tempting for teachers to over-decorate their classrooms. In some classrooms posters, pictures, numbers, and letters may conceal the walls and sometimes even the ceilings. Some teachers feel compelled to fill every nook and cranny with "something." Multiple strands of holiday-type lights are often used to decorate classrooms. But, pause for a moment to consider that a profusion of decorative additions may be overstimulating for some of the youngsters in the room. Overstimulation of the senses may induce unwanted behaviors in some students. Some children, bombarded and overwhelmed by a vast array of stimuli, child oriented as they may be, simply choose to block them out entirely, thus missing the academic learning the teacher intended. And, while the flowery scent of a room freshener may be pleasant to some, it may irritate others. Keep in mind also that in a child-centered environment it is the *children's* creations that should be showcased. Displays of students' work should be shown and changed frequently with input, when possible, from the children about their choice of work and placement. Blank walls and bulletin boards can offer a stimulus break and provide space for children to anticipate, plan, and add their own creations.

However, when teachers place posters and materials in the classroom it is important that children see examples of themselves and their families in them. Seeing visual images that look similar to themselves helps children develop a sense of belonging. Such displays might include pictures of single parent, same sex, and grandparent families as well as visuals depicting diversity in race, ethnicity, and physical challenges.

Proper height of artwork placement is also important in order for young learners to see what is being displayed. It can be helpful for the educator to bend down to a child's level for a different perspective. If there are children in wheelchairs, additional care must be taken to ensure that everyone's viewpoint is considered.

When teacher generated materials placed on classroom walls and shelves become worn, faded, or broken, the teacher sends the message that it is all right to take little or no care of the environment. It is prudent to remember the nonverbal modeling power that adults have on the children they teach.

Some teachers spend inordinate amounts of time and money furnishing the learning environment in a fashion that not only overcrowds the classroom but also overpowers and overstimulates the young occupants. Good judgment should be exercised when it comes to decorating. Sometimes subtle touches of home—comfy pillows to sit on, a cozy chair to curl up in, a well-placed lamp in the reading area, live plants to add beauty as they clean the air and also encourage responsible student care, soft area rugs to define space— are just the furnished touches a classroom needs. Therefore, when visually enhancing the classroom, a sensible teacher:

- Is wary of over-decorating and over-furnishing;
- Is mindful of the effect on the senses;
- Makes an effort to display student creations;
- Encourages input from young learners;
- Is aware of the viewers' height;
- Is mindful of the condition of materials;
- Uses cozy touches of home.

Over time, we have learned that both outdoor and indoor learning environments are instrumental in determining how and what children learn. We now know that educators need to be aware of how to adjust the physical environment to fit and include all of their young learners. Cognizance of developmentally appropriate practices is central to setting up and maintaining a physical classroom environment that supports and encourages child-centered, inquiry-based learning to integrate the curriculum.

The physical environment plays a crucial part in helping to establish a thoughtful classroom climate. In the next section we will discuss the roles the occupants of a classroom or center play in establishing and sustaining a caring, civic-minded classroom community.

## THE SOCIAL-EMOTIONAL ENVIRONMENT

You are now aware of the importance of the inside and outside physical environments and how they affect children's learning, and throughout this textbook you will be offered approaches to prepare and present curriculum in a meaningful and relevant, child-centered fashion. Although the physical environment and the curriculum may be prepared to foster integrated, inquiry-based learning centered around the children, the social and emotional environment is just as important for young learners. Even the best-equipped and laid out physical environment, coupled with an engaging and motivating curriculum, will not be effective if the social and emotional needs of the learners are not taken into consideration.

### A Caring Environment: Accepting and Safe

Teachers and the learning environment have a mighty impact on incoming young children from the very beginning of their school year. It is important to note that *their* beginning may occur at any time throughout the year, as there are children who enter a class after a formal school year has begun and youngsters who enter a childcare center at any time. It is a weighty undertaking for a child to learn to trust strangers. As children enter school they trust that the adults in charge, whom they barely know or do not know at all, will keep them safe, and they hope that they will be treated fairly and kindly by the equally unfamiliar other children. Not only do youngsters need to feel, hear, and see that their physical environment is a safe place, but they need to feel emotionally safe as well—safe to attempt the unknown and safe to establish independence. Young learners need the security of a caring environment.

Critical to establishing a caring environment is the connection the children make to one another. There is a connective power that students gain, when they bond with others, that allows them to offer unconditional support for one another's attempts and achievements. Teachers need to make time in the school day for providing bona fide opportunities for children to interact cooperatively and constructively. "Cooperation is an essentially humanizing experience that predisposes participants to take a benevolent view of others. It allows them to transcend egocentric and objectifying postures and encourages trust, sensitivity, open communication, and prosocial activity" (Kohn, 1998, p. 241). Inquiry-based learning projects provide meaningful opportunities for young investigators to apply their skills as they work cooperatively as well as individually to question, experiment, and discover new knowledge. Equally critical to establishing a caring environment is the connection young learners make with the adults in charge. Children want and need to know that the teacher has their best interests at heart, and that the teacher indisputably cares about them as individuals and as a collective group. Connections are also formed when teachers share pieces of their personal presence with their students, for such sharing sends the message that teachers, too, are human and are capable of empathizing with the young learners. For example, "When students who have been in poverty (and have successfully made it into middle class) are asked how they made the journey, the answer nine times out of 10 has to do with a relationship—a teacher, counselor, or coach who made a suggestion or took an interest in them as individuals" (Payne, 2001, p. 142).

**Figure 2.2** The first days of school are filled with both anticipation and apprehension; teachers and the learning environment play an important role in helping young learners feel safe as they begin school.

In a caring, emotionally safe environment, children know that the adults as well as their classmates are tolerant and supportive of everyone's efforts to raise questions and share novel ideas. To maximize their learning potential, children must be wrapped in the comfort of safety and acceptance because it is through such security that young learners learn trust. Further, children must trust in order to risk, and they must take risks in order to learn.

### The Teacher's Influence on the Social-Emotional Environment

The teacher in a child-centered classroom must think and behave in ways that are different from those of a teacher whose primary purpose is to transmit knowledge. The teacher who honors input from the learners must have enough self-confidence to step back and let children share in the power. He or she must be flexible as well as ever vigilant for teachable moments. The teacher in a child-centered classroom must be well versed in developmentally appropriate practices. In addition, the teacher must not only be aware of but supportive of the needs and individuality of each learner.

The influence of a teacher on the formation of the social-emotional environment is paramount indeed. Generally speaking, it is easier and faster to be authoritarian, and though authoritarianism might be suitable for knowledge transmission, it is inappropriate for child-centered learning. With some thoughtful effort and willing experimentation, however, success in being a teacher who chooses to facilitate rather than dictate is quite attainable.

### The Teacher as a Model of Behavior

One major route to success is to exploit the tendency of young children to do as we do, not as we say. Adults should never underestimate the influence that their own words and actions have in causing both desirable and undesirable behavior in children. Because young children are imitative, much can be accomplished if we model what we want the children to do and become. If we want them to treat each other with courtesy and dignity, then we must treat them with respect in return. If we speak loudly at the children, they will soon be shouting at one another. If we bend the rules, it is to be expected that the youngsters watching us will not only question why we did so but wonder why principles to guide behavior are instituted in the first place. If we present ourselves as passionate, perpetual learners, our enthusiasm for learning is transmitted. Some teachers may need to make a conscious effort to modify their own behavior if they are working toward establishing copy-worthy words and actions. On the positive side, teachers can:

- Speak softly, or at least without shouting, even to the whole class, and the children will follow the teacher's example. Not only will this encourage a tranquil classroom, but should there be an occasion when the teacher's voice must be raised, it will have much more impact. Use a normal speaking voice and refrain from using high pitched "baby talk."
- Model appropriate verbal courtesies. The power of "please," "thank you," and "excuse me, please" can never be underestimated; use them often and with sincerity. When appropriate, ask permission of a young learner before moving or erasing something of his or her creation. Never use sarcasm.
- Model appropriate nonverbal courtesies. Unless children are allowed to sit on the tables, teachers should not. Unless a snack table is set up for free use during the day, teachers should not be munching on snacks while teaching. If the children are expected to walk around, rather than through, work and play areas, then the teacher should, too. Even an adult's subtle rolling of the eyes may well be observed and imitated.
- Demonstrate polite behavior with other adults in the classroom. Introduce a visitor to the class when appropriate. Children are very interested to observe adult interaction and will frequently imitate the behaviors later.
- Remember to treat others as you would want to be treated.
- Be an enthusiastic adult learner and model the joy of learning.

Modeling behavior requires the teacher to decide what it is that children should do and then to demonstrate where possible. Do not assume that children will automatically pick up the good behavior that you want them to model. To help focus children's attention on the behavior that is being sought, it is sometimes necessary to verbalize and demonstrate what it is exactly that you are seeking. Make your words and actions work together as you model the desired behavior. Model slowly and explicitly. Then, allow time for children to practice, revisiting the behavior from time to time. For instance:

- "I'm walking carefully around Farhat's and Ray's block sculptures because I don't want to knock them down. Please follow me and see if you can do it, too."
- "I'm going to push my chair in so it goes close to my desk when I'm not using it and nobody falls over it. I'll push mine in. Now, please push in your chairs so they are close to your tables."
- "I closed the door very quietly. Adele, now it's your turn to close it very quietly as well."

To have a truly child-centered class, it is also necessary for teachers to keep their egos in check. Teachers should expect to hear children declare that "no one" taught them to read; they just did it. They need to be glad when a child says proudly, "I tied my shoe all by myself!"

### The Teacher as Facilitator

In a child-centered, inquiry-based classroom, the teacher needs to be someone who does not need, or overcomes the need, to be a strong authority figure. This teacher must be willing to relinquish some hold on power and control and let children make many of their own choices and decisions. Some teachers who take a realistic look into their own needs may discover that they would really be happier having all the power for themselves. But in a society that strives to be a democracy, it is worth helping even very small children learn the responsibilities and rights that accompany independent decision making.

We therefore call the teacher who encourages children's independent thought and action, and utilizes the curiosity of children to construct meaning, a *facilitator*. Based on the Latin root word *facilis*, meaning "easy," *facilitating* education means making academic and social learning as easy as possible for children. It does not mean that teachers should avoid giving children challenges, but it does indicate that roadblocks should be removed whenever they appear. When teachers facilitate learning, they think flexibly and may choose from a variety of teaching techniques and methods.

Children are permitted and encouraged by the facilitative teacher to learn in different ways about different topics depending on their own needs, interests, and learning styles. Children are allowed to be active in their learning rather than passive receptacles of a teacher's wisdom and knowledge. They are encouraged to think on their own, make their own decisions, and rely on their own ingenuity.

The facilitative teacher is a question asker, constantly alert to the need to pose questions that will encourage children to think about what they are doing in new and more cognitively mature ways. This teacher is acutely aware that children also need to ask their own questions, to do in-depth research on topics of their own interest, and to have avenues to make connections in their learning.

The facilitative teacher does not regard errors in knowledge, judgment, perceptions, and so on that children communicate as inadequacies. Rather, errors are viewed as teaching opportunities for continual growth. The teacher looks for the right "teachable moments" to introduce new ideas that will help a child progress.

When the facilitative teacher integrates curricular subject matter through inquiry-based learning, it soon becomes apparent that flexibility in teaching methods is the most effective way to teach. The integrated, inquiry-based curriculum is one that takes young learners' real interests into account and draws on them to apply knowledge and construct meaning and thus help them to cement their learning.

### The Teacher as Instructor

The facilitative teacher can still provide direct instruction but must decide when it is appropriate to do so. To this point we have downplayed the instructing role of the teacher, relegating it to the transmission-of-knowledge classroom. Yet, direct instruction is appropriate when the teacher has new materials to demonstrate, important information to give and little time to do it in, or when information can be given more effectively if done directly. If the decision to use direct instruction is made knowledgeably and wisely, it can often be the best teaching technique for the moment. Of prime importance when using direct instruction with young children is to avoid lecturing to them.

### The Teacher as Provider of Play

Play is crucial to all phases of children's development: motor, affective, and cognitive. While this view has traditionally been accepted for children in preschool, there has been a movement in recent years to take play away from children in kindergarten and the primary grades. Few decisions could hinder their progress more.

Children need vigorous, uninhibited play as well as fluid, gentle play in order to develop physically. Children benefit from a balance of playing in groups while also being afforded opportunities to play alone. If young learners are not encouraged to develop their motor capacities through play, they may establish patterns and habits of inactivity that will stay with them through life.

Children need time for imaginative and dramatic play. This kind of play offers children the necessary opportunity to develop social skills while stimulating creativity. These are not skills that are simply nice to have if there's time after the "real" work is done. Many children today devote hours to television, computers, and electronic devices in lieu of engaging in hands-on activities as individuals and in groups.

As children play they learn. Preprimary young ones learn to represent the real world in play. Primary children expand on such learning through play by learning about rules—useful knowledge to have as they develop understanding of cooperation and competition. Children need time to play in order to develop cognitively. Reorganizing, regrouping, rethinking, and restructuring are activities that all take place through play.

For children of any age, play provides so many benefits that when we stifle this part of their lives, we inhibit much of their growth as well. Therefore, play is a vitally important element in any preprimary or primary classroom.

One of the things we have learned in this century from people who work with children is that play is not only a way of testing reality, but also a way of creating it. The freedom of children to play creatively changes the world! When those children grow to adulthood . . . it will have a profound effect on the way we perceive, change, and respect the real world. (Schwartz, 1998, pp. 458–459)

### The Teacher as Supervisor

In a classroom that is typically reliant on direct instruction as the main teaching approach, the teacher supervises as an authority figure. This involves relying on a variety of management techniques devoted to keeping the children on task and paying attention. Supervising in a child-centered environment means something quite different. In this case, the teacher watches over and guides the children as they learn to manage themselves. The more responsibility for and ownership of the classroom environment that the children have, the more they will see a need to take care of it. And as children see reasons to manage their own behaviors, the more likely they are to want to do so. However, allowing self-reliance and management to be shouldered by the young learners does not happen overnight. Thoughtful planning on the part of the teacher is, as always, needed.

Teachers need to invest time in teaching and practicing procedures that will help young learners become independent and responsible members of the classroom. When young learners know what is expected of them and know procedures to follow to carry out the expectations, there is relatively little need for the teacher to be the manager. And the children are earning the joyful independence that comes with being self-managers. When children learn to manage themselves, the teacher can assume the role of classroom supervisor with the pleasurable role of overseer—one who helps, guides, and advises when needed but feels comfortable and pleased that the workers are in charge.

## The Young Learner's Influence on the Environment

The impact young learners have on the classroom environment can be considerable. With knowledgeable planning on the part of their teachers, children can also contribute in positive ways to the success of a curriculum that is inquiry based and integrated.

For example, when children have a voice in the care and management of the classroom environment, they not only feel valued and more personally connected to one another, they also learn to take genuine pride and ownership in the success of others' accomplishments. Life in a healthy democracy requires participation, and thus children must have opportunities to practice participation. When children are afforded opportunities to pursue actions that help them form sincere, caring relationships with others, their supportive learning community is not based on ego and competition but rather on compassion and teamwork. Such is the type of environment needed to support children as they aspire to make connections in their learning, become secure enough to ask questions, and work together to gain greater comprehension of the world around them. Just as teachers assume many diverse roles in a child-centered, inquiry-rich environment, so will their young learners.

### The Young Learner as Teacher and Mentor

It is vital that children understand that they can learn from and with one another and that they are presented with opportunities to do so.

Pause for a moment to reflect on how you would teach the art of making French toast to an adult friend. Chances are you would be careful to introduce the steps in an understandable, user-friendly fashion and would choose vocabulary that your peer would understand. Hopefully, you would encourage your friend to try repeatedly until mastery had been accomplished, and when he or she was successful you both would bask in the

**Figure 2.3** Reading a story to the whole class as a "student story reader" provides an opportunity for the child to assume a teacher role. Student story readers can also take on the responsibility of asking their classmates questions about the story.

success of achievement. As an added benefit, it is likely that you yourself would have become even more skillful making French toast through such repeated demonstrations and would become more cognizant of pertinent choices of words and actions.

Young learners also take pleasure in helping others learn. This builds self-confidence, encourages teamwork, and strengthens the skills of the teacher-learner. Often, children communicate with empathy and understanding in ways logical to them but perplexing to adults. All learners have expertise in some area that would serve to benefit their classmates. An attentive teacher is aware of the talents of each child and strives to make opportunities for learners to teach other learners.

Opportunities for children to assume a teacher role might include opportunities to:

- Teach a craft—a weaving pattern, an easy origami sculpture;
- Demonstrate the steps they took to form a play dough* object (see note on p. 52);
- Show a dance move;
- Teach a new song, poem, or finger play;
- Read a story (practice first) to a small group or the whole class;
- Demonstrate techniques for tying shoes, zipping, buttoning;
- Lead a simple game.

Every child deserves an opportunity to participate in teaching others, and every child is capable of doing so. Alert and caring teachers keep close watch to be sure that no one is left out of such activities.

### The Young Learner as Manager

In a civic-minded classroom, all occupants are guided to become responsible managers for themselves and their belongings with the goal of developing socially conscious behaviors that extend to aiding others and the environment. In addition, learners need to participate, individually and collectively, in making decisions concerning the operation of their classroom. When students have ownership and a voice in the running of their learning environment, the community of learners is strengthened, displays of respect become habitual, and discipline problems decline. However, educators are sometimes uncertain as to the extent children are able to actively practice management.

Your authors have found that children's ability to shoulder management for their learning environment is often underestimated. When allowed to gradually take on responsibility for everyday procedures and routines, and when they have developed the skills to do so, young children become quite capable of performing activities that were traditionally reserved solely for the teacher.

One way to assure that everyone has at least one daily area of management is to develop a job chart, based on student input, with enough jobs so that everyone has a daily task for which to be responsible. (The construction of a job chart is explained more fully in Chapter 7.)

Young learners, after significant modeling and guiding on the part of the teacher, can be responsible for calling roll during morning meeting time as well as guiding a calendar or weather activity. As children gain confidence in their oral communication, they can take leadership of class discussions, manage a game, or direct a procedure or a routine.

When children are afforded opportunities to become managers in their learning environment, it does not mean losing control on the part of the teacher; it means providing a framework for helping youngsters gain the appropriate control they need to become responsible, involved, and conscientious citizens of the classroom.

### The Young Learner as Rule Maker

Attentive educators who choose to avoid time-outs, detentions, and sending disruptive children to the principal's office do not ignore misbehavior. Rather, they have strategies in place for making the learning environment such a personally fulfilling and engaging place that children strive to maintain behavior worthy of such an environment. In addition, instead of singling out students as conditionally belonging in the classroom, a teacher who is keen on developing a democratic classroom works with and assists the children in developing rules and standards for their behavior. Thus, even the most challenging children know that they are an essential part of the learning environment. Within these judicial guidelines, young children not only learn to govern their own behaviors but also strive to encourage productive behaviors in their fellow classmates. Children should be invited to make classroom rules in order to see that these standards are not set merely by powerful adults but by the learners in alliance with the teacher. When collaborating to form standards for their behavior, the children themselves have a vested interest in their learning climate.

It is advisable to have no more than five basic classroom rules for younger children. Often holding a healthy large group discussion before rules are written reveals many duplicate thoughts. It is usually simple, after such a discussion, for a teacher to synthesize the children's comments into three to five rules. It is appropriate for a teacher to ask permission to add a pertinent rule of his or her own if the children have not brought it up. For example, "May I share a thought for a rule? Thank you. I think it is important that we all keep our hands and feet to ourselves so we don't hurt one another. Is it O.K. with you if I add that rule to our list?" Figure 2.4 shows a student-generated classroom rule.

Children need to understand that rules are established for the welfare of everyone, and rules should be revisited from time to time as needed. If a rule does not seem to be fitting the needs of the classroom inhabitants, then it should be reconsidered and modified or eliminated as needed.

### The Young Learner as Responsible Citizen

When challenging, disruptive children view themselves as a needed, integral part of the classroom society, with unconditional acceptance, they are most apt to behave in ways that are beneficial to a well-functioning classroom. Often it is an unfilled need—of acceptance, of worth, or of purpose—that leads to discipline problems with a student.

"If we want students to act responsibly, we have to give them responsibilities" (Kohn 1998, p. 5). And indeed, young learners relish responsibility. Children should be asked to be responsible only for what they are developmentally capable of managing. They need

**Figure 2.4** This page from a class-made book titled *All About Our School* was in the book's chapter on "Rules So You Have Fun at Recess."

to be trained in their tasks and have ample opportunity to practice them to proficiency. When responsibility is given to children, it confirms to them that not only do the adults in charge deem them worthy of responsibility, but their peers value their contributions as well. It conveys the important message of *I know you can.* Giving responsibility communicates trust; *I trust that you will carry out your task.* According to Stephen Covey (1989, p. 178):

> Trust is the highest form of human motivation. It brings out the very best in people. But it takes time and patience, and it doesn't preclude the necessity to train and develop people so that their competency can rise to the level of that trust.

## CLASSROOM MANAGEMENT: PROACTIVE AND PREDICTABLE

When a teacher is skillful in capitalizing on the desire of his or her students to shoulder control, assume responsibility, and have active voices in the learning environment, then classroom management from the teacher's perspective becomes more of an organizational endeavor with the teacher assuming the role of supervisor and advisor.

This is not to say that there is little effort on the part of the teacher to see that learning and responsibility transpire in the classroom or center. Quite the opposite is demanded. A proficiently managed learning environment takes purposeful thought and commitment on the part of the teacher.

A teacher must have deep understanding and knowledge of three main dynamics: the learners and their proclivities, an engaging and meaningful curriculum, and a child-centered environment. In addition, a teacher must know how to make these elements work together to produce successful and satisfying learning experiences supportive of young, inquisitive learners.

Many factors go into the production of a well-managed classroom or center. Your authors, through their own experiences and from consultation with and observation of others, offer these suggestions:

### Be Proactive

Consider the steps that need (or might need) to be taken to accomplish a task *before* the task is undertaken, and then plan accordingly. Here are two examples:

- *When finger painting:* Will this be done with the whole class or in small groups? Are children's names prewritten on the paper? What procedures will be used to place the paint on the paper? What hints will children receive in conjunction with trying to keep the paint on the finger-painting paper, or will newspaper be underneath, or will the tables be washed when the painting is completed? (If so, how and when will that be accomplished?) Where will the paintings be placed to dry? Will the children carry them? How will the children clean their hands? What will the first-to-finish children do?
- *Going to the gymnasium to watch an all-school assembly:* Where will the class be sitting? Will they be sitting on designated mats or on chairs? Will the children need to be told ahead of time that the gymnasium lights will be dimmed during the assembly? Will the children need to wear their coats to get to the gymnasium? If so, what will they do with their coats once they are there? What are the procedures for

arriving to and leaving from the gymnasium? What information need the children know prior to the assembly? What if a child needs to use the bathroom during the assembly?

The time periods between activities and events are very important when it comes to maintaining desired behavior and atmosphere in the classroom. When a transition is planned, take care to think not only about *what* will be done but *how* it will be done. To help facilitate the lining up process, will children who are wearing a specific color line up first? In preparation for hand washing, will paper towels be placed by the sink ahead of time for student use, or will children get them from the paper towel dispenser themselves? Will all of the youngsters get their coats for outside play in one large group or will they retrieve their outerwear in small groups designated by the number of letters in their first name? These considerations might seem to be minor, scarcely worth mentioning, but a teacher's proactive thinking to a task beforehand can mean the difference between chaotic behavior and a smoothly functioning classroom.

### Provide Routine

Routines and procedures provide the predictability in the school environment that young learners need to feel secure—secure in the predictability of the known and secure in their self-confidence to carry out known responsibilities. Children like routines and the mature feeling that comes with capably executing procedures. It is important for youngsters to understand the reasons for routines as well as to practice routines through rehearsal. Two common procedures and routines appropriate for young learners center around:

- *What to do when they enter the classroom:* Where do children hang their coats? Where do notes for the teacher go? What do children do next?
- *What to do to start their day:* Un-stack chairs from the day before? Participate in a short learning activity? Meet at a group area for a morning meeting?

In addition, other routines that help a classroom run smoothly and keep behavior problems to a minimum, focus on the students knowing:

- What to do when the teacher needs their attention;
- What to do when they need the teacher's attention;
- How to safely and cooperatively get in line;
- What to do when they need to go to the restroom;
- What to do for fire drills or other emergencies;
- What needs to be done at the end of the day.

Young children, just like most adults, are creatures of habit and enjoy having the security of planned expectations.

### Have Positive Expectations

Adult expectations of learners will influence learners' achievements. Children's expectations of themselves will influence their achievements as well. Therefore, teachers should let their young learners know that they have steadfast expectations of success for everyone, including for themselves. Teachers should believe that when young investigators are allowed to constructively pursue their curiosity, they will make profound connections to new knowledge. It is important to believe that all children can learn and will work to their greatest capability. High expectations help ensure that students will be cooperative and responsible members of their classroom community. Teachers should assure young learners that they can make grand accomplishments and that they will be supported and encouraged in their efforts to reach their goals.

Ample room should be allowed for tolerance of mistakes. Mistakes are sometimes the best teachers for what could be done next time. Mistakes provide opportunities for growth. Children who are fearful of making mistakes may be hesitant to try new activities, to volunteer their questions and observations, and they may become overly critical of themselves and others.

Teachers' expectations of themselves will influence their own achievements. It helps to keep a confident and optimistic attitude as one is challenged to reach out and connect with disruptive learners, prepare an interactive environment, and continue to seek and use best teaching practices. Teaching with an inquiry-based and child-centered mindset provides many novel learning experiences for the teacher as well as for the children fortunate enough to be in his or her class. Learning experiences that are birthed through wonder and curiosity often far exceed everyone's expectations.

## IN SUMMARY

Caring, civic-minded classrooms, developed on a foundation of physical and emotional security, provide the optimal framework to promote the integration of the curriculum through child-directed, inquiry-based learning. It is challenging for teachers to make time and give the effort needed to establish the rich, stimulating, and safe physical and social-emotional environments needed to enhance children's capacity for learning, as well as to foster harmonious social growth. But teachers must rise to that challenge as they seek ways to be supportive of each of their young charges and prepare the learning environment to nurture the strengths that each child brings to the class.

Educators must be skilled in the teaching and modeling of behaviors and expectations that promote feelings of belonging, usefulness, and respect in order to set the stage needed to create an environment that provides security for every child. A blanket of security helps children gain independence, independence that will gradually mature into interdependence. A blanket of security supports and encourages young investigators as they explore their great world.

## TO DISCUSS

1. Keep in mind how readily children mimic adults. What positive traits of yours might young learners choose to imitate? What negative traits might they also choose to imitate?
2. Think back to when you first entered school. What were your fears and concerns? How did adults in your life at the time ease your apprehensions? What, if anything, could adults have done to make you less anxious during your initial days of school? Discuss how these memories, favorable or unfavorable, could be used as a guide to

create a welcoming, reassuring foundation for young learners as they begin their school career.

3. Think of the many transitions that might take place during the school day, such as lining up, washing hands, getting coats, and so on. Identify as many possible transitions as you can, then discuss proactive measures that could be taken to ensure that these transitions go smoothly.

## TO DO

1. Take a walk outside your own school or center, or visit a nearby school. Write down academic activities that could incorporate the use of this environment. Make notes of inquiry-based learning topics that might be investigated in this out-of-doors environment.

2. From the suggested criteria for good environments discussed in this chapter, make your own checklist of those you believe are most important for an effective environment. Observe one or two early childhood settings and note incorporation of environmental criteria using your checklist as a guide. Be alert for positive environmental qualities your observations provide that may not have been mentioned in this chapter. Make one checklist for the physical environment and one checklist for the social-emotional environment.

3. Use the following situation to create a blueprint or design for optimal well-being and learning: Due to lack of regular classroom space you are teaching a preschool or first grade class (choose one) in a room that once provided storage and work space for the teachers. There is plenty of wall space because there are no windows: light comes from four large skylights in the ceiling. There is an adult-sized counter along one wall with a sink. A door leads to an outside overgrown area that used to house two large garbage dumpsters. You have 23 children, a space measuring 24 feet by 24 feet, and no school-assigned assistance.

## NOTE

*In this book, we refer to "play dough," the noncommercial equivalent of Play-Doh. Here is our recipe for play dough:

2 cups flour
2 cups water
2 tablespoons cooking oil
1 cup salt
4 tablespoons cream of tartar

Mix and cook over low heat until dough forms a ball. Then cook just a little bit longer. Knead. Add food coloring if desired. Let cool. Keep in an airtight container.

## REFERENCES

Copple, C. & Bredekamp, S. (2009). *Developmentally appropriate practice in early childhood programs serving children from birth through age 8*. Washington, DC: NAEYC.

Covey, S. (1989). *The seven habits of highly effective people*. New York, NY: Simon & Schuster.

Day, D. (1983). *Early childhood education: A human ecological approach*. Glenview, IL: Scott, Foresman.

Farm to Preschool. (n.d.). *Preschool gardens*. Retrieved from www.farmtopreschool.org.

Farm to School. (n.d.). *National farm to school network.* Retrieved from www.farmtoschool.org.

Getzels, J. (1974). Images of the classroom and visions of the learner. In David, T. & Wright, B. (Eds.), *Learning environments* (pp. 1–14). Chicago, IL: University of Chicago Press.

Jensen, E. (2005). *Teaching with the brain in mind, 2nd edition.* Alexandria, VA: ASCD.

Kohn, A. (1998). *What to look for in a classroom.* San Francisco, CA: Jossey-Bass.

Leyden, L. (2009). For forest kindergartners, class is back to nature, rain or shine. *The New York Times*, November 29, A24.

Milchem, K. (2011). Breaking through concrete—The emergence of forest school in London. In Knight, S. (Ed.), *Forest school for all.* London, UK: Sage.

Nursery School Association of Great Britain. (n.d.) *To the electors: The open-air nurseryschool.* Manchester, UK: William Morris Press.

Payne, R. (2001). *A framework for understanding poverty.* Highlands, TX: aha! Process, Inc.

Prescott, C. (2008; originally 1994). The physical environment: A powerful regulator of experience. *Exchange*, March/April, 34–37.

Schwartz, M. (1998). Introductory speech, Conference at the University of Massachusetts. In Edwards, C., Gandini, L., & Forman, G. (Eds.), *The hundred languages of children: The Reggio Emilia approach—advanced reflections.* Westport, CT: Ablex.

Seaborne, M. (1971). *Primary school design.* London, UK: Routledge & Kegan.

Slentz, K. & Krogh, S. (2001). *Teaching young children: Contexts for learning.* Mahwah, NJ: Lawrence Erlbaum Assoc.

# 3

## ASSESSMENT AND STANDARDS

*Early childhood educators must critically examine facts and theories and not be dazzled by tests just because they look scientific or because governors, legislators, and community leaders believe that tests reveal "the truth" about children's learning.*
—Constance Kamii

After reading this chapter you should be able to:

- Describe the history of assessment issues, especially those related to early education;
- Explain what current assessment issues entail and how they will affect your teaching;
- Enumerate appropriate ways to assess young children while teaching for inquiry-based learning through curriculum integration.

How do you know when an activity you've done with young children has been successful? Do you measure the results based on the smiles on their faces? Do you weigh the enthusiasm with which they answer your questions? Do you note the positive feedback you get from their parents or your supervising teacher? These are all intuitively valid ways to assess success to be sure, but intuitions alone will not ensure that the children have learned something, or learned as much as they might have. Intuitive assessment will not ensure that all the children were well served, nor will it point out which ones need more support. More concrete documentation than those very satisfying smiles is required. Those who seek such documentation include parents, supervisors, directors and principals, curriculum directors, funding agencies, and legislators. Even without such outside forces placing pressure on teachers, it can be argued that concrete documentation is essential as a way to ensure that each child's development is being addressed fully, that the physical and social/emotional environment is supportive, and that educators' teaching approaches are as effective as they could be.

In this chapter we provide an overview of assessment generally, but then focus on what is appropriate for a classroom devoted to inquiry-based learning and curriculum integration. Currently, there are plenty of controversial issues surrounding the assessment of young children and their education, but we shall see that this has always been the case.

## A BRIEF HISTORY

In 2002, a group of early childhood specialists, meeting to create a position statement on assessment, noted that even the most basic of terms seemed to have multiple meanings. A sub-group agreed to create a list of important terms with accompanying definitions. The result was a glossary titled, *The Words We Use: A Glossary of Terms for Early Childhood Education Standards and Assessment* (Council of Chief State School Officers and Early Childhood Education Assessment Consortium, 2007). Their definitions of assessment and evaluation are useful for our work with children today, as well as when the historical background of this work is considered.

*Assessment*, according to the glossary, can be defined as "a systematic procedure for obtaining information from observation, interviews, portfolios, projects, tests, and other sources that can be used to make judgments about characteristics of children or programs." Note that, according to this definition, data are collected and analyzed, and descriptions are made, but evaluative judgments have not yet been made. This, in the field of education, differentiates assessment and evaluation while a dictionary might consider them synonymous.

*Evaluation* then, is defined by the early childhood glossary as "the measurement, comparison, and judgment of the value, quality, or worth of children's work and/or of their schools, teachers, or a specific educational program based upon valid evidence gathered through assessment."

Although the functions of these two processes do overlap to some degree, separating them out can help educators understand *assessment* as a means of determining where they need and want to go next in their teaching. *Evaluation* tells educators how satisfactorily they and their students are doing, not only in their own eyes, but through the eyes of others as well.

Until the early 20th century, assessment and evaluation were largely in the hands of the teacher with all the possibilities surrounding competence and bias that entailed. As public education became more universal, and the so-called child study movement made scientific research into assessment a priority, the possibility of accurate evaluations of student progress became attractive. The first widely popular test related to education was the Thorndike Handwriting Scale, introduced in 1909. By the 1930s, most states were engaged in some sort of standardized school testing, although nowhere near to the extent that is the case today. From the 1950s onward, the volume of testing began to grow by 10% to 20% a year, parents became more informed and involved, newspapers began to report results by school and district, and students learned that their individual results would now matter much more than they had in earlier times (Perrone, 1990). High-stakes testing had arrived.

As reported in Chapter 1, two 20th-century movements affected early childhood education directly. In both cases, there were important implications for assessment and evaluation. The first movement related to the space race with the Soviet Union that led away from Dewey-based progressive education and toward a back-to-basics approach with related achievement testing. The concern about test scores drove many preschool, kindergarten, and primary teachers, as well as their supervisors at all levels, to revise curriculum as watered-down versions of the higher grades.

The second movement was the founding of Head Start in the mid-1960s. Due to the fact that every Head Start center was, and is, federally funded, accountability in the form of tests was deemed necessary. Gains in children's intelligence scores and on achievement tests, as well as positive evaluations of the many components of program design (for instance: environments, staffing, schedules, curricula, teaching methods, materials, parent involvement) were required for continued funding. Over the next decade or so, more than 200 preschool tests were published. By 1986, Head Start and other early education programs were impacted by that year's amendments to P.L. 94-142, The Education of All Handicapped Children Act (P.L. stands for Public Law.) The amended law's title was changed to the Individuals with Disabilities Education Act (IDEA) and required that states provide Special Education services to eligible preschoolers between three and five years old. It also provided incentives for states to begin providing Early Intervention services to eligible infants, toddlers, and their families. Now, new tests would be required to screen, identify, and ultimately create interventions for children at risk (Hyatt & Filler, 2013).

Widespread concern about the watered-down curricula and increased testing eventually led to position papers published by a number of education organizations and to the first edition of the National Association for the Education of Young Children's (NAEYC) *Developmentally Appropriate Practice in Early Childhood Programs* (Bredekamp & Copple, 1987). The authority with which these organizations spoke made it possible for early educators nationwide to resist not only watered-down curricula but inappropriate testing as well.

In addition, there was a concerted effort by the early childhood field to find alternative "authentic" ways of assessing young children, their teachers, and their programs. The general consensus was that such assessment would be tied to what children and teachers were actually doing in their centers and classrooms, that is to say, "performance based" assessment. A full statement of what that might look like was given as:

> the process of observing, recording, and otherwise documenting the work that children do and how they do it as a basis for educational decisions that affect those children . . . it assigns priority to the needs and accomplishments of the individual learner rather than placing primary importance on measures of program outcomes based on scores of large groups of learners . . . Authentic assessment provides continuous qualitative information that can be used by the teacher to guide the instruction of individuals. (Puckett & Black, 2001, p. 22. Based on position statements of various educational organizations.)

Although the positions on assessment taken by NAEYC and other organizations did have an effect on centers and schools, new national legislation began to negate some of the progress made, both in terms of testing and in approaches to teaching.

In 2001, the federal Elementary and Secondary Education Act of 1965 was reauthorized and updated to its new incarnation as the No Child Left Behind Act (NCLB, Public Law 107-110). The focus continued to be on both elementary and secondary schools, but introduced more stringent requirements and expectations, particularly in the field of reading, as a way of increasing the performance of schools nationwide. Because the United States does not, as many other countries do, have a national curriculum, each state was given some freedom to create its own methods and systems for meeting the law's requirements and in recent years, multistate collaborative efforts produced standards in the subject areas of language arts, math, and science.

Although the first year in which all children were to be tested in reading and math was the third grade, each school was also expected to demonstrate "annual yearly progress." Schools, districts, or states responded by creating not only annual tests for kindergarten and primary children, but often tests that would be given on a continuing basis throughout the year. In some cases, the testing even reached into the preschools. One writer said in the *Harvard Education Letter,*

> the accountability "stick" in the legislation (make progress toward your goals or lose funding) is going to give the instrument used to assess these skills considerable influence over curriculum and instructional practices. If the National Reporting System, administered recently to more than 400,000 Head Start children, is any indication of what is to come, this influence will not be positive. The test assesses recognition and knowledge completely decontextualized from meaningful activities. (Stipek, 2005, p. 3)

In addition to articles by academics such as the one just quoted, online forums and blogs were devoted to the frustrations of teachers who felt required to "teach to the test" without regard to what NAEYC would call "developmentally appropriate practices." Even the popular press entered the fray with *Newsweek* publishing a cover story devoted to "The New First Grade: Are Kids Getting Pushed Too Fast, Too Soon?" (Tyre, 2006). Much of the article's focus was on the negative effects of overtesting young children as a result of NCLB legislation. Still, many observers noted that reading and math scores actually rose in schools that were deemed failures and that education for many children in less affluent neighborhoods had most definitely improved. Thus, educational legislation remained controversial, and testing for accountability remained problematic for those concerned with early childhood.

With struggles over assessment and evaluation continuing, NAEYC's 2009 edition of *Developmentally Appropriate Practice in Early Childhood Programs* (Copple & Bredekamp, 2009) addressed their related issues directly and in depth. Referring to the importance of assessing children's development and learning appropriately, NAEYC emphasized the necessity of an approach that links assessment of children to their school and center experiences and that meets the needs of each individual child. The following five positions come from NAEYC's 2009 statement regarding sound assessment for children from birth through the primary grades.

1. *Assessment should be strategic and purposeful.* There are four specific and beneficial purposes of assessment according to NAEYC: "planning and adapting curriculum to meet each child's developmental and learning needs, helping teachers and families monitor children's progress, evaluating and improving program effectiveness, and screening and identification of children with potential disabilities or special needs" (p. 178). These purposes form the foundation of assessment across the entire curriculum and all developmental domains (cognitive, social, emotional, and physical).

2. *Assessment should be systematic and ongoing.* Every center and school should have an assessment plan in place that is "clearly written, well-organized, complete, comprehensive" (p. 179). It should be well understood by directors, principals, other administrators, teachers, and families. Assessments should be carried out at regular intervals and done by trained and appropriate personnel.

3. *Assessments should be integrated with teaching and curriculum.* Assessments and the center's or school's developmental and academic learning goals should be consistent with each other. When this is the case, assessment is used skillfully to refine teaching plans, implement curricular activities, change room setup, and acquire or develop resources. Assessments are also integrated with teaching and curriculum and are based on what children can do independently as well as on their skills in collaborative work.

4. *Assessments should be valid and reliable. Validity* indicates that an assessment tool measures what it claims to measure. If the assessment tool has high *reliability*, it will produce the same or similar results if given repeatedly. The importance of validity and reliability in the testing of young children is demonstrated when the goals of assessment are considered. For example, the information that is gleaned from testing is used for purposes such as "identifying, diagnosing, and planning for children with special needs or disabilities" but not to group or label them inappropriately. Care is taken to use assessment instruments that compare children of "similar ages, cultures, home languages, and so on" (p. 324).

5. *Assessments should be communicated and shared.* Centers and schools regularly share with families the progress their children are making in all developmental domains and academic areas. Teachers and families work together in "ways that are clear, respectful, and constructive" (p. 181). Teachers also share information with the teachers who will work with their children in upcoming grades; however, such sharing must be done "within the limits of appropriate confidentiality policies" (p. 182).

These five positions from NAEYC represent the organization's views of what is positive about assessment in early childhood care and education. Table 3.1 provides examples of what NAEYC deems inappropriate as well. The inappropriate examples are titled as being "In Contrast."

### Taking Diversity Into Consideration

The history of modern early childhood education includes increasing consideration of young children with a diversity of needs. The English McMillan sisters, whose nursery school was described in Chapter 2, were driven by an intense need to improve the poor health of urban youngsters. Maria Montessori, the sisters' Italian contemporary, began her journey as early childhood educator in response to the ill treatment of children with cognitive disabilities. In the United States, the mid-20th century's creation of Head Start was intended to meet the challenges of poverty. Federal laws such as P.L. 94-142, mentioned earlier, and P.L. 99-486—extending educational coverage down to age three and family intervention services to birth—continue to address the needs of children with special needs such as lack of English and various disabilities.

Teachers in preschool and the primary grades can expect that some of their children will have special needs that qualify them for an Individualized Education Program (IEP).

**Table 3.1** Assessing Children's Learning and Development

| Developmentally Appropriate Assessment of Young Children's Development and Learning | In Contrast |
|---|---|
| 1. Assessment is strategic and purposeful. | • No systematic assessments are done.<br>• Results of assessments are not used to adapt curriculum to meet children's needs.<br>• Teachers diagnose or label a child after only a one-time assessment.<br>• Screening is done so late in the year that children go for months without needed interventions.<br>• Tests are used to hold children back or place them in remedial classrooms. |
| 2. Assessment is systematic and ongoing. | • No plan for assessment exists.<br>• Screenings aren't often enough considering children's rapid growth and development.<br>• Assessments are rare and/or random.<br>• Teachers make diagnoses better done by specialists.<br>• Teachers are required to give tests and screenings without appropriate training. |
| 3. Assessments are integrated with teaching and curriculum. | • Assessments focus on goals not in the school's or center's curriculum.<br>• There is little focus on supporting learning and development through curriculum.<br>• Assessment results are filed away and not made use of.<br>• Teachers use quizzes and tests that tell what children got right and wrong but not whether they understood or not. |
| 4. Assessments are valid and reliable. | • Tests and measures are used that have not been sufficiently vetted for validity and reliability.<br>• Methods not suited to the children's ages are used (e.g., multiple choice tests).<br>• Families' input is not accepted or respected.<br>• Assessments assume more background knowledge than the children have. |
| 5. Assessments are communicated and shared. | • Families are not informed of assessment results.<br>• Assessment results are not shared with schools or centers that children will move to.<br>• Progress reports to parents are only in the form of letter or numerical grades. |

*Source*: Copple, C. & Bredekamp, S. (2009). *Developmentally appropriate practice in early childhood programs serving children from birth through age 8*. Washington, DC: NAEYC.

The IEP has been described as the centerpiece of the federal laws and is defined as "a written document that provides a framework for the provision of a Free Appropriate Public Education (FAPE) for an individual child with a disability" (Hyatt & Filler, 2013, p. 47). The benefits to the child of an IEP are determined by a collaborative team that includes various specialized experts as well as the child's own teacher and parents. An important aspect of the IEP pertains to appropriate assessment, as noted in NAEYC's views in Table 3.1. An IEP has both long-term goals and short-term objectives, and requires that the child's educators and caregivers provide any individually needed assistance that will ensure fair assessments and evaluations. Upcoming chapters, particularly those addressing specific academic subjects, will provide further information for assessment and evaluation in the classroom.

### Inquiry, Integrated Learning, and High Test Scores

Despite federal legislation focused on the needs of individual children and expert statements from NAEYC, as well as their influence on the work of experts in the early education field, pressure to raise test scores through rigid and scripted educational programs continues. Such pressure has been, in large part, related to the needs and requirements of the No Child Left Behind Act (NCLB) described in Chapter 1. The Obama administration's adaptation of NCLB has provided more flexibility to states in regard to both programming and assessment. The recent Race to the Top—Early Learning Challenge (RTTT—ELC) appears to provide even more flexibility with its requirement that "any use of assessments conforms with the recommendations of the National Research Council's report on early childhood" (U.S. Department of Education, 2012). As of 2013, just nine states had been approved for RTTT—ELC grants, so overnight widespread flexibility in curriculum and assessment is probably not to be expected.

Thus, it is important to question if rigid and scripted programs are really necessary to raise test scores. Can children learn in developmentally appropriate programs and still do well on tests? Your authors believe that children engaged in an integrated, meaningful curriculum infused with inquiry and wonder can perform just as well if not better on tests than their young counterparts who are subjected to a tedious, fragmented, irrelevant, "test-prepping" curriculum. Your authors believe this because they have habitually seen stellar test performance in their own and others' classrooms. And they believe it because of research-based results as demonstrated in the following description of a preschool in which the teachers refused to be afraid of assessments, but used them to evaluate and validate their developmentally appropriate curriculum.

The C. Ray Williams Early Childhood Center, located in Whitehall, Ohio, has been in operation since the early 1990s and hosts close to 100 children from varying economic levels, with a high percentage of English language learners. In recent years, the Center, along with all others in the state, has been required to administer standardized language and literacy tests to their preschoolers twice a year. In addition, an observation system, also focused on literacy behaviors, is used throughout the year. Scores on these tests are compared across area preschools and Head Start centers. In 2006, a major study focused specifically on the Williams Center (Sanders & Cutler-Osbourne, 2006).

The demographics of the Center might lead to an expectation of low test scores. This was, after all, not a privileged group of children. Of the 41 who were tested, 11 were English language learners (ELL) and 30 met federal guidelines for poverty. (All the ELL children also met poverty guidelines.) However, when scores across centers were analyzed, the Williams Center had not only achieved its hoped-for goals for the year, but at times almost doubled the scores that were considered average for a center.

What, then, was the approach used by the Center to achieve such results? With testing pressures such as these, it might have been tempting to opt for a structured, or even drill-oriented, approach to teaching, which for many schools and centers would seem to be the most direct line to high test scores. The faculty and administration at this center, however, chose to utilize a "Reggio Emilia inspired, negotiated project approach curriculum that is grounded in play and imaginative endeavors" (Sanders, 2006, Personal communication). They did this while also making sure that this very creative curriculum was aligned with their state's early learning content standards.

This study's results provide definite proof that it is not necessary to deny young children opportunities to play, research, and negotiate their own learning in order to succeed on high stakes standardized tests. The study concluded that, ". . . it is clear that C. Ray Williams provides children with a literacy-rich environment that closes gaps between 'typical' children and children who have concerns in their lives such as poverty and English as a second language" (p. 5).

## THE PART THAT STANDARDS PLAY

This book's curriculum chapters will include the Common Core State Standards for Math, the Common Core State Standards for English Language Arts, and the Next Generation Science Standards. These three sets of standards were the result of multistate collaborative efforts to provide a cohesive approach to instruction with clear and consistent understandings of what students are expected to learn. The curriculum chapters will also address the standards set by the national organizations associated with each of the separate school subjects. These standards might have somewhat different formats or emphases, depending on the sponsoring organization, but there are two positions they share regarding young children's learning: Inquiry-based learning is valid and valuable, and opportunities to integrate content across subjects will enhance true learning.

Before we discuss the function that standards play in the inquiry/integrated curriculum, we need to clarify a few definitions for early learning to provide a useful basis. These come from the online resource *The Words We Use:*

- *Content Standards:* Statements that provide a clear description of what a child should know and be able to do in a content area at a particular level.
- *Early Learning Standards:* Statements that describe expectations for the learning and development of young children across the domains of health and physical well-being, social and emotional well-being, approaches to learning, language development and symbol systems, and general knowledge about the world around them.
- *Standards:* Widely accepted statements of expectations for children's learning or the quality of schools and other programs.
- *Standards-based Assessment:* A process through which the criteria for assessment are derived directly from content and/or performance standards.

The following questions and answers provide some background information regarding the basic functions and importance of standards.

*Where do standards come from and how are they formulated?* They originate with the ideas of researchers, educational thinkers, designated panels created by sponsoring organizations, school administrators, parents, and members of legislatures. These groups then "try to project into the future to imagine what children will need to know and be able to do when they grow up" (Bowman, 2006, p. 43).

*Are standards really important or necessary in early childhood education?* Many in the field try to resist what feel to them like confining, rigid expectations, arguing that children, families, and cultures have too much variation for standards to work. In a keynote address to NAEYC, the renowned early educator Barbara Bowman argued for standards, saying that, "When a program has no standards it really means that everyone gets to use their own standards without subjecting them to scrutiny . . . In my view this is an ethical problem" (2006, p. 43). For Bowman, the concern about cultural and developmental differences should become a part of the standards themselves: "There is no such thing as developmental competence outside of a cultural context—standards recognize the importance of culture, and as social constructions they ideally represent a community compromise on what children should know and be able to do. In a multicultural world, we must compromise to arrive at common expectations" (pp. 45–46).

Further argument for early childhood standards is given by Carol Seefeldt (2005) in her book devoted to showing teachers how to work with standards in the various content areas. She avers that standards can benefit early education as they:

- Bring clarity to what young children can and should be learning;
- Foster improvement in the development of curriculum;
- Bring continuity to curriculum from preschool through primary grades;
- Help bring professionalism to the field;
- Foster accountability among teachers for what they are teaching and what young children are learning. (p. 14)

*If standards are important, how can we work with them in a classroom or center that values inquiry-based learning and an integrated curriculum?* In each of the upcoming curriculum chapters of this textbook, examples are given to demonstrate how this can be done. The standards provided by each subject-specific organization call directly for integration and also promote the idea of learning through inquiry.

Other organizations such as NAEYC and the National Association of Early Childhood Specialists in State Departments of Education, as well as individuals who are experts in curriculum and child development, also argue for assessment that relates well to inquiry and integration. As we have seen in the Williams Center example, standards-based assessment can be successful without resorting to rigid, prescribed teaching methods and content.

When teachers have clarity and understanding of what their young students should know and be able to do, such awareness can help give them the confidence to use inquiry learning through integration to help their young investigators obtain maximum growth. Therefore, wise teachers embrace standards and assessment as tools to guide them as they create and use a successful early childhood curriculum.

### Ways to Assess Children's Progress in Meeting Standards

The differences between standardized achievement tests and authentic, or performance-based, assessments were described earlier. Despite their usual inappropriateness for young children, standardized tests will probably be a required part of an educator's teaching life. Their results will possibly have little to do with an educator's ability to evaluate his or her children's true learning. There are, however, alternatives that can be regarded as authentic, useful, and developmentally appropriate. Here are some that have stood the test of time and are generally regarded highly by early childhood experts.

### Observation

Observation is an assessment method useful for focusing on individual children as well as on group interactions. For early childhood educators, especially those involved with the youngest children, observation may be the most important assessment tool to be used throughout the day, focusing as it does on what children can do rather than on what they cannot do (Beaty, 2010). Data collected through observation are valuable when used to communicate with children's families about their development and progress (Nilsen, 2010). Such observations should be written down as often as feasibly possible. Some teachers carry clipboards around with them for taking notes; others carry index cards in apron pockets. For the most part, children don't question this behavior or, if they do, it is only for the first day or two. A very basic explanation on the teacher's part is all that is necessary. Entries should be nonjudgmental. Compare one teacher comment—"Mandy is sad today"—with an alternative—"Mandy had tears in her eyes when she came in but wouldn't talk about it." The first notation closes down further thinking about Mandy's behavior, whereas the second reminds the teacher to perhaps revisit their conversation later when Mandy feels better about talking.

### Anecdotal Records

Such a record is considered "an objective account of an incident that tells what happened, when, and where. The record may be used to understand some aspect of behavior, including a problematic unusual behavior" (Wortham, 2006, p. 103). Information is usually recorded after an interesting incident is completed rather than while it is going on (Ahola & Kovacik, 2007). A strength of anecdotal records is that, over time a child's feelings can be revealed. It is possible to just make a quick note about an experience, but another approach is to write it in three parts: a beginning in which the setting, time, and list of children involved are all noted; the experience itself, noting carefully the proper sequence of events; and the conclusions you draw from the entire anecdote. It takes some skill to avoid observer bias when creating anecdotal records, but with practice and perhaps feedback from more experienced practitioners, you may find them a valuable approach to assessment. We can see how this might work in Table 3.2 where a three-part chart is applied to the concerns about Mandy's tearful attitude.

### Checklists

More direct than anecdotes and generally easier to make specific, checklists have clearly defined items that can simply be checked off as present or absent. They are especially useful for observing groups of children in a short amount of time when the teacher simply needs to know if a behavior has been observed or not. Purposes may include documenting children's growth, development, or academic progress. For example, a checklist might keep track of children's recognition of alphabet letters or numbers. Another might record the acquisition of physical skills such as hopping and running. The primary shortcoming

**Table 3.2** Three-Part Anecdotal Record

| | | |
|---|---|---|
| 8:20 Mandy entered in tears. Refused to talk to me. | Went to cubby, turned her back on me. 9:05 Mandy in housekeeping corner. I enter to play as a neighbor. Observe Mandy spank baby. Ask why. "That's what moms do when babies are bad." I ask if that's what her mom did to her this morning. M. shrugs and nods. Refuses to talk. | Parent conference next Tuesday. Consider how to discuss this with M's mother. |

of using checklists is that they provide no opportunity for commentary on the quality of performance.

## Rating Scales

A rating scale is a checklist that is modified to include commentary on quality. One version to use when observing children engage in a new activity or learning experience can be implemented in the following way: Write each child's name and after it the number "1" to indicate that the activity is over the child's head and should be re-introduced at a later time; write the number "2" to mean that the activity is challenging but not too much so and, therefore, appropriate as a learning experience; write a "3" to signify that the activity has been mastered and/or is so easy for the child as to be uninteresting. This system is easily done "on the fly" when multiple activities are going on at once and it is not possible to commit an observation to memory. More details can be filled in at a later time as necessary.

## Interviews

As a way to know more about individual children and their understandings and feelings, interviews are essential, although possibly time consuming. They can be either informal or structured. In the former case, the teacher asks children about what they are doing as they play or engage in learning activities. If the children's answers indicate that they could learn from a somewhat more advanced approach, the teacher further questions them: "What do you think will happen if you add more blocks to that tower?" or "You don't have any green paint? Are there any colors you might mix?"

Structured interviews are prepared in advance and have a planned purpose. The teacher may want to get a better understanding of a child's reading or math skill level, or determine what might be a better teaching approach to deal with a learning difficulty. It can take some practice to make this kind of interview successful. What most novice teachers find difficult is asking questions to the limit of the child's ability to answer, or at least to express the answer in words. This can result in answers that simply range from "yes" to "no" to a frustrating silence. The kinds of questions that often help get fuller responses include: "Can you tell me more about that?" or "Could you do that another way?" or "What else are you thinking?"

## Work Sampling

The end results of children's work and the processes that get them to completion are all valuable means of assessment. A teacher might, for example, provide children with a choice of flash cards, board games, work sheets, or playing cards—all in one math center and all with the single goal of providing addition practice. The products, then, will also be of great variety: some that will be best sent home for posting on the fridge, others worthy of further consideration for collecting in a learning portfolio.

## Children's Self-Evaluations

Even very young children reflect on their successes, although perhaps unconsciously. With teacher assistance, they can raise their thinking to a level that is effective for increasing their understanding and capabilities. The traditional teacher queries, "Tell me about what you're doing" and "Can you tell me more about that?" encourage youngsters to think about what they are engaged in. As children gain confidence and self-awareness, questions such as "What will you do differently next time? Why?" and "What do you want to remember from this so you can do it again?" will have meaning.

Young learners can be quite astute at assessing their own work and effort both as individuals and as group members. When children reflect on the caliber of work they produced, the amount of effort they put into a task, and their contribution to group endeavors, they gain and use insightful skills that help them to be discriminating and responsible learners. A simple assessment form with positive, neutral, and grimacing face symbols next to such statements as "I tried to do my best work," "I took my time to add detail," and "I did my share of our group's work" calls for students to reflect on their efforts with deliberate awareness. See Figure 3.1 for an example of this kind of self-assessment.

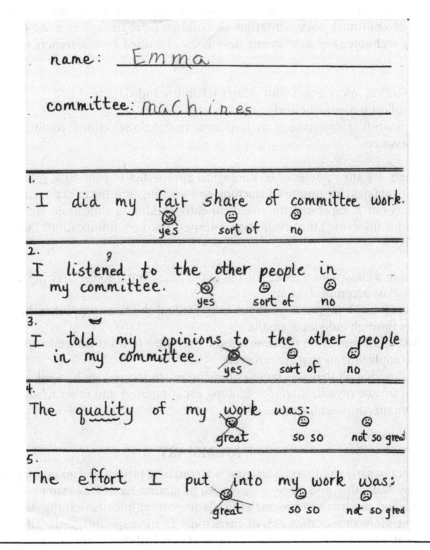

**Figure 3.1** Emma assessed her efforts on the "machines committee" as part of a pizza parlor investigation.

*Portfolios*

When teachers communicate with parents, they may well find that portfolios of work are far more meaningful and revealing than scores on achievement tests. Materials in a portfolio are real products from the actual classroom experience, not the results of an isolated testing session. Written records from the various assessment techniques that have just been described can be kept in the child's portfolio. Photos of activities, as well as work samples and products, are descriptively meaningful, especially so if the child has a voice in what is entered. A student-teacher conference to discuss what special pieces of work should be entered into the portfolio, with justifications of "why," ensures that the child is included as an integral part of the assessment process.

## THE USES OF TECHNOLOGY FOR ASSESSMENT

Technology offers methods of making sense of assessment data, important in today's climate of continual documentation of children's progress. Three major purposes for using technology in assessment have been identified by researchers (Fiore, 2012, p. 164):

1. "to collect information with greater reliability and validity;
2. to collect it more efficiently;
3. to provide a mechanism to feed into instructional efforts resulting from the assessment."

While there are any number of technological approaches to collecting, recording, sharing, and using data for improved teaching and learning, it is the engagement of families that stands out as especially important to early childhood education. Following are a few "tips for involving families through internet-based communication" (adapted from Fiore, 2012).

- Create a classroom website for many purposes, but also for drawing attention to full-class accomplishments.
- Share positive information about an individual child's accomplishments and activities through individual emails.
- Post photo stories on the class website that show how learning takes place and the accomplishments that are achieved.
- Ensure that all the class families have access to technology by applying to public and private organizations for funding for computers and other needs (see http://computersforlearning.gov).

## IN SUMMARY

Assessment in early childhood education is an ongoing process and an important one for analyzing, evaluating, and revising classroom programs. As well, assessment that focuses on individual children can provide critically important information that leads to helpful interventions or modifications of curriculum to meet specific needs. Thus, although assessment often takes place because of required standards from outside agencies, its value is continually demonstrated as programs improve and children develop in positive ways.

Assessment methods include both formal and informal or "authentic" approaches. The former is more usual when imposed from outside agencies and the latter more common when created by individual teachers and programs. Assessment methods that apply directly to the various subjects will be presented in the upcoming curriculum chapters. These will incorporate the authentic approaches discussed in this chapter and will relate specifically to the applicable content standards.

## TO DISCUSS

1. What are your main concerns related to assessment in your state or district? Discuss what you might do to overcome those concerns.
2. Does your state or district have content standards for early childhood education? Do these seem to conflict with or support inquiry learning and curriculum integration? What will they mean for you as a teacher?
3. Which of the assessment techniques in this chapter seem most reasonable and doable for you as a teacher at this stage of your career? Why? Which is the most problematic, if any? Why?

## TO DO

1. Observe the different styles of teaching used by teachers whose children must meet standards with standardized achievement tests. Interview the teachers about their teaching choices. Reflect on how these methods might work, or not work, for you.
2. If you are working in a center or school, try one of the assessment methods suggested in this chapter or one that is used by the teacher. Analyze how much you have learned about the child or children you assessed.
3. Try a second method of assessment with the same child or children. Compare its effectiveness to the first.

## REFERENCES

Ahola, D. & Kovacik, A. (2007). *Observing and understanding child development: A child study manual.* Clifton Park, NY: Thomson Delmar Learning.

Beaty, J. (2010). *Observing development of the young child* (7th ed.). Upper Saddle River, NJ: Merrill.

Bowman, B. (2006). Standards: At the heart of educational equity. *Young Children, 61* (5), 42–48.

Bredekamp, S. & Copple, C. (1987). *Developmentally appropriate practice in early childhood programs.* Washington, DC: NAEYC.

Copple, C. & Bredekamp, S. (2009). *Developmentally appropriate practice in early childhood programs serving children from birth through age 8.* Washington, DC: NAEYC.

Council of Chief State School Officers and Early Childhood Education Assessment Consortium. (2007). *The words we use: A glossary of terms for early childhood education standards and assessment.* Retrieved from www.ccsso. org/Projects/scass/projects/early_childhood_education_assessment_consortium/publications_and_prod ucts/2892.cfm.

Fiore, L. (2012). *Assessment of young children: A collaborative approach.* New York, NY: Routledge.

Hyatt, K. J. & Filler, J. W., Jr. (2013). *Writing educationally relevant and legally compliant individualized education programs (IEPs) for preschool and elementary age students with disabilities: A guide for general and special educators.* Dubuque, IA: Kendall Hunt Publishing.

Nilsen, B. (2010). *Week by week: Plans for documenting children's development* (5th ed.). Belmont, CA: Delmar.

Perrone, V. (1990). How did we get here? In Kamii, C. (Ed.), *Achievement testing in the early grades: The games grown-ups play.* Washington, DC: National Association for the Education of Young Children.

Puckett, M. & Black, J. (2001). *The young child.* Upper Saddle River, NJ: Merrill Prentice Hall.

Sanders, T. & Cutler-Osbourne, C. (2006). C. Ray Williams Early Childhood Center project: Final report to the Martha Holden Jennings Foundation, Cleveland, OH.

Seefeldt, C. (2005). *How to work with standards in the early childhood classroom.* New York, NY: Teachers College Press.

Stipek, D. (2005). Early childhood education at a crossroads. *Harvard Education Letter.* Retrieved from www.edletter.org/past/issues/2005-ja/crossroads.shtml.

Tyre, P. (2006). The new first grade: Too much too soon? *Newsweek,* September 11, 34–44.

U.S. Department of Education. (2012). *Race to the top—Early learning challenge.* Retrieved from www2.ed.gov/programs/racetothetop-earlylearningchallenge.

Wortham, S. (2006/1995). *Early childhood curriculum: Developmental bases for learning and teaching.* Upper Saddle River, NJ: Pearson, Merrill, Prentice Hall.

# 4

## CONNECTING CURRICULA THROUGH
## THEMES AND UNITS

*When you are out walking, nature does not confront you for three quarters*
*of an hour only with flowers and in the next only with animals.*
—Lionel Elvin

*. . . it is clear that when out walking, you can also sit and pick up the flowers and*
*concentrate solely on them for three-quarters of an hour and learn a great deal.*
*The problem is that in school we generally do not consider both*
*perspectives as necessary components of a child's education.*
—Heidi Hayes Jacobs

After reading this chapter you should be able to:

- Explain the importance of single-subject focus;
- Describe how themes and units can connect curricula;
- Enumerate benefits and concerns of using themes and units;
- Be attentive to inquiry-based learning opportunities within themes and units.

In his book, *Charlotte's Web*, E. B. White (1952) spun a tale of fantasy that pits a spider-heroine against a family of farmers who plan to "murder" and eat her friend, a young pig. Throughout this enchanting fantasy are woven elements of reality. In describing Charlotte's masterful spelling of words across her web, as no other spider before her had done, White chose to explain in detail the making of a real spider's web. He explained that to the unpracticed eye the completed web would appear to be a single entity of patterned thread, but that a more careful observer could see that the basis for the web was an intricate interrelationship between very distinct components. Each of these components had its separate and indispensable purpose.

For example, several types of thread are possible, and Charlotte chooses two: sticky thread for capturing insects and dry, tough thread for writing messages about the pig whose life she is trying to save. Important, too, are the spinnerets and spinning tubes that help play out the threads. The structure of the web requires that there be the circular orb lines as well as the radials that travel straight out from the center. Thus, a number of individual things work independently and together to create the finished web. Each is important in its own right, and each is also a component part of a grander design.

We can view the early childhood curriculum in much the same way. When children learn in a way that is most natural to themselves, they unconsciously integrate subject areas into a complex whole based on their current interests. Teachers who consciously adapt this method of learning to the classroom see the curriculum as a fully spun web that incorporates a number of components at one time. However, they also know that it is important to take a careful look at each of these components individually to be sure it is sufficiently represented. Without the radials to connect them, the orb lines in Charlotte's web would surely have collapsed. Without each subject area in the curriculum, the totality would lack strength. Before focusing on the positive ways in which a curriculum web can be woven, let's take a look at how these webs are weakened if the "radials," or subject areas, are deleted from the whole "web."

## THE SUBJECT AREAS

We will consider each subject area in turn, surmising what might happen if it were to be *deleted* from the curriculum. As you will see, each subject offers its own special strength that, when woven together with other subjects and embellished with child-centered inquiry, provides young learners full and richly rewarding learning experiences.

### Language and Literacy

The need to communicate is basic to human beings, and practice with using language is essential for their successful development. If children are denied the opportunity to express themselves while working and playing they are also denied the opportunity to learn effective communication. Literacy is at the foundation of our society and civilization. Without success in reading and writing, children are deprived of their rightful membership in much of today's society. This is not to say that children need to begin in preschool to be drilled in reading or even prereading exercises. In the primary grades, unfortunately, reading groups, reading instruction, and classroom-provided reading books are often so far removed from a child's experience that budding readers are frustrated, and young learners' desires to read are dampened. Children need activities and experiences that show the importance, excitement, and possibilities offered by the reading they will do one day. Real, meaningful, enjoyable reading and writing are what children crave and need. As you will see throughout this text, children, even of the youngest ages, have a keen desire to write and read when presented with real-life, meaningful purposes to do so.

### Mathematics

Particularly in the earliest years it is tempting to save mathematics for later, for "real" school. This point of view argues for a dull, drill approach to learning mathematics and divorces the subject from real life. Yet, mathematics is all around us, in everyday experiences, waiting to be discovered and explored. Without the introduction of math in the early years, children miss out on learning this important point, and this subject, too, becomes another exercise in tedium.

## Science

Teachers often feel weak in the sciences and so neglect their teaching in the early childhood classroom. To do so perpetuates this weakness in school learning in future generations. This weakness has already been observed across the grades and throughout the entire country. Worse, the deletion of science from the curriculum over recent years is beginning to have a profound effect on an entire society's ability to keep up with the rest of the world in the development of technology. If children have little or no experience with the sciences in the early years, they may never develop an interest in them, or worse yet, they may develop an antipathy toward or fear of them.

## Social Studies

This is a subject that is often left at the wayside when the day becomes too filled with demands. Yet, learning to participate in their society is one of the most important reasons for children to be educated. Simply passing down the culture from one generation to the next can be done without a study of the social sciences; for children to *understand* their culture, however, and to learn to make decisions about its future, social studies must be part of the curriculum. This includes the practice of democracy.

## Art

When the curriculum becomes crowded, this is often one of the first subjects to go. Yet when we look back through the history of the ages, the art produced by any society or culture is one of the most salient and telling things about it. The art we and our children produce will be one of the most important legacies we leave for the generations to come. Speaking for the present, art adds richness and beauty to life. It provides children with skills in observation, hand-eye coordination, and methods of communication. Without art the curriculum becomes drier, duller, more tedious.

## Movement and Drama

Young children learn not just with their eyes and ears, but with their entire bodies. Brain research from imaging sources, anatomical studies, and clinical data supports evidence of connections between movement and learning. Movement activities enhance cognitive processing and increase the number of brain cells. Not incidentally, movement helps reduce childhood obesity (Jensen, 2005). In the primary grades, organized sports are just beginning to be of interest. Throughout all the early years however, less organized experiences are also crucial to physical, emotional, and intellectual growth. Expressing themselves dramatically is an outgrowth, in part, of children's physical expression. Sometimes when children cannot verbalize what they are thinking and feeling, they can act it out. Without drama, then, a primary means of communication is eliminated from children's repertoires.

## Music

Like art, music adds richness to children's lives. And like art, it frequently disappears from the curriculum. When children are occupied in unsupervised play, they can be observed quite naturally and unconsciously singing, humming, and chanting their way through various activities and experiences. To eliminate music from the curriculum is to eliminate a primary means of children's communication and enjoyment.

It should be apparent that every curricular subject is important to the development of the children we teach. However, children do not naturally learn through isolating specific subjects with agendas determined by adults. Children's natural learning is more likely to take place across a subject of interest that is engaging to them—when they find a worm, pick a flower, examine a shoe, or interact with the first snow of winter.

Gaining acceptance for the idea of integration, as was discussed in Chapter 1, has at times been a struggle for schools and curriculum developers, although typically less so for the early childhood years. This has particularly been true since the late 1980s and early 1990s as Americans were discovering the Reggio Emilia preschools and the more American "project approach." This approach, along with the similar immersed model of integration introduced in Chapter 1, will be discussed in more detail in the next chapter.

In this chapter, the *webbed* model of integration, in which a topic or theme of interest is webbed to the subject areas, is our focus. The webbed model was introduced on p. 10 in Chapter 1. This model lets teachers connect, link, and organize the curriculum either through thematic instruction or by the creation of units. And, while themes and units share some attributes, there are important differences between them. The following two sections define units and themes separately and provide examples of each.

## USING THEMES TO CONNECT CURRICULA

Theme-based curriculum is designed to surround children with a unifying concept or broad topic in most of their study, and even play, for a predetermined period of time. All children in the class undertake the same thematic activities, which are planned in advance by the teacher.

It will be helpful to carefully define the terms *theme* and *topic* before going further. Various dictionary definitions explain that a *theme* is: a unifying element; a dominant idea; a central topic. The same dictionaries explain a *topic* as: an essential idea; the subject; a theme. No wonder there is sometimes confusion as to the definitions of these two words. Oftentimes educators describe a topic as a subdivision of a theme. In general, themes are broader than topics, themes function more as a unifying *idea*, while topics are more concrete. Because young learners need the actuality of hands-on, visible subjects, abstract themes such as: *independence, change,* or *the environment,* are not suitable for them. Therefore, in the early childhood years, a theme may take a more concrete, tangible, topic-like form—*All About Me, Farm Animals, Winter,* and so on. In this textbook we define a theme as a focus of study, topic-like in nature, that occurs over a period of time.

One popular theme is plants. For example, in a preschool grounded in the theme of plants, one might observe children color commercially drawn flower papers, piece together a puzzle of the life cycle of a flower, look at a variety of fiction and nonfiction books about plants, count seeds, move as plants would when blown by the wind, plant seeds in a cup and watch them grow, sing songs about planting, eat a mixture of crumbled Oreo cookies (which look like soil) mixed with gummy worms for snack time. The teacher and parent helpers might also have turned the classroom into a lush environment decorated with plants and flowers.

When the curriculum is devoted to a theme, the theme is usually obvious to any visitor to the classroom or center, and the children generally are aware of it as well. Fun, engaging activities may be scheduled under subjects connected by the theme. However, a theme's visibility does not ensure depth and meaningful coverage of a topic or logical connection between the various activities. Nor does visibility of a theme provide any insurance that skills within subject areas are used as tools to further student understanding of the topic. Thematic curriculum, in other words, must be created with deliberation and care.

One approach to careful planning of themes is the use of curriculum webs, which, on paper, look similar to Charlotte's own web. As in her web, the radial lines are devoted to the subject areas. However, in our planning model web demonstrated in Figure 4.1 (p. 74), a single connecting theme is placed in the middle, rather than spread in multiples through the orb lines. A major goal of creating such a web in relation to a theme is to help the teacher see how well subject areas are linked through the activities as well as how comprehensively subject areas are covered. To show how building a curriculum based on a theme can work, we will apply the idea of webbing to a topic dear to the teaching of many centers and schools: the month of December.

### Planning a December Theme Using a Curriculum Web

Most teachers create curriculum webs at one time or another, consciously or not. Often, such webs are created during various holiday seasons. As an example, let's see what one teacher might undertake as a curriculum web during the December holiday season.

In recent years, the December holidays have been the subject of dispute, controversy, and confusion as citizens and legal experts have argued the constitutional issue of church-state separation. As it becomes more understood that the Constitution denies government the right to *establish* religion but does not take away the right to *learn about* religion, schools have begun to reintroduce celebrations of the December holidays. To these have been added even more celebrations as immigrants from an array of cultures enter the schools. This wider array of possibilities suggests to teachers, in any thoughtful learning environment, that the premise of *goodwill toward all* should not only be highlighted during the December celebrations, but celebrated all year long.

Historically, the creation of a holiday curriculum web has been a popular one in the preschool and primary grades. This is often true even in classes where the day-by-day curriculum is rigid and divided into self-contained subjects. No matter what their feelings are the rest of the year, teachers seem to accept the idea that in December it is all right to plan learning around a theme. This tradition is so much a part of the culture that what it really is often goes unnoticed: It is a curriculum webbed to meet the interest and excitement of children—and adults as well. A look at some of the more common activities that take place during this time will demonstrate how the December holiday theme covers the entire curriculum.

**Language:** Introducing holiday words; learning poems; writing Christmas, Hanukkah, and Kwanza notes; reading stories of December celebrations; learning, writing, and presenting plays and programs.

**Mathematics:** Learning the sequence of songs and events in a holiday program; measuring ingredients for holiday cooking; making measurements (even primitive ones) when mounting or hanging decorations; creating decorations with repeating patterns; tracking the days, on a calendar or other construction, until a special event.

**Science:** Observing chemical and physical changes during cooking and baking experiences; noting how colors can be combined to form different colors.

**Social studies:** Working together harmoniously; learning about the music, food, and customs of other lands; learning about the varying December holidays of the cultures represented in the children's own class.

**Art:** Making greeting cards; designing and making gifts; planning and making room decorations.

**Movement, drama, and music:** Dancing to the music learned throughout the month; dramatizing songs and poems; singing carols and other traditional songs; creating accompaniments to holiday music; listening to recordings.

Presented as a straightforward list, the December holiday theme curriculum might contain most or all of the desired components, but let's see what greater possibilities there are by illustrating it as a web (Figure 4.1).

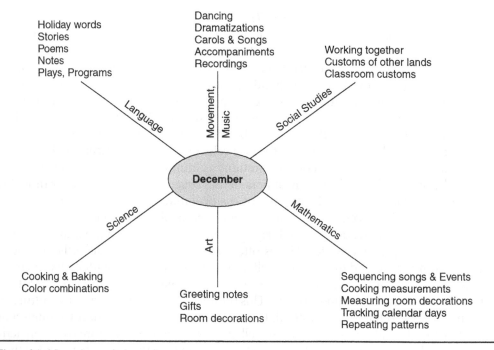

**Figure 4.1** A December curriculum web.

Here, the same activities are present, but the visual effect is quite different. The web appears less structured, more tentative, and it is these qualities that make it a useful tool for planning. The teacher can choose a theme, create a web, and then add or subtract activities as it becomes apparent that there is too much or too little emphasis in some areas.

## WHY CURRICULUM WEBS

Planning for a connected thematic curriculum can be undertaken in a variety of ways. The use of a web, however, has advantages.

### Curriculum Coverage

A major concern for any teacher considering thematic teaching should be that some curricular areas will either be overemphasized or undertaught. Planning with a web provides an overview of the entire curriculum and gives the teacher a basis for decision making of this sort. As an example, a look at the December web (Figure 4.1) tells the teacher that science is an underrepresented subject. The teacher could then choose to work in more science as a part of the theme (perhaps too contrived), to add science that is unrelated to the theme (hard to do in a hectic month such as December), or to wait perhaps until January when the children are interested in learning something entirely new (an opportunity to focus on science by making a science topic the theme of a new planning web).

### Flexibility in Planning

The making of a curriculum web provides a way of organizing that is less structured and more tentative than an outline while it still provides a focused means of organization. In the case of the December web, the teacher can see quickly that: (1) science is under-represented, (2) including both other lands and classroom cultures may be too much for one month, and (3) it will probably be better to choose between plays and more general programs in the language section. If the web is regarded as a work in progress, rather than as a finished product it can be added to or subtracted from at any given time.

Some teachers may find that after creating the web, an outline format is a good finished product. This can be done as a chronology, providing a schedule of activities in their proper sequence, and listing the subject areas. Or, the teacher may find that the web provides enough structure in itself.

## CONCERNS ABOUT CONNECTING CURRICULUM WITH THEMES

Despite the popularity of thematic teaching, there are some concerns to consider. For example, when engaged in activities that fall under a thematic umbrella youngsters may, in fact, learn certain skills and apply them in fun, albeit isolated, ways, but they may have difficulty connecting the skills to their daily lives or transferring them to future learning. John Dewey (1997/1938) offered caution concerning the linking of unrelated educational experiences and went so far as to label some experiences as "mis-educative" (p. 25). He stated, "Experiences may be so disconnected from one another that, while each is agree-able or even exciting in itself, they are not linked cumulatively to one another. Energy is then dissipated and a person becomes scatterbrained" (p. 26).

Your authors share these concerns to the extent that we prefer to move beyond connecting the curriculum with themes. Although themes can be successful if planned with great care, they are not substitutes for inquiry-based learning projects where children apply skills as they seek and then define answers to questions they have generated themselves about a topic. Inquiry-based learning projects support children's impulses to investigate things of interest to them. This results in a natural weaving or integration of the curriculum with the emphasis on skill application to further young learners' understandings.

It is important to note that while the webbed model of integration is more teacher driven and the immersed model of integration is more student driven, both use topics of study to integrate the curriculum. In Chapter 5 we will further explore integrating the curriculum through inquiry-based learning, a model described in Chapter 1 as immersed. For now, we briefly revisit the theme of plants, but used this time as a topic of an in-depth, inquiry-based project that fosters child-constructed learning connections. In this case, we might observe another class of preschool children using the topic of plants as they color student-produced observational drawings of a flower in the classroom; carry out various experiments to answer their own questions about plants and planting (such as weighing soil that is wet and soil that is dry to see which weighs more, or hypothesizing and then discovering what happens if a plant gets too much or not enough water); use magnifying glasses to spot different types of bugs on the plants; keep plant journals to record growth of the seeds they planted; or prepare to go on a field research trip to a nearby plant nursery where they can ask questions of experts and observe a broader

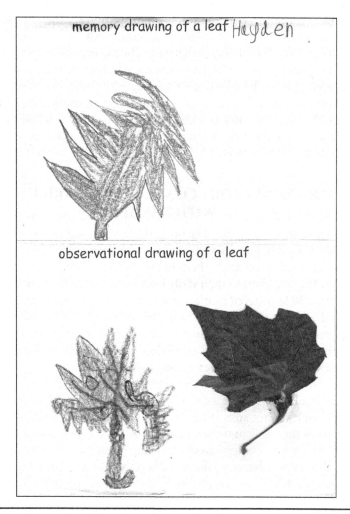

**Figure 4.2** An inquiry-based study on leaves might call on learners to compare and contrast their "memory drawing" of a leaf to their actual "observational drawing" of a leaf.

array of specimens. This classroom is adorned with child-produced representations of their learning.

Thematic curriculum can lend itself to child-centered, inquiry-based learning if children are afforded opportunities to research aspects of themes that particularly interest and motivate them. For example, in conjunction with a curriculum built around the broad theme of "Fall," children might choose to do an in-depth study on "Leaves." Young investigators might have questions about the colors of leaves, varieties of leaves, how leaves are made, why they fall, and uses of leaves. As they seek answers, the young researchers apply a variety of strategies and skills to obtain and subsequently display their new understandings. To clarify: The theme "Fall" loosely *connects* or *links* curricular activities based around the topic of fall, whereas a learner-directed, inquiry-based study on "Leaves" *interconnects* or *weaves* skills from curricular subjects with the goal of developing greater student understanding about leaves (see Figure 4.2).

Thematic curriculum, therefore, must be created with great care and with an awareness of how to make acquisition of knowledge connective, meaningful, and relevant for the young learner. Teachers should be vigilant, encouraging, and supportive of the child-initiated explorations that themes could provide.

## USING UNITS TO CONNECT CURRICULA

A *curriculum unit* is a teacher-designed body of study organized around a primary topic. A unit usually consists of preplanned lessons surrounding a topic that the teacher (or curriculum guide, or school district) deems worthy of study or of special interest to the students. Often the activities in a unit are repeated every year without particular consideration of the variety of children in each subsequent class. A unit's purpose is to provide children with what is generally the regular and expected curriculum, while working toward creating greater interest and deeper learning by incorporating the curriculum's academic subjects into the topic. Possibly making this definition confusing is the fact that, quite often, teachers refer to a unit as a "thematic unit" or even just as a "theme" when, in reality, it is an actual *unit* they are talking about.

At times, the children who become interested in a topic inspire a unit, and, at other times, the teacher realizes that there is a topic worth exploring based on observations of and discussions with the children. Most often, however, topics are determined even before a school year has started or children have been met for the first time. For example, the four kindergarten teachers in one school each assigned themselves a unit in August and then prepared lesson plans and materials, not only for themselves, but for everyone. Thus, the four teachers began the school year equipped with four completed units, but each teacher had to create only one. Each teacher also heeded opportunities to allow her children's inquisitiveness to lead to meaningful learning connections. Each knew it was necessary to be flexible and open to modifications and changes that should be made to the preplanned units.

Curriculum units share several characteristics with theme-based learning, but differ in some respects as well. While some unit study may lead to a classroom that, for a time, surrounds children with a single idea, it is not a major goal as is the case with themes. And, although several curricular subjects may be included in both approaches, a focus on subject areas is generally more intentional in the case of units. Units tend more often to carry the burden of meeting school, district, or federal guidelines and expectations and, thus, are often more formally devised. This does not ensure that the curriculum will lead to depth of knowledge and meaningful curriculum coverage, but it is a major step in that direction. The kinds of activities and learning experiences children engage in are equally important, and teachers must ask themselves, while planning, if their ideas will lead to more than surface knowledge or pleasant time filling.

Planning webs are as useful for unit creation as they are for thematic instruction. In this section we will demonstrate the use of a curriculum web that mirrors the one developed for the December theme. In addition, we will show how a second curriculum web can help teachers be sure that the needs of the whole child are being addressed. When creating curriculum units that have requirements for meeting guidelines and expectations, teachers may find that children's intellectual needs are being met at the expense of social, emotional, and physical needs. This second type of web helps circumvent that possibility.

## THE "ALL ABOUT RAIN" CURRICULUM

Let's look now at the way one first grade teacher decided to create a unit that celebrated the sometimes tediously wet weather of the Pacific Northwest. It is not a unit designed to meet governmental guidelines and expectations, although it certainly could have been extended for that purpose. The unit does, however, take children's interests and capabilities into account and demonstrates how to plan using two kinds of curriculum webs.

*The first graders never complained about sloshing through the rain to get to their classroom; it seemed that it was the adults, including the teacher, who sometimes became grumpy due to the seemingly endless drizzle. Perhaps, thought the teacher of the young want-to-be-ducklings as she watched them jump puddles, open their mouths to catch raindrops, laugh as an overflowing gutter showered them . . . perhaps by harnessing the children's enjoyment of the rain, some of their delight will splash off on me as well.*

*The teacher decided the topic of rain would be the perfect umbrella to create a unit that would be both enjoyable and of academic benefit. Before making a final decision, she made a curriculum web to determine whether the unit really could provide the kind of learning she thought her students should have.*

*It seemed to the teacher that the unit would be a manageable size, would not interfere with other curricular demands, and would apply many skills that are taught in first grade. She thought that the unit would probably not take more than two weeks, depending on the interest of the children and the continuation of the moist weather. With some potential learning experiences in mind, (and having done an in-depth study on puddles with a previous first grade class), she then jotted down some notes to determine just what it was she wanted the children to get out of a Rain Unit. Included were science, math, and language-based goals.*

### Hoped for Outcomes for a Unit on Rain

Children will:

- Practice measuring with familiar objects;
- Record and graph rain over time;
- Write, read, illustrate, and use words that describe rain and relate to rain;
- Use their five senses as applicable to rain;

- Write fiction and nonfiction stories and books with rain as the subject;
- Use music, art, and movement in a variety of forms to communicate their experiences;
- Learn facts about rain by reading books and viewing media;
- Participate in experiments relating to rain;
- Learn about other weather phenomena that occur with rain (clouds, rainbows, lightning, and so on).

*The teacher then created a planning web, inserting the learning experiences she had envisioned while attending to their relationship to her goals. Figure 4.3 demonstrates how it all came together as applied to curriculum coverage.*

*Having completed the curriculum web and feeling that, for this rather informal unit, the subject coverage and learning goals were sufficiently included, the teacher decided to experiment with a second type of web she had seen but not yet used. It is a web that shows both curriculum coverage and the ways in which the needs of the "whole child"—intellectual, social, physical, emotional—are met. Figure 4.4 demonstrates the ways in which this rather brief unit covered most curriculum areas and all aspects of development, at least at some level.*

*Knowing that this was not a lengthy unit, the teacher decided that if the students became intensely interested—and the soggy weather lingered longer than usual—there was no reason the activities couldn't be expanded. Having lived in the Pacific Northwest for some time she was keenly aware of the magical pull mud has on children as well as the eclectic raingear people wore. The teacher made a note to keep track of these and other topics within the rain unit that might be worthy of an in-depth, inquiry-based learning project in the weeks to come should the students choose to pursue a topic in greater depth.*

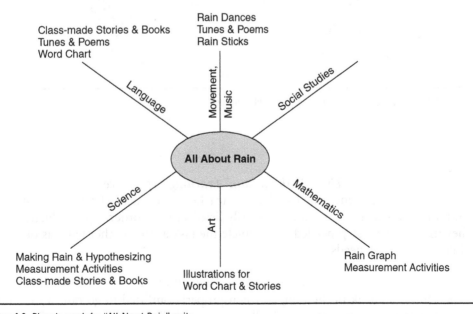

**Figure 4.3** Planning web for "All About Rain" unit.

**Figure 4.4** Whole child curriculum web for "All About Rain" unit.

### The "All About Rain" Learning Experiences

The following experiences are listed to give teachers some ideas of activities that this unit on rain included. They are not necessarily listed in their order of introduction nor do they include every step needed to complete the task as the teacher left this open to the children's learning needs.

### Measuring With Familiar Objects

- During a break in the rain, or when properly outfitted to go out in the rain, the children (as a class or individually) choose a shallow puddle to study. The children mark the depth of puddles using Unifix cubes. They keep track of the puddles' depth over time by recording the number of cubes represented on a chart in the classroom. (It is important to rinse off the Unifix cubes after use.)

- Children measure the circumference of a puddle by laying a string around puddle as close as possible to the puddle's outside and cutting the string where the two ends meet. The string is brought inside and saved. Each day (or morning and afternoon) a new string is placed around the puddle. The strings are compared over time as the puddles get larger or smaller.
- A clear plastic container with a ruler firmly attached to the side of it is placed outside to gather rain. Changes in water depth are noted, discussed, and written down over time.
- Different sized containers are placed outside to gather rainwater. The containers are brought inside and discussions are held concerning depth and volume.

### Making a Rain Graph

- Observations taken in the morning and in the afternoon are graphed over time. A simple rain/no rain graph is constructed either as a whole class or independently by students. A more intricate mist/drizzle/downpour graph can also be made.

### Writing and Reading Words That Describe Rain and Other Rain-Related Weather Phenomena

- Teacher writes as students dictate, then afterwards illustrate, words that describe rain (for example: wet, loud, heavy, gentle, and so on). These words are affixed as a word chart for all to see.
- Teacher writes as students dictate, then afterwards illustrate, other rain-related words (for example: cloud, rainbow, lightning, boots, umbrellas, and so on). Class discusses each word, providing more in-depth learning, as called for, at a later time. These words are affixed as a word chart for all to see.
- Rain descriptors and rain-related words are incorporated into individual or class-made stories and books. Such stories may center on the five senses, sequencing, cause and effect, or various rain experiences. Both fiction and nonfiction writing are encouraged.

### Using Art, Music, Movement to Communicate Rain Experiences

- Children make a rain stick by cutting a piece of aluminum foil 6 inches wide and two times the length of a cardboard tube. They first twist the foil into a coil about as long as the tube and insert it into the tube, then cover one end of the tube. A handful of beans is put into the cardboard tube and the second end is covered. The tube is decorated as desired. The sound that each rain stick makes when turned from end to end is reminiscent of rain. Such sounds are used in stories, patterns, and for movement activities.
- Children move to the beat of rain, especially fun when thunder and lightning join in.
- Children make a rain dance using their bodies: mist = rubbing fingers together, drizzle = rubbing hands together, downpour = slapping hands on knees, thunder = stomping feet on floor, lightning = clap of hands. Students take turns leading varying combinations of the rain dance as peers follow.

- Introduce tunes and poems about rain then slightly modify the words. For instance: *Rain, rain, go away. Come again another day. _____ and _____ want to play.* Students copy and fill in the blanks with names of their own choice, then illustrate (e.g., *Rain, rain, go away. Come again another day.* <u>Megan</u> *and* <u>Andy</u> *want to play*).

### *Hypothesizing and Experimenting*
- Children make rain in the classroom by filling a wide-mouth glass container with 2 inches or so of hot water (making sure it is a container that can withstand heat). Next they put an aluminum pie plate on top and fill with ice cubes, and watch for rain in the form of condensation. Finally there is a discussion of the rain cycle.
- Using elastic bands, children secure different types of material and fabrics on to jars. They then hypothesize which materials will let water through rapidly and which materials seem to be the most waterproof. As a group, with teacher direction, they record predictions and final outcomes. Materials are varied as possible. This might also lead to hypotheses and discussion as to which materials and fabrics are more water absorbent.

### *How and Why the Unit Worked*
This is one teacher's curriculum unit, using the concept of webbing both as the basic philosophy and as a tool for planning. The format she followed is very similar to the approach used in this book's curriculum chapters. Following her thought processes and planning, the unit evolved sequentially in this way:

- The children displayed an interest in a subject and seemed open to learn more about it.
- The teacher made a tentative web of curricular possibilities.
- She then listed the skills and understandings they would attain from these activities.
- To provide a comprehensive overview, both the curriculum and intellectual, social, emotional, and physical learnings were represented on a second web.
- The activities were listed and described in tentative sequential order.

This curriculum unit also displays some of the advantages for this kind of planning and teaching:

- The webs show clearly which curricular subjects are present and which are not. The teacher then has the ability to add social studies activities, for example, or to simply be aware that the subject needs addressing at another time.
- With the exception of social studies, each subject area of the curriculum was given importance. Although this was potentially a science unit, activities that integrated other subjects were also included.
- The activities were largely of the type natural to children. They had already had experiences with rain and it interested them. They would continue to have experiences with rain while learning.
- The unit would be taught because it was a topic of interest to the children. Sometimes interests can be created by the teacher through the introduction of new

ideas and topics. Other times the children themselves can inform the teacher, even unconsciously, as was the case in this unit.

- Skills were not neglected but taught in a meaningful context. The teacher did not have to say, "Children, I'm glad you're enjoying yourselves, but now it's time for math." She could move the math class outdoors where the children could see the purpose for learning.
- Although the unit had a good, sound structure, it could be readjusted as necessary.

## CONCERNS ABOUT CONNECTING CURRICULA WITH UNITS

Curriculum units do have advantages over theme-based learning as previously discussed. However, there are still dangers to be aware of. First, the convenience of being able to create intriguing, stimulating, even entertaining units in advance of a school year has its attractions. However, such planning may not work to the children's advantage or subsequently to the teacher's advantage. Suzanne learned this the hard way.

One year, three four-year-old boys came to Suzanne and pointedly asked, "When are we going to do dinosaurs?" She was a bit taken aback, not having even considered that option. A full-class discussion, however, led her to understand that almost everyone considered it their full right as students to study the topic. She then pulled together a full-fledged unit that went on for many weeks as the entire class entered into the learning with enthusiasm. The following year, she was ready for what she thought would be the inevitable interest of the next group of four-year-olds and was a bit disappointed when all her hard work was totally rejected. In fact, she never again had a class of youngsters with a rabid interest in large, extinct animals and eventually gave her materials away. Suzanne was actually pleased with the extinction of this unit, as she had lamented the availability of a crucial component of her young learners' hands-on experience: the "live" dinosaurs themselves.

A second concern, and one that leads us to our next chapter, is that curriculum units, although they are designed to take children's interests into account, are still teacher driven and teacher directed. For learning to make sense to young learners, they need to be at the center of decision making and curriculum construction. Inquiry projects can provide this element along with the thorough curriculum coverage that is essential to a successful unit.

Finally, curriculum units often provide broad coverage but don't have the depth that an inquiry-based learning project generally does. In an attempt to cover subject requirements through a topic of interest, teachers might create many entertaining activities that cover the curriculum but not delve deeply or meaningfully into it. It is sometimes better to leave some subject matter out of a unit than to try and force everything into it just for the sake of being thorough about integration. However, on a positive note, a combination of the two can work well. An observant teacher may see, during the progress of a curriculum unit, that the children are intensely interested in one specific aspect. Discussions with them might well lead to further deep inquiry on that subject alone. Think back to the unit "All About Rain." Imagine the possibilities for curriculum integration that an in-depth, inquiry-based study on mud could provide. Or perhaps young students might be very curious about how people in other parts of the world keep themselves dry. Such curiosity might be a starting point for deeper, more in-depth learning. The former study about mud would lead more deeply into science; the latter could introduce social studies issues.

In the next chapter we discuss inquiry-based learning projects in great detail. Table 4.1 points out some distinctions between units and themes and inquiry-learning projects, all of which have an important place in the early childhood curriculum when attentively implemented.

**Table 4.1** Distinctions Between Units/Themes and Inquiry-Learning Projects

| Unit or Theme | Inquiry-Learning Project |
|---|---|
| Activities and experiences are preplanned by the teacher. | Develops through: <br> - child interest/child initiation <br> - exploratory event <br> - class consensus <br> - theme/unit extension |
| Outcomes and goals are set in advance by the teacher. | Outcomes and goals are met as they are applicable to the project. |
| The teacher, or a set curriculum, determines topics of units and themes. | Children's interest is a determinant in topic selection. |
| All students in the class undertake the same work. | Students choose from a range of possibilities. |
| A field trip may or may not be included. On a field trip, information is usually given in a program directed by the expert(s) in charge. | A field research trip is an integral part of the project. It allows learners to gather information from a primary source(s) with the learners being in charge. |
| Fixed duration. | Variable duration. |
| Sequence of activities. | Process flows through three phases. |

*Source*: Adapted from Chard, S., *The project approach: A practical guide for teachers.* Edmonton, Canada: University of Alberta Press, 1992, p. 31.

## IN SUMMARY

Units and themes are means by which teachers, or curriculum developers, connect or link curricular subjects. They can be preplanned and prepared well ahead of time. Often the activities in a unit or thematic setting are repeated every year, and the results are predictable. Units and thematic teaching both have their place in the education of young children and can provide beneficial learning experiences if teachers use prudence and thought in their preparation. Units and themes can be even more beneficial to the education of young children when they honor questions that children pose as well as facilitate learning connections that young learners make to gain future knowledge.

Quality themes and units have the potential to provide interesting and motivating topics for child-initiated inquiry-learning projects.

## TO DISCUSS

1. "Yes, but . . ." See how many problems you can list that might arise when trying to develop a curriculum along the lines of a theme or curriculum unit rather than

**Figure 4.5 & 4.6** A unit on fire safety encouraged these investigators to pursue an in-depth study of firefighters and fire engines. After posing questions to this volunteer firefighter and obtaining needed fire station data (as shown in these photos), the young learners constructed a fire station in their classroom and used it for dramatic play.

according to subject areas. It may be useful to make two lists: one for preschool and one for primary grades. Then, discuss ways in which these problems might be solved.

2. If you are reading this book as part of a course, stage a formal debate in which one side argues the case for linear, subject-based curriculum in the primary grades and the other argues for linking the curriculum through the use of units and themes.

3. Using a broad thematic topic, find and talk about subtopics that you suppose would provide special interest as well as motivation for young learners to do further and more in-depth studies. Revisit this question after reading the section in Chapter 5 that discusses criteria for topic selection of inquiry-based learning projects.

## TO DO

1. Observe a class that incorporates theme learning or curriculum units. (Perhaps you can divide the two observations between you and your colleagues.) Take notes on the following:

   • Academic learning apparently planned by the teacher;
   • Academic learning arising spontaneously;
   • Social interaction;
   • Noise levels;
   • Traffic patterns and freedom of movement.

2. After observing the class, interview the teacher, as his/her time permits. Raise questions that arise from your observation. Learn the degree of formality or informality the teacher uses in planning.
3. Try your hand at either a theme curriculum or a curriculum unit. This will work best if you are currently interacting in some way with a targeted group of children. Use both types of webs demonstrated in this chapter to see how they work for your own planning needs.

## REFERENCES

Chard, S. (1992). *The project approach: A practical guide for teachers.* Edmonton, Canada: University of Alberta Press.

Dewey, J. (1997/1938). *Experience and education.* New York, NY: Kappa Delta Phi.

Jensen, E. (2005). *Teaching with the brain in mind, 2nd edition.* Alexandria, VA: Association for Supervision and Curriculum Development.

White, E. B. (1952). *Charlotte's web.* New York, NY: Harper & Row.

# 5

## INQUIRY-BASED LEARNING

*The important thing is not to stop questioning.*
—Albert Einstein

After reading this chapter you should be able to:

- Describe the history of in-depth projects in education;
- Explain why student questions are vital to student learning;
- Explain the rationale for using projects based on inquisitiveness;
- Work with frameworks for inquiry-based projects;
- Explain how elements of project work can be used in any curriculum;
- Follow an inquiry-based learning project from conception to conclusion.

Take a moment to reflect on a time when you were impassioned about learning something new. Perhaps you were determined to ski gracefully or to master a beautiful but intricate sewing project. You sought the right vegetables to survive in your garden space. You resolved to catch a bragging-rights trout. Maybe you were emboldened to learn to fly a small aircraft. Now, pause to reflect on the steps you took, or that needed to be taken, in order for you to be successful with your project.

Chances are, if you were successful at fulfilling your goal, you applied a wide array of academic, physical, and social skills. You probably sought out experts in your field of study while using a variety of print sources of information. The Internet might also have been a source of valuable knowledge. Observation and prediction were undoubtedly elements in helping you to be successful in your endeavor. Consider also the dispositions or character traits you needed to carry your project through to completion. Were you interested, motivated, challenged, and persistent? And, in addition, did you:

- Reflect on your prior knowledge of, or experience with your endeavor?
- Investigate ways to produce a satisfying, successful outcome?

- Experiment with the facts you gathered to make the project you were undertaking uniquely your own?
- Share your new expertise or product with others?
- Branch off in other connected directions?

Were you fulfilled and pleased with your accomplishments? What did you notice about your initiative and perseverance? Was your "can do" attitude reinforced enough to encourage you to attempt future projects that have since caught your attention?

Upon reflection, you will most likely remember that your project called on you to apply academic, physical, and social skills in an integrated fashion. You needed to link unknown experiences to known experiences. Chances are the skills and knowledge you had prior to beginning your new challenge became tools of understanding to help you obtain your goals. You also undoubtedly needed to learn new skills to make the final outcome of your endeavor a success or, at the least, put you on the pathway to success. Most surely, throughout your learning phase you posed countless questions—sometimes simple, sometimes more complex.

And so, upon reflection of your journey to gain new proficiency, you might ask, "What would *young* learners do?" The answer: Young learners, in their quest for knowledge and understanding of the world, do the same.

## WHAT YOUNG LEARNERS NEED

To facilitate their pursuit and grasp of knowledge, young learners need:

- Connections and relevance in learning;
- Opportunities to apply skills in meaningful, real-life situations;
- Engagement with hands-on materials;
- Worthwhile tasks to shape constructive dispositions;
- Group involvement and collaboration to hone emerging social skills.

Most important, learners of all ages need opportunities to ponder and ask questions about objects or events that engage them.

John Dewey (1900) wrote extensively throughout the first half of the 20th century about issues that focused on students' attainment of knowledge. He and his associates successfully put their educational theories into practice, most notably at the University of Chicago Laboratory School where child-centered education became the foundation of their developing theories and philosophy. Rejecting the traditional approach to education with its focus on children listening passively as teachers poured a uniform curriculum into them, Dewey sought instead to make the child the center of his or her learning universe. This did not mean, he argued, that children simply did as they pleased, flitting from one thing to another and learning not much of anything. Both discipline and knowledge are a part of child-centered education Dewey (1900, p. 37) stated, because

To satisfy an impulse or interest means to work it out, and working it out involves running up against obstacles, becoming acquainted with materials, exercising ingenuity, patience, persistence, alertness, it of necessity involves discipline—ordering of power—and supplies knowledge.

It was Dewey's observation that children brought four main "impulses" or interests to school with them, and teachers could build on these to create child-centered learning. The first impulse was "the social instinct of the children as shown in conversation, personal intercourse, and communication," which Dewey regarded as "a great, perhaps the greatest of all, educational resources" (1900, p. 43). The second was the constructive impulse or the instinct of making things, first in play and eventually in the desire to shape "material into tangible forms." The third impulse was "the instinct of investigation" that Dewey believed grew out of the "combination of the constructive impulse with the conversational." "Children simply like to do things and watch to see what will happen," he said, and this "can be taken advantage of, can be directed into ways where it gives results of value" (p. 44). Finally, "artistic expression" was included as the fourth main impulse of the child.

Reflect on the four impulses, as described by Dewey, as you pause for a moment to picture the beginning of the day in two different classrooms. Snow is falling heavily, and as the

**Figure 5.1** Although the snow outside of this classroom did not linger for long, the knowledge the students gained from their research on snow did.

students enter their classrooms they are excitedly discussing this first and most likely only snowfall of the season. Mesmerized by the falling snow, the students wonder aloud how much snow will accumulate and how long it will last. In one classroom the teacher allows the electricity of wonder to flow through her students as the youngsters create and set up experiments to determine not only how long the snow will remain but also how much will accumulate and how rapidly. The teacher, preparing to assume a role as facilitator, is already mentally assessing the multiple directions the students' many other snow queries might take; how the students' questions about snow will be used as opportunities for learning during and after the school day; and ways this mini snow project will integrate curricular areas.

By contrast, in the other classroom the equally excited students are told by their teacher that, yes, it is indeed snowing rapidly, and they will have opportunities to play in it at recess time, but the snow will most likely be melted by nighttime. And thus the students resignedly return to the lessons that are planned for the day.

It is a mindful teacher who embraces the wonder in his or her students as a tool to construct knowledge; such use of wonder is at the heart of using inquiry throughout the integrated curriculum.

## DISPOSITIONS TOWARD LEARNING

Dispositions are habits of mind or tendencies to act in a particular way. Teachers can help children develop certain dispositions that enable them to be functional and effective learners in the classroom. When tasks are engaging, children's dispositions to be interested in their work are reinforced, and this facilitates their learning and energizes their effort (Chard, 1992).

Desirable dispositions include curiosity, creativity, persistence, humor, empathy, helpfulness, openness, reflection, and responsibility. Conversely, undesirable dispositions include aggressiveness, selfishness, indolence, and apathy. Often, undesirable dispositions can be discouraged and healthy dispositions encouraged when youngsters team together to solve problems, seek answers to questions, and work to form a learning environment that is stimulating, satisfying, and safe.

Dispositions and their effect on learning have been recognized for decades. John Dewey (1938) believed a great teaching fallacy of some was the belief that a person learned only the information that was being studied at the time. He compared collateral, or indirect, learning to the learning that takes place in a singular, isolated lesson. Dewey proposed, "Collateral learning in the way of formation of enduring attitudes, of likes and dislikes, may be and often is more important than [a] spelling lesson . . . For these attitudes are fundamentally what count in the future. The most important attitude that can be formed is that of desire to go on learning" (p. 48). And even more riveting to educators should be Dewey's admonition, concerning the desire to go on learning, that

> If impetus in this direction is weakened instead of being intensified, something much more than mere lack of preparation takes place. The pupil is actually robbed of native capacities which otherwise would enable him to cope with the circumstances that he meets in the course of his life. (p. 48)

Arthur L. Costa and Bena Kallick (2000), in their quest to help educators cultivate passionate and compassionate human beings, have identified 16 habits of mind. Costa and Kallick suggest that the list of 16 habits will undoubtedly be added to by others in the future. See if you can think of additional pertinent habits of mind that would warrant placement on the following list:

1. Persisting
2. Managing impulsivity
3. Listening with understanding and empathy
4. Thinking flexibly
5. Thinking about thinking (metacognition)
6. Striving for accuracy
7. Questioning and posing problems
8. Applying past knowledge to new situations
9. Thinking and communicating with clarity and precision
10. Gathering data through all senses
11. Creating, imagining, innovating
12. Responding with wonderment and awe
13. Taking responsible risks
14. Finding humor
15. Thinking interdependently
16. Remaining open to continuous learning

To reinforce the message that it is crucial for students to know not only how to obtain knowledge but also how to appropriately apply knowledge, Costa and Kallick declare with hopeful caution that "[t]eaching with the habits of mind requires a shift toward a broader conception of educational outcomes and how they are cultivated, assessed, and communicated" (2000, p. xiv).

## TEACHING FOR UNDERSTANDING: TRANSFER, RELEVANCE, AND ENGAGEMENT

Howard Gardner, known for his views on multiple intelligences, spoke to the importance of teaching for understanding. In an interview almost 20 years ago, but still quite relevant to education today, Gardner expressed concern with the lack of *transfer* in student learning (the inability to apply skills successfully in new situations), which demonstrates an absence of understanding. He further conveyed concern that educators do not fully appreciate how difficult it is for students to transfer knowledge from one situation to another: "In the absence of such flexibility and adaptability, the education that the students receive is worth little. I suspect that this problem exists in other countries as well, but our American fixation on the mastery of facts and the administration of short-answer instruments of assessment makes the problem particularly acute here" (quoted in Stegel & Shaughnessy, 1994, p. 563).

When asked if it was realistic to believe that all students, even those of low IQ, could obtain "deep understanding," Gardner replied that he was not interested in a student's IQ but, rather more importantly, he was concerned with a student's current understanding and what could be done to enhance such understanding (p. 564):

No human understands everything; every human being understands some things. Education should strive to improve understanding as much as possible, whatever the student's proclivities and potential might be.

Gardner went on to assert (p. 564):

> When a child does not learn, it is premature to blame the child, because, more often than not, the failure lies with the educator. When we educate better and when we can educate in a more personalized way, then children will learn better.

As was discussed earlier in this text, the influences of John Dewey, Jean Piaget, and Lev Vygotsky; the schools of Reggio Emilia, Italy; and the Project Approach as prescribed by Lilian Katz and Sylvia Chard all repeatedly emphasize the necessity and importance of applying academic skills and concepts in real-life contexts with hands-on experiences in order to facilitate transfer of knowledge in personalized, purposeful ways. Dewey (1938) lamented the contrariness of learning subjects in isolation, disconnected to the actual conditions of life. Dewey concluded, "It is contrary to the laws of experience that learning of this kind, no matter how thoroughly engrained at the time, should give genuine preparation" (p. 48).

When a student is engaged in learning with a focus and reason to learn, academic connections happen with minimal effort. When working in groups on an engaging, thought-provoking project, children have genuine opportunities to apply social skills as they share ideas and opinions, assist one another with tasks, resolve differences of opinion, and work together toward common goals. As this chapter progresses you will see how educators can meet the demands that are asked and expected of them while honoring the tenets of sound child-centered and developmentally appropriate education. We will demonstrate how to integrate the curriculum of young learners by embracing their curiosity and inquisitiveness.

## INQUISITIVENESS AND YOUNG LEARNERS: THE POWER OF "WHY?"

The apposite use of inquiry and wonder to seek and obtain information is perhaps one of the most valuable and powerful tools children can acquire to equip them in their business of being lifelong learners.

Young learners need to be permitted to ask questions. The natural tendency of a child to be inquisitive should be respected and encouraged. Think back to the new endeavor referred to at the start of this chapter and to the innumerable questions you must have had when learning and undertaking it. Your questions and the answers you received were, no doubt, a vital part of your success, or lack of success. A challenge for educators of young children is not only to be aware of and responsive to queries of their students, but to actively pursue avenues that allow for inquisitiveness in the classroom. Educators must know how to capitalize on children's natural predisposition to wonder and then use such curiosity to help integrate the curriculum and make learning meaningful.

Toddlers' curiosity seems to have no limits. Toddlers have questions all day long. Mostly the questions are connected to concrete life: *Who, what, when,* and *where* are typical sentence starters. *Why* is soon added, although it takes toddlers some practice to understand what it really means. These young children seemingly ask "why?" about everything. Toddlers often use this bombardment of "whyness" to connect with and gain attention from adults, rather than to know "why." They are more enthralled with the verbal exchange and the attention that follows their questioning rather than the precise, correct answer.

As toddlers grow and mature and their communication skills become more refined, they constantly spew questions about the people and world around them in order to make sense of their environment: "Whazzat?" "Why, Daddy?" "See, Gramma?" Children also handle objects to help satisfy and engage their nonverbal curiosity, often manipulating the same object repeatedly over an extended period of time. Youngsters can spend hours and days playing in the magical land of a cardboard box. A variety of containers, a shovel, and sand will present a continent of possibilities to a child. Think of all the alter egos a mere stick possesses. The natural anthropological drive in children calls to them to explore and experiment with the environment—and the people and things in it. Such exploration helps to build bridges of understanding that connect what young learners know and have learned to their future learning experiences. These bridges of understanding, formed by both verbal and nonverbal experimentation, are the connections of learning that are invaluable to young learners as they grow and mature.

The responses children receive to their questions and their own explorations link what the person is telling them or what they have discovered to what they already know. Sometimes this requires a child to ask the same question repeatedly or to experiment until he or she has connected the unknown to the known, which results in understanding at the child's level. Replies and reactions young learners receive to their questions encourage them to ask more questions, or inhibit them from asking more questions, at least temporarily.

Adults who grow weary of the seemingly constant barrage of questioning by these youngest learners need to be heedful that it is through such questioning that children establish knowledge at their own level of inquiry. It is important, therefore, to provide ample opportunities for children of all ages to ask questions.

Preschoolers may continue their incessant questioning at home, but at school they have more distractions and fewer opportunities to bombard every nearby adult. Nevertheless, they remain curious about the world and now have an increased understanding of it, thus adding complexity and maturity to their questioning. They are ready, in short, to begin investigative projects, most of them short-term at first. By the primary grades, youngsters are excited about being in "real" school and bring their enthusiasm for learning with them, hoping—even assuming—that their questions about their world will be answered, that this is the purpose of attending school. Providing them with inquiry-learning opportunities can only enhance their excitement about being in school.

Offering avenues for children to utilize their inquisitiveness not only helps them gain awareness of the world around them but also helps them establish frameworks for making sense of future knowledge. Educators who are intent on covering a predetermined amount of material in a finite time span might find it difficult and frustrating to allow the inquisitiveness of their students to emerge. Often, under the constraint of district and state guidelines, educators fall into the habit of teaching material in such a hurried fashion that there is little time for their learners to apply or use newly acquired skills. Unfortunately, for the teacher and young learners, such lack of relevant connection through application often results in the need to reteach materials.

## THE ART OF QUESTIONING

Young learners are not always aware of the properties of a question. When a young child is asked, "Do you have any questions?" a likely response will be to tell something that is often totally unrelated to the context of the question. For instance, in one classroom setting, during a school district sponsored "stranger/danger" program, the students were asked by a visiting police officer if they had any questions. A small boy solemnly raised his hand, and when called on announced, "My dog died." The youngster had a most sincere statement that he wanted to share with the officer, but the officer was rather befuddled as to how to answer the boy's "question."

Young learners often lack the experience and maturation needed to understand the use of questions to gain answers. Therefore, when confronted with, "Do you have any questions?" youngsters often emit statements completely unrelated to the topic of the question. Young students need experience formulating and asking questions, and they need opportunities to pose questions throughout the day in both structured (teacher-directed) and non-structured (child-directed) activities. The topic of a question posed to a child needs to be meaningful and pertinent to the child. Young inquisitors need encouragement and support from adults and peers as they formulate their questions. They need to feel secure in their attempts to ask questions and know that they will not be subject to ridicule by either their classmates or the teacher. Teachers must make conscious efforts to employ developmentally appropriate questioning strategies and use purposeful and relevant opportunities to draw out and encourage questioning in their students.

The following lists some examples and ways to help young students think about and formulate their own questions. Also see Figure 5.2 for an additional example of how students can practice question formulation.

- Rather than asking students "Do you have any questions about ants?" inquire:
  "What do you wonder about ants?"
  "What wonders do you have about ants?"
  "What do you want to find out about ants?"
  "What do you want to ask about ants?"
- Model the first part of the question for the child, then let the child repeat the whole question. For example:
  "How do ants _____?" (Let the child fill in the blank.)
  "Can ants _____?" (Let the child fill in the blank.)
  "Why do ants _____?" (Let the child fill in the blank.)
- To help change a child's statement into a question, try:
  "You wonder if ants can swim. Let's ask that in a question: Can ants swim?"
  "You want to find out if ants like sun. Let's ask that in a question: "Do ants like the sun?"
- Help children understand that a question is not a "tell" but something that one says (asks) to someone to gain information (an answer). In the case of the befuddled police officer, the teacher offered assistance by saying, "Tommy, I hear what you told about your dog, and I am very sorry that he died. While Officer Maria is here, maybe you could ask if she has a police dog that works with her." Tommy accepted the teacher's prompt readily and found out to the delight of the class that yes, indeed, two dogs were on the force although they did not work directly with Officer Maria.

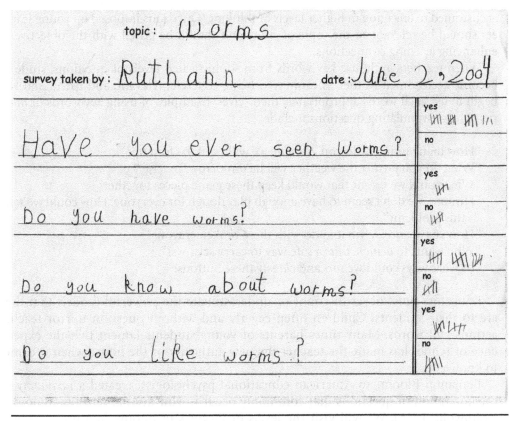

topic: Worms

survey taken by: Ruthann          date: June 2, 2004

| | yes / no |
|---|---|
| Have you ever seen worms? | yes: ⅥⅠ ⅥⅠ ⅥⅠ Ⅰ/ⅰ<br>no: |
| Do you have worms? | yes: ⅥⅠ<br>no: ⅥⅠ |
| Do you know about worms? | yes: ⅢⅠ ⅥⅠ ⅣⅠ<br>no: ⅥⅠ |
| Do you like worms? | yes: ⅥⅠ ⅣⅠ<br>no: ⅥⅠ |

**Figure 5.2** Student surveys not only integrate language and math skills (and, in this case, science), they also help learners become aware of the properties of a question. This survey was conducted as part of an inquiry-learning study on worms.

Teachers also teach questioning by example. When teachers ask their students meaningful questions of varying complexity, not only are students respectfully challenged, but they will also elevate their own thinking powers to a higher level.

## CATEGORIZATION OF QUESTIONS

Even at young ages, students are adept at tackling complex questions and can be sophisticated in formulating complex answers when they are allowed to use their own wisdom without fear of a "right answer." For example, Pam's kindergarten–first-grade students did an in-depth study on fast food restaurants. One of the student-generated research questions was, "Do the workers like their jobs?" The group of students who interviewed the workers and kept a "yes/no/sometimes" tally of worker responses on a graphic organizer knew the answer. But other students chimed in that they also knew the workers liked their jobs. When asked how they knew this, the children had the following replies: "Because the workers smiled a lot at the customers." "They talked in 'kind' voices." "They had clean uniforms."

Young children are keen on following adults' modeling, good and bad as it may be. When teachers ask high-level questions—questions that require more elaborate thought and speculation than a one-word answer—students become comfortable with and accustomed to engaging in higher levels of thinking. Questions imposed on young learners should be relevant to the topic of study and should be posed with the objective of enhancing learning connections.

When teachers aptly use key words from sophisticated levels of questions, students become accustomed to their meanings as being concrete, relevant, and useful and will begin to use such words appropriately themselves. Examples of using key words or *question cues* in stimulating questions include:

"How many minutes do you *estimate* we will need to clean up?"
"What do you *predict* the weather will be tomorrow?"
"What could we *invent* that would keep these game pieces together?"
"Hmmm, we don't seem to have enough play dough for everyone. How could we *solve* this problem?"
"How can we *decide* what to do with these broken crayons?"
"Who wants to *demonstrate* a safe way to carry scissors?"
"In what ways could we *sort* and *classify* these buttons?"

Educators must never discount or underestimate the powerful models that they are to their students. Children often eagerly and without question mirror teacher actions and words. Many times parents of young students lament that the experience of school has made the teacher the new authority of the house when it comes to knowledge.

Benjamin Bloom, an American educational psychologist, created a *taxonomy* or categorization of questions that commonly occur in educational settings (Bloom & Krathwohl, 1956). We will visit the levels of Bloom's taxonomy in a practical way, analyzing each category as it might apply to children's queries. As you might expect, the younger the children are, the closer their questions relate to the most basic levels of "Knowledge" and "Comprehension." However, as seen in the preceding section, young children can surprise us, and as adults we are wise not to underestimate the capabilities of young learners. In Table 5.1 we give examples of questions children might ask and answer that would, from the perspective of most adults, normally be reserved for their older peers. In addition, we provide examples of teacher questions at all levels.

**Table 5.1** Skills, Question Cues, and Examples Using Bloom's Taxonomy

| Competence | Skills Demonstrated, Question Cues, Examples |
|---|---|
| *Knowledge* | • **Skills:** observation, recall of information, simple knowledge, mastery of subject matter<br>• **Question cues:** *list, tell, describe, identify, show, label, collect, examine, name, who, when, where,* etc.<br>• **Child questions:** "Where's Daddy?" "What is that bug called?" "Who was that lady that sang to us?"<br>• **Teacher questions:** "How much is 5 minus 3?" "Where do your mittens go?" "What color is this?" |
| *Comprehension* | • **Skills:** understand information, order, group, translate knowledge into new context<br>• **Question cues:** *describe, interpret, associate, estimate, extend, discuss, differentiate*<br>• **Child questions:** "Who do you think is faster, a dog or a cat?" "Water is a liquid, so is milk a liquid, too?"<br>• **Teacher questions:** "Can you tell me some differences between a spider and a fly?" "How can we put all of these different-sized circles in order?" |

| Competence | Skills Demonstrated, Question Cues, Examples |
|---|---|
| *Application* | • **Skills:** use information, apply concepts in new situations, solve problems using required skills or knowledge<br>• **Question cues:** *apply, demonstrate, illustrate, show, solve, examine, classify, discover*<br>• **Child questions:** "I wonder if I can fix my bike like this book picture shows me." "If red and white paint makes pink, what will red and white crayon make?"<br>• **Teacher questions:** "Can you find some new ways to classify these shells?" "What did you think would happen if this time you added white paint to black paint? |
| *Analysis* | • **Skills:** see patterns, organize parts, identify components, recognize hidden meanings<br>• **Question cues:** *separate, order, explain, connect, classify, arrange, divide, compare and contrast, select, explain*<br>• **Child questions:** "How come she is smiling in this picture if she's really feeling sad?" "Do you want to try to make a pattern with all of these crayons?"<br>• **Teacher questions:** "Why would she smile if she is really feeling sad? When have you ever done that?" "What color pattern do you see in this line of blocks?" |
| *Synthesis* | • **Skills:** predict, draw conclusions, relate knowledge from several areas, generalize from given facts, use old ideas to create new ones<br>• **Question cues:** *combine, rearrange, substitute, plan, create, design, invent, rewrite, what if?*<br>• **Child questions:** "What would the story of *The Three Little Pigs* be like if there were dogs instead of pigs?" "I wonder what my school would be like if we lived when the Pilgrims did."<br>• **Teacher questions:** "What do you think would happen if no one had any cars or trucks?" "If you could go to George Washington's house, what do you think he would have in his house that you have in your house?" |
| *Evaluation* | • **Skills:** discriminate between ideas, make choices based on reasoned argument, assess value of theories and presentations, recognize subjectivity<br>• **Question cues:** *decide, rank, test, measure, recommend, convince, select, judge, discriminate, support, conclude*<br>• **Child questions:** "Do you want to know what my favorite ice creams are? I'll make the best one number one and the next best one number two and . . ." "I don't think that cloud can really be behind the far away moon. Do you think it's just a teeny cloud?"<br>• **Teacher questions:** "That painting is your favorite. Why do you think it is better than the others?" "Some of you think this metal boat will float, some of you think it will sink. Why do you think this? |

As these examples demonstrate, young children can question and be questioned at all levels of Bloom's taxonomy. It should be noted however, that "Synthesis" and "Evaluation" are generally considered to be applicable to children above the ages we consider in this text, both in terms of what children will ask and what teachers should consider asking. Therefore, expectations in these categories should be made very cautiously.

## QUESTIONS AND "WONDERS" THROUGHOUT THE SCHOOL DAY

Questions and "wonders" can be embedded in everyday routines. The flow of the school day can be structured in such a manner that student questioning is encouraged and fortified. Children can anticipate opportunities to ask and answer questions during everyday routines. As soon as the teacher feels the students are capable and it is appropriate, the role of the questioner should be transferred from the teacher to the children. When a student asks a question and gains pertinent feedback, the relationship of question to answer to solicit information gains meaning. In other words, children learn that forming questions to gain knowledge will garner more satisfying results to their queries than uttering declarative statements.

We offer the following ways to employ questions during everyday classroom routines and activities. The routines offer a mix of applicability for preprimary as well as primary children. Each individual teacher is the best judge as to which routines and questions fit the maturation level of the children he or she instructs. Some of these routine procedures will be revisited in greater depth and with different emphases in subsequent chapters, as daily classroom routines offer excellent opportunities to integrate the curriculum.

### Morning Procedures

Most classrooms and early childhood centers have procedures and routines for discussing information relative to the starting of the school day. In the beginning of the year, the teacher utilizes these routines to ask moderately simple questions of the students. Gradually and with encouragement, in each activity the role of questioner can shift from the teacher to the children in the class. An astute teacher takes care and thought in providing a variety of age-appropriate questions, peppered with challenging questions, knowing that the students will eventually model them.

### Questions Centering on a Weather Graph Activity

"What do you observe our weather outside to be right now?"

"How many rainy days have we had so far this month?'

"How many more sunny days have we had than rainy days?" followed by "How did you figure this out?"

"What do you predict the weather after lunch might be?"

**Figure 5.3** Children become skilled at asking questions when they are afforded opportunities to practice. The morning routine of taking a lunch count tally not only ensures that every child will have a chance to participate as a respondent, but also incorporates math questions into the routine.

*Questions Centering on a Visual Lunch Count*

"Which is more, hot lunch or cold lunch?"

"How many more hot lunches are there than cold lunches?"

"Why do you think there are more hot lunches today?"

"How many lunches do we have altogether?"

*Questions Centering on School Arrival*

"Did you walk to school?"

"Why do you walk to school?"

"How many other people rode in the same car with you?"

"Why do some people ride in a car to school and some people ride in a bus to school?"

"What was one interesting thing you saw on your way to school?"

The calendar can generate numerous questions, especially if it has hands-on appeal. The individual numbers that correspond to the dates of the days of school for the month can be written on various paper shapes—square, circle, triangle, and so on—and placed around the perimeter of the calendar. The "calendar person," with the verbal help of the class, then locates and affixes the appropriate paper shape to the day's date on the calendar. This is an easy task that affords success for children when they feel comfortable to don the role of questioner.

*Questions Centering on the Daily Calendar*

"If yesterday's date was _____, what is today's date?"

"If today's date is _____, what will tomorrow's date be?"

"Is tomorrow a day we come to school?"

"How many days are there in this month?"

"How many days in this month are Mondays?"

To verbally help the "calendar person" find the corresponding date shape to fasten onto the calendar, ask the class such questions as:

"Is the shape with today's date on the right or the left side of the calendar?"

"Is the shape placed high, medium, or low around the calendar?"

"What shape is today's marker?"

"What pattern do you see in the shapes on the calendar?"

"What shape do you predict tomorrow's marker will be?"

*Classroom Surprise Box*

A colorful, decorated shoebox can be transformed into a classroom surprise box containing an object or preview representative of the day's activities. Questions are posed to the "surprise box opener" with the objective of enabling class members to guess the box's contents. After each question is answered, classmates have an opportunity to guess what is inside the surprise box based on the answer's clues. This is an arena of question asking

**Figure 5.4** Children have many opportunities to pose and answer questions centering on the daily calendar.

that will enthusiastically be shouldered by students after the teacher has done sufficient modeling. Thought-provoking questions include:

"Is the surprise box heavy or light?"
"Is there something that rolls around inside of it?"
"Can you smell anything through the box? What do you smell?"
"Does it feel or sound like there is more than one thing in it?"
"Does the thing inside of it feel hot or cold?"
"Does it feel like something that has been in there before?" followed by "In what way?"

*Classroom Stories*

*Before* reading a story, discuss briefly with the students the title, cover of the book, and, depending on the familiarity, the author. Initially, the teacher will pose questions to engage the students and focus their awareness of the book. As the school year progresses, the children will eagerly take on the responsibility of asking questions in reference to the story about to be read. Depending on the cover of the story and the contents of the book, examples of teacher questions (later to become student-asked questions) might include:

"Have we read this story before?" or "Is it new?"
"What do you think, or predict, this story is about?"
"Who do you think the main character might be?"
"Does the boy look happy or sad?"
"Why do you think this boy looks happy?"
"Do you think this book is fact or fiction?" followed by "Why?"
"What other things has this author written about?"
"Did this book remind you of other books we have read?" followed by "Why?" and "Which ones?"

*After* a story, questions asked might include:

"Who was the main character?"
"What happened in the story?"
"Was the girl happy or sad? Or was she both?" followed by "Can someone be both sad and happy at the same time?"
"Why do you think _____ did _____?"
"What could have happened if _____?"
"What happened that made you happy for the character in this book?"
"If you were the main character, what would you have done?"
"How did this story remind you of the story _____ we read yesterday?"
"Should we read this story again another day?"

## SUMMARIZING SO FAR

Questioning and wondering are the cornerstones of inquiry learning. Children question and experiment not only to make sense of their world but to craft connections in their learning. Children need to know that they will not be subject to ridicule when asking questions in front of their peers. Young learners need a variety of occasions to ask and practice asking questions. An astute teacher will be constantly vigilant for opportunities to model and encourage question asking in the classroom. It is a wise teacher who values and encourages wonder, inquisitiveness, and curiosity throughout the school day and capitalizes on such wonder to integrate the curriculum.

We have shown the significance of questions and the vital part they play in the education of young learners. Now we will introduce strategies that educators use for promoting and honoring inquisitiveness and curiosity in students while integrating subjects within the curriculum.

## INTEGRATING THE CURRICULUM: THE FOUNDATION

According to brain-based-teaching specialist Eric Jensen (2005), learning takes place when students can:

- Identify or predict the relevant associations among variables in the learning situation;
- Predict and express accurately the appropriate concepts or actions;
- Store, retrieve, and apply that prediction in context next time.

Jensen's understanding of the influence educators have over children's learning has stirred him to warn educators, "You have much, much more to do with how your students turn out than you may have thought" (p. 32). He adds, "You have far more influence over the volition and engagement of your students than you may realize" (p. 102). Educators are very cognizant of the fact that there is considerable pressure to teach more and more content during the school year. It would seem like common sense, but Jensen reminds us that "you can teach more and faster, but students will simply forget more and faster" (p. 42). This common-sense notion coupled with Jensen's advocating of hands-on, relevant, and meaningful experiences to enhance the brain's complex learning capacity makes for a compelling reason to use inquiry-based learning to integrate the curriculum.

Integration is a strategy that allows learners to be immersed in activities surrounding a topic within their range of experience while drawing on goals from one or more subject-matter disciplines. When teachers "integrate ideas and content from multiple domains and disciplines . . . children are able to develop an understanding of concepts and make connections across content areas" (Copple & Bredekamp, 2009, p. 161).

For learning to make sense to children, they need to have avenues of skill application that are engaging, thought provoking, and meaningful (Chard, 1992). An integrated curriculum embracing inquiry promotes this kind of active student engagement, with the goal of strengthening and expanding student understanding through the connectivity of subjects and the meaningful application of skills.

There are many strategies for integrating a child-centered curriculum but no one "right" strategy. Educators who are knowledgeable about developmentally appropriate practices and about the subject matter, who honor similarities and differences and unique needs in their students, and who believe in establishing a "community of learners" to promote success for all are most likely already employing strategies that effectively integrate the curriculum.

The *first* step to effectively integrate the curriculum demands that teachers have thorough knowledge of their children and their developmental levels. Teachers must recognize and capitalize on children's individual and collective social, emotional, and intellectual needs as well as employ developmentally appropriate practices. In addition, for each age or grade level a teacher must:

- Know singular skills to be taught at the level as well as above and below the level of the children being taught;
- Be well versed in the individual curriculum areas (subjects);
- Be conscious of and know state and local school district or child center mandates, including exiting goals and learning objectives;
- Know how to administer appropriate and thoughtful methods of evaluation and assessment.

The *second* step to effectively integrate the curriculum is to *interconnect* or *weave* rather than simply connect or link subject areas. This calls for a teacher to:

- Respect and utilize the inquisitiveness of young learners;
- Embrace engaging topics worthy of student interest;

- Become well versed in strategies that knit subject areas together in support of skill application to further student understanding;
- Be open and adaptable to paths that integrated curriculum might travel.

It should go without saying that no teacher will successfully integrate the curriculum around student-driven topics if he or she is not skilled in ways to establish and support independence and interdependence among learners. (Review the key factors that help build a positive classroom climate as well as support a cohesive community of young learners in Chapter 2.)

## THEMES, INTEGRATION, AND INQUIRY-BASED LEARNING

Units and themes have been discussed in depth in Chapter 4. Here we will briefly revisit themes in order to view differences between the use of thematic courses of study and inquiry-based projects to integrate the curriculum.

A theme has a recurring and unifying characteristic, and producers of thematic units often go to great lengths to spotlight all subject areas. The theme may be visually obvious to students and visitors entering the classroom, and it may appear in various academic endeavors and group activities. However, a theme's visibility does not ensure depth and meaningful coverage of the topic, nor does it ensure that skills within subject areas have opportunities to be used as tools to further student understanding of the topic.

In an effort to add more dimension to the concept of integration, and as was mentioned in the second step of effectively integrating the curriculum, we propose the word *interconnect* to describe the integrative process of weaving skills and curricular areas together in order for students to gain personalized understanding of a topic. Interconnection in this text is used in comparison to connection, or linking by proximity. A question to ponder with regard to thematic integration is, "Is the topic of the theme a student-driven study used to interconnect curricular subjects with the goal of furthering student understanding of the topic?"

For instance, in a classroom using apples as a thematic topic to connect or link subjects by proximity, one might see one group of children painting and cutting out predrawn apples while another group is counting paper apple seeds. Apple-shaped nametags are placed on the tables. One might observe children practicing writing their names on lines drawn on large paper apples. Fiction and nonfiction books about apples line the classroom library. A parent helper is cooking applesauce in a pan on the back counter of the room. The teacher has copiously decorated the classroom with assorted shapes and sizes of apples. As you can see, in this classroom many subject areas are linked by the apple thematic topic. But the students in this class do not use skills in the subject areas to learn or further their understanding about apples, nor do they have opportunities to apply their skills as they research answers to questions and wonders they have generated surrounding apples. Think about the way the apple theme is used in this classroom; then ask yourself the question posed at the end of the preceding paragraph.

Subject areas may be present and observed in thematic units, but the subjects are not necessarily woven and interconnected. Activities in thematic units are often loosely related to a central theme but do not necessarily form the student-constructed connections children need in order to gain a deep and meaningful understanding of the theme's topic.

**Table 5.2** An Integrated Curriculum

* Is organized around topics within children's understanding and that help children make sense of their world
* Is organized around topics that provide opportunities to apply academic and social skills with the goal of transference of knowledge to future learning
* Encourages in-depth exploration of a topic worthy of study
* Stimulates and facilitates personal inquiry, problem solving, self-regulation, and independence and interdependence
* Integrates by weaving and interconnecting the content and processes of many disciplines

*Source*: Adapted from Wishon, Crabtree, & Jones, 1998, p. 73.

Sometimes thematic units work vigorously to include all subject areas, resulting in insubstantial attempts to genuinely integrate the curriculum. Not all subjects need to be integrated just for the sake of integration, nor do all activities need to relate to a central topic or theme (Wishon, Crabtree, & Jones, 1998). Subjects and skills should be integrated only as they add to the understanding of the topic of study and help children to make sense of their learning. Table 5.2 shows elements of a cohesive, integrated curriculum.

To visualize what interconnecting or weaving curricular subjects and skills in a cohesive, integrated curriculum looks like, we visit another classroom. As in the classroom previously described in this section, the young students in this classroom are also learning about apples. However, in this classroom, the depth and coverage of the topic are much different and there is a variety of ways the young learners are applying their skills. On the wall is a chart depicting "What we know about apples." Next to it is a chart that reads "What we want to find out about apples." Child-drawn observational drawings of apples dot the classroom walls as well. Some of the experiments and displays on the counters and walls show labeled apple parts, scales to weigh different sizes of apples, a child-charted depiction of the life cycle of seed-to-apple. A visitor to the classroom would also see rotting apples placed next to a flip-over calendar used to record how many days they have been sitting there. In the corner, near the library of fiction and nonfiction apple books, is a live potted apple tree placed next to a yardstick. A variety of graphs, tallies, and sequence charts show data obtained by the young investigators on a recent field research trip to an apple orchard. The children are now in the process of transforming a corner of the classroom into an apple stand that will eventually sell child-constructed papier-mâché apples and will also provide consumer-friendly apple fact information.

## PROJECT WORK AND INTEGRATION

There are multiple curricular models that speak to integrating the curriculum in an interdisciplinary fashion in order to make learning meaningful and relevant. Project-based learning, inquiry-based learning, project method, and investigative learning are all descriptors for methods that encourage children to apply their fledgling research skills in open-ended, real-life, and meaningful situations. All have at their core a reverence for students' questions and use the explorations of a topic or a theme to promote greater understanding as well as to support transference of knowledge to future learning.

Regardless of the nomenclature given, any method of integration that calls for active, meaningful student involvement based on inquisitiveness has common components, as noted in Table 5.3.

**Table 5.3** Integrated Learning Based on Inquisitiveness

---

- The curriculum is not bound to a text, a guide, or a particular sequence. However, curricular expectations are respected.
- Activities build on information across disciplines and across content areas.
- The environment and the learning experiences are characterized by novelty and engagement.
- Time is flexible; learning experiences are not restricted to fixed increments.
- The method is not unstructured. Rather, the structure flows through phases of learning generated by the investigations of a topic.

---

*Source*: Adapted from Wishon, Crabtree, & Jones, 1998, p. 15.

The Project Approach, as introduced by Lilian Katz and Sylvia Chard (1989), utilizes a child-centered worthwhile topic or theme as a catalyst for an in-depth study. Project work follows a framework of three general phases that typically merge into each other. Katz and Chard believe that an overall aim of project work is to cultivate the life of a child's mind. The roots of what is now called the Project Approach grew from John Dewey's studies and philosophy as well as from the structure and beliefs held by many British educators in the 1970s about child-centered curriculum. In a subsequent publication, Katz and Chard (2000) revisit the idea of the application of emerging social and academic skills in open-ended activities reflective of real-life situations in order to enhance students' understandings of the world in which they live.

It is important to note that inquiry-based learning projects do not fill every day of every week. Instead, they should be regarded as avenues for young learners to apply their social and academic skills in meaningful contexts. While some skills are certainly picked up through the experience of a project, it is more the case that children generally acquire specific skills through systematic, or direct, instruction. "Systematic instruction is an approach to teaching individual children a progression of interrelated sub-skills, each of which contributes to greater overall proficiency in skills such as those involved in reading, writing, and arithmetic" (Katz & Chard, 2000, p. 13). The teacher can provide the skills she or he knows in advance will be needed for a project, or address deficiencies as they become apparent. "Project work can thus complement and enhance what children learn through other parts of their curriculum" (p. 12). For example: If a teacher knows that a topic of in-depth study might call on students to take measurements, the teacher would take time, before the project commenced, to teach any needed measurement skills to the students. In doing so, direct instruction will have been delivered in a meaningful way, one that has purposeful application to the integrated curriculum project.

The authors of this text are supporters and advocates of the work of Katz and Chard. Through experience in using the framework of a project approach with young learners in public schools and child centers, and by observing how other educators use project work, we are able to offer our insights into the successful use of project work in inquiry-based learning. After describing the phases of project work, we will present a vivid picture of what learning based on an inquiry project looks like.

### Phase 1: The Beginning

A topic worthy of study is decided upon by the teacher, by the students in collaboration with the teacher, or by the children with parameters given by the teacher. Typically, younger learners are successful studying simple, concrete topics such as a class pet,

**Figure 5.5** Young investigators enjoy displaying pieces of work depicting the three phases of their in-depth study on hospitals. Note the boxes that store ongoing committee work.

machines, or objects in nature. Older students have the sophistication to do studies on more complex topics including public establishments, community helpers, and occupations. Wise topic selection takes the following into account:

- Is it worthy of study?
- Does it relate to the young learners' everyday, firsthand experiences?
- Does it build on what the children already know?
- Will the majority of the students have some familiarity with it?
- Can curricular and social skills be applied in its study?
- Are there reasonably close and suitable resources for field research work?
- Is it specific enough for the age group that will be studying it?
- Does it have future learning value?

Throughout the first week or so of the project, the young learners reflect on their knowledge of the topic in a variety of ways that include verbal discussion, written/scribed and illustrated memory stories, paintings, models, and dramatizations. The children, with the teacher as a scribe, make a chart of what they know about the topic to further communicate their prior knowledge and basic understanding of the inquiry-learning topic. Common vocabulary and concepts become evident when a baseline of understanding about the topic of investigation is formed. Family members as well as the classroom or center library can be very helpful in providing books and other media along with other information that focuses on the topic of study.

Before moving on to the next phase of the inquiry project, a list of questions centering on what the young learners want to know or find out about the topic is constructed, again with the teacher as the scribe. A quick-sketch drawing made by the teacher next to each question helps nonreaders. The more the topic is discussed, the greater the familiarity the students have with the topic, which in turn tends to produce a greater variety and number of questions. Questions can be added to the list over the course of a few days or, depending on the age of the children, the chart may be completed in a short time. After the chart is completed, depending on the learners' abilities, commonalities among questions can be pointed out, and the group can discuss how to derive the answer to each question.

If a field research trip to a site outside of the classroom or center is to be undertaken, it is planned at this time. Experts who might provide first-hand, primary resource knowledge for the inquiry study should be contacted now. It is helpful to share with adult experts how children learn through the investigative learning study, as a field research trip and interviewing with an expert differs greatly from a typical field trip.

### Phase 2: The Middle

With the creation of a list of essential questions to be answered by the young investigators, the inquiry project flows to the next phase. It is during this phase that the children will focus their efforts on collecting data as they seek answers to their questions.

Preparation for the field research trip is crucial. The students will not be merely passive listeners but, rather, active solicitors of data. They should have ample opportunity to practice their research skills in the classroom before undertaking field research work. Appropriate social skills should be in place.

Plan, in conjunction with the children, how the field research will be carried out. Will the young investigators work individually or in groups (usually called "committees")? What questions will each individual or committee seek to answer? What equipment (paper, crayons, stopwatches, and so on) will be needed? Will teacher-made graphic organizer sheets be needed for students to record data, and if so, which ones would be most helpful? What other notes could be made at the field research site? If the site is a place of business, appropriate protocols need to also be discussed.

Coach the adults who will be accompanying the children. A field research trip during which the children are charged with the task of gathering data might be a new experience for them. Along with clearly written, specific duties with which you want assistance, adult supervisors should be reminded that the students will be actively and independently obtaining information necessary for their research. For example, a note to adults supervising a field research trip to a pet shop might read like this:

Thank you very much for helping us on our field research trip to the pet shop today. The students have reviewed (and practiced) protocols that will be needed on this trip. However, please remind the students, as needed, to:

• use "inside voices"
• focus attention to the store owner when she is speaking to the total group

- remember that the "customers" have the right-of-way
- use polite manners: please; thank you; excuse me; please; etc.

The students will be obtaining information in a variety of ways; please allow them to work at their own level. The students are very independent and have learned to rely on their peers for assistance when it is needed.

Again, thank you and we hope that you will enjoy this field research experience as much as all of us in room 4 will.

During the field research trip, be flexible and open to avenues that might provide additional learning experiences. Perhaps a machine at the site commands the learners' attention. Would observational drawings by the students capture the details? Inquiry-based learning projects may encourage future in-depth studies of related topics; be alert for these opportunities.

It is important to note that the field research may also take place within the classroom, school, or center. In other words, field research does not necessarily have to go far afield.

### Phase 3: The Conclusion

Some kind of culminating event brings the study to a close. The young learners tell the story of their project to others outside of their classroom or center. Other classes, family members, the principal or director, community members, and so on might be invited to see and hear details about the inquiry-learning project and to observe what the children have learned.

Displays around the room will illuminate the knowledge children gained as a result of the study. Such displays might include the charts compiled in Phase 1, memory drawings and stories, graphic organizers, observational drawings, drawings and stories of what was learned on the field research trip, charts and pictures that depict gained knowledge, and artifacts that help to tell the story of the topic under study.

The young learners might construct a representation of the researched topic, thus consolidating new understandings gained through the study. Some topics of an in-depth investigation might beg the students to reconstruct them in such a manner that they can be used for dramatic play in the classroom. Thus inquiry-learning through integration can be taken to an even higher level of applicability as will be described in the next section.

As the young investigators reflect on their undertakings and accomplishments, new questions and topics that warrant future study may arise. Thus, new projects may present themselves, and the class begins again with a new Phase 1.

The following is a brief review of the three-phase structure recommended for projects:

- Phase 1: Review the children's current knowledge and interest.
- Phase 2: Give the children new experience and research opportunities.
- Phase 3: Evaluate, reflect on, and share the project work.

(Chard, 1994, p. 2)

Figure 5.6 demonstrates how the phases work together to create the whole.

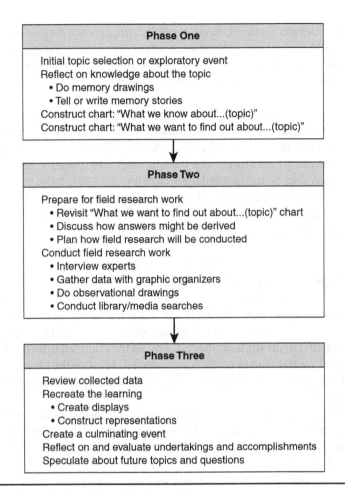

**Phase One**

Initial topic selection or exploratory event
Reflect on knowledge about the topic
  • Do memory drawings
  • Tell or write memory stories
Construct chart: "What we know about...(topic)"
Construct chart: "What we want to find out about...(topic)"

**Phase Two**

Prepare for field research work
  • Revisit "What we want to find out about...(topic)" chart
  • Discuss how answers might be derived
  • Plan how field research will be conducted
Conduct field research work
  • Interview experts
  • Gather data with graphic organizers
  • Do observational drawings
  • Conduct library/media searches

**Phase Three**

Review collected data
Recreate the learning
  • Create displays
  • Construct representations
Create a culminating event
Reflect on and evaluate undertakings and accomplishments
Speculate about future topics and questions

**Figure 5.6** The three phases of an inquiry-based learning project.

## INQUIRY-BASED LEARNING IN ACTION

Now that the elements and phases of investigative projects have been explained, we will visit Pam's public school classroom to observe project work based on inquiry. The following pages describe a project that was undertaken by the whole class and lasted nearly two months. The class worked on the project with varying durations and intensity during each school day. The teacher is well seasoned in facilitating project work to integrate subject areas and is cognizant of the power of a democratically functioning class of students. However, as you journey through this project, do not be intimidated by its vastness or complexity; rather, marvel at the investigative skill that young learners possess. This project takes you from initial topic-choosing activities, continues through various phases, and culminates in a remarkable facsimile of an often-visited community establishment.

As you read the following inquiry-based learning project, be observant of the many ways subjects are naturally integrated. Watch how social and academic skills are readily applied in meaningful, real-life situations. See how connections are made between school and community as well as between school and life as students research a topic that is realistic and relevant to them. Read carefully through the following project and note pieces that could be used by an educator eager to begin infusing inquiry-learning projects in his or her own classroom. But first, take a leap and envision yourself as a young learner and active participant in the following environment.

### The Pizza Parlor Inquiry Learning Project

Pam's room 4 kindergarteners and first graders are used to having their classroom's physical appearance change to meet and reflect their needs as learners. Tables and chairs can be easily rearranged to accommodate various activities. Smaller shelves, cabinets, and furniture are movable. Some of the larger cabinets are stationary, but for the most part the classroom can be metamorphosed according to avenues of study. In room 4, one corner sees regular alteration, as it is an area conducive to displaying work-in-progress and outcomes of project work.

### Phase 1: The Beginning

**Choosing a Topic for Inquiry-Based Study**

The children were keen on transforming the classroom corner into "something" that could facilitate dramatic play during their daily workshop activity time. The teacher knew the "something" would be an engaging topic for an inquiry-based research project since it was evolving from student interest. And so the children informally discussed various ideas about how the corner could be remodeled. Most of the ideas had strong student appeal, good potential for integration of disciplines, and provided opportunities for field research within the community.

In a classroom that encourages all voices and opinions to be heard, Pam chose to experiment with a unique way to select a topic of study. Each student who chose to do so could present an idea of a study topic to the class. Pam gave the following parameters for the students' choice of topic: (1) It had to be a topic worthy of research; (2) there had to be opportunities to do field research available in the community; and (3) all the students had to be able to use the finished project within the classroom. For each topic the young presenters also were asked to give at least one way that math, reading, and writing skills could be used in the finished outcome.

With admirable composure, six students individually presented a well thought-out topic choice to a very attentive audience: (1) hospital, (2) bakery, (3) gas station, (4) pizza parlor, (5) grocery store, and (6) hat shop. The seemingly difficult decision of a final choice was not problematic at all as each topic of study was charming in its own right, and the students were anxious to commence their research. A written vote was taken, and the journey to produce the Room 4 Pizza Parlor began.

Conveniently, and maybe not coincidentally, there are three pizza parlors within 5 miles of the school.

**Accessing Prior Knowledge**

The children accessed their prior knowledge of the inquiry-based study of pizza parlors in verbal, written, and artistic forms. The students wrote or asked Pam to scribe recollections about their experience, or lack of experience, with pizza parlors. A student-drawn picture that illustrated the memory accompanied each memory story. These memory story pages were placed in view around the classroom. At a later date they were collected and bound together into a class book.

The children made a class experience chart by dictating to Pam what they knew about pizza parlors. The "What We Know about Pizza Parlors" chart had entries representing astute observations such as:

- Some have candles on the tables and the lights off.
- They don't all have bathrooms.
- Some have cameras to see strangers.
- Some workers have hats on so their hair doesn't get in the pizza.
- They make the pizzas different sizes.
- Some pizza parlors have smoke because of the cooking.
- Some have people that sing and dance in them.

The engaging topic of pizza parlors stimulated the children for weeks. The Room 4 Weekly Newsletter, produced and taken home by the students, always contained reports of learning activities surrounding the pizza parlor investigative project. Illustrated word charts from the children's experience were hung around the room: "Pizza Adjectives," "Pizza Parlor Words," "Pizza Toppings." These words were used extensively in writing activities, particularly by the first-graders. Flexible play-dough pizzas were cut and recut in math lessons. Hardened play-dough pizza toppings were used in counting, sorting, and classifying activities. Pizzas were made in different shapes and sizes. Surveys of pizza choices were conducted. Pizza became the number one entree choice of the students during lunchtime.

### Investigative Questions

One day's activities called for the children to generate an extensive list of questions centering on "What We Want (and Need) to Know about Pizza Parlors." A small sample of the questions included:

- How many kinds of toppings do they have?
- How do they make the pizzas?
- What things other than pizza do they sell?
- Do breadsticks or pizzas cook faster?
- What kind of uniforms do the workers wear?
- How do they decide what jobs the workers do?
- What is the workers' agenda for the day?
- What shapes are their tables?
- What do those cameras see?
- Why did they decide to build another pizza parlor when there were already two others?

Pam wrote each question on a chart that was then displayed in the classroom. The next day the children engaged in a sophisticated discussion about how answers to each question might be obtained. The young learners deduced, with some guiding input from Pam, that there were three ways they could gather answers: (1) ask experts, (2) observe, and (3) use books, the Internet, or other media sources. Pam suggested to the students that she write, in a space after each question, the ways or combination of ways the answers could be obtained. To introduce the concept of using a symbol key, after each question she wrote, as directed by the children, "B" for books/Internet/media, "O" for observing, and/or "E" for asking experts. The children agreed that it helped, indeed, to think about different ways to get answers to questions.

## Phase 2: The Middle

### Prior to Field Research

The children wrote a letter to a local pizza parlor asking if they could visit the parlor in order to get answers to some of their questions and to do observations. The pizza parlor manager gladly welcomed the young investigators' visit, and a field research trip was arranged.

Meanwhile, as the list of pizza parlor questions was lengthy, common connections were discovered among the variety of questions. The students, with Pam as the facilitator, organized the questions according to the commonalities. This made it much easier for the student-formed committees of three and four children to develop a plan to comprehensively answer the questions relating to the committee on which they chose to work. The committees formed included the machine committee, the workers committee, the furniture and walls committee, the food committee, and the menu committee.

In their committees during the next few days the students collaborated to decide what equipment they would need to collect data that would answer their questions. Paper, pencils, crayons, rulers, tape measures, stopwatches, and the ever-versatile clipboard became the equipment of choice. For each question, the children determined whether they would ask, observe, or use books or other media to acquire an answer.

The young learners were accustomed to using a variety of teacher-created graphic organizer pages on which to record data: to tally, to make graphs, to sequence events, to jot down time notations, to record cause and effect, and to note oral survey interview information. In addition, the students were very adept at making observational drawings in which they homed in on even the tiniest of details. Graphic organizers and observational drawing paper were included as part of the equipment the young investigators planned to use to gather data on their field research trip to the pizza parlor. For examples, see Figures 5.7 and 5.8.

Throughout their inquiry study the children also gained valuable information by perusing books from the library and various sources on the classroom Internet concerning pizza and pizza parlors. And, as reported to Pam by the children's parents, there were many engrossing conversations at home about pizza and pizza parlors.

### Field Research

The children embarked on their field research trip to the local pizza parlor with excited control. As they moved about the parlor, the young investigators professionally and politely gathered data even though they did not always stick to their planned techniques for doing so. For instance, one child became so entranced with the conveyor-type pizza oven that her complete focus was devoted to producing a very realistic and detailed observational drawing of it. According to which question they were seeking to answer, the young investigators used graphic organizers to sequence the steps that go into making a pizza, graph the shapes and numbers of the tables, time how long it took to bake a pizza, tally how much of each ingredient went into the pizza dough, record the measurements of breadsticks, and so on. Each child used one or two graphic organizers and did an observational drawing of at least one object that was especially intriguing. Figure 5.8

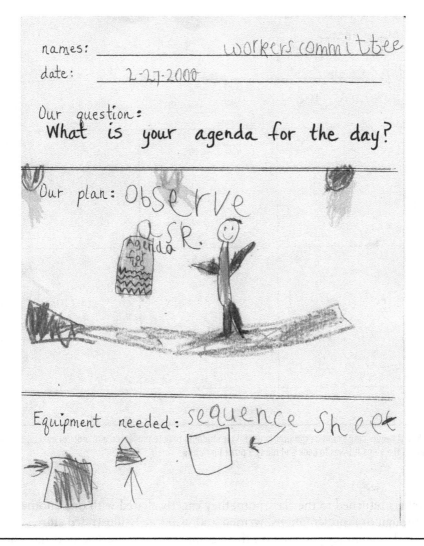

names: _____ workers committee

date: _____2-27-2000_____

Our question:
What is your agenda for the day?

Our plan: Observe
ask.

Equipment needed: sequence sheet

**Figure 5.7** Before embarking on a field research trip, children plan how they will be obtaining answers to their questions and note equipment that they will need.

shows Nicole's sequencing graphic organizer, and Figure 5.9 shows Nicole's observational drawing.

The pizza parlor manager and a worker, the two on-site primary resources, were impressed with the caliber of social skills and expertise the young interviewers possessed. The interviewers from the workers committee did detailed observational drawings of their two interviewees; used a yes/no/sometimes survey to record pertinent job-related information; jotted down notes in phonetic, sometimes hieroglyphic K–1 writing; and committed other details to memory to be shared at a later time with the rest of the class.

### Field Research Debriefing

The children were rather amazed, but quite proud, that they had obtained more firsthand information than what they had sought in their original questions. When the young

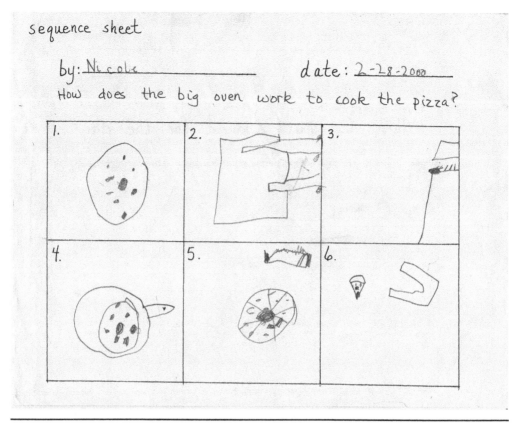

**Figure 5.8** A sequencing graphic organizer is useful for students to note processes and order of events. On this organizer, Nicole notes the steps it takes to cook and ready a pizza for eating.

researchers returned to the classroom, they eagerly shared with one another their findings through oral presentations, written and elaborately illustrated stories, and discussions of the data they gathered on their graphic organizers. The next day, the children wrote a detailed thank-you letter to the pizza parlor people who had helped them with their research.

### Phase 3: The Conclusion

Armed with valuable information the young investigators now set out to construct a pizza parlor of their own in the corner of room 4. Again, committees were formed to more efficiently assume the responsibilities of the workload: food, workers, parlor, machine, money, and menu.

At varying times during the day and throughout the next few weeks, the young entrepreneurs worked to ready the Room 4 Pizza Parlor. Play-dough pizza dough was kept in a container ready to be rolled out into three sizes. A variety of pizza toppings, made of paper and in labeled containers, were waiting to be placed on the dough when it was flattened and shaped. The children decided that the toppings could not be made of play dough because they would stick to the dough and could not be reused. An ingenious cardboard box machine for "cooking" the pizza was devised, open on both ends and complete with

observational drawing   name: Nicole

date: 2-28-2000

object: oven.

**Figure 5.9** In her observational drawing of a pizza oven, Nicole focused on the details of the pizza oven in order to help her make a replica of it back in the classroom.

rollers to expedite the pizza production. Brightly decorated menus and menu boards spelled out prices for the variety of pizzas and beverages. The cash register was readied. The single table in the restaurant was equipped to welcome student-customers with flowers and place settings for two.

Workers, attired with real cloth aprons, were prepared to sign in on the worker time chart to document the length of their work shift. Customers entering the Room 4 Pizza Parlor were greeted with a most unusual feature: They got to choose a decorated wallet filled with a predetermined amount of money to use for their food purchases.

Family members and the principal enjoyed a ribbon-cutting ceremony and a brief child-provided account of the history of the Room 4 Pizza Parlor. And, at last, the parlor was open business.

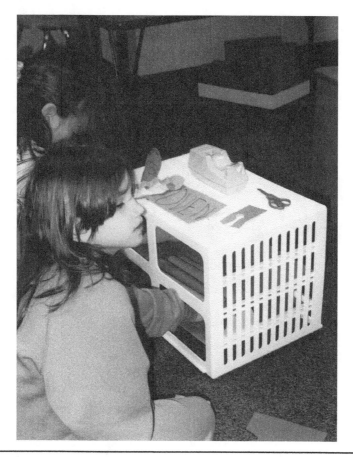

**Figure 5.10** These inventors spent many hours getting this pizza oven to "cook" pizzas on rollers just like the real model they observed.

## SUGGESTIONS FOR PROJECT WORK BASED ON INQUIRY

Novices at using inquiry-based learning to integrate the curriculum may be intimidated by the prospect of undertaking an unfamiliar type of instruction. We suggest that starting small can be helpful and also offer the following tips.

### Before You Begin to Use Inquiry-Based Learning Projects

- Provide opportunities for children to become savvy questioners. Refer to the techniques suggested earlier in this chapter.
- Teach young learners to use a variety of graphic organizers and ways to collect data, as is developmentally appropriate.
- Expose children to measurement devices and creative ways to measure, as is developmentally appropriate.
- Reassess your classroom management strategies to see if they are supportive of investigative project work. Chapter 2 offers helpful suggestions.
- Assure your principal and your students' parents that you will be addressing the curricular goals and objectives.
- If possible, collaborate with a colleague.

### *As You Begin to Use Inquiry-Based Learning Projects*

- Start by using "pieces" of investigative learning: observational drawings, memory drawings and stories, discussions about a certain person, place, or object.
- Use an inquiry-based learning topic that you are comfortable with and have knowledge about—the less complex the topic, the easier.
- Look for areas in your curriculum that are conducive to in-depth studies. For example, in a unit with plants as a topic, worms could be an engaging topic for further study.
- Be persistent in your attempts to teach with inquiry learning; learn with the students; revel in positive outcomes.

## IN SUMMARY

The utilization of inquiry-based learning in early childhood curriculum is not new. It is, however, an avenue that enables children to gather and utilize knowledge in meaningful and relevant ways with the goal of helping them become lifelong learners. It may not be an overstatement to argue that using inquiry-based learning to integrate the curriculum can be a panacea—to counter the lament of too much curriculum to cover; to overcome the lack of transference in student knowledge; and to address the misfortune of under-stimulated, disengaged young learners.

## TO DISCUSS

1. Discuss possibilities of topics for in-depth, inquiry-based learning projects for young learners. Using the criteria in this chapter for topic selection, discuss why or why not each topic could or should be used. Keeping in mind that younger children need less complex topics, include discussion of the children's age and developmental appropriateness of each topic.
2. Choose a topic worthy of study from your list in Item 1. Discuss or write down what might take place in each phase if the inquiry-learning study traveled through three phases similar to the phases of a project approach.
3. Using the pizza parlor project at the end of this chapter, comment on the young investigators' social skills and interactions. What skills were they using? Discuss how many subject areas were covered and how academic skills under each of these disciplines were applied. As you were not able to see the complete depth of the project, what other possibilities for academic skill application might there have been?
4. Discuss pros and cons of doing project work based on inquiry learning. For each of the cons, suggest ways they might be overcome.

## TO DO

1. Think back on a time when you were embarking on a new endeavor. Record the steps you took to become successful in your undertaking. If you were not pleased with the outcome, reflect on what you could have done (or should not have done) to obtain a more desirable result.

2. Using the same endeavor as in Item 1, write down the skills you used in math, reading, writing, social studies, science, art, music, and/or movement. Write down what social skills you applied.
3. Make observations of young children at work or play (school setting, park, home, etc.). Write down at least 10 questions that you hear them ask. Categorize these questions according to the levels of Bloom's taxonomy.
4. Refer to the two classrooms in this chapter that used apples as a topic of study: one as a theme and one as an inquiry-based study. Compare and contrast the learning that you perceived to take place in both of the classrooms. Comment on and then discuss your findings.

## REFERENCES

Bloom, B. & Krathwohl, D. (1956). *Taxonomy of educational objectives.* New York, NY: Longman.

Chard, S. (1992). *The project approach: A practical guide for teachers*: Edmonton, Canada: University of Alberta Press.

Chard, S. (1994). *The project approach: A second practical guide for teachers.* Edmonton, Canada: Quality Color Press, Inc.

Copple, C. & Bredekamp, S. (2009). *Developmentally appropriate practice in early childhood programs serving children from birth through age 8.* Washington, DC: NAEYC.

Costa, A. & Kallick, B. (2000). *Activating and engaging habits of mind.* Alexandria, VA: Association for Supervision and Curriculum Development.

Dewey, J. (1990/1900). *The school and society.* Chicago, IL: University of Chicago Press.

Dewey, J. (1997/1938). *Experience and education.* New York, NY: Kappa Delta Phi.

Jensen, E. (2005). *Teaching with the brain in mind.* Alexandria, VA: Association for Supervision and Curriculum Development.

Katz, L. & Chard, S. (1989). *Engaging children's minds: The project approach.* Norwood, NJ: Ablex.

Katz, L. & Chard, S. (2000). *Engaging children's minds: The project approach* (2nd ed.). Norwood, CT: Ablex.

Stegel, J. & Shaughnessy, M. (1994). Educating for understanding: An interview with Howard Gardner. *Phi Delta Kappan,* 75 (7), 563–567.

Wishon, P., Crabtree, K., & Jones, M. (1998). *Curriculum for the primary years: An integrative approach.* New York, NY: Prentice-Hall.

# Part Two
## The Subject Areas

In Chapter 1, we noted that there are those who object to curriculum integration on the grounds that the importance of individual subjects can be diverted or even lost. Part Two is devoted to ensuring that this will not happen. This textbook offers educators ideas to try in their classrooms and learning centers that embrace and promote children's natural curiosity. This can be done with an integrated curriculum that maintains the integrity of individual subjects. As well, these ideas are intended to spur educators to think of additional ways to make learning vibrant and meaningful for their young learners. Each of the next six chapters focuses on a single subject and includes discussion of curriculum standards laid out by its related national organization or, in some cases, through the work of a multistate consortium. It is only after a subject has been treated in depth that suggestions are provided for integrating it with other areas of the curriculum and for application to inquiry learning. On that topic, we have two items for our readers to consider.

## PREPRIMARY AND PRIMARY EXPERIENCES FOR AN INTEGRATED CURRICULUM

You will note that often activities that some teachers would designate as preschool or primary level can actually be successful at either level. This success depends on the teachers using the activities with an awareness of the developmental maturity of the children. Such awareness will allow the teacher to modify the activities as needed in order to provide the most beneficial academic learning for the students. In some of the subject chapters, we show how preprimary activities can be expanded to provide appropriate challenge for those preprimary students who are ready.

## INQUIRY-BASED LEARNING PROJECTS FROM THE INTEGRATED CURRICULUM

Toward the end of the discussion of each individual subject, you will find suggestions of inquiry-based learning topics that could originate from activities presented in the chapter. In each subject chapter, we have purposely echoed the words describing what constitutes an appropriate topic. This is done to reinforce the attributes of topic selection, as well as to stress the importance of choosing topics that are worthy of in-depth investigations by children.

In addition, suggested topics for inquiry-based learning in the following chapters have not always been delineated according to preprimary or primary age children, as each age will not only bring their own level of understanding to the proposed topics, but also carry out investigations as is developmentally appropriate to their skill level. To demonstrate, consider for a moment how dramatically different the study of an inquiry-based learning project on the topic of leaves would look at the preschool level, the primary level, the junior high level, and even the college level.

# 6

## LANGUAGE AND LITERACY

*The more you read, the more things you will know. The more that*
*you learn, the more places you'll go.*
—*Dr. Seuss (Theodor Geisel)*

After reading this chapter you should be able to:

- Explain language and literacy as the foundation of inquiry learning and integrated curriculum;
- Describe child development across the various components of literacy;
- Explain the new Common Core State Standards for English language arts;
- Describe how language and literacy can and should be incorporated throughout the day;
- Explain ways to use language and literacy as the core of an integrated curriculum.

Suppose a national polling organization were to pose this question about education: "What is the single most important reason that young children should attend school to be educated?" Then suppose we could take this question back through generations and centuries. It is highly likely that across the ages a single answer would stand out: "They need to learn to read and write. Especially read." Although the reasons for learning to read and write have been different for different generations, this accomplishment has long had such importance in the minds of adults that obsession has sometimes outweighed reason in the quest for the perfect literacy education.

Is there a single best way to teach literacy? There have been numerous bandwagons to hop on for those who believe, for a while at least, that they have found it. Today, we seem to have found some peace in the conclusion that there are any number of best ways depending on the needs of individual children. Before looking at the research and the history of reading and other language instruction that led to this position, we describe the experience of a small child who, surrounded by reading, writing, and oral language both at home and at preschool, broke the reading code on her own.

Every young reader's story is his or her own, of course. In Frances's case, it is interesting to note that her preschool had mixed ages so that there were older children to emulate; that the school itself was academically oriented and formal reading instruction of the older children was in evidence if Frances cared to notice; and that at home there was no attempt to teach reading, although older members of the family read constantly, both to themselves and, quite frequently, to Frances. Further, in this educated middle-class family, dinner table conversation was often intellectual and spirited, and even Frances sometimes participated. Frequent trips in the car provided opportunities to play games with rhyming words, to learn new songs, and to read simple and familiar signs along the road. Magnetic letters covered the front of the refrigerator, and at times Frances would move these around, quietly mouthing a few sounds. The importance of all these details of Frances's literacy experiences is demonstrated by the research indicating that in the first four years of life, children of middle- to upper-class families hear 30 million more words via interaction with those in their environment than do children from the poorest families (Hart & Risley, 1995). Continuing research has confirmed similar findings over time (Hoff, 2003). Although Frances's experiences did not guarantee or promise that she would read early, they certainly provided extensive support should she be so inclined.

Frances was four, close to five, when she rather suddenly, or so it seemed, learned to read. As her story unfolds, note the very natural, unforced, almost unconscious way in which this preschooler discovered that all those phonics skills she had thought to be some sort of game older children played actually had a practical application.

Frances attended an academically oriented school in which children between the ages of three and six were placed in one classroom. One of her favorite ways to spend the morning was to follow along after "the biggest kids" as they engaged in various reading and math activities. Especially fascinating to her were various phonics games in which she could help match pictures to labels, sound out letter combinations, or place labels next to tiny objects. Although she seemed to understand that certain letters referred to names of objects or pictures, Frances did not grasp the idea that writing and reading were for communication purposes. Before long she knew the sound of every letter of the alphabet and many combinations as well, but it did not occur to her that they could be put together into words to mean something. To Frances it was just learning to play a game that the biggest kids had mastered. She enjoyed the status that came with being able to do what they did.

It was after she had achieved the ability to rattle off letter sounds out of context that her mother began to observe a change in behavior. Each afternoon after school, the mother would sit in the living room with a cup of coffee and the evening newspaper. One day Frances decided that she wanted to be there, too, rather than in the yard. She entered the room with a small pile of her favorite books and snuggled down next to her mother. At first she looked at the pictures as she always had, but then her mother became conscious that she was not turning the pages. Frances was staring at the top line of a Dr. Seuss book—staring and staring. Finally she turned the page and again stared a long time at the top line. This behavior continued for about 10 minutes.

The next day the pattern was repeated, but by the third day Frances was looking over the entire page. At first her mother considered discussing the new experience with her but decided that it might be better to let Frances work through the process on her own. By the beginning of the second week, Frances occasionally looked over her mother's shoulder at the newspaper but said nothing. She continued to look silently at the words of her books, seemingly having lost interest in the pictures.

After about two weeks, something new appeared in Frances's behavior. Instead of just glancing at the newspaper, she draped herself across her mother's arm and leaned into her lap, although she seemed unconscious that she was doing it. She appeared fascinated with a full-page ad for a major sale in a local department store. Frances's mother wondered if she were able to read the easier words and if Frances could pick up on such things as the fact that Co. stood for "company." Just as she was thinking that the time had come to intervene, Frances asked, "Why is the Hecht Co. having a sale?"

Her mother marveled at the natural way the question came out. She had rather expected a drum roll and an excited announcement, "Now I can read!" Instead, this new ability had just quietly and naturally emerged. She did find herself a little puzzled by the fact that Frances could pronounce Hecht correctly with its hard "ch" sound but had not intuited that Co. stood for "company," since Frances had often visited there and knew the correct name.

Curious as to how well Frances really could read, her mother pointed to a short news story on the opposite page and said, "Can you tell me what this says?" Frances read it with barely a pause!

A few weeks later when a visitor asked Frances who had taught her to read, she answered with a trace of indignation, "I did!" And she had, of course.

## WHY LITERACY MATTERS: A BRIEF HISTORY

In recounting Frances's experience, we focused on the evolution of her ability to read; yet her language experiences were wrapped up in more than just reading. She sang in the car, participated in discussions at the dinner table, listened to bedtime stories, and moved letters around on the fridge. It may be surmised that these experiences had as much to do with her learning to read as did the actual exposure to older children's reading lessons at school. The whole of language was present in Frances's life experience, with each piece contributing to progress in the others. The view that all these pieces fit together in the young child's literacy life, and that unstructured, self-directed learning can be powerful, is a relatively recent one.

In this country's colonial period, children concentrated first on learning their ABCs, usually using a hornbook. These could be made of wood, various metals, perhaps ivory, and occasionally even gingerbread—an early attempt to encourage interest. The underlying reason for learning to read had primarily to do with attaining the ability to read the Scriptures. Over the succeeding centuries, motivation became more secular, and various teaching methods were tried.

After the turn of the 20th century, interest in reading instruction rather suddenly became the source of much research and newly devised methodologies. In 1909 Edward Thorndike introduced a handwriting scale, and shortly thereafter numerous other tests began to follow, thus instituting this century's scientific movement in the study of education. The major change in teaching reading that came from this period was a complete switch from a centuries-long emphasis on oral reading to an equally strong emphasis on silent reading.

In the next decade, from the mid-1920s to the mid-1930s, the idea of reading readiness became an issue as awareness developed that all children were not ready in the same way at the same time and that too many were failing to learn to read. There was also the beginning of an argument that exists today: Should children be given carefully planned work in sequential skills? Or should they learn to read as part of what was called an "activity program" in which children chose studies according to their own interests, and teachers tried to incorporate these into the larger picture of an integrated curriculum?

In the period from 1935 to 1950 interrelationships between the other language arts and reading began to be part of teaching methodology. In the 1960s, a focus on assisting the economically disadvantaged attain higher educational and societal benefits led to government support of new reading programs. New materials were published, basal programs were expanded, and help for reading disabilities increased. Not since 1910 had there been such a focus on helping children learn to read.

Yet, for all the excitement, the questions about methodology still were not answered. There was no general agreement then, and there is none now on the best way to teach a child to read. From the mid-1960s to the mid-1970s the power of the basal reader as the core of reading instruction was undisputed. Other language arts were integrated according to the basal programs' instructions, but the basal was the all-important foundation.

However, a new movement quietly but persistently rose up to challenge the power of the basal programs. This challenger argued that we should abandon trying to find the one best method and instead attempt to find the methods that work best for each child. It also argued that reading should not be separated from the other language arts but that they should all be incorporated into a whole, just as children do when they learn language naturally and on their own. Just as learning to read is incorporated into the other language arts, so can language arts be integrated with other areas of the curriculum. Thus, reading is not an isolated skill to be taught in a specified, skill-oriented reading time, but it is part of the everyday life of the classroom.

The name given this challenger to the status quo was *whole language instruction*. This method of teaching did not provide the security of a kit or program, but it did give the teacher the freedom to make choices based on his or her knowledge of the children and their needs. While most teaching methods and materials have historically been imposed from above, teachers themselves were a driving force behind the whole language movement.

Because of the difference between the whole language approach and the skills-oriented basal approach, the teachers who chose to explore whole language often found themselves regarded as courageous pioneers. Before long, however, they were supported in their views by professional associations such as the International Reading Association (IRA). Positive school environments for young children, the IRA said in 1985, "provide reading and writing opportunities that focus on meaningful experiences and meaningful language rather than merely on abstract skill development, because teaching skills out of context does not ensure use in effective reading and writing" (p. 1).

Despite the support of the IRA, as well as an impressive list of other educational organizations associated with young children's learning, whole language did not gain total acceptance among educators, school officials, and parents. Even whole language-oriented teachers found that there was often a gap between theory and practice, due in part to the demanding nature of such teaching. Parents, school officials, and others expressed alarm as statistics began to show that children submersed solely in whole language teaching were scoring poorly on standardized tests.

However, the widespread notion of *balance* had emerged, as it became apparent that neither side in the so-called reading wars could claim anything like a research-based victory. Reading and the other aspects of language learning—writing and oral skills—were to be taught as would best fit individual children, classes, ages, and cultures.

Most recently, The Common Core State Standards for English Language Arts and Literacy (National Governors Association Center for Best Practices & Council of Chief State School Officers, 2010) were crafted to provide consistent English language arts structure across grades K–12 with emphasis on real world relevancy. These Standards are based on the most recent research from numerous sources and focus on core understandings and procedures. Yet these Standards were written with the intention of being "a living work: as new and better evidence emerges, the Standards will be revised accordingly" (National Governors Association Center for Best Practices & Council of Chief State School Officers, 2010, n.p.). These Standards will be displayed later in the chapter.

Possibly more important than teaching methodology are the enthusiasm, interest, and curiosity expressed by children and their teachers. With that in mind, this chapter is dedicated in part to the belief that, when children have something interesting to read, write, and speak about, they will be more engaged as they learn to read, write, and speak. Integrating other areas of the curriculum with literacy learning thus becomes a logical, appropriate, and positive direction to take. And immersing youngsters in research of their own choosing, with enough direction and structure from their teachers, can help children on their way toward competence in language and literacy. In other words, when children have meaningful and relevant opportunities to apply the academic skills that they have been taught, and in some cases even learned by themselves, their learning becomes real and valuable to them.

## LITERACY AND CHILD DEVELOPMENT

Language and literacy are basic and integral to the entire early childhood curriculum. They simply cannot be taught in isolation because there must be some sort of content to listening, speaking, reading, and writing. How children are able to engage in these skills, however, depends on their level of development. The level of inquiry learning they can engage in is also determined to a great extent by their level of language and literacy development. According to the National Reading Panel (2000), the two goals of literacy are to obtain meaning from what is heard and read and to successfully communicate meaning through writing and speaking. To best support young learners in their beginning steps toward these goals, teachers must have a good understanding of how each communication element develops. The next section details the development of these elements.

### Oral Expression

Infants respond to speech as soon as they are born. Some, for example, have been observed responding to their own names as early as six or seven days after birth, or synchronizing their body movements with adult speech (Charlesworth, 1996). Oral language has already entered their lives in a major way and will continue to permeate their development in all areas. It is only a short while before babbling appears, first as pseudo-crying, which adults recognize as an expression of discontent or attention getting. Soon there is also experimentation with vowel sounds, then, by four or five months, an interest in consonants (researchers include the ever-popular "raspberry" noise here). By 10 or

11 months, infants often carry on with extensive, complex babbles that sound like adults talking but that are totally incomprehensible (Trawick-Smith, 2000).

At the same time, between eight and 18 months, babies can be expected to speak their first words. By 15 months, a vocabulary of about 10 words is normal with six or seven of these words nouns. At 18 to 20 months, words are sometimes put together in what has been called "telegraphic speech" because it leaves out the little connecting words that telegrams also leave out (Dale, 1976).

By the age of three, most children are moving from telegraphic speech to more complex sentences. By the time they are four, complex sentences make up between 20% and 25% of children's speech (Garrard, 1987). Sometime between ages five and seven, children attain most of their grammatical understanding, although some children do not master complex structures completely until they are as much as 10 years old.

## Reading

Before children can learn to read, they need to understand what the purpose of reading actually is. And they need to understand, too, why all those strange little marks are on the page. A knowledge of this is called "print awareness." One source of confusion for youngsters is the presence of both pictures and print on the same page. While it is obvious to the adult reading a story to a child that pictures are to be looked at and words are to be read, this may not be grasped by the young child. There are some children as old as five who believe that pictures can be read just as words are, although there are also children as young as three who have not only figured out the difference but have learned to read in the adult sense of the word.

In recent years, research has demonstrated that children and adults alike develop literacy capabilities through five general stages (Cooper, 2006). The first stage, called *early emergent literacy*, requires that there is at least a basic understanding of the purpose of reading and of developing oral language. The child is generally in preschool or about to begin kindergarten and writes by drawing or scribbling. A child at the second stage, *emergent literacy*, has developed standard patterns of oral language and can form or name letters. Single-word recognition is also a capability. *Beginning reading and writing* constitutes the third stage and, for most children, continues through the first grade or, in some cases, through the primary grades. At this time, children begin to read in the conventional way, including figuring out new words and reading with some *fluency* (automatically and at a normal pace). The fourth stage, *almost fluent reading and writing*, begins for most children late in the second grade. More silent reading is now possible, and oral vocabulary makes good strides. Finally, children reach the *fluent reading and writing* stage, generally in about the fourth grade. Now, reading, writing, and oral language can be used for many purposes, and the student is truly at home in a literate society. Although this description of stages includes general ages, children can vary widely in their development and still remain within what is considered a normal range of ability.

## Writing

Much of writing development parallels reading development, at least conceptually. In fact, there have been several methods for teaching reading based on the idea that children learn to read through writing. However, the ability to control pencil or crayon varies from child to child, with some more capable than others. Like reading, writing develops through a series of stages (Trawick-Smith, 2000). The *prephonemic* stage includes

**Figure 6.1** At age three months, Daniel was already hearing both Japanese and English at home.

random letters, perhaps scribbled, that represent whole stories. The chosen letters have no relationship to the actual sounds in the story. In the *phonemic* stage, children begin to understand that a story should be written using letters that make the sounds of the story's words. However, reading such stories usually takes much effort on the part of the reader who must usually ask the writer what the "words" say. The next stage is referred to as the *transitional* stage in which the writer's ability to spell out whole words increases, but often with the use of invented spelling. A common error at this stage is the neglect of the "silent e" at the end of a word with a long vowel. Finally, children achieve the stage of *conventional writing* in which spelling and writing conventions look like those of adults. Some children, but certainly not all, arrive at his stage during the primary grades.

### Diversity in Development

When infants babble, they do so in imitation of their mother tongues. Thus, the sounds they make take on different tones and shapes. Babies in bilingual or multilingual families adopt sounds from all the languages they hear, and their first words come from every language around them, although their interpretation is as if they were learning a single language. In other words, toddlers typically name each object in their environment from just one of the languages they hear, happily mixing the languages as they go along (see Figures 6.2 and 6.3). For example, a child from an English-Spanish home might refer to the "lamp" that is "on the mesa." Or, the child might actually combine two languages in one name, for example calling a cat a "kittygato" (Trawick-Smith, 2000).

**Figure 6.2** Now, at age six, Daniel feels comfortable reading and illustrating books from both Japanese and English. This picture, and the picture in Figure 6.3, were drawn in one sitting.

Once bilingual children start putting words together in sentences, they are faced with the problem of word order. In Spanish, for example, adjectives typically come after the noun rather than before it as in English. Some languages, such as Japanese with its verbs appearing at the very end of the sentence, require a completely different mind-set for the speaker and writer. With their usual creative approach to making sense of their world, toddlers learn to cope, sometimes selecting the grammatical structure of one of their home languages and applying it to both, or even creating a grammatical structure of their own (Trawick-Smith, 2000). By their preschool years, this usually gets sorted out, and their teachers can best help them by simply modeling standard grammar themselves. Primary teachers might find it advantageous, if incorrect structures persist, to intervene with one-on-one coaching.

Cognitive delays and physical disabilities present somewhat different challenges to young children learning language and beginning literacy activities. Delays may be caused

**Figure 6.3** At age six, Daniel feels comfortable reading and illustrating books from two languages.

by cognitive disability or by physical problems, such as ear infections, that can cause long-term hearing impairment. The fact that both oral and written language are essentially symbol systems makes them problematically abstract for some children. Thus, simple modeling on the part of the teacher, even when repeated many times, may not be sufficient. There are a multitude of techniques that teachers can use to assist such children. As examples, it can sometimes be helpful for children with delays to learn a collection of sight words used in everyday life if they are unable to master true reading; children can be enlisted to help other children; and the teacher can draw explicit attention to the written word as it appears in and around the entire classroom but that may not be apparent to the child with special needs. Whenever possible, it is best to keep children in their own classroom surrounded by their peers and with the stability of the usual classroom schedule. If special intervention is necessary, however, there are many resources available to assist children with delays, from federally funded reading specialists to an ever-growing array of tools and utensils that help children hold and turn pages, write, or use computers.

Children who break reading's abstract code early are gifted—not only with convenient skills mastery but also with the opportunity to explore and enjoy where others often have to struggle. This chapter opened with the early reading story of Frances. Not only did this child have an exceptional innate gift, she was also exposed to many other

**Figure 6.4** Some young children have the advantage of having an older sibling read to them.

advantages in her life. If you return to her story and remind yourself of what all these were, it will become apparent that these advantages can be shared with all children in your own classes.

## INCORPORATING LITERACY INTO DAILY ROUTINES

When children have meaningful and purposeful experiences with literacy on a daily basis, they have consistent and predictable avenues that call on them to apply their budding literacy skills and strategies. Such routines, depending on the developmental level of the children, include:

- At the beginning of the school day, point to and read children's names from a student-visible class list and have each child respond in a predetermined way (such as replying "good morning" in a choice of foreign languages) to signify his/her presence. This reading task might be delegated to the students after the teacher has done sufficient modeling of this routine.

- At the beginning of the school day (or another routinely scheduled time), have children read simple but daily-changing silly rhyme sentences that are placed in an area for all to see. For example, "Today I saw a cat sitting on a rat." Or, "Today I saw a goat singing in a boat." Change the sophistication of the sentences as children's skills advance. This also might be a task that the children assume by putting in their own rhyming words.
- Prewrite a short "morning message" each day for the children to read, with teacher assistance as needed. Examples of fitting preschool messages: "It is sunny today" and "I like your smiles." A primary message, of course, will be lengthier depending on the learners. For example, "Good morning. It was cold last night. Did you see frost on the ground on your way to school?" Sometimes, young learners can shoulder the task of being "morning message writer."
- Write each child's first name (add surnames as skill level dictates) on 3 in. × 8 in. cardstock paper. Show the cards and have the whole class read each name to transition to another area in the room or to line up.
- As part of the "morning business" routine, rotate and affix the proper days in the sentence strip blanks and have students read:
Yesterday was (<u>Monday</u>).
Today is (<u>Tuesday</u>).
Tomorrow will be (<u>Wednesday</u>).

**Figure 6.5** Parent readers are scheduled to come into this K–1 class on a regular basis. On this day, a child's mother is reading one of the students' favorite stories, *Are You My Mother?*, in the Spanish language.

- Provide a scheduled time when young learners can be "student story readers." After sufficient home practice reading a student-chosen book, student story readers sign up on a chart to signify that they are prepared to read a story to the whole class. If many students sign up to read in one day, the class could be divided up into small groups for each reader, depending on the allotted time.
- Story reading by teachers, parents visiting the class, or other adults should always be routinely incorporated into the day's schedule.
- Almost any time of the school day is a good time to burst into song to reinforce a variety of language skills such as vocabulary, pronunciation, sentence patterns, rhythm, and parts of speech. The repetitive nature of songs is of value to ELL students and, in turn, learning songs in non-English languages may be enjoyable to all students. Literacy skills can be integrated even further when children write their own words to familiar tunes with the option to publish them to share with others.

## A CHILD-INITIATED INQUIRY EXPERIENCE

In each of the curriculum chapters, a real-life project or experience demonstrates how children's curiosity, wonder, concerns, and inquiries can be the inspiration for school- or center-based studies. In this first example, the children in the childcare center were just three and four years old, yet their concern about a sudden change in their environment was such that a project seemed important. Perhaps it would best be called a mini-project because it lasted a relatively brief time. This, however, is to be expected for children who are so young and with little academic experience. In subsequent chapters, the inquiries of somewhat older children are discussed, as they evolve through more lengthy in-depth learning. Although the experience presented here crosses curriculum lines, it is the emphasized literacy elements that are important to note.

*Hayley, age three, walked into the childcare center wondering what the loud noise on the other side of the building was. It was early still, and most of the children had not yet arrived. The three who were there, however, were lined up at the window, watching the gardener and his very noisy leaf blower. Before long, he put it down and picked up an equally noisy trimmer. In dismay, the children watched as he began to cut back the bushes they liked to hide in. As a group, they ran to Teacher Moira to voice their complaint and concern. But the noise suddenly stopped, and when Moira checked outside, she observed that the gardener, carrying his tools, was on his way back to his truck.*

*"But what if he comes back?" the youngsters asked in unison, all looking exceptionally worried. And Hayley added, "Isn't there something we can do to stop him?" At that point Teacher Moira had an idea, exciting but a bit intimidating. She had read about the Project Approach by Lilian Katz and Sylvia Chard (2000), but she had been uncertain as to how it might work with her preschoolers. In addition, she knew just a little about the schools in Reggio Emilia and the investigative learning that preschool children do there. But she had never had the courage to try anything on her own. Further, her administrator was not inclined to support such experimentation, and each week published, for staff and parents, a curriculum schedule based on "The Theme of the Week."*

Now, however, Teacher Moira wondered if she might take this simple but profound concern of the children and imbue it with the structure of a project. Using what she recalled of the Project Approach, she decided that the children's expression of concern and their question about what they might do could be called Phase 1 and that they could complete the phase by considering alternative courses of action. So, she asked her aide to take care of newcomers as they arrived, then took the other four to a quiet place to discuss what might be done. At first, their answers were quite fanciful and impractical, but soon Hayley, who had recent practice dictating thank-you notes to her mother, suggested that they could send a note to the gardener. The idea appealed to everyone, and it was decided that Teacher Moira would write what they dictated and that the note would then be posted on the fence.

Phase 2, Teacher Moira knew, was the actual investigation, but she realized that no actual investigation had been discussed or planned. However, the children had informally discussed the gardener's negative impact on their environment and sought to find solutions to this problem. Her very young investigators were taking their first steps toward civic action, and they needed to research, with her help, ways to do this. She began with the note itself, asking the children what they could say that would be most polite to the gardener and make him actually want to follow through. They decided that courtesy words such as please and thank you would be important, and the note ended up reading: "Dear Mr. Gardener, Please do not cut these bushes. We like to hide in them. Thank you." The children all signed their names to the best of their ability, and then decorated the note with pictures of trees or their best scribbles.

The entire group then went out to the front of the building and taped the note to the fence. Suddenly, the children began to wonder which bushes were most important to them and experimented with hiding to see which ones worked best. With Teacher Moira's encouragement, they began to observe more about the bushes than they ever had before, noting leaf and branch sizes, shades of green and brown, and bush height as compared to their own.

It was three days before the gardener returned, and, charmed by the children's written request, he wrote a note back promising to be more careful. He invited the children to show him what their preferences would be. Teacher Moira read the note to the group of four and accompanied them on a trip back to the fence. Discussions were held, decisions were made, and the children left with a feeling of great satisfaction. At this point, Teacher Moira felt that the children had successfully engaged in Phase 2 of their research into community activism, but what, she asked herself, about Phase 3? Teacher Moira sat the children down and asked what, if anything, should happen next. Again, Hayley remembered about thank-you notes and suggested they write one. One of the boys said they should tell the whole class what had happened. Teacher Moira suggested that each child tell one thing, and the youngsters agreed, carefully determining who should say what and which experiences were most important to share. And that, Teacher Moira decided, was plenty for a Phase 3 conclusion. However, the enthusiasm that her young learners showed for engaging in this child-directed project encouraged Moira to be observant for other learning opportunities that would center around her youngsters' interests.

When children, even at preprimary levels, have support and encouragement to use their natural curiosity to pose questions and solve problems, the outcomes can be profound. In this case, the budding activists of the childcare center learned that politely voicing opinions could have positive results. Language and literacy skills were put to action in purposeful ways, and were subtly woven into the students' experience.

## THE LANGUAGE AND LITERACY CURRICULUM

Knowledge of academic skills is crucial when integrating the curriculum and using inquiry-based learning. When a teacher is well versed in the student learning expectations for the grade level he or she is teaching—when the grade level skills are at the forefront of the teacher's mind—the use of inquiry to integrate the curriculum becomes more automatic and more easily achievable. With the Common Core standards securely in mind, teachers can self-confidently delve into the use of integration and inquiry, and thus, the opportunities to make the curriculum rich and meaningful for young learners is limited only by the imaginations of the teachers and the students.

Hence, in this textbook the often very lengthy, but pertinent, academic standards, for literacy as well as for each subject covered, are presented in a user-friendly, concise manner with hopes that educators will readily use them.

The National Governors Association Center for Best Practices and the Council of Chief State School Officers (NGACBP/CCSSO) drew on international models and numerous sources to design standards that clearly communicate what is expected of students at each grade level. The standards provide all K–12 students, from all states, an equal opportunity to reach high academic standards in English Language Arts and in short, "Students

**Figure 6.6** This high school teacher enjoys reading to these young children just as much as he enjoys reading to his much older students.

who meet the Standards develop the skills in reading, writing, speaking, and listening that are the foundation for any creative and purposeful expression in language" (National Governors Association Center for Best Practices & Council of Chief State School Officers, 2010, n.p.). The skills and understandings students are expected to demonstrate have meaningful applicability outside the classroom.

It is important to note that the Standards focus on what is most essential for students to know and be able to do. They do not describe all that can or should be taught, nor do they command how teachers should teach. A great deal is left to the discretion of teachers and curriculum developers. The complete Common Core State Standards in English Language Arts can be found at www.corestandards.org/.

The Standards in K–2 concentrate on students reading a wide range of literature and informational text; fostering understanding and working knowledge of concepts of print, alphabetic principle, and other basic English writing conventions; and focusing instruction to help ensure that students gain sophistication in all aspects of language use. In order to ensure continuity across the grade levels each grade level section is divided into *strands* followed by a strand-specific *anchor standard*. Each anchor standard is followed by grade specific skills (in italics) that develop the anchor standards into end-of-school-year expectations. The Common Core Standards in English Language Arts are as follows:

### Kindergarten
#### Reading: Literature

1. Key Ideas and Details
   (*With prompting and support: ask and answer questions about key text details; retell familiar stories; identify characters, settings, major events.*)
2. Craft and Structure
   (*Ask and answer questions about unknown words; recognize common types of texts— e.g., storybooks, poems; name author and illustrator.*)
3. Integration of Knowledge and Ideas
   (*With prompting and support: describe the relationship between illustrations and the story; compare and contrast the adventure experiences of characters in familiar stories.*)
4. Range of Reading and Level of Text Complexity
   (*Actively engage in group reading activities with purpose and understanding.*)

#### Reading: Informational Text

1. Key Ideas and Details
   (*With prompting and support: ask and answer questions about key text details; identify the main topic; describe connections between two pieces of information.*)
2. Craft and Structure
   (*Identify front and back cover, title page; name author and illustrator; with prompt and support ask and answer questions about unknown words.*)
3. Integration of Knowledge and Ideas
   (*With prompting and support: describe relationship between illustrations and text; identify basic similarities and differences between two texts on the same topic—e.g., illustrations, descriptions.*)
4. Range of Reading Level of Text Complexity
   (*Actively engage in group reading activities with purpose and understanding.*)

## Reading: Foundational Skills

1. Print Concepts
   (*Demonstrate understanding of the organization and basic features of print—follow words left to right, top to bottom, page by page; understand that spoken words are represented by letters; understand that words are separated by spaces; recognize and name all upper and lowercase letters.*)
2. Phonological Awareness
   (*Demonstrate understanding of spoken words, syllables, and sounds [phonemes]—recognize and produce rhyming words; interact with syllables in spoken words; isolate and pronounce sounds in consonant-vowel-consonant [CVC] words; change phonemes in one-syllable words to make new words.*)
3. Phonics and Word Recognition
   (*Know and apply phonics and word analysis skills in decoding words—one-to-one letter-sound correspondence; long and short vowel sounds; high-frequency sight words.*)
4. Fluency
   (*Read emergent-reader texts with purpose and understanding.*)

## Writing

1. Text Types and Purposes
   (*Draw, dictate, and write to compose opinion pieces, informative texts, narrate events—.g., I like ___; This dog can ___; Yesterday I ___*)
2. Production and Distribution of Writing
   (*With adult guidance and support: respond to questions and suggestions from peers to strengthen writing as needed; use digital tools to produce and publish writing.*)
3. Research to Build and Present Knowledge
   (*Participate in shared research and writing projects; with adult guidance and support, use information from provided sources to answer a question.*)

## Speaking and Listening

1. Comprehension and Collaboration
   (*Participate in collaborative conversations about kindergarten appropriate topics by listening, taking turns, staying on topic; ask and answer questions to seek help, get information, or for clarification.*)
2. Presentation of Knowledge and Ideas
   (*Describe people, places, things, and events adding drawings or other visual displays to provide additional detail; speak audibly, express thoughts, feelings, and ideas clearly.*)

## Language

1. Conventions of Standard English
   (*Demonstrate command of the conventions of standard English grammar and usage when writing or speaking—print upper and lowercase letters; use frequently occurring nouns and verbs, plurals, question words [interrogatives], and prepositions. Demonstrate command of the conventions of standard English—capitalize first word in a sentence, end punctuation, write letters for most consonant and short-vowel sounds [phonemes], spell simple words phonetically.*)

**Figure 6.7** These young gentlemen enjoy reading collaboratively.

2. Vocabulary Acquisition and Use
   (*Determine or clarify meanings of unknown or multiple-meaning words, use affixes (e.g., -ed, -s, re-, un-, pre-, -less) as clues. With adult guidance and support explore word relationships and nuances in word meanings—categories [e.g., shapes, foods], word opposites, shades of meaning [e.g., walk, march, prance]. Use words acquired through conversations, reading, being read to.*)
   (National Governors Association Center for Best Practices & Council of Chief State School Officers, 2010, n.p.)

### First Grade
#### Reading: Literature

1. Key Ideas and Details
   (*Ask and answer questions about key text details; retell stories; describe a story's characters, settings, major events.*)
2. Craft and Structure
   (*Identify words/phrases that suggest feelings; explain difference between story books and information books; identify the story teller.*)
3. Integration of Knowledge and Ideas
   (*Use story illustrations and details to describe characters; compare/contrast experiences of characters in different stories.*)
4. Range of Reading and Level of Text Complexity
   (*With prompting and support, read prose and poetry of appropriate complexity for Grade 1.*)

## Reading: Informational Text

1. Key Ideas and Details
   (*Ask and answer questions about key details in a text; identify main topic and retell details; describe the connection between two individuals, events, ideas or information.*)
2. Craft and Structure
   (*Ask and answer questions to clarify meaning; know and use text features—e.g., headings, tables of contents, icons—to locate facts; distinguish between information from illustrations or from words.*)
3. Integration of Knowledge and Ideas
   (*Use illustrations and details to describe key ideas; identify reasons given to support points; identify basic similarities and differences between two texts on the same topic— e.g., in illustrations, descriptions.*)
4. Range of Reading and Level of Text Complexity
   (*With prompting and support, read informational texts appropriately complex for Grade 1.*)

## Reading: Foundational Skills

1. Print Concepts
   (*Demonstrate understanding of basic features of print—e.g., first word, capitalization, ending punctuation.*)
2. Phonological Awareness
   (*Demonstrate understanding of spoken words, syllables, sounds: distinguish long from short vowel sounds; produce single-syllable words; isolate and pronounce sounds in spoken single-syllable words.*)
3. Phonics and Word Recognition
   (*Know and apply grade-level phonics and word analysis skills in decoding words: know the spelling-sound correspondences for consonant digraphs; decode regularly spelled one-syllable words; know final-e and vowel team conventions; decode two-syllable words; read words with inflectional endings; read grade-appropriate irregularly spelled words.*)
4. Fluency
   (*Read with sufficient accuracy and fluency to support comprehension: read with purpose and understanding; orally with accuracy, rate, and expression; use context to confirm or self-correct.*)

## Writing

1. Text Types and Purposes
   (*Write opinion pieces; write informative/explanatory texts; write narratives.*)
2. Production and Distribution of Writing
   (*With adult guidance and support: focus on a topic and respond to questions and suggestions from peers; use a variety of digital tools to produce and publish writing.*)
3. Research to Build and Present Knowledge
   (*Participate in shared research and writing projects; with adult guidance and support, recall information or gather information from provided sources to answer questions.*)

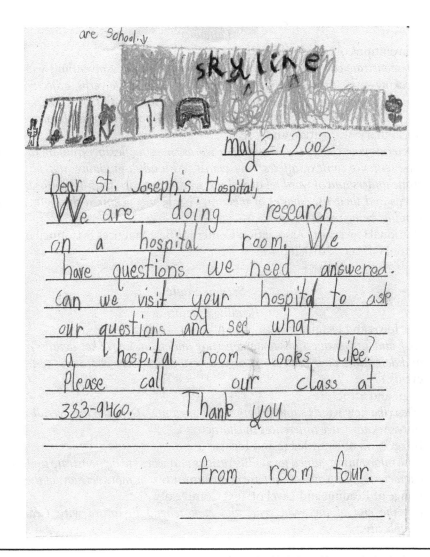

are School..v

skyline

may 2, 2002

Dear St. Joseph's Hospital,
We are doing research
on a hospital room. We
have questions we need answered.
Can we visit your hospital to ask
our questions and see what
a hospital room looks like?
Please call our class at
383-9460. Thank you

from room four.

**Figure 6.8** Writing has purpose in inquiry-based learning, as shown by this letter asking permission to do research at a hospital.

### Speaking and Listening
1. Comprehension and Collaboration
   (*Participate in collaborative conversations about Grade 1 appropriate topics by listening, taking turns, staying on topic; ask and answer questions to seek help, get information, or for clarification.*)
2. Presentation of Knowledge and Ideas
   (*Describe people, places, things, and events adding drawings or other visual displays to provide additional detail; produce complete sentences appropriate to task and situation.*)

*Language*

1. Conventions of Standard English
   (*Demonstrate command of standard English grammar conventions when writing or speaking—e.g., print all upper and lowercase letters; use verbs, adjectives, pronouns, articles, prepositions. Demonstrate command of standard English when writing—e.g., capitalization, end punctuation, commas, spell untaught words phonetically.*)
2. Vocabulary Acquisition and Use
   (*Determine or clarify the meaning or words choosing flexibly from an array of strategies: sentence context, affixes, root words. With adult guidance and support demonstrate understand of word relationships: word categories, real-life connections between words and their use, shades of meaning. Use words acquired through conversations, reading, being read to.*)
   (National Governors Association Center for Best Practices & Council of Chief State School Officers, 2010, n.p.)

## Second Grade

### Reading: Literature

1. Key Ideas and Details
   (*Ask and answer questions to demonstrate understanding of key details; recount stories and determine their central message; describe how story characters respond to major events.*)
2. Craft and Structure
   (*Describe how words supply rhythm and meaning. Describe the overall structure of a story. Acknowledge differences in characters.*)
3. Integration of Knowledge and Ideas
   (*Use information gained from illustrations and words to demonstrate understanding of characters, setting, plot. Compare and contrast two or more versions of the same story.*)
4. Range of Reading and Level of Text Complexity
   (*By the end of the year, read and comprehend literature with Grades 2–3 text complexity.*)

### Reading: Informational Text

1. Key Ideas and Details
   (*Ask and answer questions to demonstrate understanding of text details. Identify the main topic of paragraphs. Describe connections between series of events, concepts, steps of procedures.*)
2. Craft and Structure
   (*Determine meanings of words and phrases. Know and use text features—e.g., glossaries, indexes, icons. Identify main purpose of a text.*)
3. Integration of Knowledge and Ideas
   (*Explain how specific images clarify a text. Describe, compare, and contrast important points.*)
4. Range of Reading and Level of Text Complexity
   (*By the end of the year, read and comprehend informational texts with Grades 2–3 text complexity.*)

*Reading: Foundational Skills*

1. Phonics and Word Recognition
   (*Know and apply grade-level phonics and word analysis skills in decoding words by using: long/short vowels; spelling-sound correspondences; common prefixes and suffixes; recognize and read grade-appropriate irregularly spelled words.*)
2. Fluency
   (*Read with sufficient accuracy and fluency to support comprehension; read orally with accuracy and expression; use context to confirm or self-correct words and understanding.*)

*Writing*

1. Text Types and Purposes
   (*Write opinion pieces, informative/explanatory texts, narratives of events.*)
2. Production and Distribution of Writing
   (*With adult guidance and support: focus on a topic, revising as needed; use a variety of digital tools to produce and publish writing.*)
3. Research to Build and Present Knowledge
   (*Participate in shared research and writing projects; recall information or gather information from provided sources to answer questions.*)

*Speaking and Listening*

1. Comprehension and Collaboration
   (*Participate in collaborative conversations about Grade 2 appropriate topics by listening, taking turns, staying on topic; ask and answer questions to seek help, get information, or for clarification.*)
2. Presentation of Knowledge and Ideas
   (*Describe people, places, things, and events adding drawings or other visual displays to provide additional detail; produce complete sentences appropriate to task and situation.*)

*Language*

1. Conventions of Standard English
   (*Demonstrate command of the conventions of standard English usage when writing or speaking by using: collective nouns—e.g., group; irregular plurals—e.g., fish; reflexive pronouns—e.g., myself; irregular verb past tense—e.g., sat; adjectives and adverbs; producing and expanding sentences. Demonstrate command of the conventions of standard English capitalization, punctuation, and spelling when writing: capitalization; commas; apostrophes; generalize learned spelling patterns.*)
2. Knowledge of Language
   (*Use knowledge of language and its conventions when writing, speaking, reading, or listening; compare formal and informal uses of English.*)
3. Vocabulary Acquisition and Use
   (*Determine or clarify the meaning of words choosing flexibly from an array of strategies: sentence context, prefixes, root words, compound words, use of glossaries and dictionaries. Demonstrate understanding of word relationships: real-life connections*

**Figure 6.9** This young investigator uses oral language, as well as reading and writing skills, as he interviews an adult during an inquiry-learning project on ice cream.

*between words and their use; distinguish shades of meaning. Use words acquired through conversations, reading, being read to.)*
(National Governors Association Center for Best Practices & Council of Chief State School Officers, 2010, n.p.)

The Common Core State Standards for English Language Arts do not cover the years before kindergarten. However, the skills that learners obtain in their early years form the foundation on which the subsequent grade level skills are built. The next section details elements that help to form a literacy foundation in the preprimary years.

### The Preprimary Years

#### Listening and Speaking

From birth, and probably from their time in the womb, infants use their listening skills to learn about their environment. In their very first days they begin to differentiate between the voices of the people in their lives and start to understand the meaning of various environmental sounds. Attention to these sounds—including language, music, machinery, meal preparations, and much more—can be considered preparation for communication for the infant and linguistic skill building for children old enough to talk.

The early speech of infants is typically in single words: *mama, dada, dinner, kitty*. These can often be interpreted as complete sentences: "Mama, give me my dinner!" although it is, at times, difficult to intuit an entire meaning such as this. Once two-word sentences appear, understanding becomes easier: "Kitty dinner" might well mean that the kitty is eating dinner or wants to be fed. Teachers and caregivers can help young children expand their sentence structure by repeating back this telegraphic speech using more complete grammar: "Yes, the kitty is eating her dinner." For some native speakers of English, this kind of assistance may prove helpful through the primary grades. For children learning English as a new language, teachers should carry on in this conversational fashion whenever possible.

Children should be provided with an opportunity to talk to the whole group while not being pushed to do so. Virtually every early childhood classroom has circle time, or a total group gathering time, during some period of the day. Although young children (like many adults) are more tied to their own need to express themselves than they are to the needs of their listeners, some suggestions to them may improve their communication skills and sense of audience. To the child who talks and talks: "What is the most important thing you want to share? Just share that one thing right now." To the child who assumes that his or her own life details are interesting to everyone: "What do you think will be most interesting for others to hear? Can you tell why?"

Children should be able to both ask and answer questions, calling for patience and guidance on the part of the teacher as preprimary children work to form their words into questions. Circle time, as just described, is one venue for this. The rest of the day, however, does not just belong to the teacher to ask all questions while children are tested as they provide answers. An inquiry-learning model of education presupposes that questions from children will be a major part of any day. The teacher's role is to model respect while listening to the questions and answering them, or while having an entire group consider what the answers might be. The children also should learn to listen and respond with respect.

### Reading

Listening to stories helps pave the way for the thrilling time when young learners begin to read and write stories on their own. Listening to daily stories, both oral and written, provides children with new content information as well as opportunities to learn about story structure, vocabulary, grammar, and the sounds of letters and language. The teacher who is a skilled reader to any age level finds ways to address all these elements (although certainly not all of them at once), while still maintaining youngsters' interest in what is being told or read. Teachers who invest the time to hone their oral reading and storytelling skills and choose engaging and appropriate story material set a good example for their students.

*Modeling* on the part of the teacher can begin in infancy as parents and caregivers read stories to their young charges. A baby, sitting in a reader's lap, can learn the direction that pages turn and even to turn the pages correctly, that the words in stories sound the same even with many repetitions, that pictures are related to the plot, and that reading is an enjoyable activity. From preschool onward, read-alouds provide endless opportunities for teachers to model reading to the whole class.

The first step toward independent reading is typically considered to be *shared reading*. Shared reading is an instructional approach in which the teacher and students read a story together. With the teacher explicitly modeling skills and strategies of proficient readers, the students participate as they can. At home, the small child might learn to

**Figure 6.10** People of all ages enjoy hearing and reading a good story.

recognize a single word or phrase in a popular story. At school, the teacher might use a Big Book or PowerPoint to do a shared reading activity. These activities can include noting how print moves from left to right and top to bottom, recognizing repeated words by sight and chanting them together whenever they appear, and filling in predictable words. Time is also taken to identify letter-sound associations.

*Phonemic awareness* is the understanding that words are made up of various and specific sounds. For example, a child who can hear a string of words and identify which ones have the same beginning sound is demonstrating this awareness. Other examples include identification of rhyming sounds and being able to clap to the sounds of separate syllables. Success in achieving phonemic awareness has been identified as important to reading success (National Reading Panel, 2000).

### Writing

Just as infants and toddlers can be introduced to the joys of reading through engaging in picture books, so they—and older children as well—can be introduced to the pleasures and challenges of writing through the making of pictures. For the very young, just holding a pencil, crayon, or marker is a learning experience, and much of what goes on paper is simply for the purpose of observing what happens when the tool is moved around on it. As youngsters learn to create actual pictures, they often tell a story. Once this happens, the opportunity is ripe for the teacher to take dictation and write down on the picture, or near it, what the child has to say. At about this time in children's development, the teacher can also help children begin the process of learning to write. As students become more skillful they will write their own words to correspond to their pictures.

Modeling can be done by writing aloud. The teacher demonstrates writing in front of the class and talks out loud while doing it. Anything that children are ready to learn is appropriate for sharing, from saying that the writing goes from left to right to demonstrating how to write in a journal.

Shared writing parallels shared reading in which teacher and children create a document or story together. Recall Hayley's experience on p. 132 in which the three- and four-year-olds worked with the teacher to write a letter to the gardener, then signed their names as they could. Shared writing is especially appropriate for children at this developmental level.

Young children, no matter the level of writing they are ready for, are intensely interested in learning to do what bigger and older people can do. One writing consultant has said that "in my work teaching writing across the United States, I have seen firsthand the desire of young writers to be taken seriously, to be treated as young artists in the studio—not just students completing assignments" (Lane, 2004, p. vii). Another author has said that, although young children may not yet know the conventions or be able to shape letters, they are already writing in their heads:

> They are thinking of ideas and expressing them orally with remarkable voice and (often) memorable word choice and fluency. In time, given encouragement and opportunity to write, their capacity for conceptualizing their world and putting their own voice on those interpretations is captured on paper. They learn to write by trying it out, by writing often, by copying what they see in the environment, by listening to good literature read well, and by imitating what they hear and see—as well as, of course, turning their imaginative spirits loose. (Spandel, 2004, p. ix)

Although independence is viewed as the end of a continuum that begins with basic introduction to each of the literacy components, it is not necessary or even desirable to drop off earlier activities entirely, or to deny the youngest children some activities associated with their older peers. For example, just because infants and very young children love having stories read to them does not mean that older children cannot also benefit from the experience. Conversely, older children become capable of writing stories independently, but preschoolers also enjoy mimicking them as they make scribbles on paper all by themselves.

## THE IMPORTANCE OF PLAY

Throughout this book, the influence of play on each academic subject will be discussed. While research has demonstrated that play is a successful approach to teaching and learning in all subjects, it is no doubt language that has been the subject that has been studied in most depth and over the most time. This includes all aspects of language discussed in this chapter: speaking, listening, reading, and writing.

Referring to oral language and as stated by NAEYC (Copple & Bredekamp, 2009), "research shows the links between play and foundational capacities such as . . . oral language abilities, social skills, and success in school" (p. 14). Play can help native speakers and language learners alike improve their oral capacities. "Young children organize their knowledge of events into words that communicate their experience, which enhances some elements of carrying on a conversation" (Saracho, 2012, p. 145).

Play has been shown to foster children's reading and writing skills as well, providing far more opportunities for imaginative thinking than can direct instruction (Katz & Chard, 2000).

For example, preschool children can learn about the purposes of reading and writing before they can actually read or write. In their play they can make shopping lists, "write" prescriptions, or follow recipes. Play or pretend writing may take the form of scribbling even after children are receiving writing instruction. (p. 98)

Literature offers many play opportunities. Storytelling, for example, can include dramatizations, follow-up play in dramatic play centers, and the use of puppets. These same activities encourage the development of literacy as children learn more about story structure and increase their vocabularies. Literacy play centers can include activities such as "pretend reading, reading pictures, learning the letters of the alphabet, and writing stories" (Saracho, 2012, p. 212).

## TECHNOLOGY AND EARLY CHILDHOOD LITERACY

Media and technology are entwined in everyday life in the 21st century. Even the youngest of children explore their world using keypads and touch screens on an ever-expanding range of technological devices as they view, browse, navigate and produce original works long before they enter school. Young children see family members engage in shared literacy practices when they network with email, text messaging, and instant chat; youngsters are often invited to participate as well. Handheld, portable electronic devices are seemingly everywhere. Even when young children don't have the actual devices, they can be seen mimicking the use of them in their play—a small rectangular block makes an excellent "cell phone."

But, oftentimes the tech world of young children changes when they come to school and enter the classroom. The focus on print-based literacy text, on phonics, word-decoding, pencil and paper can be a jarring shift from interacting with an image on a screen and a keypad. An equally jarring effect may strike a child who enters a tech-rich classroom environment having had limited access to technological devices at home.

According to the most recent position statement by NAEYC as related to technology and interactive media in early childhood programs, "There has never been a more important time to apply principles of development and learning when considering the use of cutting-edge technologies and media" (NAEYC & Fred Rogers Center for Early Learning, 2012, p. 1).

There are conflicting studies on the value of technology in children's development: Are screen media inherently harmful to young children? Does technology help or hinder children's socialization? Are electronic resources positive tools for effective reading instruction? The research findings remain divided. The amount of time children spend with technology is an issue but *how* children spend time with technology is also an issue. One area that studies seem to agree with centers on concerns with child health issues such as obesity. Several professional and public health organizations and child advocacy groups have recommended "passive, non-interactive technology and screen media not be used in early childhood programs and that there be no screen time for infants and toddlers" (NAEYC & Fred Rogers Center for Early Learning, 2012, p. 2).

However, there are many benefits of using media and technology in the classroom. Technologies that are interactive, allow children to use their curiosity, and encourage problem solving and independent thinking skills can be valuable in the school setting. In addition, the use of technology can support early learners with English as their second language, children with special needs, and those who need assistance with language development.

Please note how important the words *developmentally appropriate* are. There are plenty of computer-based reading, writing, and storybook activities available, as well as a plethora of technological tools and media that are marketed to enhance learning in the language arts, but an alert teacher must closely examine their quality and appropriateness. In addition, "Educators should provide a balance of activities in programs for young children, and technology and media should be recognized as tools that are valuable when used intentionally with children to extend and support active, hands-on, creative, and authentic engagement with those around them and with their world" (NAEYC & Fred Rogers Center for Early Learning, 2012, p. 12).

## ASSESSMENT AND EVALUATION

It is important to assess children's progress in language and literacy continually and adjust curriculum accordingly. The once- or twice-a-year standardized tests will not provide the sufficient or timely information that is necessary to work with children effectively. Try these approaches as adapted from Seefeldt (2005):

- Observe how children are moving from incomplete to more complete sentences in their everyday language.
- Record when and how children name materials in their environment.
- Note children's use of verbs as they describe actions.
- Keep some drawings and observe over time the increasing abilities in dictation to the teacher, as well as the complexity of the drawings.
- Observe children's responses to stories and their growing ability to interact during shared reading.
- Interview individual children about their likes and dislikes, noting their use of parts of speech.
- Note, record, and analyze invented spelling, numbers of correct letters used, and the use of conventional spelling.

As children are introduced to writing, it becomes possible to assess using a helpful approach originally created by a group of teachers in Oregon: the "six traits to enrich writing process" (Spandel, 2004). The traits are applicable to anyone writing at any age and include ideas, organization, voice, word choice, sentence fluency, and conventions. Table 6.1 is a summary of what to look for, as adapted from Vicki Spandel's book and from the Northwest Regional Educational Laboratory in Portland, Oregon.

## PREPRIMARY EXPERIENCES: A STORYBOOK CURRICULUM

Young children everywhere love to hear stories. And they love to hear the same ones over and over again. The familiarity of favorite characters, the opportunity to join in on remembered words and phrases, pictures to see again and again—all these contribute to repeated enjoyment of a story.

It is not necessary, however, to treat a story repetition in the same way each time it is brought back into the classroom. Yes, children love to hear the same story again and

**Table 6.1** Six Traits Writing Process

| Traits | Assessment levels |
| --- | --- |
| ***Ideas*** The main thesis and/or plot line. Include details to help the reader's understanding or maintain interest. | *Emerging:* Some recognizable words present; drawings used for detail. *Developing:* Attempts to make a point or tell a story; some ideas still fuzzy. *Experienced:* Topic is focused and ideas fresh; writer understands topic well. |
| ***Organization*** The internal structure, including lead, developing middle section, close. | *Emerging:* Writes left to right and top down; experiments with beginnings. *Developing:* Limited transitions; attempts at sequencing. *Experienced:* Transitions connect main ideas; good opening and close; important ideas stand out. |
| ***Voice*** The writer speaking to the reader. | *Emerging:* Predictable treatment of topic; audience could be anyone anywhere. *Developing:* Awareness that someone else will be reading piece; characters' feelings evident but predictable. *Experienced:* A variety of emotions present; point of view evident. |
| ***Word Choice*** Using language to paint a word picture. | *Emerging:* Uses recognizable words; makes attempts at phrases. *Developing:* Uses ordinary words unless in an attempt to impress readers; new words don't always fit. *Experienced:* Ordinary words are used well; avoids repetition, clichés; attempts figurative language. |
| ***Sentence Fluency*** Well-crafted sentences with rhythm, logic, variety. | *Emerging:* Strings words into phrases; attempts simple sentences; short, repetitive patterns. *Developing:* Uses simple sentences that tend to begin the same; reader may have to reread to understand. *Experienced:* Sentence structure |
| ***Conventions*** Punctuation, spelling, grammar, usage, capitalization, paragraphing. | *Emerging:* Attempts partially phonetic spelling; random punctuation; nonstandard grammar. *Developing:* Uses phonetic, if incorrect, spelling; punctuation at end of sentence usually correct; attempts standard grammar. *Experienced:* High-frequency words spelled correctly, most others close; basic punctuation correct; has control over standard grammar. |

again, but they also enjoy acting it out, singing about it, role-playing the characters in the dress-up corner, and seeing it appear during activities that—to adult eyes—might not seem at first to be related. In short, it is possible to really live a story for a while.

In recent decades, use of fantasy literature with young children, has been the source of some controversy. The work of Jean Piaget (1971) has consistently reminded us that young children are concrete thinkers and that it is only gradually, throughout the elementary and high school years, that they become capable of abstract thinking. On the surface, at least, today's education of young children reflects this theory. Yet, we continue to tell and read stories with metaphors and morals to these same children, and we often expect that the children will understand these abstractions. These most frequently appear in traditional fairy and folk tales.

Canadian educator Kieran Egan (2006) has argued that young children are not nearly as constricted by the need for concrete learning as Piaget theorized. Referring to psychologist Bruno Bettelheim's (1976) observation that children bring order to their emotional worlds by placing conflicting ideas into opposites, Egan points out the many "binary concepts" that are familiar to children's fairy tales: "One of the most obvious structural features of these stories is that they are based on powerful conflicts between security and danger, courage and cowardice, cleverness and stupidity, hope and despair, and good and evil" (p. 35). Thus, Egan concludes,

> We are familiar with claims that young children's thinking is in some sense "concrete," and that if we want to make material accessible to them we need to present it in concrete terms. But the implication of the above observation is that young children's thinking is also "abstract," or at least children's ability to make sense of the kinds of stories they find readily engaging. . . . Far from young children being unable to deal with abstractions, in such narratives they deploy easily and readily the most abstract ideas we ever learn. (1999, p. 36)

The stories chosen for this chapter are traditional ones, and they all contain conflicts between binary concepts such as good and evil or security and danger. That these conflicts always end on the side of good and of security is important for young children who need such reassurance in their emotional lives. The activities that accompany the stories can help make the abstractions of the conflicts more concrete. Figure 6.11 webs the activities and learning opportunities associated with these stories. The stories in this chapter and other traditional fairy and folk tales can often be found online.

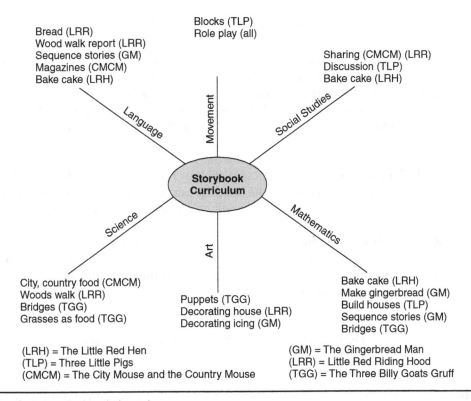

**Figure 6.11** A storybook curriculum web.

### The Little Red Hen (LRH)

#### Summary of Story

A number of animals live in the barnyard, all of them lazy with the exception of the Little Red Hen. When she decides to make bread (or a cake), none of the animals will help her in the processes that are necessary: planting the seeds, cutting the wheat, threshing it, carrying it to the mill for grinding into flour, baking the bread or cake. So she does it all herself. When the animals volunteer to help with the final stage—eating—the hen responds that they didn't help make it so they can't help eat it. She and her chicks eat it all.

#### Activities

- Bake a small, simple loaf cake with children, using picture instructions for the recipe. Stuffed animals can represent the animals who do not get to eat. While the "chicks" eat their cake, they can discuss whether the other animals should get any or not.
- For very young children, the dramatization may work best if the teacher takes the role of the hen. If there is a child who can do the job, the teacher may wish to play the part of a chick, making comments or asking questions to help move the story along.
- Children toward the end of the preschool years are beginning to think about what is and is not fair. After reading the story two or three times, hold a brief discussion about this issue as it appears in the story.

### The Three Little Pigs (TLP)

#### Summary of Story

Three young pigs leave home to seek their fortune. Each builds himself a house: one of straw, one of wood, and one of brick. When the big, bad wolf comes to eat them up, he huffs and puffs but can only blow down the first two houses. Each of the pigs, in turn, runs to the brick house for safety. When the wolf then tries to climb down the chimney of the brick house, the pigs are ready to catch him with a kettle of boiling water.

#### Activities

- In the block corner or outside, have children replicate the pigs' homes. This can be part of a role-play effort, or the building can be done for its own sake. Informal discussion as the project progresses will help point up the obvious superiority of brick as a building material.
- Role-play this story using tables that can be crawled under as houses. For younger children, the teacher should play the part of one of the pigs to help the story movement. Sometimes an entire class will refuse to play the part of the (scary) wolf. This then becomes the teacher's part.

### The City Mouse and the Country Mouse (CMCM)

#### Summary of Story

The city mouse comes to stay with his country cousin and is somewhat condescending about the inelegant surroundings and food. He extends a return invitation to come to his more sophisticated city home, and the two of them set off. At first the country mouse is impressed with city living but is soon happy to return to the more simple country life when their safety is threatened by snarling attack dogs.

### Activities
- From magazines cut a large collection of city and country pictures. After discussing the differences, mix them in one pile and let children classify them. Label each pile, or label two shallow boxes.
- For snack on the first day, eat small samples of "city" food as shown in the version the children are reading. "Country" food will follow the next day.
- Most versions of this story stress the idea that the country mouse was a host who acted from a motive of sharing. Discuss with children the unmannered behavior of the city mouse. Role-play more appropriate behavior.

## The Gingerbread Man (GM)

### Summary of Story

While a little old man is out working in the fields, his little old wife bakes a gingerbread man who surprises her by jumping out of the oven and running away. The man and woman give chase, as do other people and animals, but no one can catch the gingerbread man. At the end he is outsmarted by a fox who offers him a ride across a river if the gingerbread man stands on the fox's head. The fox lures the unsuspecting gingerbread man close enough to his mouth to do what is supposed to be done to gingerbread men: The fox eats him.

### Activities
- Use packaged gingerbread mix to make dough, providing a picture chart for directions. As a math experience, have children count out specific numbers of raisins or candies for prebaking decorations.
- Photocopy the pictures in the story and mount them on tagboard. On the backs write the numbers that place them in sequential order. Make a tagboard strip with sections marked off for placing the pictures. Each of these should be numbered. Children place the pictures in order, checking the backs for accuracy. They can then tell the story to each other, to themselves, or to the teacher.
- This is a good story to role-play because so many children can have a turn. Lay out the "escape route" and chasing rules very clearly before beginning.

## Little Red Riding Hood (LRR)

### Summary of Story

Little Red Riding Hood's mother sends her through the woods to visit her sick grandmother. On the way she is waylaid by the wolf, who has evil intentions. Unsuspecting, she tells the wolf where she is going, and he then sneaks to the grandmother's house and eats her up. When Red Riding Hood arrives, she encounters the wolf tucked into bed and thinks it is her grandmother. After discussing "grandmother's" strange appearance, the wolf attacks Red Riding Hood, intending to eat her. She is saved by a woodsman passing by, who then saves the grandmother as well. (Some books reduce the traditional gore of this tale by having Grandma hide in a closet.)

*Activities*

- The plot of this story is direct and simple enough that it is appropriate for the dress-up corner or for independent role-play.
- Take a walk through the woods (it need only be a small area with trees). Find flowers, acorns, pine cones, and so on for decorating Grandma's house. Write an experience chart about the trip.
- Make stick puppets using paper plates, pipe cleaners, fur, and construction paper. Let each child make favorite characters for more role-play, either directed or free.
- Make bread or cupcakes to take to Grandma. Children can all pretend to be Red Riding Hood taking them to Grandma. The teacher can be Grandma, who then shares the gift with all the Red Riding Hoods.

### The Three Billy Goats Gruff (TGG)

*Summary of Story*

The three goats have eaten all the grass in their usual territory and decide to head for the very green grass in the meadow on the other side of the bridge. However, under the bridge lives a fearsome troll who may eat them up. They then follow a unique plan for arriving safely. First, the smallest goat crosses the bridge and answers the troll's challenge with the suggestion that he wait for a larger goat to eat. The middle-sized goat does the same. After each has arrived safely in the meadow, the largest goat responds to the troll's challenge with one of his own. The two fight, and the goat succeeds in knocking the troll off the bridge and permanently downstream.

*Activities*

- The simple sequence of events makes this a good story to role-play. Choose a sturdy, low table to use as a bridge. Use a strong chair at each end as a step.
- In the block corner, design bridges of varying styles and sizes. Use available dolls to determine which styles and sizes of bridge are the most useful and appropriate.
- Using a homemade bridge, enact the play with stick puppets.
- People eat parts of edible grasses and some greens that resemble grasses. Further, they chew them with teeth similar to those of goats. Point out these teeth to the children and then have them consciously use these teeth to eat such things as bean sprouts and finely shredded lettuce.

### Inquiry Projects That Might Emerge From the Preprimary Storybook Curriculum

In-depth studies from these fairy tales might take any number of directions. Depending on the proximity of a neighborhood farm, individual barnyard animals are good topics for further study as young learners seek to answer such questions as: What do they eat? Where do they sleep? How many babies do they have? What sounds do they make? A more specific topic might center around animal feet—how many feet animals have, the variety of feet shapes, what protects feet, and so on. An interesting twist to a study on animal feet might present itself when children discover that humans are animals as well.

## PRIMARY EXPERIENCES: USING LITERACY AS THE BACKBONE OF INQUIRY-BASED LEARNING

Literacy is the glue that is needed to connect inquiry-based learning observations to paper, that affords young investigators a means to gather and represent their findings, and that enables learners to recreate and share—in a permanent fashion—information gathered on a field research trip. There are many textbooks and "how to" manuals available that specifically present activities that teach and reinforce literacy skills. Therefore, this section focuses on literacy activities that specifically support integrating the curriculum through the use of inquiry learning. These literacy activities have been developed and successfully used by your authors to reinforce inquiry skills and facilitate data collection.

### Literacy Activities That Support the Use of Inquiry Learning

- The use of a *survey sheet* to gather information can be modified to fit different occasions. For example: After making a class list of verbs that describe actions displayed at recess, a "Did you_____?" survey could ask "Did you jump?" "Did you slide?" "Did you skip?" After writing the questions, students survey one another and tally the yes/no answers. Compile a class list of favorite foods and use the survey question of "Do you like to eat_____?" After a field research trip, "Did you see_____?"
- *Sequence charts* can record in written and pictorial form the steps of a creation or an occurrence through time. For example: the steps taken to make a snowperson; the actions students follow as they get ready for school; the process of making a pizza.
- A *scripted interview form*, containing relatively simple questions that encourage easily written answers, is a way to reinforce reading, writing, and interpersonal communication, and sets the stage for more advanced interviews as students become more sophisticated. Questions might include: What is your favorite color? How old are you? What is your favorite food? How many sisters do you have?
- A *make-a-card* area encourages writing and reading with a purpose, especially when outfitted with various shapes and sizes of pre-folded paper and messages to copy, including: I hope you are feeling better. I love you. Thank you. Please come see our research.
- *Papers to write and illustrate observations* encourage descriptive writing and attention to detail. For example: I observed a_____. It was_____. It was_____. It was not_____. This is what it looked like: _____.
- A *form for writing friendly letters*, strategically placed for viewing with a sample letter written on it, gives a structured model for writing letters. Envelopes add a personal touch.
- A *committee-work form* encourages young investigators to think about how they will seek answers as well as what equipment might be needed to obtain data. This form can be used by a research committee, as well as a single student, and addresses: "This is what I (we) will do to research the question. These are the materials and supplies I (we) need." These forms can be used any time a young learner has a compelling question that begs for an answer.

In addition to the preceding activities, young investigators might apply their literacy skills, depending on the topics they are researching, as they construct menus, prepare price lists, design signs, detail instructions, produce informational pamphlets, label artifacts, and compose charts of questions and charts of what they know. See Figure 6.12 for an example of a menu the class created for their pizza parlor project.

### Inquiry Projects From Children's Interest in Literacy

Even in a complex subject such as literacy, there are many topic possibilities that are sufficiently interesting to warrant a child-centered, inquiry-based learning project. Your authors advise teachers to be mindful of the criteria that make a topic worthy of study.

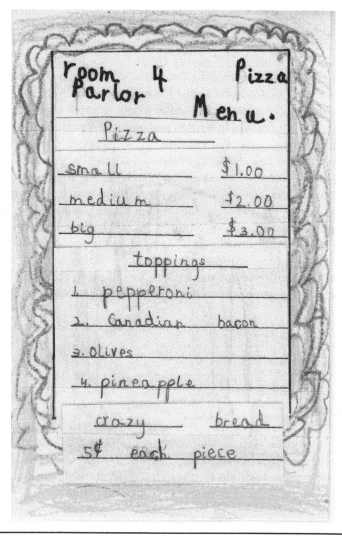

**Figure 6.12** After doing in-depth research on pizza parlors, the students made menus to use in the pizza parlor they constructed in their classroom.

*Will the Study of the Topic:*
- Build on what children already know?
- Offer hands-on relevance to the children?
- Encourage application of social and academic skills?
- Integrate subjects by interconnecting and weaving them, with the goal of furthering student understanding of the topic?
- Support transference of knowledge to future learning?

The following possibilities for inquiry-based learning projects may arise as children are immersed in the magical joy of reading and writing. Each suggested topic would be appropriate for preprimary as well as primary students, as each age of young learners will not only bring their own level of understanding to the proposed topics but also carry out investigations as is developmentally appropriate to their skill level.

- Tools used to enhance readers' vision may intrigue young investigators, especially since some of their classmates may be relying on their use. Glasses, magnifying glasses, or binoculars may encompass history and other cultures, including how they are made, how they work, and of what they are constructed, while also tying in health and safety issues.
- Implements for writing—including pencils, pens, chalk, even typewriters—have excellent potential for in-depth inquiry and investigation as children explore their construction, different varieties and uses, and evolution through the ages. Such investigations may lead to children creating their own writing implements.
- Books and paper may be very intriguing to young learners, calling them to explore their creation and production as well as their use over time. A variety of books including books for the blind, audio books, books composed solely of pictures or photos, and diaries may be of interest to young learners. Paper comes in different textures, colors, and weights and might encourage students to experiment with making paper.

Through experience, we have found that when the interest and enthusiasm of young learners is attentively observed it is easy to develop a wide variety of topics worthy of in-depth study. Therefore, teachers should be aware that such potential areas of interest, when turned into a topic of inquiry-based study, can be used to logically and meaningfully integrate the curriculum.

## THE POWER OF INQUIRY LEARNING THROUGH INTEGRATION

Oral language, reading, and writing are the backbone tools of inquiry learning. Young learners can apply their literacy skills at their own level of proficiency when engaged in a topic of research. Working in a small group, or committee, provides modeling from children who may have more advanced skills.

The elements of language and literacy—oral, written, and reading language—are totally interrelated, and if that is remembered when the curriculum is planned, then language learning will have much more meaning for children. It is important to remember this whether children are very small and reading simply means looking at pictures, or they are older and have "cracked the code" of reading; whether they are small and writing is merely scribbling while telling a story, or they are older and ready to make their own books.

Regarding integration with other subjects, it is important to realize that children will write better if they have some actual content to write about, and that reading, listening, talking, and writing are all important roads to enriching children's knowledge. In the words of Carol Seefeldt (2005), "Just as the language and literacy standards are tightly integrated with each other, language learning simply cannot be separated out from the school day. Language learning is a vital part of everything that takes place in good schools for young children" (p. 78).

**Figure 6.13** In conjunction with their study of hospitals, the first-graders thought up and illustrated adjectives to describe doctors. These adjectives were then incorporated into their writing.

An inquiry learning approach to integration gives students the opportunity to not only apply the many English Language Arts skills they have learned, it gives students the opportunity to apply the many skills needed to be lifelong learners.

## TO DISCUSS

1. No matter what type of reading instruction is used in a primary classroom, some children will be more advanced than others. Discuss first the feelings that children of all levels might have about these unavoidable inequities. Then discuss approaches you might take to alleviate negative feelings.
2. Prepare an adult interview based on six college subjects you took or are currently taking. Use the format of "Did you take_____?" Or "Did you like_____?" Use your classmates as interviewees and tally their yes/no responses. Discuss the merit or lack of merit a survey activity would have with the young learners you teach or plan to teach.
3. Reflect on the technology and media you used in your early childhood and the technology and media you use at present. Discuss with your classmates how tech and media have changed over the years. Also discuss the pros and cons of using today's tech and media in early childhood environments; include in your discussion how such usage could enhance learning in language arts and how it might hinder student progress.

## TO DO

1. Practice reading a picture book to others in your class, modeling some of the ways a teacher might involve students in shared reading. Ask for feedback; then read the story to a group or class of children. Compare the responses.
2. Skip ahead to one of the inquiry-based learning projects listed in another chapter in this text. List all the ways that literacy skills are applied in the project.
3. Choose a K–2 grade level that you would like to teach or are already teaching. Using that grade level, organize the CCSS for English Language Arts in a way that best enables you to remember the main skills for each standard. Keep in mind that, while it might be impossible to memorize all of the skills under each anchor standard, knowing a large percentage of them will help make you more confident as you integrate the curriculum using inquiry learning.

## REFERENCES

Bettelheim, B. (1976). *The uses of enchantment: The meaning and importance of fairy tales.* New York, NY: Knopf.

Charlesworth, R. (1996). *Understanding child development.* Albany, NY: Delmar Publishers.

Cooper, J. (2006). *Literacy: Helping children construct meaning.* Boston, MA: Houghton Mifflin.

Copple, C. & Bredekamp, S. (2009). *Developmentally appropriate practice in early childhood programs serving children from birth through age 8.* Washington, DC: NAEYC.

Dale, P. (1976). *Language development.* New York, NY: Holt, Rinehart & Winston.

Egan, K. (2006). *Teaching literacy: Engaging the imagination of new readers and writers.* Thousand Oaks, CA: Corwin Press.

Garrard, K. (1987). Helping young children develop mature speech patterns. *Young Children, 42* (3), 16–21.

Hart, B. & Risley, T. (1995). *Meaningful differences in everyday parenting and intellectual development in young American children*. Baltimore, MD: Brookes.

Hoff, E. (2003). The specificity of environmental influence: Socioeconomic status affects early vocabulary development via maternal speech. *Child Development*, 74 (5), 1368–1378.

International Reading Association. (1985). *Board position statement on reading and writing in early childhood*. Newark, DE: International Reading Association.

Katz, L. & Chard, S. (2000). *Engaging children's minds: The project approach* (2nd ed.). Norwood, NJ: Ablex.

Lane, B. (2004). Foreword. In V. Spandel (Ed.), *Creating young writers: Using the six traits to enrich writing process in primary classrooms*. Boston, MA: Pearson.

NAEYC & Fred Rogers Center for Early Learning. (2012). *NAEYC position statement: Technology and interactive media as tools in early childhood programs serving children from birth through age 8*. Washington, DC: NAEYC.

National Governors Association Center for Best Practices & Council of Chief State School Officers. (2010). *Common core state standards English language arts*. Washington, DC: National Governors Association Center for Best Practices, Council of Chief State School Officers.

National Reading Panel. (2000). *Teaching children to read: An evidence-based assessment of the scientific research literature on reading and its implications for reading instruction*. Washington, DC: National Institute of Child Health and Human Development.

Piaget, J. (1971). *Psychology and epistemology*. New York, NY: Viking Press.

Saracho, O. (2012). *An integrated play-based curriculum for young children*. New York, NY: Routledge.

Seefeldt, C. (2005). *How to work with standards in the early childhood classroom*. New York, NY: Teachers College Press.

Spandel, V. (2004). *Creating young writers: Using the six traits to enrich writing process in primary classrooms*. Boston, MA: Pearson.

Trawick-Smith, J. (2000). *Early childhood development*. Upper Saddle River, NJ: Merrill Prentice-Hall.

# 7

## MATHEMATICS

*How important it is not to correct every error. Instead, encourage investigation,*
*and remember that children construct their own knowledge.*
*What an important lesson for someone teaching mathematics!*
—Juanita V. Copley

After reading this chapter you should be able to:

- Review the history of mathematics teaching and learning for young children;
- Explain current research-based ideas about teaching mathematics;
- Describe ways to apply today's best methods to the early childhood classroom;
- Enumerate ways to incorporate mathematics learning into the fabric of everyday classroom life.

The world of the written word is an obvious one. Billboards, road signs, digital media, newspapers, magazines, and books surround us. Mathematical messages are more subtle, although equally part of our everyday life. Looking out across a cityscape, we see buildings that could not have been constructed without extensive use of mathematical principles. In the grocery store we buy a vast variety of food, knowing that every item we pay for has been measured, weighed, or packed according to volume. To get to the store we climb into a car that has been built using mathematical calculations, fill it with carefully measured gasoline, and drive mathematically derived distances. Once our food is home, we can put it into a refrigerator cooled to a mathematically calculated temperature or into an oven heated with similar calculations. Even the simple act of making a bed is a mathematical one as we toss fresh (rectangular) sheets into the air, let them land in a symmetrical position, and, at least casually, calculate the measurements of bed and sheets to ensure a reasonably ordered finished product.

Somehow, as adults we often neglect to communicate to children the mathematical nature of the world around them. We are much more conscious of providing exposure to the written word. Perhaps it is because the messages of mathematics are so subtle that both adults and children absorb them without awareness of them. Yet our days are full of mathematical problem solving, and it would be well if we made ourselves more conscious of these incidents and communicated them to children. Then when it is time to introduce children to sophisticated mathematical systems, they will be able to see the long-term payoff because they will have had sufficient real-life experiences. Learning mathematics and learning to read can both be exciting and engaging, but they also require effort. Children need to know that in both cases there is a real-life reward waiting for them.

A primary focus of this chapter is the real-life purpose and application of mathematics. We start with a daily mathematical activity in a primary age classroom. This demonstrates how a simple daily routine can encompass multiple mathematical principles. The discussion that follows includes a look at two views of mathematics learning: the concept of math as fact learning and a focus on real-life problem solving. Historically, the two views have been at odds with each other, but recent research (including the widely published dismal scores of American students as opposed to those of many other countries) has led us to understand that both are important.

As the chapter progresses, practical, meaningful ways to integrate mathematics into the classroom routine will be shown. Both the preprimary and primary curriculum sections will focus on ways teachers can increase math experiences through everyday classroom routines, routines that are engaging and that foster high levels of thinking. Throughout this chapter, and as is evidenced in many others of this text, it is clear that play is a critical part of the primary curriculum. Through the self-expressive medium of play and playful learning, children learn to make sense of the world and to develop social and cultural understandings. In addition, through play children naturally integrate their learning across the curriculum and incorporate inquiry approaches into their activities. As you read through the examples of real-life mathematical situations, we hope that you will be fueled to think of additional ways you can provide integrated and meaningful mathematical connections for your students.

## BEGINNING THE DAY WITH A MATH ROUTINE

*Each day, the 24 kindergarten and first-grade students arrive in room 4, greet their teacher, hang up their coats, and check backpacks for notes needing to be returned. The earlier arrivers have already unstacked chairs that had been stacked the afternoon before in groups of five. Each student now eagerly goes to observe the "estimating jar"—a clear, pint-sized jar filled with a frequently changing array of objects. Today, the jar contains a number of green and blue pattern-block triangles. Some children turn the jar from side to side, while others just contemplate it. The students' mission: to estimate how many objects the jar contains, then note their prediction. Overheard are comments such as, "Blue is my favorite color—I'm thinking there will be more blues than greens," "I know these things aren't squares," "The jar isn't full today so I'm guessing smaller," and "Of course there are more than 10 but not as many as 100—that's too big to fit in the jar" and even, "She's trying to fool us—yesterday there were big nuts in there, full up, but not so many."*

*The students all write numerals that correspond to their predictions on a 1 in. × 1 in. sticky note from a pad (custom cut by the teacher to this small size) located in a box next to the estimating jar. Then, the students place their sticky notes underneath the corresponding numbers on a number line of numerals 0–100, which is attached to the classroom whiteboard. The more capable students gladly help the struggling numeral writers; one even helps*

*demonstrate the correct formation of the numeral by placing her hand over that of the strug-*
*gling writer. Adam, in particular, has difficulty placing his prediction on the number line.*
*"I can't find the number with six and one," he laments. Nicki comes over to help him. After*
*scrutinizing his scrawling, Nicki turns it upside down and states, "Maybe you just meant one*
*and nine. Here, I can help you find it." And so the task continues as independent and inter-*
*dependent learners carry out one of room 4's morning routines.*

## WHY MATH MATTERS: A BRIEF HISTORY

The use of estimation in this daily classroom routine is showcased because of the importance of estimation both in mathematics and in everyday life. People use estimation
out of necessity (think ballpark guesses) and as a tool in solving problems or checking
answers. Skill with estimation takes years to develop and requires a variety of learned
strategies, and exposure to estimation activities at early ages helps children develop number, shape, and volume sense. Very young children will not be accurate estimators until
they understand concepts such as *smaller, bigger, close to, more, less,* and *fewer.* Estimating
also increases children's comfort in taking risks in prediction while helping to dismiss the
notion that there is always one right answer. The routine of estimation used in room 4
allows other mathematical and social concepts to be incorporated while also permitting
skills to be varied and easily expanded. We can see that it takes only a little effort to turn
everyday routines into integrated learning opportunities.

Estimation is just one example that shows why math matters. In this section we
discuss the basic goals of mathematics education now and throughout history. Sometimes these goals have demonstrated awareness that math matters because of its applications to real life; at other times, the goals are learning the math skills as an end in
themselves.

Today, those who are involved in mathematics education and research believe that the
ultimate reason for learning mathematics is to solve problems that present themselves
in many phases of life; it is not just to solve problems on a worksheet. We are discovering that young children are capable of mathematical thinking that is much deeper
and broader than educators had ever before realized (Ginsburg, Lee, & Boyd, 2008).
Even infants have been observed demonstrating a basic and intuitive understanding of
mathematics.

From the vantage point of the early 21st century, some ideas seem very simple: reading
a number, using it as a symbol for a known quantity, doing basic addition and subtraction. Such simplicity has not always been so apparent. The first time someone tried to
represent a number symbolically, it probably came out as a series of hash marks. The
earliest record we have of this attempt is on a wolf bone from the Paleolithic times, and
the hash marks were divided into groups of five. Perhaps our ancestors of 30,000 years
ago were already using their fingers as counting aids and as bases for numbering systems.

The symbol for zero was invented by the Babylonians, probably about 700 B.C.E., later
by the Mayans around 400 C.E., and again by the Hindus in 800. If the invention of the
zero does not seem earthshaking, think how much trouble the last sentence would have
been to write without it.

By the Middle Ages finger reckoning was still the order of the European school day,
and children were considered sufficiently educated if they could count. Today we assume
that even the youngest children can use their fingers to count to five and that a zero means

something is "all gone." Older children are expected to go much further. In the first part of the 18th century, algebra, geometry, and trigonometry were introduced into colleges. A century later these subjects were moved down to the high school level. By the end of the 19th century, there were recommendations that children from the sixth grade onward should be exposed to concrete forms of geometry and introductory algebra. After centuries of grappling with these mathematical concepts, people were finding them so easily understood that they were trickling down from the colleges to the elementary schools. Today we routinely expect children in kindergarten to have a rudimentary understanding of numbers and geometry.

In addition to expecting more of today's children, we have also spent this century pondering the method by which mathematics should be taught. When nothing more was expected of children than that they could count, rote learning and memorization reigned supreme as the logical methodology. In fact, this is still the preferred approach for some of today's educational professionals.

Stimulus-response methods based on behaviorist techniques have been the primary way of updating the centuries-old tradition of rote learning. For example, B. F. Skinner, in the mid-20th century, assumed that arithmetic was one of "the drill subjects." His point of view led to the invention of teaching machines, later replaced by computers, that could introduce new skills, present related drills, and provide tests of children's learning.

The controversy over the definition of arithmetic as a drill or non-drill subject was already taking place by the 1930s. At that time William Brownell argued that "children must understand the basic concepts that underlie what they are learning if learning is to be permanent" (Kennedy, 1986, p. 6). Brownell and others attacked the drill theory of arithmetic for a number of reasons: Children do not understand or enjoy arithmetic, they cannot apply their skills to new situations, they forget quickly, the focus is on the subject rather than on the needs of the learner, and, finally, this type of learning has almost no relationship to the real world. Theorists and researchers of that time began to consider a newly controversial question: Should children learn mathematics incidentally as a part of their natural environment?

By the end of World War II, the general consensus, and the position of the National Council of Teachers of Mathematics (NCTM), was "Mathematics, including arithmetic, has an inherent organization. This organization must be respected in learning. Teaching, to be effective, must be orderly and systematic; hence, arithmetic cannot be taught informally or incidentally" (Trafton, 1975, p. 21). This did not mean, however, that systematic instruction had to be formal. The needs, interests, and developmental level of the child were all to be taken into consideration. Thus, a compromise position between learning by drill and incidental, real-life learning was effected.

The mid-1950s brought yet another major reform movement, which was often referred to under the umbrella term of *new math*. The concern of educators moved from methodology to content. The ability of the Russians to send the satellite Sputnik into orbit led to a questioning by Americans of mathematical training in schools. After looking at math instruction across the country, it seemed that there was a need for greater substance and higher expectations.

As mathematics programs were reconstructed, the early years were viewed as an appropriate time to learn geometry and graphing, sets, open sentences, and properties. The use of computational skills was newly emphasized, although there was controversy over the importance of memorizing facts or of discovering them through work with meaningful problems. This issue was never settled during the approximately 20 years in which new math evolved. Other unsettled issues concerned the training of teachers, who learned more substance but less about how to impart it to children, and the problem of focusing on materials that could best be understood by top students but might leave others behind.

Although the era of new math has been labeled by some as a mistake or failure, there was much progress that we can apply today to early education: Revitalization in curriculum and pedagogy accompanied the searching for answers; new content such as geometry and graphing was introduced into the early years; planned but informal programs became accepted for young children; mathematics became more exciting to teach and to learn; more research was done on the content and processes of children's thinking (Trafton, 1975). In other words, this period of ferment was a time for much thinking and growth.

Continuing research has led to the understanding that some topics can be introduced much earlier than was thought possible and vice versa. We now know, for example, that infants learn math concepts from birth as they constantly order, classify, and integrate the information they get from seeing, hearing, feeling, tasting, and touching. Surprisingly perhaps, "Their mathematical concepts are both concrete and abstract and can be extended spontaneously." Thus, it is the case that by kindergarten and first grade, "Young children can learn more and deeper mathematics than teachers usually expect," even solving "informal addition and subtraction problems during their play" (Ginsburg, Lee, & Boyd, 2008, quoted in Saracho, 2012, p. 254).

Early in the 21st century, an important document set the stage for developments in the teaching of mathematics to young children: the first-ever early childhood position statement by the National Council of Teachers of Mathematics. In its *Principles and Standards for School Mathematics* (National Council of Teachers of Mathematics, 2000), the NCTM stated that, "The foundation for children's mathematical development is established in the earliest years" and that "it is imperative to provide all students with high-quality programs that include significant mathematics presented in a manner that respects both the mathematics and the nature of young children" (National Council of Teachers of Mathematics, 2000, pp. 73, 76). Teachers, they said, "need to be knowledgeable about the many ways students learn mathematics, and they need to have high expectations for what can be learned during these early years" (p. 75).

Today, the value of applying and integrating critical concepts in science, technology, engineering and mathematics as put forth in STEM education has become a focus of attention. The acronym STEM originated with the National Science Foundation and refers to the disciplines of science, technology, engineering, and mathematics. President Barack Obama championed the cause for quality STEM education when he launched the "Educate to Innovate" campaign, a nationwide effort to help improve the quality of math and science teaching. In a press release the president said, "Leadership tomorrow depends on how we educate our students today, especially in math, science, technology, and engineering" (January 6, 2010). Recently, some educators have proposed that the acronym STEM be changed to STEAM, with the letter A designating *art*, as indeed, mathematics and science are deeply implanted in both art and music (Moomaw, 2013).

In 2010, The Common Core State Standards Initiative, established through a state-led effort and with review from the National Council of Teachers of Mathematics (NCTM), teacher organizations, and experts in the field, put forth clear and succinct standards in mathematics. These K–12 standards help ensure that teachers, parents, and students, no matter where they live, have a clear understanding of schools' expectations (National Governors Association Center for Best Practices and Council of Chief State School Officers, 2010). We will delve into these mathematics standards later in this chapter.

A strong understanding of child development is essential when teachers make decisions about curriculum and instruction. The next section details stages of children's development in mathematics.

## MATHEMATICS AND CHILD DEVELOPMENT

A review of research (Saracho, 2012) demonstrates that "children are born mathematicians" (p. 254). For example, in their very first days, newborns can tell the difference between sets of two and sets of three objects. Over the next half year, this skill expands to include such abilities as matching a set of three sounds to a set of three objects.

Through the toddler years, practical application of quantitative understanding continues to develop such that between the preprimary and primary years a great change takes place in children's mathematical development. The preprimary child has limited abilities in conservation, classification, seriation, and ordering of numbers. The primary child has gained, or is gaining, competence in all of these. Because children make their developmental transitions at their own individual rates, it is important for teachers to observe the current understandings of each child before making curriculum choices. This means that one size cannot fit all when it comes to planning math activities. An entire class of preschoolers may be able to count quickly and in unison to 20, but some of them will have a mental picture of 20 objects while others are simply making noises learned by rote. The dangers of thinking that the latter group of children know as much as the former have been addressed by one teacher-researcher (Richardson, 2004) who maintains that these children "leave their preschool experience appearing to know what is necessary but without the underlying ideas to build on" and that they "will continue to fall behind if these needs are not met" (p. 323). Some of the facets of cognitive development that pertain to mathematical understandings are described in fuller detail in the next sections.

Understanding children's affective development is also an important component of our decision making about mathematics teaching. For example, children in the primary grades may have deep concerns about their performance and about how that performance looks to the teacher and other children. Erik Erikson's (1964) theory of child development explains that children of this age are at the beginning of a stage that pits an ethic of industriousness against potential feelings of inferiority. As such, it is a time when it is important for children to feel positive about their own ability to perform mathematically in order to avoid long-term negative feelings about themselves and the subject. The NCTM reflects this concern in its statement, "Young students are building beliefs about what mathematics is, about what it means to know and do mathematics, and about themselves as mathematics learners. These beliefs influence their thinking about, performance in, and attitudes toward, mathematics and decisions related to studying mathematics in later years" (2000, p. 76).

Affective development related to mathematics has also been addressed by Jean Piaget's (1932) theory of development. Children in the preprimary years are egocentric in their play and work, often preferring to have their own materials, perhaps while working next to (but usually not with) someone else. Children in the primary grades, however, have begun to be intrigued by games played in teams, by the rules that accompany them, and by the negotiations that must take place for a game to progress smoothly. The implications for teaching are that children of primary age generally learn best in small groups or teams, particularly when the work is presented in the form of games. Research has demonstrated that, using this approach, children will actually learn arithmetic skills and facts as completely as, or better than, children who have learned through drills and worksheets (Kamii & Housman, 2000; Kamii, Miyakawa, & Kato, 2004). Piaget's developmental theory also addresses cognition as it relates to mathematics learning. The following sections describe his views on the ways in which children develop their understanding of conservation, classification, seriation, ordering, and number.

### Conservation

*Conservation* refers to the child's ability to realize that two equal quantities or groups remain equal in amount or number, no matter how they may be transformed in shape or position. Conservation comprehension can be applied to number, liquid, mass, or length. The following experience demonstrates both the theory about conservation of number as well as the controversy surrounding it.

A Head Start teacher had been studying Piagetian tasks and decided to prove, or disprove, their correctness with his own children. He began with the conservation of number and, knowing that pennies were important and interesting to children, chose them as his testing materials.

The teacher began with Lola, a four year old. Placing the pennies in parallel rows of eight each, he asked Lola to count the number in each row. She did so with no difficulty, declaring that she saw "the same much" in each row. Then the teacher spread out one row of eight so that it produced a longer line. This time Lola stated, with great assurance, that the spread-out row had more pennies.

Here, the teacher tried to help Lola relate the experience to real life. "Suppose you wanted to buy some candy," he said. "Which row would be best to take?" Lola chose the spread-out row because "it has mucher."

After attaining the same results with several other children, the teacher interviewed Samantha, also four years old. At first she also believed that the spread-out row contained more pennies. But when the teacher asked her which she would choose if planning to buy candy, she looked thoughtful for a moment and then said, "What does it matter? They're both the same!"

The teacher, wanting to see how far Samantha's reasoning could go, restocked the rows so that one had nine pennies, the other seven. He then squeezed the nine pennies close together and spread out the seven to make a longer row. "Now," he asked, "which row do you want to spend?"

"You're trying to trick me, aren't you?" she asked. "I want the row that has nine."

This experience, a variation of a classic Piaget test of conservation ability, demonstrates in two ways the controversial aspect of tests of this ability. Piaget's observations indicated that children obtain conservation between the ages of six and eight, and yet Samantha clearly was acquiring understanding at age four. This surprising finding is related to a second one in which researchers have found that children can conserve earlier if the objects are more interesting to them or related to their lives in some way.

One explanation for this apparent departure from Piaget's findings was provided by Constance Kamii (Castle, 1986). In her work with the Piaget research institute in Geneva,

Switzerland, she learned that children were achieving conservation at earlier ages than they had a generation ago. The important issue, she argued, is that children do attain conservation developmentally and that they cannot truly understand number and numeration without an understanding of conservation.

Other types of conservation were mentioned earlier in this section, and they, too, are related to early mathematics learning. The ability to conserve length and area will influence the type of geometry learnings children can attain. An example of a test for conservation of length includes laying four sticks of equal length in a straight line. Four more sticks of the same length are then laid below them in a zigzag pattern. Children must have attained conservation of length in order to understand that the two rows are equal.

To test for conservation of area, four square pieces of paper can be laid out in a row with their sides touching. Below this are placed four equally large sheets of paper, placed so that the four squares create a larger square. Again, it is necessary to have achieved conservation in order to see that the areas of both configurations are the same.

### Classification

When a child draws a picture of assorted animals and then circles all the birds, then all the dogs, and so on, she is placing them in classes. An infant just learning to talk may learn to say "dog" and then apply that label to all furry animals. This, too, is *classification*, although primitive, and it soon gives way to more accurate labeling. In both cases just described, the classification is a simple and singular one: Birds are understood as different from dogs, but the concept of them as part of a larger group called animals is as yet too complex. Young children can classify on just one level at a time.

An experience in a childcare center illustrates how this can cause limitations. Suzanne stopped by a small table to visit with a two-and-a-half-year-old boy who sat clutching, in his left hand, a collection of yellow plastic circles. Mixed in among them was a single yellow hexagon. The child smiled at Suzanne, and then triumphantly took from a nearby basket another yellow circle. Suzanne pointed at the yellow shapes in his hand and asked, "Are those all the same?" Silently the child nodded his head yes. Suzanne reached into the basket and took out a yellow circle and a yellow square. "Which *one* (she emphasized the "one") would go with the others you have?" The little boy said nothing but, with a wide grin, snatched them both and hung on tight. He then sat for some time, staring at all the other children and their activities, content to clutch his collection of yellow plastic circles—and one square and one hexagon. This experience is quite typical for children of this age, who normally classify by color to the exclusion of other choices, although they might momentarily intuit that there are other, more complex, possibilities. Older children might be more apt to add size to the mix right from the beginning, making an arrangement of small yellow circles and another of large yellow circles.

Another limitation in early attempts at classification is that of class inclusion. If a child is given six miniature dogs and two cats and asked if there are more dogs or more animals, the answer will vary depending on age. A preschooler will generally answer that there are more dogs, whereas the child in the primary grades can usually see that one class (dogs) is included in another (animals).

Piaget's colleagues observed that the understanding of class inclusion is developmental and subsequent researchers have concluded that the "wrong" answers young children give to mathematical questions are actually developmental steps. At each progressive stage, these wrong answers will be better coordinated and closer to the adult perception of correct (Kamii & Housman, 2000). This finding is important to consider when offering children activities that include classification. The experiences are necessary to help children achieve more adequate understanding, and teachers need to express patience with them as they work their way through a hierarchy of wrong-to-right answers. It is entirely possible to push children to give the adult-defined right answers, but they may be simply parroting us, lacking any real understanding.

### Seriation, Ordering, and the Understanding of Number

Alex was new to preschool, and his mother was explaining to the teacher that he already knew a lot about math. For example, she said, this three-year-old could count to 20. When asked to perform, Alex at first refused and then shyly counted quickly and accurately to 20.

The teacher praised him and then asked Alex to count a row of 10 Popsicle sticks. Alex began accurately enough until he got to the fourth stick. This one became "four, five." He then skipped over the next stick and described the following one as "six, seven." By the time Alex finished there were 12 sticks as far as he was concerned.

His mother looked embarrassed. The teacher assured her, however, that Alex's behavior was quite normal and that in preschool there would be a focus on *understanding numbers,* rather than simply repeating them. It would be a while, in fact, before Alex even needed to work with numbers directly.

Understanding the *ordering* of numbers and placement of objects in a *series* is yet another skill that needs to emerge before number can be understood and used as a tool for mathematics learning. At times children can point to objects and name the numbers that go with them, but they do not always think of the numbers in the same way adults do. If the teacher had asked Alex to show her the number-10 stick, Alex might well have thought its name was actually "Ten," just as if it had been Sam or Amjad.

A further difficulty emerges when children are asked to place objects in a row in order of size. Preschoolers tend to have difficulty doing more than finding the smallest and the largest. Even through the first or second grade, children often need to find the proper order through trial and error. It is only in second or third grade that most children can logically lay out a series correctly or place a second series of objects below the first one so that they are matched one to one.

Conservation, classification, and seriation are important attainments in their own right. Additionally, as children learn these concepts they prepare for a later understanding of number. For example, when they play with their toys and place a group of dolls on one side of the room and a pile of books on the other, they are classifying their belongings into mathematical sets. Although when they are very young, they will not consciously count the dolls and the books, the children will perceive that there are more objects than one. Arranging the dolls in a row with the biggest at one end and the smallest at the other teaches seriation and precounting. And while the pile of books and the row of dolls may be too many objects to count, there are other objects in the children's lives that can be understood in the plural. The concept of *two* comes naturally when it is noticed that there are two shoes to wear or two cookies to eat.

These early learning experiences are intuitive and natural ones. For true mathematical understanding, real thinking is eventually needed. During the years that children comprehend prenumber and number concepts, they are not yet conscious of their thinking. In the primary years, first steps in making children conscious of their thinking should be taken, although they have not yet grown completely out of intuitive thinking. To make their learning experiences most beneficial, it is important to let children construct their own learning and understanding. If they are drilled and pushed, they will probably perform fairly well, but they will simply be mimicking adult behaviors. Long-term learning will be achieved more readily if children are permitted to invent their own ways of dealing with their new concepts.

### Diversity in Development

The sections above have touched on the fact that children do not all learn mathematics at the same rate and that getting them all to the same level on any kind of test does not guarantee that everyone understands at the same depth, or even at all. Because mimicry is so often possible and rote memory so frequently relied on, math is an academic subject that can be "passed" with no understanding. Making sure this does not happen is an important responsibility of early childhood teachers, whose job is to instill in their children a positive and adventuresome attitude toward mathematical problem solving. Understanding variations in development is helpful in reaching all children.

Let's return to room 4's estimation activity to see how it turned out and to observe how diversity in development is honored. Just before lunch, the students congregated at the "work rug" area in front of the whiteboard to count out, with teacher assistance, how many objects were in the estimating jar. Discussion was conducted so that children could hear each other's thoughts about how they formulated their answers. Chynna, according to the student-generated job chart, was the day's "estimate-counter-outer."

*The teacher asked, "Chynna, in what way would you like the class to count out these triangles with you today?" Chynna decided that she would like to count them out by odd and even numbers, with the girls counting the even numbers with her and the boys counting the odd numbers with the teacher. Her comments elicited puzzled looks from some of her classmates. One child suggested that the girls just count the green ones and the boys count the blue ones and that they could take turns. "Yeah, we'd count out in a pattern then," Howard said. "Okay," Chynna agreed.*

*The students enthusiastically counted out the blue and green pattern, most of them oblivious to the fact that they were also counting out by odds and evens. Each group of 10 was placed in a see-through container with "10" marked on it. Other containers marked with "20," "30," "40," and so on to "100" as well as "ones" were also available. The objects from the estimating jar that day filled one "10" container, and the remaining nine triangles were placed in the "ones" container. These containers were then placed on the whiteboard tray. The corresponding number was written above each jar: Over the single "10" container was written the number one, and over the "ones" container was written a nine.*

*Suddenly, a shriek went out. "I got it! I got 19!" Adam, who had earlier needed help from Nicki to understand that his upside-down number could be a 19, was the exactly "right on" estimator for the day. He proudly stood up and took a bow to the applause of the class. Even though the children in room 4 understand that estimations do not generally approach total accuracy, it is always a special occasion when it does happen, and they greet these occurrences with great glee.*

From beginning to end, this two-part estimation activity took into account children's varying levels of development. In the morning, children who were more confident could help those who weren't. While there was no specific focus on estimation methods, the more confident children would, no doubt, intuit more sophisticated ideas. At lunchtime, Chynna's understanding was clearly superior to some of the other children's, but adjustments were made that would include something for everyone. While Adam's lucky guess did not, in itself, demonstrate any advanced development, his subsequent good feelings about himself might well encourage him to keep trying in a subject that was often overly challenging for him.

Cognitive delays can especially put young children at risk for learning math. For example, the dangers of such children learning to count without understanding number or of having difficulty engaging in semi-abstract activities such as addition and subtraction are very real. In addition to the naturalistic and integrated activities suggested throughout this text, more direct tutoring or instruction may be especially useful. A very few minutes each day can be sufficient, particularly just before the more creative activities begin. Routines that allow for repetition of skill application, eventually in a flexible fashion, are found beneficial for this group of children. In addition, children with cognitive delays may need to learn concepts and skills that are more basic than those learned by more typically developing classmates (Saracho, 2012).

Other delays or impairments that can cause difficulty are physical. Children who cannot hear well must be spoken to carefully and directly to be sure they understand instructions and other information. Those who have vision problems need to be given extra time to explore materials with their hands. Children with visual impairments will find manipulatives such as a Braille abacus helpful (Saracho, 2012).

Increasingly, students with special needs are being included in general education classrooms. These students are most often held to the same standards as their general education classmates. And even though "the consensus among general education mathematics professionals has been a move toward more inquiry-based teaching and away from direct instruction," using appropriate direct instruction with inquiry-based teaching strategies has been shown to improve student outcomes for all students (Cole & Washburn-Moses, 2010, p. 16).

While poverty may not at first seem to be a controversial issue for math learning, the common use of food items for counting and other calculations has been troublesome. Children who have had little or nothing for breakfast are likely to have a hard time concentrating on the math implications of a handful of fish-shaped crackers. Their parents may be appalled to see schoolwork coming home that includes numerical groupings of dry macaroni glued to construction paper.

In addition to the children who are at risk for not keeping up with their class, there are others who are equally at risk for not reaching their full potential. Mathematical giftedness can often be observed in very young children who should be challenged with new materials and problem-solving opportunities. These can be just as natural as other activities in the curriculum. Examples of such activities are asking one of these children to add up play materials as they come in from the playground, to be sure they are all there, or to lead the class in discovering how many children are left when two are absent for the day. In the primary grades when math teaching becomes more formal, these youngsters can be asked to explain to the rest how they solved a particular problem. As the class listens, those who are ready to advance will expand their knowledge and ability to use new approaches to problem solving themselves. Additional suggestions for supporting talented math students include teaching with an emphasis on inquiry-based learning approaches, using higher order "why" and "what if . . .?" questioning to discuss problems, and providing concrete experiences, because "although talented learners may be capable of abstract thought, they still benefit from the use of manipulatives and hands-on activities" (Deal & Wismer, 2010, p. 60).

Math can be a difficult subject for children who do not yet understand the language of instruction. Suzanne, for example, recalls when her granddaughter attended first grade in Kiev, Ukraine, and was failing arithmetic. This was a mystery to her parents who were coaching her, in the evenings, through American second-grade textbooks. Eventually the mystery was solved when it was learned that all the work was paper and pencil; there were no manipulatives. The teacher did not realize that Hayley did not understand the Ukrainian words for *add* and *subtract* and therefore never understood what process she was expected to be doing. Although American schools generally seem to be aware of providing the right kind of help, this is not always the case; the following list of teaching ideas should serve as reminders to all teachers (Northwest Regional Educational Laboratory, 2005):

- *Make it visual:* PowerPoint projections, posters, graphs, charts, and flash cards can all prove helpful.
- *Make instruction hands-on:* Use manipulatives whenever possible.
- *Introduce new vocabulary at the beginning of a lesson:* Think what words might stymie English language learners and deal with those upfront.
- *Use direct instruction:* Demonstrate when appropriate, using more action and fewer words.
- *Use group-based work:* Children teaching other children can be exceptionally helpful, especially if some of them know the ELL child's language.
- *Simplify instructions:* Teachers do tend to talk—and talk; keep instructions basic and, therefore, less confusing.
- *Make it personal:* Redo worksheets to make them relate to children's own lives and understanding.
- *Supplement with bilingual materials if they are available.*

To this list we would add:

- *Make it meaningful and relevant:* Encourage children to apply math concepts in ways that build on their natural curiosity at their own level of understanding.

As you read the upcoming section on curriculum, remember that teachers must always balance curricular concepts and methods with the developmental needs of their individual children. It is an approach that the NCTM itself always takes.

## INCORPORATING MATHEMATICS INTO DAILY ROUTINES

Children of all ages need routine—not rigid, uncompromising routine, but experiences that reinforce the predictability of upcoming events of the day. Routines help build responsibility and independence while also providing a framework for repeated practice and use of skills. The predictability of routine helps children feel comfortable and secure. Such security makes children feel empowered and confident enough to then take healthy risks and engage in thoughtful questioning.

When mathematics is regarded as an integral part of the school day, teaching is actually made easier. Children learn from one another as well as from the teacher, making youngsters both independent and interdependent problem solvers. Such collaboration is essential in establishing classroom climate, whether the children are in the preprimary or primary grades. Later in the chapter we provide specific experiences to foster this collaboration.

Equally important as incorporating mathematics in daily routines is the application of mathematical skills in classroom endeavors. The inquiry-based learning project in the next section reveals the young learners' impressive collaborative skills as well as their real-life application of mathematical skills during their research, construction, and use of a classroom fishing lake.

## A CHILD-INITIATED INQUIRY EXPERIENCE

*A fishing lake in the classroom? Many adults might be skeptical of not only the learning value but also the feasibility of researching such a topic. As the teacher of the class of youngsters who proposed this topic, Pam also needed to be convinced. To prove fishing lakes worthy of study, the four children who presented this topic for consideration were asked to describe how skills in the subjects of reading, writing, and math might be applied. After a very persuasive presentation, Pam and the rest of her young students unanimously agreed that yes, indeed, the research and construction of a fishing lake in the classroom had enormous potential. Although a number of disciplines were covered in this inquiry experience, we will show some of the ways math skills were integrated and applied in this unusual but "catchy" endeavor.*

*A parent, a commercial fisherman, and Pam's husband were invited to come to Pam's K–1 class to share their expertise and wisdom pertaining to fishing and fishing lakes. The learners were serious as they sought to gather answers to the questions they had formulated days before the experts arrived. The experts were equally serious as they imparted years of fishing wisdom to the young future fishers.*

*Many of the answers to the children's questions included reference to math standards. For instance, the children learned that fishing rods, fishing line, and fishing hooks come in many lengths as well as different weights and colors; different sizes of fish are sometimes caught in different depths of water; weather and wind affect fishing productivity as does the turbidity of the water; and live and artificial bait comes in all different shapes, sizes, and weights as well as colors and smells.*

*After listening to the safety admonitions of Pam and the experts, the young investigators measured, weighed, sorted, classified, and graphed various fishing lines, sinkers, floats, lures, and artificial flies. Surveys were used to predict which baits might be most successful. Survey data were tallied and put on charts.*

*But one vital question remained to be answered: How do you catch a fish in a fishing lake? And so the children, with Pam as a facilitator, planned a field research trip to nearby Lake Terrell. Their main goal was to gain firsthand knowledge of fishing in a fishing lake. Upon arrival at the lake (with ample adult help and multiple safety warnings), the young investigators carefully, even stealthily, walked out on the pier jutting into the lake. Armed with homemade bamboo poles, an assortment of bait with which to experiment, measuring tools, and graphic organizers on which to record data, the young fishers got down to business. It was not long before a fish-catching frenzy began. Each child caught numerous perch and obeyed the "catch and release" and "be respectful to nature" rules. With the assistance of the adults, data were quickly and harmlessly collected on each fish. The most difficult part of this field research trip was extracting the children and adults from their fishing fun in order to return to school.*

*During the next few weeks, the children's Lake Terrell experience and fishing lake data were used to transform part of the classroom into the room 4 Fishing Lake. This paper lake took up nearly 5 square feet of floor space and was surrounded with appropriate flora and fauna. Many different colors and sizes of stuffed paper fish (with a small magnet attached to each) were swimming in the lake. Child-sized fishing poles, strung with small magnets on the end of their lines, were for sale alongside of an assortment of play dough bait at the nearby room 4 Bait and Tackle Shop. Children created the fishing rules that stipulated how many fish could be caught and released each day. Every fish caught had to be measured and weighed. For many weeks, the classroom fishing lake was the site of much excited learning and only concluded because it was the end of the school year.*

**Figure 7.1** A field research trip to a nearby lake proved to be a catchy experience for the young investigators.

# THE MATHEMATICS CURRICULUM

We now return to the recently developed Common Core State Standards in Mathematics (CCSSM, National Governors Association Center for Best Practices & Council of Chief State School Officers, 2010). The standards in K–2 are organized under four domains: Operations and Algebraic Thinking; Number and Operations in Base 10; Measurement and Data; and Geometry. Kindergarten has an additional domain, Counting and Cardinality. These domains are designed to bring emphasis to the standards at each grade as well as to draw attention to the importance of continuity of understanding through the grade levels and the necessity of building on previous knowledge. Under each domain, a main idea statement summarizes the subsequent content standards. A condensed description of student understanding for the content standards is included after each main idea. The complete Common Core State Standards in Mathematics can be found at www.corestandards.org/.

The content standards' expectations of understanding define to teachers what students should understand and be able to do, but they do not mandate how teachers should teach. Educators can use the standards to build their curriculum and to guide instruction. As the Common Core State Standards in Mathematics begin at the kindergarten level, preprimary understandings will be discussed later in this section.

## Kindergarten

Instructional time in kindergarten should focus on two significant areas: (1) representing and comparing whole numbers and (2) describing shapes and space. Importance is placed on devoting ample learning time to number.

### Counting and Cardinality

*   Know number names and the count sequence.
    (*Count to 100 by ones and by tens; count forward beginning from a given number; write numbers from zero to 20.*)
*   Count to tell the number of objects.
    (*Understand the relationship between numbers and quantities; count to answer "how many?" about 1–20 objects.*)
*   Compare numbers.
    (*Identify whether the number of objects in one group is greater than, less than, or equal to the number of objects in another group.*)
*   Understand addition as putting together and adding to, and understand subtraction as taking apart and taking from.
    (*Represent and solve addition and subtraction problems within 10 using objects, sounds—e.g., claps, and so on; decompose numbers 10 and less and record each decomposition—e.g. 6 = 3 + 3 and 6 = 4 + 2; fluently add and subtract within five.*)

### Number and Operations in Base 10

*   Work with numbers 11–19 to gain foundations for place value.
    (*Compose, decompose numbers from 11 to 19 into 10 and ones; record each composition or decomposition by a drawing or equation—e.g., 17 = 10 + 7.*)

### Measurement and Data

- Describe and compare measurable attributes.
  (*Describe measureable attributes—e.g., length, weight—of objects; directly compare two objects to see which one has "more of"/"less of" the attribute—e.g., compare the heights of two chairs and describe one chair as taller/shorter.*)
- Classify objects and count the number of objects in each category.
  (*Classify objects into given categories; count the number of objects in each category and sort the categories by count of 10 or less.*)

### Geometry

- Identify and describe shapes.
  (*Describe objects in the environment using names of shapes and describe the objects' relative positions—e.g., above, behind, next to; identify shapes as two dimensional— "flat" or three-dimensional—"solid."*)
- Analyze, compare, create, and compose shapes.
  (*Use informal language to describe and compare shapes—e.g., some have four corners, some have equal length sides; build shapes using sticks, clay, and so on; compose simple shapes to form larger shapes—e.g., How can two triangles make a rectangle?*)
  (National Governors Association Center for Best Practices & Council of Chief State School Officers, 2010, n.p.)

### First Grade

The standards in Grade 1 concentrate on four critical areas: (1) developing understanding and strategies for addition and subtraction within a value of 20; (2) understanding of whole number relationships and place value; (3) developing understanding of linear measurement; and (4) reasoning about attributes of geometric shapes.

### Operations and Algebraic Thinking

- Represent and solve problems involving addition and subtraction.
  (*Use objects, drawings to solve addition and subtraction word problems within 20; solve word problems that call for addition of three whole numbers less than or equal to 20.*)
- Understand and apply properties of operations and the relationship between addition and subtraction.
  (*Apply properties of operations as strategies to add and subtract—e.g., If $9 + 3 = 12$ is known, then $3 + 9 = 12$ is also known.*)
- Add and subtract within 20.
  (*Relate counting to addition and subtraction—e.g., by counting on two to add two; use relationships between addition and subtraction to create sums—e.g. $7 + 7 = 14$, therefore $7 + 7 + 1 = 15$.*)
- Work with addition and subtraction equations.
  (*Understand the meaning of the equal sign; determine the unknown whole number in an addition or subtraction equation—e.g. $6 + ? = 11$; $4 = ? - 9$; $3 + 5 = ?$.*)

*Number and Operations in Base 10*

- Extend the counting sequence.
  (*Count to 120; read, write, and represent a number of objects within this range.*)
- Understand place value.
  (*Understand that a two-digit number represents digits in the amounts of 10s and ones; compare two two-digit numbers with symbols representing more, less, or equal to.*)
- Use place value understanding and properties of operations to add and subtract.
  (*Add and subtract, mentally and in written form, multiples of 10 within 100; relate strategies and explain reasoning using concrete models or drawings.*)

*Measurement and Data*

- Measure lengths indirectly and by iterating length units.
  (*Order three objects by length and compare the lengths of two objects indirectly by using a third object; express the length of an object as a whole number of length units.*)
- Tell and write time.
  (*Tell and write time in hours and half·hours using digital and analog timepieces.*)
- Represent and interpret data.
  (*Organize, represent, and interpret data with up to three categories.*)

## GEOMETRY

- Reason with shapes and their attributes.
  (*Distinguish between defining and nondefining attributes—e.g., squares are closed and are four-sided versus squares can be big or red; compose two-dimensional shapes—e.g., squares, trapezoids, and three-dimensional shapes—e.g., cubes, cylinders; understand halves, fourths, quarters as they apply to circles and rectangles.*)
  (National Governors Association Center for Best Practices & Council of Chief State School Officers, 2010, n.p.)

*Second Grade*

In Grade 2, the standards focus instructional time on four critical areas: (1) extending understanding of Base 10 notation; (2) building fluency with addition and subtraction; (3) using standard units of measure; and (4) describing and analyzing shapes.

*Operations and Algebraic Thinking*

- Represent and solve problems involving addition and subtraction.
  (*Use addition and subtraction within 100 to solve one- and two-step word problems using drawings and equations to represent the problem.*)
- Add and subtract within 20.
  (*Fluently add and subtract within 20 using mental strategies. By the end of Grade 2, know from memory all sums of two one-digit numbers.*)
- Work with equal groups of objects to gain foundations for multiplication.
  (*Determine whether a group of up to 20 objects has an odd or even number of members—e.g., by pairing up the objects or counting them by twos; use addition to*

*find the total number of objects arranged in rectangular arrays with up to five rows and five columns and write an equation to express the total.)*

## Number and Operations in Base 10

- Understand place value.
  (*Understand the amounts represented in a three-digit number—100s, 10s, and ones; count within 1,000 by fives, 10s, 1,000s; read and write numbers to 1,000; compare two three-digit numbers using more, less, equal to.*)
- Use place value understanding and properties of operations to add and subtract.
  (*Fluently add and subtract within 100; add up to four two-digit numbers; add and subtract within 1,000 using concrete models or drawings with the understanding that it is sometimes necessary to compose or decompose tens or hundreds; mentally add or subtract 10 or 100 to or from a given number 100–900; explain why addition and subtraction strategies work.*)

## Measurement and Data

- Measure and estimate lengths in standard units.
  (*Select and use the appropriate tool—e.g., ruler, yardstick—to measure the length of an object; estimate lengths using units of inches, feet, centimeters, meters; measure to determine how much longer one object is than another.*)
- Relate addition and subtraction to length.
  (*Use addition and subtraction within 100 to solve word problems involving lengths using drawings and equations; represent whole numbers as lengths on a number diagram.*)
- Work with time and money.
  (*Tell and write time from analog and digital clocks to the nearest minutes, using a.m. and p.m.; solve word problems involving dollar bills and coins, using dollar and cent symbols appropriately.*)
- Represent and interpret data.
  (*Generate measurement data by measuring lengths of several objects to the nearest whole unit; draw a picture graph and a bar graph to represent data; use information presented in a bar graph.*)

## Geometry

- Reason with shapes and their attributes.
  (*Recognize and draw shapes having specified attributes; identify triangles, quadrilaterals, pentagons, hexagons, and cubes; partition a rectangle into rows and columns of same-size squares and find the total; use the words* halves, thirds, half of, *and so on as they pertain to circles and rectangles.*)
  (National Governors Association Center for Best Practices & Council of Chief State School Officers, 2010, n.p.)

### Standards for Mathematical Practice

In addition to the skill sets provided for each grade as described above, the CCSSM Initiative includes a list of vital mathematical actions that should permeate the pedagogy of mathematics. The Standards for Mathematical Practice describe the ways in which students, throughout their K–12 school years, ought to actively engage with the CCSSM. These practices are built on important processes and proficiencies that have longstanding importance in mathematics education.

As you consider the items on the list, note that these Mathematical Practice Standards resonate with the principles of inquiry learning through integration in that they encourage students to conceptualize, analyze, and solve problems using appropriate tools and strategies. Children are subsequently able to formulate explanations to others, thus demonstrating their deeper understanding of the work they have done. The Standards for Mathematical Practice are as follows:

- Make sense of problems and persevere in solving them.
- Reason abstractly and quantitatively.
- Construct viable arguments and critique the reasoning of others.
- Model with mathematics.
- Use appropriate tools strategically.
- Attend to precision.
- Look for and make use of structure.
- Look for and express regularity in repeated reasoning.

> (National Governors Association Center for Best Practices & Council of Chief State School Officers, 2010, n.p.)

### The Preprimary Years

Although the NCTM has not created standards for the years before kindergarten, it has taken positions about what is developmentally appropriate for the youngest children in preschools and centers. It has stated, for example, that "The foundation for children's mathematical development is established in the earliest years" and that "it is imperative to provide all students with high-quality programs that include significant mathematics presented in a manner that respects both the mathematics and the nature of young children" (National Council of Teachers of Mathematics, 2000, pp. 73, 76). Teachers "need to be knowledgeable about the many ways students learn mathematics, and they need to have high expectations for what can be learned during these early years" (p. 75).

In the beginning of their preschool years children cannot be expected to engage fully and understand meanings of operations and how they relate to one another. As Arthur Baroody (2004) states, "An understanding of cardinal number . . . deepens gradually over the course of early childhood. It can begin by recognizing the number of items in small collections . . . even before children learn to count objects reliably. The use of object counting and then written numbers develops" (p. 184). Some research has shown that young children entering school have a nonadult understanding of the meaning of counting, assuming that it is for the purpose of conforming to others' expectations or for their own entertainment. Thus, it is important for children's first teachers to actually explain and demonstrate that counting is for the purpose of learning "how many" while respecting children's own interpretations as well (Munn, 1997).

Ordinal numbers are understood, at an intuitive level, from as early as 12 months, a little later than infants intuit cardinal numbers. Although research has not yet shown how young children develop a precise understanding of how ordinal numbers work, Baroody surmises that it may derive from an understanding of such relational terms as *more* and *less*.

Very young children are interested in sorting objects in various ways, according to their attributes. In addition, they develop the ability to count how many of each kind of collection they observe. Representations of data must begin with concrete objects, then move to pictures, and later to the more abstract. For example, preschoolers might make a simple graph with colored shapes glued to construction paper according to their classifications.

Again, as in the concept of number, geometric understandings develop over time. Children from the earliest ages, however, can and must be given opportunities to fully manipulate geometric forms and to make predictions about them. It is this kind of activity that helps children develop their spatial sense, rather than the more basic experiences of just observing and naming geometric shapes. Although it is not known why, children with well-developed spatial sense have been found to be more competent in mathematics generally (Clements, 2004a). In addition, concepts about shapes that begin forming as children leave toddlerhood may be stabilized as early as age six. Thus, it is important to move beyond the typical introduction of just the four usual shapes (circle, triangle, square, rectangle) and include others as well. The use of pattern blocks, for example, encourages the concept of constructing shapes from other shapes through the use of hands-on materials

"Algebra begins" according to Douglas Clements (2004b, p. 52) "with a search for patterns. Identifying patterns helps bring order, cohesion, and predictability to seemingly unorganized situations and allows one to make generalizations beyond the information directly available." Preschool children can duplicate simple patterns.

"Measurement is one of the main real-world applications of mathematics" (Clements, 2004b, p. 43). Although preschool children are unable to accurately measure or quantify, they have a beginning understanding of differences in mass, length, and weight. They are, at this age, strongly swayed by what they think they see rather than what adult forms of measurement would tell them (Clements & Stephan, 2004). Measurement activities can begin, however, once children can compare for equality and inequality. They may not yet be ready to use a standard ruler marked off in segments, but they can, for example, predict if a table could go through a nearby doorway.

The importance of incorporating high-quality mathematics in the lives of preprimary children has been stated forcefully in a joint position statement set forth by National Association for the Education of Young Children and National Council of Teachers of Mathematics (2010/2002, n.p.). To help achieve this goal, 10 research-based recommendations to guide classroom practice are described. The joint position statement was adopted in 2002 and updated in 2010 and reads as follows:

"In high-quality mathematics education for 3–6 year-old children, teachers and other key professionals should:

1. enhance children's natural interest in mathematics and their disposition to use it to make sense of their physical and social worlds
2. build on children's experience and knowledge, including their family, linguistic, cultural, and community backgrounds; their individual approaches to learning; and their informal-knowledge
3. base mathematics curriculum and teaching practices on knowledge of young children's cognitive, linguistic, physical, and social-emotional development

4. use curriculum and teaching practices that strengthen children's problem-solving and reasoning processes as well as representing, communicating, and connecting mathematical ideas
5. ensure that the curriculum is coherent and compatible with known relationships and sequences of important mathematical ideas
6. provide for children's deep and sustained interaction with key mathematical ideas
7. integrate mathematics with other activities and other activities with mathematics
8. provide ample time, materials, and teacher support for children to engage in play, a context in which they explore and manipulate mathematical ideas with keen interest
9. actively introduce mathematical concepts, methods, and language through a range of appropriate experiences and teaching strategies
10. support children's learning by thoughtfully and continually assessing all children's mathematical knowledge, skills and strategies."

## THE IMPORTANCE OF PLAY

Those in the field of early childhood education have long supported the notion that play can and should lead to effective development. Constance Kamii, a researcher of early childhood math learning and previously a student of Jean Piaget's, has spent several decades demonstrating the superiority of play over other methods of teaching math to young children (Kamii & DeClark, 1985; Kamii & DeVries, 1980; Kamii & Joseph, 1989; Kamii, Miyakawa, & Kato, 2004; Kato, Honda, & Kamii, 2006). For example, playing specially designed card games helped young learners develop their understanding of spatial organizing, categorizing, seriating, counting, and temporal relationships as well as their ability to read numbers (Kato, Honda, & Kamii, 2006).

It should be noted that the games Kamii and her colleagues have devised are carefully created to promote constructivist learning and are based on analyzing play "with depth and precision." Additionally, Kamii and her colleagues take issue with the step-by-step approach to learning math concepts that comes from position statements made by the NCTM and NAEYC. "Logico-mathematical relationships are messier and more complex, and they develop in interrelated ways. Developing activities that challenge children to think logico-mathematically in their play may be a more fruitful focus of our efforts than trying to specify standards that may well be off the mark" (Kato, Honda, & Kamii, 2006, p. 88). (see Note, p. 194).

The challenge for teachers is to provide learning experiences that incorporate meaningful play while still meeting required standards. In addition to teacher-constructed card games such as those devised by Kamii and her colleagues, other play experiences can be adapted for young children. For example, a play pizza parlor with pizzas to cut encourages an informal understanding of fractions. Play money in a classroom "store" provides addition and subtraction experience. Some products need to be weighed before they are sold. Others might need to be divided into groups for sharing.

Providing children with mathematics play experiences has the potential for the natural development of inquiry learning projects because "play experiences motivate and nurture the children's inquisitive minds." When students are given sufficient materials and time for learning through play, their interest in what they are doing "can be the basis for a classroom-wide, extended investigation or project that will build rich mathematical learning" (Saracho, 2012, p. 262).

## TECHNOLOGY AND EARLY CHILDHOOD MATHEMATICS

One recommendation made by the early childhood conference that followed the introduction of the 2000 NCTM standards was that "Children should benefit from the thoughtful, appropriate, ongoing use of various types of technology. Especially useful are computer tools that enrich and extend mathematical experiences" (Clements, 2004b, p. 60). From our point of view, the most important phrase in this recommendation is "enrich and extend." Technology, in other words, does not provide the basis from which the early childhood curriculum grows. It does, however, provide an alternative or additional approach to learning *when it is appropriate*. The conference recommendation also comes with a warning: Adults and children may see situations, problems, and their solutions in very different ways. It is important, therefore, for teachers (and administrators) to do their best to see computer-based math activities from their children's point of view, not just their own, and to adjust experiences accordingly.

Computers can be used for students to date and record thoughts and information, often in journal form. In addition, audio-visual equipment is commonplace in most classrooms and can be used to document change and to compare and contrast over time. Older children can use technology to research mathematical aspects in an area of interest. For example, in an inquiry project about butterflies, they might gather information on the web about the distance of butterfly migration and compare and contrast the facts.

Although actual hands-on experience with mathematical manipulatives is generally more meaningful to children, computers, when used appropriately, have some unique advantages. Computers can increase children's ability to be more flexible with manipulatives because the onscreen objects can be moved, cut, even resized, something that is often difficult, or even impossible, to do with real objects. In addition, objects on screen are not awkward to handle as compared to the handling difficulty their real-life counterparts might pose (Lee & Ginsburg, 2009). At all costs, however, the use of the computer for mere "drill and grill" should be avoided.

## ASSESSMENT AND EVALUATION

The NCTM states strongly that "assessment should enhance students' learning," citing research from 250 studies demonstrating that "making assessment an integral part of classroom practice is associated with improved student learning" (National Council of Teachers of Mathematics, 2000, p. 22). The NCTM points out that the kinds of tasks required of children in their assessments demonstrate to them what kinds of knowledge and performance are valued, thus inspiring them to focus further in those areas. Conversations and interviews with the teacher, as well as interactive journals, help youngsters learn to articulate their ideas to themselves and others. Feedback from assessments "can also help students in setting goals, assuming responsibility for their own learning, and becoming more independent learners" (p. 22). And, when children share with their peers their approaches to solving problems, they begin to learn (perhaps only intuitively at first) the difference between excellence and mediocrity.

As you reflect on your teaching and plan for the future, think about the time and extent of mathematical experiences in your classroom in relationship to other subject-area experiences. Be sure that children have continual opportunities to work with mathematical ideas and plan for new ones as they outgrow the old. Lynn C. Hart et al. (1992) suggest several questions the teacher might use to reflect on the success of mathematics teaching:

- Is it possible to make the problem realistic and grounded in real-world experience?
- Is it possible to represent the problem concretely, pictorially, and abstractly?
- Am I exploring alternative strategies posed by different students?
- Am I modeling mathematical thinking?
- Are my students talking to one another—disagreeing, challenging, and debating?
- Are my students willing to take risks?
- Are my students taking time to think about the problem?
- Are my students encouraged to show respect for, and listen to, other students?

## PREPRIMARY EXPERIENCES INCORPORATING MATHEMATICS IN CLASS ROUTINES

As has been pointed out throughout this chapter, the possibility for mathematics learning is around us at all times, and it is up to the teacher to exploit the continual opportunities that arise. To demonstrate what is meant by this, consider the usual morning circle time in which roll, informal or formal, is taken, often by the teacher. If that is all that happens, a valuable learning opportunity is lost. If the experience is expanded just slightly, children can count those present, consider how many are usually in attendance, and then discuss the difference. In just a few minutes some math has been taught and learned. A thoughtful teacher, with a solid background of district and school expectations and the capability to think open-endedly, will come up with a variety of activities that fit and challenge the abilities of the youngsters being taught.

The following section presents a collection of potential math experiences that can be attached to the daily routine. As you observe preprimary classrooms, take note of these and other ways in which math can become embedded in the day's routines.

In this chapter, we will make use of circular webs that inform the teacher of the degree to which the whole child's needs are addressed by the classroom experiences. The webs are found at the end of each activities section in Figures 7.2 and 7.12. Be sure to make note of the ways in which children's developmental domains are addressed, and the ways they are not. The strength of this model of web is in the information it provides visually to help address future planning.

### *Activities*

#### *Silver Sorting*

This experience provides children with practice in placing objects in sets while engaging in a typical classroom community routine. Use plastic tableware drawer inserts that have the shapes of the different pieces indented in them. When silverware has recently been washed, place all the pieces in a mixed pile, and leave it to no more than a few children to sort and replace the pieces in their correct containers. For the sake of the experience, if only one type of utensil has been used and washed, the teacher can still place everything in the pile for sorting.

### Table Setting

It is difficult for young children to figure out how to set both sides of a table when, visually, everything appears upside down on the opposite side. Placemats can be made from construction paper on which outlines of the eating utensils and dishes are drawn. Laminating them ensures long life. With help, children can first put the placemats around the table, and then, on their own, place the utensils and dishes on top.

### Distribution of Materials

When children sit at tables in small groups, they can get experience in one-to-one correspondence if they are permitted to bring the necessary materials for upcoming activities. As possible, provide each child a turn. Perhaps one can bring crayons, another paper, and so on. Encourage correct problem solving with instructions such as "You have one table, so you need that number of crayon boxes" or "Each child at your table needs one sheet of paper, so bring what you will need."

### Snacks for Everyone

The teacher should precount the number of crackers and so on that will be given to each small group of children. A designated child then is asked to share them fairly with the group. Youngsters who are comfortable with this activity and ready for a challenge can be given a plate or basket containing a number that does not divide evenly. The group is then encouraged to solve the problem in a way that all agree is fair. Preprimary children are frequently ready to grapple with the concept of fractions; or, particularly by kindergarten, they may find the social implications of possible unfairness too much to deal with and will turn to the nearest adult to arbitrate. In either case, the teacher should use the opportunity to ask leading questions to move children's learning along. "Is there a way to break up those two extra crackers so that everyone has the same amount?" or, "There aren't any more crackers to give you, so what do you think you might do now?" are examples of such questions.

### Storytime Counting

Since reading stories to young children is typically a daily occurrence in preprimary classrooms, we include this idea in our collection of math-oriented routines. Many books for young children are designed to elicit counting experiences, but virtually any book, with a bit of teacher creativity, can offer these. When you read to children and show them pictures, help them find and count various items. You might focus on placing items in sets ("How many yellow things can you see?") or on class inclusion ("Are there more bears or more animals?") or on expanding the children's ability to count ("Shall we see how many pages are in this book?").

### Counting Verses

Consider using verses throughout the day that incorporate counting: at line-up time, on the playground, on the way back from a field trip. Repetition helps children remember and provides them with a basis for later generalizations and transfer. For example, "Ten Little Monkeys," below, is an exercise in subtraction, while "One Little Brown Bird" focuses on addition. Children who are cognitively ready will be able to transfer their experience with them to other situations, whether their level of understanding is intuitive or more formal. While the wording given below for each verse is traditional, it may be desirable to change the subjects (monkeys, birds) or their activities (jumping, flying) from time to time.

> Ten little monkeys jumping on the bed.
> One fell off and bumped his head.
> Called the doctor and the doctor said,
> "That's what you get for jumping on the bed."

As the monkey "falls off," he or she moves to the side to reveal that there is now one fewer. The verse continues accordingly until there are no monkeys left. This is a good whole body exercise. In general, choose the most active children to be the final monkeys out.

> One little brown bird, up and up she flew.
> Along came another one, and that made two.
> Two little brown birds, sitting in a tree.
> Along came another one, and that made three.
> Three little brown birds, here comes one more.
> What's all the noise about? That made four.
> Four little brown birds and one makes five.
> Singing in the sun, glad to be alive.

For the youngest children, counting and matching "birds" to five will be sufficient. You might want to invent new verses to take the number higher if children are ready for it.

### Hand Rhythms

When it is time to get everyone's attention, try basic hand claps that the children repeat back. The sound of hands clapping cuts through almost any level of noise and over much space. Math operations include many kinds of patterns, and here is one way to make them meaningful to youngsters. In addition to using this activity to get attention, you can include it in circle time, between other activities, or while standing in line or waiting for an upcoming event. The clapping patterns can be made more or less complex depending on the situation and children's capabilities. A note of caution: Any attention-getting device, including hand clapping, may eventually become ineffective and actually lead to negative behavior. Observe children carefully as time goes by for any changes in their receptivity to this activity.

### Inquiry Projects That Might Emerge From Preprimary Daily Routines

If youngsters become interested in such housekeeping activities as silver sorting and table setting, they might be interested in investigating the ways in which they can be helpful at home and/or learn more about the ways in which parents keep their home organized and clean. An in-depth study on brooms or sweeping devices could be fascinating for young learners. Another totally different direction might relate to a study of healthy snacks, or perhaps an in-depth study on the dizzying array of containers that enclose healthy snacks.

**Figure 7.2** Preprimary web—meeting children's needs.

## PRIMARY EXPERIENCES FOR INCORPORATING MATH INTO CLASS ROUTINES

At the primary level, when children become more aware of themselves as a community, effective teachers use routines to provide opportunities for children to learn from one another. In this section, we show how mathematical activities can be embedded in the beginning of the day or "morning business" routines. Because these activities are ideal for fostering curriculum integration and elements of inquiry learning, some of them will be revisited in subsequent chapters.

### Activities

#### Job Chart

In the beginning of the year (and later as necessary), use class discussion to determine what jobs will be needed to run the classroom smoothly. There should be enough jobs so that everyone in the class will have something to do each day (with some jobs having a morning and an afternoon person assigned if it is not possible to come up with enough ideas). On card pockets typically found in library books, write the jobs and have the students illustrate them. Then glue the pockets (or something similar if library card pockets can't be found) on a large tagboard and place it on the wall (Figure 7.4). Write students'

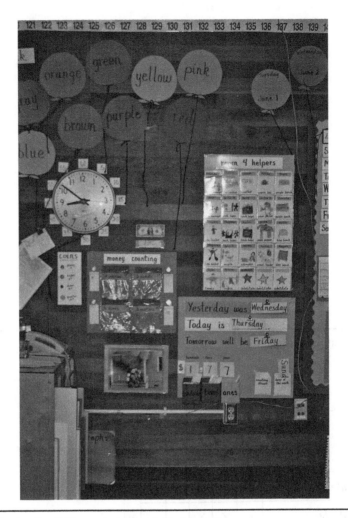

**Figure 7.3** A variety of math activities can be incorporated in daily routines.

names on tagboard cards to place in the pockets. Rotate the students' names daily. The job chart can be used to make mathematical predictions. For example, children can predict what job they will be responsible for the next day, five days ahead, and so on. They can also revisit what job they did yesterday or two days ago.

*Attendance*

The gathering of class data via attendance can provide some engaging mathematical activities (Figure 7.5):

- An attendance chart may be kept with students putting an "X" each day next to their names as they enter the classroom. These may be formatted to allow attendance tracking on a weekly or monthly basis. Math-related teacher questions might include, "Which day had the most children here?" or, "What were the total absences in March?"

**Figure 7.4** Job chart.

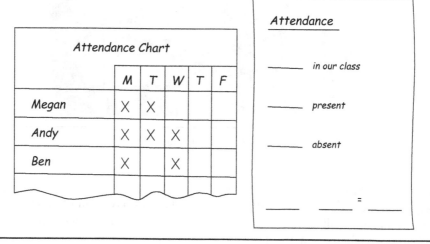

**Figure 7.5** Attendance.

- Attendance data depicting numbers of children present can be gathered over time by simply putting an "X" on a graph grid corresponding to the number of students present. If done monthly, these graphs can be used to compare and contrast trends and used in discussion of cause/effect and prediction. "Why do you think so many students were absent in December?" or, "Can you estimate how many students will be absent in April?" are possible teacher queries.
- Wipe-off charts can be used daily to record numbers of students present and absent and then added together for the total. Number stories using this information can be

created. "We usually have 24 students in our class. Two are not here today, so today we have 22 students in class."

- Always allow for children's observations and questions. It is often astounding to hear their creative and interesting thoughts.

### Lunch Count

If students have a choice of school lunch (usually "hot") or lunch brought from home (usually "cold"), they or the teacher can lead the daily tally for an experience that goes beyond routine to a math experience (Figure 7.6). Use a laminated wipe-off chart with two headings, one for hot lunch and one for cold. The teacher (or child) calls each student's name with the student replying "hot lunch, please" or "cold lunch, please." The students' responses are tallied by groups of five using four small vertical marks crossed by one horizontal mark, as needed, in the appropriate rows. After everyone has responded, any of the following experiences might be chosen:

- The tally bundles can be counted by groups of five.
- The hot lunch and cold lunch numbers can be added. These numbers may be written under the headings of "tens" and "ones" to easily facilitate regrouping if necessary.
- The hot lunch and cold lunch quantities can be compared and contrasted. "How many more students would we need to have hot lunch tie with cold lunch?" or, "How many more cold lunches are there than hot lunches?" are possible questions.
- The use of mathematical directions can be addressed: *vertical, horizontal.*

### Calendar

Although calendar skills of time and place are generally not mastered until around the fourth grade, use and exposure to the calendar in the early years aids in this mastery and provides many ways to apply mathematical skills. It is important for the younger children to see the complete calendar written for each month, thus helping provide a feeling for "quantity of days" in a month. This also allows for the matching and placing of dates on an existing calendar.

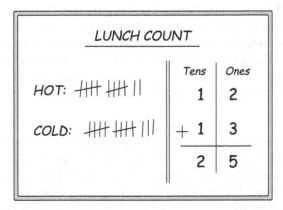

**Figure 7.6** Lunch count.

Calendars can be made to reflect different times of the year. For example, a calendar produced on the belly of a snowman to represent January could include snowflakes of different geometric shapes for each day (Figure 7.7). These snowflake dates can be scattered on the area just outside the calendar to be found, as needed, and affixed in their proper space each day. Children identify not only the numbers but the shapes as well.

The mere placing of the dates on the calendar requires mathematical skills as the students search for the daily date. "Is today's number on the right or left side of the calendar?" and, "Is it placed high, medium, or low along the sides of the calendar?" are questions that direct children to consider placements.

The use of the class calendar encourages whole-group, interactive thinking and problem solving with such questions as:

- How many days are in this month?
- How many days have six in the "ones" place?
- Can you pick two days with the sum of 19?
- On what day of the week does this month begin? End?
- What will the date be tomorrow? Two days from today?
- What was yesterday's date?
- What are the dates of all the Saturdays?
- Why does the year stay the same day after day?

Encourage the use of calendars outside the classroom. At the beginning of each month have students make a calendar to take home. Special events can be prewritten on it. Provide the calendar grid with the days of the week already written in, but have the students fill in the dates. This calendar grid can then be glued onto any variety of backgrounds and makes an appealing tool for the children and their families to use at home.

### Place Value Straws

One way for students to observe the progression of the school year while incorporating integration of place value skills is to represent the passing of each day by adding a straw to the "place value boxes." Affix to the wall half-pint milk containers covered with contact paper and labeled "ones," "tens," and "hundreds." Each school day, as part of the morning business routine, the "calendar person" can add a straw to the "ones" box (Figure 7.8). When there are 10 straws in the "ones" box they are bundled and secured with a rubber band, then placed in the "tens" box. Then, all of the previously placed straws are taken out of the boxes and counted to establish the current school-day number. Above each place value box is a strip that has been laminated so that it can be written on and erased daily. Hence, two bundles of 10 in the "tens" box and six single straws in the "ones" box would read "26," signifying that day as being the 26th day of school.

### Money Exchange

A unique way for students to observe the progression of the school year is to incorporate the passing of time with a money exchange. Attach four small plastic bags to the wall and label them "penny," "nickel," "dime," and "quarter" (Figure 7.9). Each day a penny is added to the penny bag. Subsequent coin exchanges are made as needed, and the written amounts are noted on the wipe-off tagboard strip above each plastic bag. The money

**Figure 7.7** Calendar.

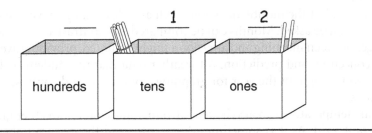

**Figure 7.8** Place value straws.

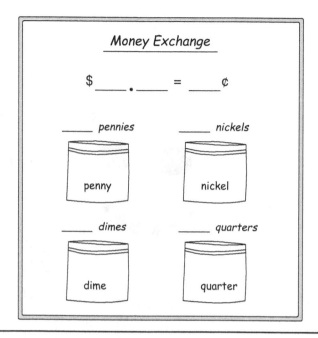

**Figure 7.9** Money exchange.

in the bags is counted each day with the total corresponding to the current school-day number. This activity is best carried out with the teacher performing the logistics while the students give input as to how the exchanges should be made. This daily routine helps children distinguish among coins, observe connections among coins' values, and see how exchanges from one coin to another are linked.

### Weather Graph

General weather conditions can be observed, discussed, and recorded. The "weather person" (perhaps called the "meteorologist") observes and records the weather as is seen each day. Tally marks for each day's weather can be placed under pictorial representations of the weather. A graph grid with weather pictures depicting sunny, cloudy, rainy, snowy, and weather combinations on the left side might be used as students fill in the graph each day with the weather they observe (Figure 7.10). Oral observations by classmates can incorporate mathematical observations such as, "I see that two more days are sunny than cloudy."

At the end of the month, questions such as, "How many snowy days did we have this month?" can be asked. Months can be compared and contrasted with each other. Weather changes between morning and afternoon might be noted, providing avenues for observation, collection, and prediction. All weather data that the students collect can be saved and used throughout the year for graphing, comparing and contrasting, and predicting activities.

Daily temperature can also be recorded in a space on the weather graph or on a separate graph grid. As it is sometimes difficult to read the exact number of degrees on a temperature scale, the thermometer might be sectioned into color-coded chunks. For example, 16°–32° could be labeled as blue/cold, 34°–50° could be labeled as green/cool,

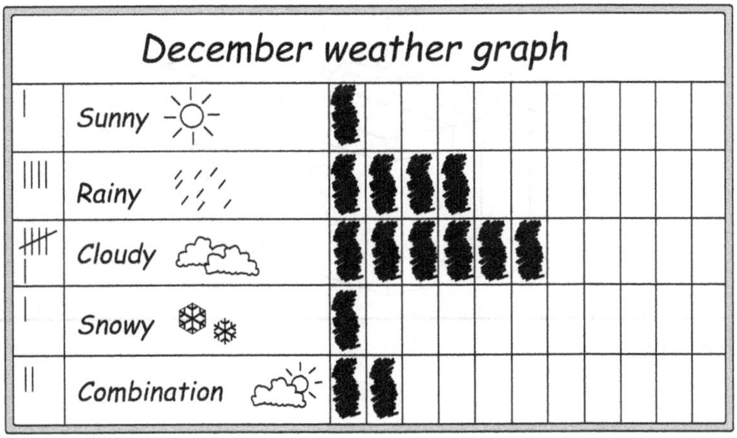

**Figure 7.10** Weather graph.

and so on. Each day, a corresponding color dot can be placed directly on the grid. Reflection and comparisons can then be made later just as they are with other parts of the weather graph.

In conjunction with making a calendar each month for home use (see the calendar activity above), a blank weather graph for each month can be used at home to provide students opportunities to collect weather information each day, with (or without) family participation.

### Surprise Box

A very engaging way to begin the day is by using a "surprise box." This box can be any container that is large enough to hold a variety of objects. One version is a large shoebox covered with sparkly colored contact paper tied with hardy ribbon (Figure 7.11). The job of the "surprise box person" is to stand before the class and carefully shake the box while listening to and perhaps feeling the motion or temperature of the contents inside. Usually, the students can also hear and see the motion in the box. The surprise box person answers questions from the audience based on the known and perceived data. "Is it heavy or light?" and, "Do you think there are a lot of things in there or just two?" and, "Does it feel like it's rounded/curved or angled?" are questions children might ask. After questions are fielded, the surprise box person has the joy of opening up the box and showing its contents to the class. This activity offers opportunities to consider geometric and other shapes, as well as to predict and estimate.

The incorporation of mathematics principles in everyday routines, as well as in real-life activities, reinforces the fact that mathematics is everywhere in an amazing combination of different concepts. But, most important, children see that math relates to things we do and skills we need in the real world every day.

### Inquiry Projects That Might Emerge From Primary Daily Routines

Taking responsibility for much of what goes on in class can lead to an increasingly democratic classroom model. Children might be interested in investigating new ways in which they can be responsible for the room's, or even the school's, welfare. Other inquiry

**Figure 7.11** Surprise box.

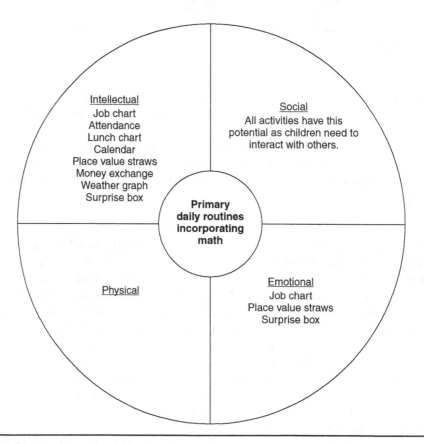

**Figure 7.12** Primary web—meeting children's needs.

projects might grow from an activity such as the money exchange (perhaps children are curious about where money comes from and how it is made) or the weather graph (with studies of weather, climates, clouds, including cause and effect on the environment as it relates to weather).

Even the daily opening of the surprise box might pique youngsters' interest, leading them to explore and study other containers that enclose objects—what they are made of and why, how they are made, what functions they have, and where the containers come from. Young investigators might thus be inclined to make their own containers to hold things, thereby hypothesizing, experimenting, noting cause and effect, as well as using skills in measurement.

## THE POWER OF INQUIRY LEARNING THROUGH INTEGRATION

As you have seen, math learning in room 4 is incorporated into the fabric of everyday life. There are social studies and science experiences requiring mathematical calculations, storybooks with mathematics as part of the plot, art that reflects knowledge of geometric shapes and beginning measurement, even music that embraces rhythmic patterns. Sometimes concepts in math are obvious to the outside viewer of the classroom, but most times they are embedded in the real-life experiences of the students' active learning as the young learners engage in play, use math to find answers to their questions, and carry out daily routines.

Teachers who respect a child's need to explore, discover, and make sense of the world will seek to make math an integral part of classroom life. Integrating mathematics naturally into the students' classroom curriculum and daily routines helps children feel comfortable about a subject area that will have applications throughout their lives. As children use math authentically they will begin to see themselves as capable in a world of numbers. And this confidence, buoyed by a strong foundation in understanding the way numbers work, will give students their best chance at being successful with challenging mathematical material in later grades as well as in their journey of life-long learning.

## TO DISCUSS

1. Discuss the routines used in either the preprimary or primary classroom as shown in this chapter. What additional mathematical skills could be incorporated within these routines? What social implications would they have?
2. Discuss classroom routines that have not been showcased in this chapter. In what ways could mathematical skills be embedded naturally in these routines?
3. In your class, divide into groups according to the ages or grades of your students. Brainstorm the greatest number of ways possible in which mathematics learning might be incorporated naturally into the day.
4. Discuss the two webs in the activity sections. Is it clear as to why titles were placed where they were? Would you position them differently? Why?

## TO DO

1. Observe morning opening procedures in a classroom. What evidence of math skill incorporation do you see? If you are a classroom teacher, assess the use of mathematical skills in your own opening procedures.
2. In your own daily personal routines, keep a mental note of the multitude of ways math is infused in your life. Compare and discuss your observations with other adults.
3. Observe a group of children at play and note any formal or informal use of mathematics skills.

4. Choose any single Common Core State Standard in Math and devise a way to meet it through play. For very small children this might mean simply providing inspiring materials. For older children, creation of a game might be in order.

5. Try implementing any of the ideas suggested in this chapter. Then write about or discuss your successes and problems. Analyze why some things went better than others.

6. In the primary web in Figure 7.12, you will observe that the listed activities provide no direct physical experience. Try revising any of the activities to provide for children's physical needs or suggest daily routines that will do this. Reflect on your additions and inventions and determine if these are a good idea when it comes to routines. Would it be better to incorporate physical activity in other ways? Why or why not?

## NOTE

* Logico-mathematical reasoning refers to children's using their own thinking about mathematical problems and ideas. It can be differentiated from social or conventional knowledge, which refers to memorization of facts and symbols.

## REFERENCES

Baroody, A. (2004). The developmental bases for early childhood number and operations standards. In Clements, D., Sarama, J., & DiBiase, A. (Eds.), *Engaging young children in mathematics: Standards for early childhood mathematics education* (pp. 173–219). Mahwah, NJ: Erlbaum.

Castle, K. (1986). Conference update: 1985 NAECTE keynote address. *National Association of Early Childhood Educators Bulletin,* 7 (1), 1–2.

Clements, D. (2004a). Geometric and spatial thinking in early childhood education. In Clements, D., Sarama, J., & DiBiase A. (Eds.), *Engaging young children in mathematics: Standards for early childhood mathematics education* (pp. 267–297). Mahwah, NJ: Erlbaum.

Clements, D. (2004b). Major themes and recommendations. In Clements, D., Sarama, J., & DiBiase A. (Eds.), *Engaging young children in mathematics: Standards for early childhood mathematics education* (pp. 7–72). Mahwah, NJ: Erlbaum.

Clements, D. & Stephan, M. (2004). Measurement in pre-K to grade 2 mathematics. In Clements, D., Sarama, J., & DiBiase A. (Eds.), *Engaging young children in mathematics: Standards for early childhood mathematics education* (pp. 299–317). Mahwah, NJ: Erlbaum.

Cole, J. & Washburn-Moses, L. (2010). Going beyond the "math wars". *Teaching Exceptional Children,* 42 (4), 14–20.

Deal, L. & Wismer, M. (2010). NCTM principles and standards for mathematically talented students. *Gifted Child Today,* 33 (3), 55–65.

Erikson, E. (1964). *Childhood and society.* New York, NY: Norton.

Ginsburg, H., Lee, J., & Boyd, J. (2008). Mathematics education for young children: What it is and how to promote it. *Social policy report giving child and youth development knowledge away,* 22 (1), 3–24.

Hart, L., Schultz, K., Najee-ullah, D., & Nash, L. (1992). Implementing the professional standards for teaching mathematics: The role of reflection in teaching. *Arithmetic Teacher,* 40 (1), 40–42.

Kamii, C. & DeClark, G. (1985). *Young children reinvent arithmetic: Implications of Piaget's theory.* New York, NY: Teachers College Press.

Kamii, C. & DeVries, R. (1980). *Group games in early education.* Washington, DC: NAEYC.

Kamii, C. & Housman, L. (2000). *Young children reinvent arithmetic: Implications of Piaget's theory* (2nd ed.). New York, NY: Teachers College Press.

Kamii, C. & Joseph, L. (1989). *Young children continue to reinvent arithmetic—2nd grade—Implications of Piaget's theory.* New York, NY: Teachers College Press.

Kamii, C., Miyakawa, Y., & Kato, Y. (2004). The development of logic-mathematical knowledge in a block-building activity at ages 1–4. *Journal of Research in Childhood Education,* 19 (1), 44–57.

Kato, K., Honda, M., & Kamii, C. (2006). Kindergartners play lining up the 5s: A card game to encourage logico-mathematical thinking. *Young Children,* 61 (4), 82–88.

Kennedy, L. (1986). A rationale. *Arithmetic Teacher,* 33 (6), 6–7.

Lee, J. & Ginsburg, H. (2009). Early childhood teachers' misconceptions about mathematics education for young children in the United States. *Australasian Journal of Early Childhood*, 34 (4), 37–45.

Moomaw, S. (2013). *Teaching STEM in the early years*. St. Paul, MN: Redleaf Press.

Munn, P. (1997). Children's beliefs about counting. In Thompson, I. (Ed.), *Teaching & learning early number*. Buckingham, UK: Open University Press.

National Association for the Education of Young Children & National Council of Teachers of Mathematics (2010/2002). *Early childhood mathematics: Promoting good beginnings* (electronic version). Retrieved from www.naeyc.org/positionstatements/mathematics.

National Council of Teachers of Mathematics. (2000). *Principles and standards for school mathematics*. Reston, VA: NCTM.

National Governors Association Center for Best Practices & Council of Chief State School Officers. (2010). *Common core state standards mathematics*. Washington, DC: National Governors Association Center for Best Practices, Council of Chief State School Officers.

Northwest Regional Educational Laboratory. (2005). Teaching math to English language learners. *Northwest Education*, 11 (2), 14–15.

Obama, B. (2010). *Honoring educators in math and science*. Retrieved from www.whitehouse.gov.

Piaget, J. (1965/1932). *The moral judgment of the child*. New York, NY: Free Press.

Richardson, K. (2004). Making sense. In Clements, D., Sarama, J., & DiBiase A. (Eds.), *Engaging young children in mathematics: Standards for early childhood mathematics education* (pp. 321–324). Mahwah, NJ: Erlbaum.

Saracho, O. (2012). *An integrated play-based curriculum for young children*. New York, NY: Routledge.

Trafton, P. (1975). The curriculum. In Payne, J. (Ed.), *Mathematics learning in early childhood*. Reston, VA: NCTM.

# 8

## SCIENCE

*Except for children (who don't know enough not to ask the important questions), few of us spend much time wondering about why nature is the way it is. . . . In our society it is still customary for parents and teachers to answer most of these questions with a shrug.*
—Carl Sagan

After reading this chapter you should be able to:

- Explain why science learning is important for all children;
- Describe the history of science teaching and learning for young children;
- Enumerate important learnings as presented by the Next Generation Science Standards;
- Share ways to employ children's natural wonder and curiosity about the world to integrate science into the curriculum.

Science is central to the lives of all of us. In our complex and rapidly changing world science knowledge is critical to making sense of it all. However, in spite of the importance of science education, today's emphasis on meeting standards in reading and mathematics has at times meant that science takes a back seat in the curriculum, sometimes disappearing altogether. This can happen not only in the primary grades but in preschool and kindergarten as well. Yet young children are natural born scientists in the broadest sense of what a scientist is—one engaged in a systematic activity to gain knowledge—as they enthusiastically continue about their business of making sense of their real, tangible world by acting on their curiosity, experimenting with their environment, and asking questions. Experiences impact a child's understanding of his or her world, and hands-on science activities that respect exploration are essential components of any early childhood setting. Add to that a setting that values curriculum integration and inquiry learning and a teacher will find that it is completely possible to incorporate science to honor children's needs while still meeting today's academic standards.

As well, today's environmental crises require a citizenry that is committed to sustaining the earth and everything in it. People who, from the early days of their schooling, have learned to appreciate the environment and to take active steps away from its demise are most likely to continue taking steps, large and small, toward its survival. The story that follows describes the experiences of one first-grade teacher who began planting a vegetable garden with her children but then realized she was embarking onto something much, much larger. With the full support of a forward-looking principal and the help of parents and community members, a class of first graders began taking their own steps toward environmental conscientiousness.

## FIRST GRADERS LEARN ABOUT SUSTAINABILITY

Jamine Moss-Owen, a first-grade teacher in Washington State, believes strongly in involving parents and community members in the education of her children. When she learned that one of the mothers was taking a master composting class, Jamine knew that somehow her class would benefit from the new knowledge. After a discussion with the parent, the teacher decided that the class would plant a vegetable garden using organic techniques. They selected a space with good exposure to the sun but away from trampling feet and stray playground balls. A field trip to a major composting center informed the children of that process from beginning to end. Coincidentally, Jamine's school was already participating in a "Food to Flowers" composting program sponsored by the local garbage pick-up company. This meant that every child in school was already engaged in sorting lunchtime leftovers for the purpose of composting and that well-composted soil from their own efforts was available to get the first-grade garden started.

The complexity of creating a garden using organic techniques, with the aid of the school's composting program, made some class-time research necessary. Over time, the research itself grew in complexity, but it was all tied to a theme of sustainability and was based on the children's own interests. The following are some experiences that transpired over a two-month period:

- Exploring at a nearby pond led to an interest in the concept of habitat. The children began to consider issues surrounding habitat as they worked in their garden.
- The field trip to the composting center led to interest in the worms' feeding habits and needs. This, in turn, led to more hands-on involvement in the feeding and nurturing of worms back at the school's own bins, not to mention a growing understanding of the chain of events leading from their lunchroom throwaways to composting to gardening.
- Curiosity about the different flavors and textures of various kinds of lettuce led the children to experiment by planting different varieties.
- Rising interest in sustainability issues led to concern on the part of several boys about the role of oil in the quest for world peace. Here was a case of children transferring conversations from home to their studies at school; a community member was enlisted to engage those who had an interest in creating an environmentally oriented mural.
- Music was incorporated when the class wrote a song about the watershed their school resides in. A community member helped with a guitar accompaniment.

- Once the theme of sustainability became deeply imbedded in the children's studies, they created posters about the subject using recycled materials.
- Finally, a Sustainability Fair pulled everything together. With the help of various community members, centers were created in the classroom—some of them designed to extend the children's learning, some to consolidate it.

As the school year came to an end, Jamine asked her class to create their own definition of sustainability. This is what came from the collaborative thinking of 22 seven year olds: "Thinking not just about yourself but about the world and everything in it, on it, and around it. Taking care of these things for the future. Everything is connected."

Jamine's own view about teaching for care of the environment is summed up in this statement: "To not teach that would make you off-task as a teacher, if you're supposed to teach children to live in the future."

## WHY SCIENCE MATTERS: A BRIEF HISTORY

Young children have a natural curiosity about the world that is important to address. First, it has been widely noted that professional scientists most often seem to have gained their first interest in their field when they were young children (Rubin, 2006). Additionally, children's appreciation for their world as well as an understanding of it will aid in the creation of adult citizens who are not only scientifically aware but socially responsible. In a time when we are learning that human actions have been having a profound effect on global conditions, this has become a crucial consideration. "The challenges we face now and in the near future will require citizens and experts well versed in cycles of nature, in specific knowledge of living things, and in asking the right questions that can lead to useful investigations and, ultimately, answers" (Meier & Sisk-Hilton, 2013, p. 218).

Historically, science education in the United States has always had a moral dimension to it, but for quite different reasons. For example, in the last half of the 18th century, nature books were imported from England with the intention that children would glean from them a greater appreciation of God's handiwork. As one book review of the time stated:

In infant and elementary schools generally these volumes will be found of great service, in awakening the mind to an early interest in the study of Life, that peculiar manifestation of creative Wisdom. (Underhill, 1941, p. 26)

The study of science was generally a hands-on affair, with little time devoted to hypothesizing or studying theory. This was due partly to the influence of the views of the English philosopher John Locke and the Swiss philosopher Jean-Jacques Rousseau, both of whom argued for concrete learning experiences for children. It was also due to the belief that children would appreciate God's handiwork most if given the objects themselves to admire.

It is important to point out that during the late 1700s education was primarily for those who could afford to pay for it. By the beginning of the 19th century, universal schooling had evolved, and schools were becoming more and more crowded. Although the desire to teach science through the use of objects remained, the need to provide an education for many children at one time meant that discussion and pictures began to be more the norm.

Toward the end of the 19th century an attempt was made to return to the use of objects, but the teaching methods promoted rote learning of isolated bits of information. With the advent of a new explosion in technological expertise and invention, it became clear that something more was needed. An "elementary science movement" grew out of educators' concerns, and soon a structured, knowledge-based approach was recommended for children's learning.

A counterforce was at work, however, prompted by influential religious interests and by the fact that the economy was still largely agrarian. The "nature study movement" promoted nature study that would be unstructured and build on children's interests, emotional development, and imagination. For some, such an approach provided children with appreciation for their creator and for the fruits of the earth, thus making them more content with rural life. For many early childhood educators, a further benefit seemed to be that the nature study approach was more in the spirit of Friedrich Froebel, founder of the kindergarten, and, thus, theoretically acceptable.

In hindsight it is not difficult to see that in the battle between these two opposing approaches to science education, it was inevitable that the more structured, knowledge-based approach would win out in an increasingly technological society. The issue was not dead, but dormant, and it has erupted once again in recent years. In the meantime, the elementary science movement provided the materials and methodology until the mid-1950s. Kindergartens were the site of experiential hands-on exploration while elementary children studied science topics from graded readers developed largely in the 1920s. Then in 1957 an alarming thing happened: The Soviet Union launched the world's first satellite, and the entire United States asked how Soviet technology had become more advanced than ours. Part of the answer seemed to be the out-of-date school science programs in the United States, and, shaken from its complacency, the science community responded.

Unfortunately, administrators and curriculum leaders, nervous about the need to raise test scores in an era of keeping up with the Soviets, soon reverted to traditional methods, and process approaches disappeared. However, at the same time, research showed that a focus on process actually raised scores in content knowledge (Lind, 1997; Martin, 1997), and once these results, as well as the views of Piaget and Vygotsky, became more widely known and accepted, engaging children in inquiry-based learning again became an acceptable way to teach science. For the next 20 years, with funds provided by the federal government, projects were instituted ranging from course development to graduate degrees for science teachers. Of importance to the early childhood field during this time was the development of a variety of curricula that school systems could purchase, all of which focused on and provided materials for carefully programmed hands-on exploration.

Throughout the second decade of federally supported programs, concerns for and problems arising from the civil rights movement replaced worries about Russian technological superiority. Science education took a backseat to study about human rights, and, in 1976, when the National Science Foundation studied the status of science education in the United States, it was found that study of science in the elementary schools had virtually disappeared. By 1982, when the National Science Teachers Association wrote its first position paper stating that "there is a crisis in science education," the civil rights issue had been replaced by the back-to-basics movement. Science was not considered basic.

Noting that the devaluing of science education had produced a situation in which American schools no longer produced graduates sufficiently knowledgeable to take on scientific and technological jobs and that the populace as a whole had become, yet again, scientifically illiterate, the National Science Foundation (NSF) announced in early 1989 a $50 million development project for elementary education. The NSF, a federal agency, thus began a four-year project to upgrade and expand elementary science study through the development of books, learning materials, software, and teacher training. One major intent of the project was to move away from text-oriented, read-and-recite learning; another was to integrate science with other curricular areas.

In the 1990s, the American Association for the Advancement of Science (AAAS) (1993) published the results of its Project 2061. Named for the year that Halley's Comet will next appear, the project pulled together scientists, school administrators, mathematicians, engineers, historians, and teachers to set standards for the improvement of science literacy in grades K–12. The focus of their work was to lay out a series of "benchmarks" for different grade levels in all areas of science learning. Grades 2, 5, 8, and 12 were chosen as the times to take stock of children's progress. At each of these benchmarks, a common core of learning was identified with the understanding that many children would also have their own interests and ambitions that would extend beyond the core while other children would have learning difficulties that must be taken into account.

A number of principles guided the project, including the idea that less is more, meaning that it is better to study fewer topics in depth than to try to accomplish a lot of coverage. Another principle was that science should be integrated with other subjects when appropriate (Martin et al., 1994).

Today, those engaged in theorizing and researching how young children best learn science are generally in agreement that appropriate teaching takes place when "teachers cultivate and build on children's curiosity to emphasize inquiry in science experiences. Children are encouraged to observe and ask questions about the natural world and to think about what might happen during various scientific processes" (Copple & Bredekamp, 2009, p. 315). Another basic premise is that it is much more important for young children to learn scientific process skills than to learn scientific facts. Put another way, learning about science is far less valuable than learning to do science. "Young children need to engage in learning experiences that assist them to learn the nature of scientific inquiries" (Saracho, 2012, p. 226). And finally, although it might not be desirable to feed scientific facts to young children, it is good to include the acquisition of concepts, "not only from life science/nature but also from physical science . . . and earth science. . . . Teachers use a variety of strategies to help children develop important scientific concepts and skills" (Copple & Bredekamp, 2009, p. 315). How to make this all happen is the subject of our upcoming section on the science curriculum.

## SCIENCE AND CHILD DEVELOPMENT

The developmental attributes children acquire that are related to science learning are, in some respects, similar or identical to those in other areas of learning. For example, the understanding of conservation, classification, and seriation and ordering is necessary to children's understanding of number; thus, we have discussed these attributes extensively in the mathematics chapter. As children develop their understanding of time and space their ability to comprehend science concepts expands. These developmental attributes are also related to the social studies and are discussed at length in that chapter. We shall not, then, give more than a brief review of each as it applies to science in particular.

Conservation, it will be recalled, is the ability to understand that two equal quantities or groups remain equal in amount or number even when they are transformed in space or position. In doing science experiments, this understanding may be crucial if liquids are poured into containers of different sizes and shapes or if mud, sand, or play dough is used to understand the stability of weight and mass.

The discussion on classification in the mathematics chapter described the difficulties of preprimary science in focusing on more than one class at a time. Classes of animals were used as one example, and these will relate to numerous science experiences, as will classification of plants. In other words, the preschool child may see that there are red flowers and white flowers but have difficulty understanding that they are both roses or that one is a carnation but that both are flowers. The child in the primary grades should be more capable of grasping class inclusion and can participate in more complex science experiences.

Seriation and ordering of numbers or objects are as important to science as they are to mathematics. Very young children cannot place things in any kind of order, but by the preschool years they can do so through trial and error. Logical thinking begins to appear anywhere from kindergarten through the second grade. Thinking in logical order is necessary to many kinds of science experiences, such as determining the processes that contribute to the successful growth of plants or understanding the importance of keeping the steps of an experiment in order.

Children's concepts about time are discussed in the social studies chapter in relation to the study of history. The confusion that young children feel about the passage of history will be felt also in their attempts to understand prehistoric animals, extinction, and other aspects of science history. On a more immediate level, it will be difficult for preprimary children to do experiments that require many days' duration or observation over time.

The concept of space is related, in the social studies chapter, to the study of geography. There the discussion focuses on the need for young children to see geographic use of space as immediate, related to self, and three-dimensional. Children who have achieved concrete operations can begin to use two-dimensional materials such as maps and will have some idea of scale. As related to science learning, this growth in the concept of space means that primary children will enjoy making realistic drawings of their experiments and will be able to comprehend visually the changes and measurements that are made in them.

Other aspects of development are related most specifically to science learnings. A discussion of them will demonstrate why true scientific experimentation is impossible with very young children and why it must be carefully introduced in the most basic way in the primary grades. How children look at concrete objects is an important place to begin.

### Concrete Information

At the preoperational stage, children understand objects by physically handling them, turning them over to see all sides, and feeling the differences in surface. Objects that present optical illusions or those that look different from different perspectives cause confusion. However, concrete operational children can take varying viewpoints in stride because they are not so bound by their perceptions.

Yet concrete operational children have their own limitations. Although they can see varying viewpoints and physical relationships, they have a hard time theorizing about possibilities. If given an experiment in which they must find possible solutions to a problem, they will probably assume that the first solution they find is the only one. For an example of this phenomenon, note the behavior of young Timmy in the next section.

### Isolating, Controlling, and Testing Variables

In doing science experiments, the manipulation of variables is often a necessary capability. A graduate student in child development once used his three children—ages five, eight and a half, and 13—to test this capability, and his description of the results provides a good illustration of the way children develop.

Five identical clear plastic bottles were placed in a row with each one filled with its own clear liquid (diluted sulfuric acid, water, hydrogen peroxide, sodium thiosulfate, and potassium iodide). Two small open dishes each held a clear liquid also (water in one, a combination of the sulfuric acid and hydrogen peroxide in the other). As each child was called into the kitchen, the father added just a little potassium iodide to the open dishes, and they both watched while one of the liquids turned greenish yellow. The child was then told to try to duplicate the color by mixing as he or she desired. Each child took a different approach illustrative of his or her developmental levels:

Janie (Age 5) After staring silently for a few moments at the open dishes she murmured, "It's gotta be magic." Her father assured her that it wasn't, and Janie began a random selection of containers, from which she poured and mixed, with increasing frustration. Finally, she pushed the experimental container away from herself, announced, "I'm too little for this," and departed in disgust.

Timmy (Age 8 ½) After observing his father, Timmy began by combining water and sodium thiosulfate. His father asked how he chose them, and he answered incongruously, "If I knew what they were, I'd probably figure it out." For a time he tried various combinations, realizing aloud that he might have already done some of them. Finally, he combined the sulfuric acid and hydrogen peroxide and got a faint yellow. His father suggested that a third liquid might be in order, and suddenly Timmy remembered seeing him add the potassium iodide. He watched in great satisfaction as the proper color appeared and excitedly declared, "I did a sinetific expermint!"

Audra (Age 13) Audra began by adding the potassium iodide to each of the liquids in order. When nothing happened, she exclaimed, "Wait, maybe it could take three mixtures or all five." She then mixed all five together and expressed disappointment that it didn't "at least turn a light *shade* of yellow." Audra then wished she had a piece of paper to organize her efforts, but turned down her father's offer of one. She then tried to remember which combinations she had made as one by one she attempted to replicate the correct color. At last the correct combination was stumbled upon.

Looking back at the efforts of the three children, we see that Janie's attempts were primitively random, that Timmy was vaguely aware that some kind of system was possible but acted as randomly as Janie, and that Audra had yet to reach a truly formal operational stage in which she could methodically isolate, control, and test the variable.

It should be obvious from this illustration that science experiences that require systematic manipulation of this sort are beyond the capabilities of younger children.

### Rules, Procedures, and Models

In order to accomplish scientific experiments in the fullest sense, it is necessary to set up procedures, develop theoretical models, and create rules for handling objects or situations.

One Saturday, Richard (age 15) discovered some large, half-dead batteries in a box in his house. Always one for scavenging and experimenting, he carefully and methodically analyzed the properties and uses of the batteries. With the addition of miscellaneous wires, old flashlight parts, and coins, he then creatively experimented with some new ways to use them. It wasn't long before one of the neighbor boys, Carlos (age 13), came by and joined in the experimentation. Carlos worked systematically and methodically following Richard's lead, with no apparent interest in doing the original research. When Carlos' little brother Victor (age eight) came looking for him, he, too, got caught up in the spirit of invention. His participation, however, was limited to observation and occasional menial jobs as new materials were needed. The next day, quite on his own, Victor repeated the processes of the day before as well as his memory would serve him.

Here it can be seen that a child of primary-grade age can take part in scientific processes if there are strong models for him or her to follow. Victor was quite content in this case to follow the lead of others but would not have known, much as Timmy (in our last section) did not know, how to create the processes on his own. If we were to add a preschool child to this account, he or she would more than likely have no interest in the processes at all. The preschool child, if drawn by a desire to be with the other children, might, however, enjoy doing some of the mundane work involved.

### Causality

To carry out science experiences with real understanding, it is necessary for children to grasp logical cause and effect beyond the early childhood dependence on animism, artificialism, or magic as explanations of various phenomena. Piaget explained animism as being the belief that things, such as objects in nature, act the way they do because they want to, with minds of their own (for example, the flowers move to make the bees leave them or the sun might set because it is tired.) Artificialism, Piaget said, is the belief that God or man has made the entire world and its contents in human fashion. (God might be seen as both creator of wind and inventor of sailboat building so that the wind might be enjoyed.) The concept of magic is used by children to link cause and effect. (When Suzanne was six she saw her first shooting stars and assumed that they must have sent the tooth fairy who, shortly afterward, flew in her window and left 25 cents under her pillow.)

At times, teachers may need to address misunderstandings and even fears children might have about natural phenomena: Will earthworms bite? Are dragonflies baby dragons? Do tree branches really swish down and grab unaware children? Involvement in nature-related projects can help clear up misunderstandings for children and "any fears they have based on misinformation can be replaced by informed respect for their environment" (Mendoza & Katz, 2013, p. 168).

In the primary years, some children will still occasionally lapse into inventive, albeit incorrect, explanations when there seem to be no others available. For the most part, however, they are beginning to understand scientific causality if concrete materials are present.

## Transformation

Perhaps one reason that small children have a tendency to believe that changes may be caused by magic is that they are unable to see transformations taking place. They can focus on the beginning and on the end, but the change process can elude them until they are in the primary grades. The story has been told (Forman & Kuschner, 1983) of a teacher who showed a four-year-old boy a caterpillar and an anesthetized butterfly. The butterfly, she told him, used to be a caterpillar. The child was completely confused and no doubt wondered how the apparently dead butterfly could ever have been a caterpillar—perhaps even that caterpillar—when the caterpillar was still alive and in its caterpillar state. Children this young do not have the capability to imagine what transformations might have taken place unless given the opportunity to witness them firsthand and at a speed that helps them make sense of the world, hence the need for actual hands-on learning and observation.

Throughout our discussion of children's development in science-related concepts, young children can be seen trying to make sense of their world. Logical thought is beyond possibility for the very young, and so they rely on their ability to invent answers that seem quite sensible to them at the time. Based on observation and work with children, however, it has long been known that the confusions about causality, natural phenomena, animism, and so on may not be dropped through simple maturation (Howe, 1975). What is needed is experience coupled with maturation, or children may not progress in their scientific thinking as they could and may continue to rely on fanciful explanations. With experience and maturation of thought, it becomes possible in the primary years to drop most of the reliance on such fanciful explanations. With guidance and concrete experiences some logical thought is possible in science learnings. In choosing activities for the science curriculum, it thus becomes essential to help children sort out fantasy from reality, to observe how phenomena change, and to present all activities in the most concrete way possible.

## Diversity in Development

One approach to promoting science learning to a wide array of children at different stages of development and abilities is to create science learning centers in the classroom that are open-ended and nonthreatening (Irwin, Nucci, & Beckett, 2006). These centers can focus on concept review or lead to new but related directions. They can include cultural objects or geological specimens, such as rocks or soil, from children's homelands or states of origin. The materials should be fairly indestructible as well as nontoxic, particularly if some children are developmentally delayed. Directions should be simple, clear, and posted at each center; for preliterate children or non-English speakers, the directions should include simple pictures for each step. The setup for each center should be such that no child is denied entry due to disability or the extra room required for a wheelchair. Children should be allowed to work at the centers in groups, with encouragement for combinations that cross ability levels and or English-speaking capabilities. Children with disabilities can learn much in centers such as these, particularly if they are given more instructional and practice time. They may also need to have the experiences simplified (Saracho, 2012). When children learn from one another in less formal settings such as centers, the results often expand beyond what the teacher had expected.

Centers such as these can be recommended for almost any area of the curriculum at some time or other. For science, hands-on learning centers that encourage exploration can be an especially powerful teaching tool, and we recommend to our readers that this approach be explored when possible.

## INCORPORATING SCIENCE INTO DAILY ROUTINES

One way to make science an integral part of children's lives is to incorporate it automatically in classroom activities. Some suggestions:

- If there is a classroom aquarium or terrarium, it will need continuing attention. However, young children will need careful supervision so that fish and other animals are not lovingly attended to death.
- Classroom plants need weekly, or semiweekly, watering as well as occasional fertilizing. Again, careful supervision is essential.
- Lining up and moving in and out of doors provides an opportunity to observe nature. Note the movement of clouds, the ambient feel of temperature changes, the seasonal developments of trees and other plants.
- A daily classroom ritual can be created to check and record weather.
- Older students might choose to make and be in charge of a device that collects rainwater, thereby recording, on a regular basis, the amount of rainfall (or lack of it).
- Some locales have daily air quality statistics; older children might choose to keep track of them, noting causes and effects as well as patterns over time.

## A CHILD-INITIATED INQUIRY EXPERIENCE

It sometimes happens that teachers who have come through an educational system that has de-emphasized science study are often unaware of the potential science offers for exciting learning. Yet science learning is such a natural part of everyday life that it occasionally appears, unbidden, as an unexpected and serendipitous experience. Such was the case in the experience described below. Here was a situation in which the teacher had the best of intentions for her children's progress, but it took a rabbit and a few messy construction workers to show her what broader possibilities existed.

*Jan had just begun her first teaching job in a small southern town. Her county had recently become devoted to achieving higher scores on standardized tests. Perhaps it was her principal's concern about this that led to his strong encouragement for using a back-to-basics approach in her classroom. Although Jan's teacher education had focused on a broader-based, child-oriented philosophy, she was too conscientious and nervous about doing well in her first job to be very worried about any discrepancies in point of view.*

*Early on it was made clear to Jan by the veteran teachers that there was little or no time for such traditional kindergarten "frills" as a dramatic play center or any kind of inquiry-based learning. Children in the school's kindergarten classrooms were typically seated at tables facing the front for most of the day. Any toys had disappeared into the dark corners of closets. Recesses were few and far between.*

*One break in the routine was provided when Jan took the children to a small wooded area at the edge of the school property for their lunch. There they could listen to the wind in the trees and hear water flowing in a nearby stream. An occasional rabbit or less frequent garter snake provided added interest. It did not occur to Jan that curricular opportunities were available until a change in the idyllic surroundings suddenly took place, and the children themselves caused something to happen.*

*Across the street, work began on a small shopping center. During their breaks the construction workers found refuge from the hot sun in the little woods. The children began to notice discarded aluminum cans and cigarette stubs. Then, more alarming changes took place as the creek began to fill with silt and discarded building materials. The rabbits were nowhere to be seen. One day it occurred to a few of the girls that the construction workers were directly to blame, not only for the refuse in the woods but for the disappearance of the rabbits as well. Jan, who had been fairly disturbed by the changing environment, became angry herself.*

*"Is there anything we could do about this?" she asked the class. "Would you like to talk to the construction workers and see if they could change some of the things they do?" At the suggestion of a direct confrontation, the children immediately lost courage. They did, however, suggest that it would be helpful to draw pictures of the creek and the woods around it that "someday" they could show to the construction workers.*

*Returning to their classroom, the children made individual pictures showing trees, creek, and outsize pieces of litter. As they drew, Jan engaged them in some discussion. "Do you think that the woods and creek will look the same tomorrow and next week?" she asked. Some children assumed that all damage had been done and that now nothing would change; others weren't so sure. Remembering that simple graphs were on the district requirements for kindergarten math, Jan asked the class if they would like to learn a way to keep a record of what changed and what didn't.*

*The class responded enthusiastically, and Jan began to realize that it might be possible to provide her children with inquiry learning while at the same time meeting required guidelines. Over the next weeks, the children documented everything they could think of: anthills, rabbits (or no rabbits), snakes, litter items, and so on. They used very basic bar graph techniques, enhanced by pictures. They role-played animals and falling or blowing pieces of litter and divided themselves into "sets" for addition and subtraction. Journal entries were dictated to Jan, who used the opportunity to demonstrate writing conventions and to review letters and sounds.*

*In the middle of all this, the foreman from the construction project ambled across the street to say hello to the children. "Someday" had arrived, and suddenly the young investigators had the courage to share their concerns. The foreman not only had a genuine liking for children but a sense of humor as well. Immediately, he made sure the workers changed their behavior. Just as immediately, the graphs took on a different look, and the journal entries began to read differently. The foreman even came to class one day to explain the shopping center project and to assure the children that rabbits and garter snakes would eventually return, and the creek water would no longer be filled with silt.*

*There was no grand finale to this project. The children began to tire, quite naturally, of the sameness of what they were doing and went on to other explorations. They did, however, spend the entire year referring back to their charts and pictures, which were kept in a special corner of their library area. The journal was there, too, and one or two children eventually could read it to the others. As weather permitted, occasional lunchtime trips were still made to the woods, and the children were happy to observe the improving environment.*

## THE SCIENCE CURRICULUM

In 1990, President George H. W. Bush met with the states' governors to discuss national education policy. An ambitious set of goals was laid out, eventually titled Goals 2000. Optimistically, one of these goals declared that, by the year 2000, U.S. students would score first in the world in both mathematics and science. Anyone who has read international reviews of student performance in subsequent years knows that this goal was overly optimistic. However, it did lead to much curriculum development as well as to theoretical and philosophical position statements by mathematics and science organizations.

The major organizations that developed nationally disseminated positions might have stated things differently, but they had similarities as well (Martin, 1997). Importantly, they agreed that:

- Children should learn investigation skills.
- There should be less focus on content.
- *The inquiry method of learning should be emphasized.* *
- *The teaching perspective should be interdisciplinary.* *
- Teachers should focus on teaching all children.
- Children's interest in science should be stimulated.
- It is important to develop scientifically literate citizens.

  (*emphasis added)

### The Next Generation Science Standards

In 2013, with the belief that science education should reflect how domains of science are interconnected and practiced in the real world, the National Science Teachers Association (NSTA), the American Association for the Advancement of Science (AAAS), and the National Research Council (NRC), along with other notable and influential organizations, completed a two-step process that produced the Next Generation Science Standards (NGSS). These new guidelines build a comprehensible progression of science skills kindergarten through Grade 12.

The Framework, the first critical step developed in the NGSS, identifies core ideas in science, articulates them across grade bands, and describes a vision of what it means for students to be knowledgeable in science. The Framework's goal of using children's curiosity to build on their knowledge in a developmental progression, presents three dimensions that subsequently combine to form each standard: Science and Engineering Practices; Crosscutting Concepts; and Disciplinary Core Ideas (National Research Council, 2012). We briefly describe each of the three dimensions:

### 1) Science and Engineering Practices

This dimension describes behaviors, or skills, that scientists engage in as they investigate and theorize. The Science and Engineering Practices run constant in the K–2 standards as emphasis is placed on children knowing how to:

- Ask questions, make observations, and gather information about a situation people want to change to define a simple problem that can be solved through the development of a new or improved object or tool;
- Develop a simple sketch, drawing, or physical model to illustrate how the shape of an object helps it function as needed to solve a given problem;
- Analyze data from tests of two objects designed to solve the same problem to compare the strengths and weaknesses of how each performs.

**Figure 8.1 & 8.2** Exploration, observation, and hands-on experiences are critical to inquiry-based learning. These young investigators are applying their research skills in their in-depth study of pumpkins.

As students in K–2 strategize and carry out investigations to answer questions or test solutions, they use their prior experiences and *fair tests* (scientific tests in which just one variable at a time is changed). Data are collected from observations (firsthand or from media), analyzed, and interpreted. It should be noted that preprimary children are not yet ready to engage in a step-by-step scientific method. Most specifically, they are not yet ready to learn how to design or perform a fair test. For verification of this position, we need only to return to this chapter's section on child development and the description of isolating, controlling, and testing variables in which even the oldest child was unable to perform a fair test with skill.

What preprimary children can do is ask questions, make observations, and use simple equipment and tools to gather data. Preschool children, for example, might make use of various kinds of sticks to measure, while primary children will develop an interest in actual rulers and begin to use them accurately. (Preschool children also enjoy using real rulers, but their teachers must resist any impulse to insist that they use them in adult fashion.) Magnifying glasses, microscopes, thermometers, beam balances, and spring scales can be introduced as children demonstrate an interest in them. Focus should be on the inquiry process rather than on accuracy with the tools or with emerging content knowledge.

## 2) Crosscutting Concepts

Crosscutting concepts are a way of linking the different domains of science. Such linking helps students interrelate knowledge from science into other aspects of their world. The crosscutting concepts are themes that help students to gain deeper understanding of core ideas in science. These core ideas will be listed in the upcoming section. The seven crosscutting concepts of the NGSS, as applied to K–12, include:

- patterns;
- cause and effect;
- scale, proportion, and quantity;
- systems and system models;
- energy and matter;
- structure and function;
- stability and change.

In keeping with the focus of integration as touted by this text we show how the cross-cutting concepts themselves can be integrated when a science curriculum is based on inquiry and investigation.

Young children apply *patterns* and *cause and effect* concepts when they recognize patterns in the natural world and use them to make predictions and describe phenomena such as the sun rising and setting or flowers budding, blossoming, and dying. As well, certain events have patterns of cause and effect and thus generate observable patterns such as when a plant does not receive enough water and wilts. When children are older they are equipped to use patterns in waves in water to predict how fast an object in water will move and can use this information to make predictions when observing causal effects of stormy or clear weather.

Young students utilize *scale, proportions, and quantity*, and *systems and models* concepts when they use comparative scales such as bigger/smaller, shorter/taller, and faster/slower to describe objects and organisms in terms of their parts and systems in the natural world. They continue to use these concepts when they observe the growth of various plants' roots, stems, and leaves over time. Older children might use certain descriptors to note the effects of environmental changes on plants and animals or to make a claim about the merit of a solution to remedy negative environmental effects on plant and animal systems.

And last, the cross-cutting concepts of *energy and matter, structure and function*, as well as *stability and change* can be applied as young inquirers watch the changing effects of water eroding a sandy-bedded channel and wonder if the devices they have constructed, and placed in the water, will speed up or slow down the erosion of the sand. What changes will they note if the same devices are used in a channel of water with a gravelly or solid rock bed? What modifications might they need to make in their devices to produce the changes they desire?

### 3) Disciplinary Core Ideas

The ideas in this third and final dimension help focus the K–12 science curriculum, instruction, and assessment on the most vital aspects of science, in reaction to the lament that too often science standards are long lists of detailed and disconnected facts. Disciplinary ideas are grouped in four domains: the *physical science* standards; the *life science* standards; the *earth and space science* standards; and *engineering, technology, and applications of science* standards (National Research Council, 2012).

### Core Ideas: What Each Student Should Know

The second step in the development of the Next Generation Science Standards produced a set of standards based on the initial Framework. The approach used in developing these standards is "built on the notion of learning as a developmental progression. It is designed to help children continually build on and revise their knowledge and abilities, starting from their curiosity about what they see around them and their initial conceptions about how the world works" (Achieve, Inc., 2013, Appendix E, n.p.).

You will note that the NGSS student performance standards provide a common understanding of what students are expected to learn; they are not the curriculum. In addition, they deal with children K–2 at the youngest. With that in mind, we will show you, later in this chapter, how teachers of preprimary as well as primary aged children can deliver instruction, in engaging and meaningful ways, to support the standards.

The following sections entitled "Core Ideas" and "What each student should know" are from *A Framework for K-12 Science Education: Practices, Cross-Cutting Concepts, and Core Ideas* (Achieve, Inc., 2013).

### Kindergarten Performance Expectations

The performance expectations in kindergarten help students to discover answers to questions such as: "Does a bigger push make things speed up or slow down?," "Where do animals live and why do they live there?," "What do plants need to survive?," and "Why is the weather different today than it was yesterday?"

## Forces and Interactions: Pushes and Pulls

*(Core Ideas: Forces and Motion; Types of Interactions; Relationship Between Energy and Forces; Defining Engineering Problems)*

Students who demonstrate understanding can:

- Plan and conduct an investigation to compare the effects of different strengths or different directions of pushes and pulls on the motion of an object.
- Analyze data to determine if a design solution works as intended to change the speed or direction of an object with a push or pull.

## Interdependent Relationships in Ecosystems: Animals, Plants, and Their Environment

*(Core Ideas: Organization for Matter and Energy flow in Organisms; Biogeology (plants and animals can change their environment); Natural Resources; Human Impacts on Earth Systems; Developing Possible Solutions)*

Students who demonstrate understanding can:

- Use observations to describe patterns of what plants and animals (including humans) need to survive.
- Construct an argument supported by evidence for how plants and animals (including humans) can change the environment to meet their needs.
- Use a model to represent the relationship between the needs of different plants or animals (including humans) and the places they live.
- Communicate solutions that will reduce the impact of humans on the land, water, air, and/or other living things in the local environment.

## Weather and Climate

*(Core Ideas: Conservation of Energy and Energy Transfer; Weather and Climate; Natural Hazards; Defining and Delimiting an Engineering Problem)*

Students who demonstrate understanding can:

- Make observations to determine the effect of sunlight on Earth's surface.
- Use tools and materials to design and build a structure that will reduce the warming effect of sunlight on an area.
- Use and share observations of local weather conditions to describe patterns over time.
- Ask questions to obtain information about the purpose of weather forecasting to prepare for, and respond to, severe weather. (Emphasis is on local forms of severe weather.)

(Achieve, Inc., 2013, n.p.)

*First Grade Performance Expectations*

By using performance expectations in first grade, students discover answers to questions such as: "Do some materials vibrate more than others?," "What are the effects of placing objects of different materials in the path of a beam of light?," "How are young plants and animals similar to their parents?," and "What objects in the sky move, and is there a pattern to their movement?"

**Waves: Light and Sound**
*(Core Ideas: Wave Properties; Electromagnetic Radiation; Information Technologies and Instrumentation.)*
Students who demonstrate understanding can:

- Plan and conduct investigations to provide evidence that vibrating materials can make sound and that sound can make materials vibrate.
- Make observations to construct an evidence-based account that objects can be seen only when illuminated.
- Plan and conduct an investigation to determine the effect of placing objects made with different materials in the path of a beam of light.
- Use tools and materials to design and build a device that uses light or sound to solve the problem of communicating over a distance.

**Structure, Function, and Information Processing**
Students who demonstrate understanding can:

- Use materials to design a solution to a human problem by mimicking how plants and/or animals use their external parts to help them survive, grow, and meet their needs.
- Read texts and use media to determine patterns in behavior of parents and offspring that help offspring survive.
- Make observations to construct an evidence-based account that young plants and animals are like, but not exactly like, their parents.

**Space Systems: Patterns and Cycles**
*(Core Ideas: The Universe and its Stars; Earth and the Solar System)*
Students who demonstrate understanding can:

- Use observations of the sun, moon, and stars to describe patterns that can be predicted.
- Make observations at different times of year to relate the amount of daylight to the time of year.
    (Achieve, Inc., 2013, n.p.)

*Second Grade Performance Expectations*
Performance expectations in the second grade help students to generate and seek answers to questions such as: "How and why do plants depend on animals?," "What are things that cause land to change and how does that change happen?," "How can an object made of a small set of pieces be disassembled and made into a new object?," and "Which changes caused by heating and cooling can be reversed and which changes cannot?"

**Interdependent Relationships in Ecosystems**
*(Core Ideas: Interdependent Relationships in Ecosystems; Biodiversity and Humans; Developing Possible Solutions)*
Students who demonstrate understanding can:

- Plan and conduct an investigation to determine if plants need sunlight and water to grow.

- Develop a simple model that mimics the function of an animal in dispersing seeds or pollinating plants.
- Make observations of plants and animals to compare the diversity of life in different habitats.

### Earth's Systems: Processes That Shape the Earth
*(Core Ideas: The History of Planet Earth; Earth Materials and Systems; Plate Tectonics and Large-Scale System Interactions; The Roles of Water in Earth's Surface Processes; Optimizing the Design Solution)*
Students who demonstrate understanding can:

- Make observations from media to construct an evidence-based account that Earth events can occur quickly or slowly.
- Compare multiple solutions designed to slow or prevent wind or water from changing the shape of the land.
- Develop a model to represent the shapes and kinds of land and bodies of water in an area.
- Obtain information to identify where water is found on Earth and that it can be solid or liquid.

### Structure and Properties of Matter
*(Core Ideas: Structure and Properties of Matter; Chemical Reactions)*
Students who demonstrate understanding can:

- Plan and conduct an investigation to describe and classify different kinds of materials by their observable properties.
- Analyze data obtained from testing different materials to determine which materials have the properties that are best suited for an intended purpose.
- Make observations to construct an evidence-based account of how an object made of a small set of pieces can be disassembled and made into a new object.
- Construct an argument with evidence that some changes caused by heating or cooling can be reversed and some cannot.

(Achieve, Inc., 2013, n.p.)

### *Quality Science Learning in the Preschool*
Using science learning as a prime example, NAEYC points out that "In high quality learning environments, children become increasingly persistent, flexible, and proficient problem solvers—and they learn to *enjoy* solving problems" (Copple & Bredekamp, 2009, p. 140). NAEYC's sources for applying this statement to preschool science experiences are scientist Karen Worth and education researcher Sharon Grollman. According to these two experts, a high-quality science program:

- Builds on children's prior experiences, backgrounds, and early theories. "Rather than being designed to correct early ideas, teach information, or provide explanations, new experiences provide children with opportunities to broaden their thinking and build new understandings."
- Draws on children's curiosity and encourages children to pursue their own questions and develop their own ideas. "In good science programs, questioning, trying things out, and taking risks are expected and valued."

- Engages children in in-depth exploration of a topic over time in a carefully prepared environment. "When children explore a few topics . . . they are able to organize what they know into deeper and more powerful theories or ideas."
- Encourages children to reflect on, represent, and document their experiences and share and discuss their ideas with others. "Children . . . need to analyze their experiences, think about ideas such as patterns and relationships, try out new theories, and communicate with others."
- Is embedded in children's daily work and play and is integrated with other domains. "A good science program is skillfully integrated into the total life of the classroom."
- Provides access to science experiences for all children. " . . . teachers are aware of each child's strengths, interests, needs, and challenges."

(Copple & Bredekamp, 2009, pp. 140–141)

## THE IMPORTANCE OF PLAY

Suggesting that play is as necessary to scientific inquiry as is systematic behavior, Olivia Saracho (2012, p. 230) calls upon the wisdom of Albert Einstein as her inspiration. Believing that play and inquiry must ultimately be intertwined, she points to his view of inquiry learning as a "holy curiosity" that requires the "enjoyment of seeing and searching." A number of writers see play as a part of a sequence related to inquiry learning. First, young children observe something new and interesting, then they approach and touch it, next they inquire about it in ways that interest them, and finally—as the experience feels somewhat familiar—they play to learn more. The view we must have as educators, Taylor argues, is that "Science requires thinking and doing; play and science are natural companions" (1993, p. 73). Or, to put that sentiment another way, "The fact of the matter is that child's play is practice in learning to think" (Beaty, 1990, p. 203).

Young children are so curious about the world around them that, without adult prodding or coercive teaching methods, they are excited to use playful approaches to learning everything they can. The more teachers can stay out of the way of such playful activities, the more their children will experiment and therefore the more science they will learn.

## TECHNOLOGY AND EARLY CHILDHOOD SCIENCE

As our society becomes more and more dependent on technology in virtually all aspects of modern day life it is valuable for teachers to be cognizant of how a child's home technological environment is reflected in the classroom. Just as technology is helpful in everyday life outside of school so can the appropriate use of current technologies be used to support the growth and learning of young children in the school setting (Parette, Quesenberry, & Blum, 2010).

Science and technology for young children are more than using the computer to practice isolated skills. Some Internet-based software applications have child-friendly interfaces which offer new avenues for children to obtain information, including online virtual tours of real-world places; there are technologically-advanced types of chalkboards which use special "markers" to display and share information with others; older students can use PowerPoint presentations and animation software to present information in an interactive way; and there is a variety of digital devices that offer even younger students the ability to record objects, including the sounds that go with them. In addition, there is technology that allows students to network their findings with other students in classrooms around the world.

But technology utilized in science for young children also includes tools that investigators use as they gather information first-hand: magnifying glasses to observe tiny critters; child-friendly microscopes to look at the world invisible to the naked eye; binoculars for viewing animals from afar; balance scales for weight comparisons; and so on. We are reminded of a speech once given at a college technology conference, in which the speaker, to great applause, held up his "favorite piece of technological equipment." It was a pencil. When teaching young children about technology and providing them with opportunities to explore, it is important to remember that the simplest things, which are often the most important to daily life, should be studied first.

In the spirit of inquiry, opportunities should also be provided for children's inventive solutions to everyday technological problems. Design and inquiry, in fact, are often intertwined when children's activities are informal and based on an interest in or need for the creation of objects, models, or systems. The study of familiar objects such as zippers, buttons, door latches, kitchen gadgets, and the safer automotive parts introduces children to the idea that human inventions can alter their experience in the world. From there, child-created solutions to fastening, locking, and movement are appropriate, particularly in the primary grades.

## ASSESSMENT AND EVALUATION

The National Science Education Standards (National Research Council, 1996) deal with assessment at length. As applied to early childhood, the following statement may be most important: "Assessment tasks must be developmentally appropriate, must be set in contexts that are familiar to the students, must not require reading skills or vocabulary that are inappropriate to the students' grade level, and must be as free from bias as possible" (p. 84). In addition, assessment tasks should be authentic, that is, children should find them "similar in form to tasks in which they will engage in their lives outside the classroom or are similar to the activities of scientists" (p. 83).

Informal observation is of the utmost importance in early childhood education, but documentation must accompany it. For example, a teacher might write down concepts that are reflected in a child's activity or intentionally created assessment task. Examples might include: An 18 month old who dumps shape blocks on the rug, then stacks up all the circles showing he can sort and organize; a four year old who carefully sets her place for lunch showing she understands one-to-one correspondence; two seven year olds who compare their baseball card collections and figure out who owns more, thus demonstrating their understanding of more and less (Lind, 1996).

Another assessment technique is the one-on-one interview between teacher and child. Like the observation, this might be connected to informal learning or to a predetermined assessment task. Several issues are important to this approach: Rightness of answers is not as important as the child's thinking process; the teacher must interview in an accepting manner, demonstrating that the child's answers are valued whether right or wrong; a quiet site should be chosen if possible; if the interview is formally scheduled, the teacher should let the child know that this is a "special" activity that they are doing together (Lind, 1996).

Collecting multiple forms of evidence over time is also a good way to gauge children's growing science understandings. This should be done both for individual children and for groups. Forms of evidence might include drawings, with or without dictation or independent writing; photographs of children involved in activities; and records of children's conversations and questions (Jones & Courtney, 2002).

Truly, science is appropriate for integration into the curriculum as well as having an importance of its own. Our welfare as a civilized culture depends heavily on the advances of science. At the same time, we have learned that science can be (and has been) used to negative effect. As world population grows and science discoveries increase, it will become increasingly necessary to combine our science knowledge with high ethical standards. This combination can and should begin at the earliest ages. The following science units focus on this kind of integration.

## PREPRIMARY EXPERIENCES: APPRECIATING NATURE

Most very young children are fascinated by nature. They take delight in the colors and shapes of flowers, the changing scenery of the sky, and the antics of animals. It takes little encouragement to make them aware of the beauty around them. Without that encouragement, many children eventually become oblivious to much of nature as they are increasingly lured away by friends, television, and electronic games.

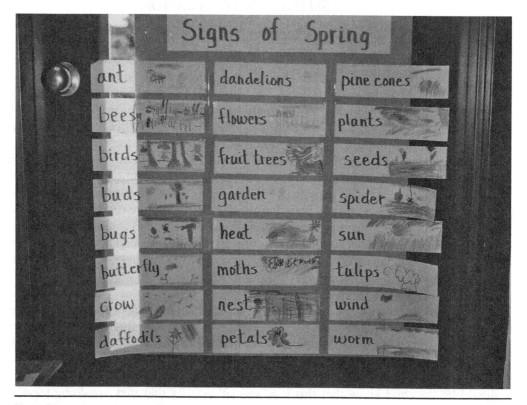

**Figure 8.3** After an outdoors nature walk, the teacher was the scribe for the young learners' words and illustrations of spring words.

The purpose of the experiences that follow is to heighten children's awareness of the natural beauty in their world. The appreciation of nature they develop at this age can be continued and augmented by environmental awareness and activism.

Although other scientific processes are used in these experiences, observation is used most prominently. The activities can be taught as a curriculum unit or as individual activities integrated throughout the year into the broader curriculum. The curriculum web for this unit is shown in Figure 8.4.

### One Beautiful Thing

Use the entire schoolyard or mark off a permissible search area. Ask children to find one beautiful thing and bring it to you. When the collection is complete, return the objects to their owners and have the children sit in a circle. One by one have each child explain why the found object is beautiful and then share it with another child as a gift (only one gift for each child).

### The Sky's the Limit

On a day when there are fast-moving cumulus clouds, have everyone lie down looking skyward. (This may well be the children's first opportunity to play the age-old game of finding shapes in the clouds.) Focus the discussion on the beauty of the shapes and sky colors also. After returning to the classroom, have children use crayons to draw white clouds on light blue paper or shape cotton and glue it on the paper.

### Matching Nature's Colors

Take a tray containing paints in the primary colors (as well as white, black, and brown) outside to the garden or woods. In empty pots let children attempt to mix colors that match those they observe in individual plants. Follow up with paintbrushes and art paper attached to clipboards. While still in the environment, have children paint as they are inspired.

### The Calming Aquarium

Psychologists have long recommended aquariums for their calming effect. Permit children to simply sit and gaze at the fish and other aquarium life whenever they need to take a break from interacting with others. Rules for caring for the fish should be given to the children as the aquarium is introduced into the classroom. As a group they can decide the rules for observation.

### Wonderful Webs

Before school each morning check the grounds for spider webs woven the night before. Teach children to keep a respectful distance but gather around close enough to observe. If the group is small, children may want to watch the spider and its web for some time. Although most young children cannot achieve much in the way of representational art, a web with a single spider (and possibly a victim) may emerge in drawing.

### Leaf Rubbings

This well-known art project becomes a science and math learning when children are asked to find two leaves whose shapes and or sizes are different from each other. Most children will be able to tape the leaves to a piece of paper on their own, tape a second sheet of paper over the top, and choose any color crayon to make a rubbing by using the side of the crayon. Keep both sheets of paper for comparisons.

## Squaring Off

Have children choose any measuring stick they prefer, whether it is something from the classroom or a stick dropped by a tree. Assist them in using their measuring stick to lay out a straight line and then, with another small stick, to draw the line in the dirt. Repeat on three other sides to make a square. Ask each child to observe his or her own plot for a few minutes and then share with others interesting observations about insect life or plants.

## The Daytime Moon

Keep track of the moon's orbit, and when it is in the sky during the daytime, take the children outside to observe it. This may assist them in growing out of such misconceptions as the idea that the sun goes to bed, and the moon wakes up at night.

## Classifying Litter*

Take a walk through the nearest park or wooded area that is visited frequently by people. Give each child a bag in which to put litter dropped by plants or by people. (It is recommended that children wear plastic gloves, often found in the health room. See notes at the end of this chapter.) Returning to the classroom, give children time to classify on their own for a while, using characteristics of their own choosing. Then, with the class as a whole, classify the entire collection into litter dropped by plants or left by people. Discuss the implications for the beauty of the area when people leave litter behind. Collages can be made with the natural litter such as leaves, lightweight flat stones, and small sticks. Some older children may be interested in adding one piece of litter made by people to the collage and then dictating a story about its ugliness.

## Dandy Dandelions

If your schoolyard is beset with dandelions, make full use of them. Pull growing plants apart to see how the flowers are constructed. When the pappus (seed parachute apparatus) has appeared, have the children blow the seeds away and observe where they land. Uproot a plant and admire its strong root, a major factor in promoting its success as a plant. Have children dance as if they were dandelions swaying in the wind or as if they were the pappus blowing away.

## Rock Collections and What to Do With Them

Children often begin collecting rocks because they admire their beauty. When this happens, start a classroom rock collection in the science or nature corner. Carefully hammer one of each type of rock (as the children watch) to see which are soft and will break up. Have older children search in rock reference books for pictures of similar examples. Search for fossils in the rocks. Use a magnifying glass to observe differences in each group. Have children dictate stories about what they have observed. Place written stories on the wall above the rock collection.

## The Classroom as Forest

From the ceiling, hang assorted plants as there is room. Be sure to hang them low enough that the children are aware of them, even if it means that adults must carefully wend their way through the forest. Bring them down as necessary for the children to water. Large plants in on-the-floor planters also add a woodsy touch. Have a class discussion about the way having the plants in the room makes the atmosphere different.

### Appreciating Rain

When a rainstorm is coming, children small and large (like animals!) often respond to the change in atmosphere and their behavior changes. Make use of this time. Have them sit still and sense the change in the temperature and the feeling of the air, listen to the wind, smell the earth as the first drops hit, and simply sit and stare out the window at the rain. If the storm is not electrical, the weather is warm, and children have raincoats, take a walk in the rain, or stand in a covered area to observe. Splash in puddles, feel the rain on the face, listen to the differences in sound as it hits varying surfaces. Observe the effect it has on different plants.

### I Am Part of Nature Too

When having a picnic outdoors, practice leaving the environment as clean, or cleaner, than when it was entered. When walking anywhere where footprints are left, observe their sizes and shapes. Emphasize that footprints are the only things people should leave behind when they hike.

### Appreciating Trees

Sit very quietly under a group of trees or choose one special tree. Notice the birds, squirrels, or other animals that regard the tree(s) as their habitat. Feel the bark of the tree(s) and discuss the texture. Follow up by making rubbings on sturdy paper. Join hands around individual tree trunks, and count how many children it takes to encircle each one; discuss which is larger, which is smaller. Collect, compare, and make rubbings from the leaves as in the leaf rubbing activity.

### Mud and Dirt Play

Section off a small area outside that is just for exploring dirt and mud. Equip it with small sprinkling cans, small cans of water, and assorted spoons. Have on hand old rubber boots to wear or, in warm weather, go barefooted. Let children experiment with different textures, asking them occasional questions about their observations.

### Plant Dissection

Provide a center in which children can pull plants apart to see how they are constructed. Have one of each type as a model that is off limits to experimentation. Be sure that the plants you choose are nontoxic.

### Inquiry Projects That Might Emerge From These Preprimary Experiences

Although the preceding experiences all relate to the appreciation of the natural world, they lack the coherence of an inquiry project. Almost any of the activities might be the inspiration for further study that would provide such coherence. For example, observing a spider's web could lead to a study of spiders and/or insects; the aquarium might spark interest in knowing more about parts of the fish and their functions, as well as a study of the differences among kinds of fish; the dandelion experience could lead to a study of seeds; and the appreciating trees experience might foster an interest in learning about different kinds of trees and where they grow.

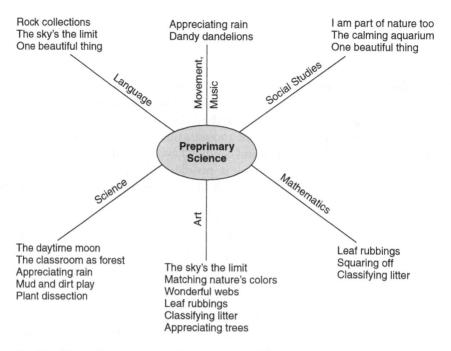

Rock collections
The sky's the limit
One beautiful thing

Appreciating rain
Dandy dandelions

I am part of nature too
The calming aquarium
One beautiful thing

Language

Movement,
Music

Social Studies

**Preprimary Science**

Science

Art

Mathematics

The daytime moon
The classroom as forest
Appreciating rain
Mud and dirt play
Plant dissection

The sky's the limit
Matching nature's colors
Wonderful webs
Leaf rubbings
Classifying litter
Appreciating trees

Leaf rubbings
Squaring off
Classifying litter

Note that all the activities are science-based. The five listed here are not integrated with other subjects.
Note that some activities are listed twice because they are integrated into more than
one area of the curriculum.

**Figure 8.4** A nature curriculum web.

## PRIMARY EXPERIENCES: ARE WE HELPING OR HURTING OUR ENVIRONMENT?

Even without our help the environment is always changing: Volcanoes erupt, tornadoes realign whole communities, hills erode, and coastlines expand and contract. In more primitive times, human beings interacted with nature and its changes with a certain respect for the power of natural phenomena. But as societies have grown in size and knowledge, the human tendency has been to try to interfere and to grasp some of nature's power. In early Egypt building dams and other irrigation projects was a budding science; today, we build huge sequential dams on ever-larger rivers. In earlier centuries we walked or rode horses on trails that animals had created; today we have built extensive road systems over those same trails or have created roads in whatever directions provide convenience for us. To shelter our families and businesses, we blast out hillsides, drain swamps, and create landfills. The list goes on. The growth of the technology that has made it possible to create so many changes has been so rapid that it is only in recent years that we have begun to be aware of what we are doing to the environment. Some changes are reversible; some are not. Some changes are benign; most are harmful.

In recent years, various organizations and study groups have tried to warn us of the consequences of our actions. In order to slow the tide of irreversible harmful changes, it is important for children to learn at the earliest possible time that what they do to the environment affects more than themselves. During the primary years, children are developmentally ready to begin to look at the consequences of their actions. They are beginning to understand the concepts of conservation and reversibility. As they reach out in a social way to their community, they are also able to reach out in an environmentally responsible way.

This unit is designed to help children in the primary years understand that natural changes are taking place constantly, that some changes are positive for humans and some are negative, that some can be reversed and some cannot. Most important, a major purpose of this unit is to help children understand that they can have some effect on the condition of the environment and have a right and a responsibility to help others in the community understand also. The web is shown in Figure 8.5.

The experiences for this unit are divided into two sections: an awareness-informational section and an activist section. Activism should follow knowledge, but within each section experiences may be done in any order or adapted to individual needs.

### Experiences to Increase Awareness of Change

#### Identifying Irreversible Changes

Make a class mural that demonstrates changes in nature that cannot be reversed. Use photos, drawings, or pictures from magazines to illustrate. Examples might be small animals that have grown large, baby humans that have become adults, raw vegetables that

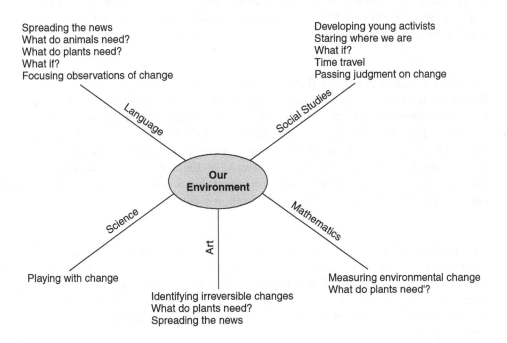

Note that all the activities are science-based. Only 'Playing with Change' is not integrated with other subjects.
Note that some activities are listed twice because they are integrated into more than one area of the curriculum.

**Figure 8.5** An environmental curriculum web.

have been cooked, milk that has come from the cow. Small objects can also be taped or tacked on the mural; worn-down pencils from the classroom and leaves that have turned brown are examples.

### Measuring Environmental Change

Be alert to measurement opportunities. Use whatever measuring tools and system (English or metric) you are using in your math curriculum. Keep records of changes in temperature, size of melting ice cubes, length of worn-down pencils, height of a pile of writing paper or books, size of growing plants, and so on. These changes can be charted. One suggestion is to divide the chart into human-made changes and nature-made changes; this will increase awareness of societal responsibilities.

### Passing Judgment on Change

Divide a chart into three columns labeled "Good," "Bad," and "Neutral." Each day children observe changes in weather, the natural environment, and the human-made environment both at home and at school. These are discussed as a class and entered in the appropriate column based on the class decision.

### Focusing Observations of Change

As part of any activity concerning change, divide children into small groups or pairs. Assign each team to observe and list changes according to a single word such as color, population, environment, habitat, organisms, or structure. This activity is best done outside if a natural environment for observation is available.

### Time Travel

Choose a modern invention that children take for granted as part of everyday life. Research what was used to serve the same purpose in previous cultures. Determine which invention, resource, or change altered the environment more and in what ways. If irreversible changes were made, these should be noted. Changes can be charted according to centuries or by dividing between good, bad, or neutral changes or between reversible and irreversible changes. (It may well be discovered by the children that earlier societies also used the environment unwisely. Discussion may focus on our greater awareness today and the resulting increase in our need for responsibility.)

### What If?

Ask children to look at the long-range consequences of environmental change by writing about them. Individualized essays can be written, but more ideas may emerge from small group brainstorming. Present each child or group with a question at the top of a page. Some examples: "What would happen if all the water on earth got polluted?," "What would happen if all the dogs became extinct?," and "What would happen if all the garbage landfills got filled up?"

### What Do Plants Need?

Purchase four small, flowering potted plants. Deprive one of light by placing it in a dark closet (but give it necessary water). Deprive a second one of water by placing it in sufficient sunlight and giving it no care. Deprive a third one of soil by pulling the plant from its dirt and placing it in a pot of water. The fourth plant is provided with all the necessities. Divide the class into four teams to draw before, during, and after pictures; to graph sizes of plants over time; and to write a diary of observations. Have a final discussion in which there is a focus on people's responsibility toward plants that come under their care.

### What Do Animals Need?

Obtain several animals of different classes so that children can compare the needs of mammals to those of fish, reptiles, or birds. Introduce the animals one at a time, giving careful instructions for the care of each. After they are all in the classroom, divide the children into study teams to research the food and habitat needs of each animal and then determine if their needs could be better met. Make changes as appropriate. Through discussion between groups, compare the needs of one class with the others. "What If?" essays may be written focusing on the consequences of each animal not having its needs met (see the What If? activity).

### Playing With Change

Create a center in which children can experiment to learn what changes are reversible and which are permanent. Some suggestions: making mud from dirt; mixing water that has had different shades of food coloring added; collecting magazine pages to cut up; trying to get toothpaste back into the tube; hammering soft rocks into dust. As you pass by, informally question the children about the implications of what they are finding.

## Experiences to Promote Active Environmentalism

### Starting Where We Are

Have children help identify consumables used in the classroom. Discuss ways in which conservation efforts would be beneficial and then follow through. Some examples: Use both sides of paper when possible; use washable cotton towels in place of paper ones; if the thermostat is controlled in individual rooms, encourage children to wear sweaters and to keep the temperature turned down; never leave the drinking fountain on longer than necessary.

### Moving Outward

Encourage the use of the three Rs (reduce, reuse, recycle) not only in the classroom setting, but at home as well. Children can make posters touting the positives of recycling. These posters can be displayed at school or taken home. Repurposed "junk" from school as well as from home can be made into very imaginative creations.

### Spreading the News

As children become aware and interested in conserving, they can make posters to be placed school-wide. Short articles can be written for the school newspaper describing their conservation efforts. It may even be possible for the class to start a school-wide conservation and/or recycling program.

### Developing Young Activists

Make students aware of human-made and natural environmental changes as described in newspapers, television, and other media. Discuss whether the changes are good, bad, or neutral. If they are good, it may be appropriate to write a brief class letter of thanks.

If they are bad, another kind of letter may be in order. If changes are local, there may be more the children can do. Second and third graders, for example, can be enthusiastic members of neighborhood cleanup campaigns. The important consideration is to be certain that the chosen tasks are suitable for young children.

### *Inquiry Projects That Might Emerge From These Primary Experiences*

Units of study for young children are most frequently organized around tangible subjects. Examples in science might include mammals or animal homes or the life cycles of plants. Less frequently, a unit is organized around an intangible concept, as this one was. If children are interested in exploring the concept of change further, this would be one direction an inquiry project might head. Identifying irreversible change might beckon students to do in-depth studies of specific vegetables, including the different ways they are changed to be used as food around the world. "What if?" discussions of long-range environmental consequences might provoke young activists to delve deeper into the how, what, why, and where of landfills and other ways garbage is dealt with. "What do plants need?" might lead to further experiments with plants or the creation of a garden or the study of how plants contribute to the survival of various animals.

When making a decision to continue on with a topic as an in-depth, inquiry-based learning project, it is prudent for a teacher to reflect on what the study of this topic will provide. Will the study of the topic:

- Build on what children already know?
- Offer hands-on relevance to the children?
- Encourage application of social and academic skills?
- Weave and integrate curricular subjects with the goal of furthering student understanding of the topic?
- Support transference of knowledge to future learning?

## THE POWER OF INQUIRY LEARNING THROUGH INTEGRATION

Humans have a need to know and understand the world around them. Sometimes it is comes from a natural curiosity and, in other cases, from a need to help build a better, more comfortable life without harmful effects to the environment. Optimum science learning, as we have seen, is all about inquiry and it is through integration that the real world of science begins to make sense to children as they apply skills that they have learned in meaningful, genuine ways.

The Next Generation Science Standards encourage the use of cross-cutting concepts to integrate the various domains of science. Thus, integration can begin with combining subjects within general science as, for example, when children study the effects of local geology on an animal's choice of a home. Integration can also take place across the wider curriculum when children use math concepts such as counting, measuring, and graphing as they observe and record data; literacy concepts as they prepare a presentation on objects they have studied; concepts of art, drama, and movement, as they share their new knowledge in an informal dramatic presentation.

And, as you have learned, a child's ability to ask questions, make observations, gather information, and experiment, coupled with knowledgeable encouragement by adults is key to it all.

# TO DISCUSS

1. Collect a number of books for very young children. Survey them to discover how many portray a fantasy view of natural events (sun rising, wind blowing, flowers growing, animals talking, and so on). Are there more that portray fantasy or more that portray reality? Discuss the implications for young children's understanding and cognitive growth. Will they become more confused than they already are about natural events? Should books such as these be saved for a time when fantasy and reality are sorted out in children's minds, or is it better to simply accept the idea of fantasy books for very young children?

2. Discuss ways in which science can become part of the school day. Divide this discussion into two parts: preprimary and primary. Discuss what regular events and classroom (or outdoor) materials lend themselves to incorporation of science without actually taking time for formal science activities.

3. Choose science-related topics that might be good contenders for an inquiry-based learning project. For each topic, discuss ways that other subjects could be woven and interconnected during the study of this topic.

# TO DO

1. Use this chapter or any science activities book. Find an activity that could be presented to children as a teacher demonstration or that could emerge as an inquiry experience. Experiment in one of the following ways:

   • Pair up with another student. Each choose one method of teaching (teacher demonstration or inquiry experience) and observe each other. Compare results in terms of child learning, enjoyment, and receptivity.
   • If you have access to two classes of similar age, try both methods yourself. Compare results as above.

2. Explore primary grade science textbooks. Do the textbooks encourage much inquiry for children or are they more teacher driven? Would you want or need to make any alterations to learning activities? If you made alterations, what would they be?

3. If you have access to a science activity kit designed for a ready-to-use lesson, explore its contents. Is it more teacher driven or does it encourage student exploration and inquiry? Would this lesson have the potential to continue into an inquiry-based learning project? If so, describe what the project might look like and what subjects could be integrated in the process.

4. Use a lesson from either a primary grade science textbook or a science activity kit and describe what NGSS would be met. If needed, how would you adapt the lesson to meet the standards?

# NOTE

\* Safety regarding litter, both natural and human, is an issue. It is recommended that you walk through first and remove anything that might prove dangerous. In addition, you might consider making a rule about touching human litter. Perhaps only you will do this and demonstrate carefully picking things up while wearing protective gloves. And we do know teachers who accompany their pre-experience walkthrough with the dropping of a few pieces of litter for the children to find.

# REFERENCES

Achieve, Inc. (2013). *Next generation science standards.* Achieve, Inc. on behalf of the 26 states and partners that collaborated on the NGSS. Retrieved from www.nextgenscience.org/.

American Association for the Advancement of Science. (1993). *Benchmarks for science literacy: Project 2061.* New York, NY: Oxford University Press.

Beaty, J. (1990). *Observing development of the young child.* Columbus, OH: Merrill.

Copple, C. & Bredekamp, S. (2009). *Developmentally appropriate practice in early childhood programs serving children from birth through age 8.* Washington, DC: NAEYC.

Forman, G. & Kuschner, D. (1983). *The child's construction of knowledge.* Washington, DC: NAEYC.

Howe, A. (1975). A rationale for science in early childhood education. *Science Education, 59* (1), 95–101.

Irwin, L., Nucci, C., & Beckett, E. (2006). Science centers for all. In McNair, S. (Ed.), *Start young! Early childhood science activities.* Arlington, VA: National Science Teachers Association.

Jones, J. & Courtney, R. (2002). Documenting early science learning. *Young Children, 58* (1), 34–38.

Lind, K. (1996). *Exploring science in early childhood: A developmental approach.* Albany, NY: Delmar.

Lind, K. (1997). Science in the developmentally appropriate integrated curriculum. In Hart, C., Burts, D., & Charlesworth, R. (Eds.), *Integrated curriculum and developmentally appropriate practice: Birth to age eight.* Albany, NY: SUNY Press.

Martin, D. (1997). *Elementary science methods; A constructivist approach.* Albany, NY: Delmar.

Martin, R., Jr., Sexton, C., Wagner, K., & Gerlovich, J. (1994). *Teaching science for all children.* Boston, MA: Allyn & Bacon.

Meier, D. & Sisk-Hilton, S. (2013). *Nature education with young children.* New York, NY: Routledge.

Mendoza, J. & Katz, L. (2013). Nature education and the project approach. In Meier, D. & Sisk-Hilton, S. (Eds.), *Nature education with young children* (pp. 153–171). New York, NY: Routledge.

National Research Council. (1996). *National science education standards.* Washington, DC: National Academy Press.

National Research Council. (2012). *A framework for K–12 science education: Practices, crosscutting concepts, and core ideas.* Washington, DC: The National Academies Press.

Parette, H., Quesenberry, A., & Blum, C. (2010). Missing the boat with technology usage in early childhood settings: A 21st century view of developmentally appropriate practice. *Early Childhood Education Journal, 37* (5), 335–343.

Rubin, P. (2006). Start young! In McNair, S. (Ed.), *Start young! Early childhood science activities.* Arlington, VA: National Science Teachers Association.

Saracho, O. (2012). *An integrated play-based curriculum for young children.* New York, NY: Routledge.

Taylor, B. (1993). *Science everywhere: Opportunities for very young children.* Fort Worth, TX: Harcourt, Brace, Jovanovich.

Underhill, O. (1941). *The origins and development of elementary-school science.* Chicago, IL: Scott Foresman.

# 9

## SOCIAL STUDIES

*Community begins in the classroom. . . . The vision of community that the classroom
provides can color a child's ideas and expectations about equity,
cooperation and citizenship for a lifetime.*
—Jim Carnes

After reading this chapter you should be able to:

- Describe historical approaches to teaching social studies to young children;
- Apply today's best approaches to teaching social studies to young children, in both center and classroom;
- Explain how to integrate social studies content with other curriculum subjects and how to integrate content across all the fields of the social studies;
- Describe ways in which social studies promotes civic competencies in everyday classroom life;
- Describe ways in which social studies standards can be incorporated into inquiry learning.

Defining social studies is more complex than defining any other curricular subject. At its core, the term social studies refers to the study of human beings in their societies, and this leads to any number of school subjects. Demonstrating the complexity of this group of academic subjects, the National Council for the Social Studies (NCSS) states that: "Social studies is the integrated study of the social sciences and humanities to promote civic competence. . . . The primary purpose of social studies is to help young people make informed and reasoned decisions for the public good as citizens of a culturally diverse, democratic society in an interdependent world" (National Council for the Social Studies, 2010, p. 9). The NCSS lists the following subjects that pertain: anthropology, archaeology, economics, geography, history, law, philosophy, political science, psychology, religion, and sociology. As appropriate, we might sometimes add aspects of the humanities and even mathematics and the natural sciences.

To explain how all these subjects can work together or alone, the NCSS (1994) has used the metaphor of an orchestra. The orchestra can be viewed as the entire social studies program performing some specific music. An instrument playing a solo represents a single subject—history or geography perhaps. Just as the quality of a musical performance relies on the quality of the composition and of individual instruments, the acoustics of the hall, and the abilities of musicians and conductor, so does the quality of social studies learning depend on curriculum design, contributions from each discipline, expertise of the adult planners, and the abilities of children and teachers.

The complexity of social studies makes a good argument for integrated curriculum, and years of related research have demonstrated the importance of inquiry learning to children's deeper understanding of the entire "orchestra" of social issues. This chapter presents a short history of how today's teaching came to be, the areas of child development related to the social studies, the current national standards, and practical ideas for teaching.

We open with a kindergarten experience that demonstrates some of the complexities just mentioned as children learn about another culture as a way to know themselves better, to discover that they themselves might be members of that culture, and to determinedly grapple with learning activities outside the teacher's definition of developmentally appropriate kindergarten experience. As you read this story, note the very natural, perhaps unconscious, use the American Indians* made of an integrated curriculum. Their purpose was to teach an overview of their culture, not to break it down into lessons in art, literature, dance, and so on.

## KINDERGARTENERS EMBRACE ANTHROPOLOGY AND SOCIOLOGY

Trudi taught kindergarten in Oregon. One year, two of her students were American Indian boys from two different Plains tribes. They had been adopted by White families who each hoped that their son would develop an appreciation of his heritage. During that year a local coalition of American Indians received a government grant to develop an awareness program for use in the elementary schools. Although the program was to be targeted for third grade and up, Trudi decided that interaction with the Indians would help provide self-esteem for the two boys and expand cultural awareness for all the children. She invited the Native American group to work with her class, and enthusiastically they agreed to pilot their eight-week program in the kindergarten.

On the first day, American Indians, all adults, arrived and gathered the class around them to explain a little of their background. It was the first time that the subject of American Indians had been brought up in the classroom, and the children were unaware that two boys, Gil and Aaron, were themselves Indian. The two did not even know it about each other.

As a first activity, one of the men gave a simple pretest. "Tell me what you know about Indians," he said. The general consensus seemed to be that "Indians are bad guys who shoot cowboys." Without looking the least surprised, he responded, "Well, we're Indians and we're here to show you that Indians are a lot more than that. Let me tell you a story . . ."

For more than an hour the class sat transfixed as he told one Native American legend after another. Although Trudi worried that the children would become restless, no one moved. Clearly the occasion was an important one. Over the following weeks, more stories were added, and old ones were revisited. Women taught beadwork, bringing in a collection of the tiniest beads in a multitude of colors. Again, Trudi worried about the appropriateness of the materials for five year olds. After all, she had just recently shown the children how to string complex patterns in wooden beads many times larger than those of the Native Americans. But one of their children, herself five years old, came with her mother bringing her own intricate beadwork and demonstrated that even a very young child could manipulate small materials if the motivation was there. The other children were impressed and tackled the challenge with enthusiasm, never losing patience despite the many frustrations.

Games, songs, and dances were introduced with ever-increasing complexity, and most of the children caught on. They began to look at books about Native Americans and to ask for stories during the daily story hour. Native American themes began to appear in the children's fantasy play. Clearly, the curriculum had become integrated and related to a single theme with the children themselves responsible for much of the trend.

As the weeks went by, many of the children began to talk informally about the differences they observed between Native American culture and their own. Trudi observed that the two Indian boys, Gil and Aaron, never joined in these conversations. She wondered what they were thinking but hesitated to force the issue. Then, late one morning the two boys, quite suddenly and on their own, awoke to their heritage together. It was just after an extended free-play period. The entire class had finished cleaning up and was headed for the story corner. By coincidence, Gil and Aaron were the last two to finish cleaning. They came from opposite sides of the room, nearly ran into each other, and then, in unison, stopped and stared. Gil put a hand on Aaron's dark, straight hair. "Are you Indian?" he asked, looking startled.

"Yeah," Aaron answered with a shy smile.

"So am I." Gil smiled back and put his arm around Aaron's shoulder, while Aaron did the same to Gil. Arm in arm, they walked to the story corner to join the others.

With that experience, Trudi felt she had achieved her goal: All the children had had the experience of comparing and contrasting two cultures, and two American Indian boys had achieved an appreciative awareness of their native culture. Further, they all learned something about themselves—that they were capable of participating successfully in another culture's traditions, even if the skills required (such as bead stringing and complex dancing) were difficult to acquire. Thus, in increasing their self-esteem and their appreciation of another culture, the children had taken an important step toward the ultimate goal of attaining the skills necessary for living in a democratic and pluralistic society.

Once they reached the upper elementary years, it would be appropriate for these children to study about their cultural heritage. They would be able to study more fully about Native American culture and anthropology as well as to learn about conflicts between Indians and the U.S. government. Such formal studies are appropriate for older children, whereas in the preprimary and primary years, concrete involvements, such as those experienced in Trudi's kindergarten class, provide more meaningful learning. This learning may not always work smoothly toward a predetermined goal as it did in the case of Aaron's and Gil's recognition of their common heritage. But one purpose of such early concrete learning is to plant the motivational and cognitive seeds from which later social studies learnings can emerge.

These concrete social studies experiences might take various directions. The social studies unit in Trudi's classroom was an adult-designed unit that crossed curricular lines.

From such a unit might grow a specific interest on the part of some or all of the children, leading to an in-depth study that would add yet another dimension to their knowledge. For example, the children might want to continue to learn new dances with their cultural implications, or they might want to study the housing traditions of Indians in different environments. This interest could then evolve into an inquiry project complete with the various types of research you learned about in Chapter 5.

## WHY SOCIAL STUDIES MATTERS: A BRIEF HISTORY

At present in our nation's history, social studies has lost much of its importance at all levels of education. The original *Standards for Social Studies* were published in 1994 "when the standards movement was still in its infancy, and NCSS believed that it should provide social studies educators and curriculum specialists with a document, which could serve as a vehicle for curriculum development" (Goldberg, 2010, p. 7). Since that time, the language and mathematics focus of No Child Left Behind has ensured that social studies has become less of a presence at all age levels, practically disappearing in some states. One writer, declaring the situation "a crisis," attributes the loss to "increased attention to math and language arts under the federal No Child Left Behind law" and argues that "without being attached to a high-stakes test, the subject has lost ground" (Pascopella, 2005, p. 30). She adds that, although social studies might still be taught in middle and high school, students at those levels now lack the basic knowledge that should have been provided in the earlier years.

With the advent of updated NCSS Standards in 2010, the observation was made by an early childhood/elementary task force of the NCSS that there is still a need for citizenship learning. In a commentary on the importance of the newly revised NCSS Standards, one writer stated, ". . . though civic competence is the responsibility of an entire school curriculum, it is more central to social studies than other subject areas . . ." (Herczog, 2010, p. 217).

The early childhood classroom is a positive place for beginning the journey toward full citizenship, for starting to understand something of the rights and responsibilities of people living in a democratic society. Of course, privileges are more attractive than duties, so that children (and probably most adults) will be more easily drawn to the former. It is much more pleasant, for example, to take your turn telling the class about your weekend than to listen quietly to others. And it is certainly more enjoyable to be involved in a limited-access learning center than to wait impatiently for a turn. But learning the kind of fairness required for living in a cooperative society with limited resources is an essential step in learning to be a successful citizen. While home and neighborhood contribute much to children's development as citizens, the school or center also offers an excellent opportunity for learning to relate well to people of varying races, abilities, and opinions. Thus, it becomes both the right and the responsibility of teachers to assist young children as they grow toward effective citizenship.

Educating the youngest children for citizenship is a concept that first took root in the United States in the last half of the 19th century. At that time there was a dramatic increase in the number of preschools and kindergartens, including many provided for children of recent immigrants. Parent involvement was an integral part of this new early education movement, and mothers, particularly, were encouraged to participate. The ultimate goal for both parent and child was the same: socialization to a new culture and responsible citizenship.

Over the decades, early childhood settings evolved along with society. In the 1970s, the National Council for the Social Studies (NCSS) created an early childhood committee. It was their view that

> It is increasingly clear that early childhood is a formative period for the rapid development of the concept of the political self, a sense of self marked by growing attitudes about how the system works. The ingathering of experiences and the shaping of attitudes through interactions in the environment are part of the process of children becoming citizens, setting foundations for adult citizen actions. (Pagano, 1978, p. 14)

A few years later, the NCSS stated that social studies enables children to "participate effectively now in the groups to which they belong and not to look only to their future participation as adults. . . . Democratic and participatory school and classroom environments are essential to this type of real-world learning (National Council for the Social Studies, 1989, p. 15).

Another view of social studies that evolved in the 20th century was the idea of a spiral curriculum in which very young children would study first about themselves, then their families, then neighborhoods, and so on until, in the elementary grades, the entire world was appropriate for investigation. Although the idea of a spiral curriculum from the early years of the 20th century remains popular, today it is difficult to focus only on the self and the neighborhood with younger children when, through ever-developing technology, they have become so highly exposed to global issues. Thus, today's educators must look for ways to incorporate a worldview into young children's egocentric interests.

Still another 20th-century development, one based on the philosophy of John Dewey, emphasized the need for young children not to study *about* the various social sciences, but to *become* social scientists themselves. Those who have written about social studies education for young children over the past century have emphasized the need for active involvement that regards youngsters as geographers, historians, anthropologists, and so forth, rather than as passive students of the subjects.

In recent decades, curriculum planners for all levels of education, including early childhood, have become increasingly focused on the growing diversity of our society and the need to prepare children for life in this complex democracy. For example, in California an antibias curriculum task force created a curriculum for children as young as two (Derman-Sparks, 1989). In 2010, an updated second edition provided curriculum not only for young children, but for their caregivers and teachers as well. Its title is the appropriate *Anti-Bias Education for Young Children and Ourselves* (Derman-Sparks & Edwards, 2010). The curriculum provides practical suggestions to accompany four goals that "provide a safe, supportive learning environment for all children" (p. 1):

1. Each child will demonstrate self-awareness, confidence, family pride, and positive social identities.
2. Each child will express comfort and joy with human diversity; accurate language for human differences; and deep, caring human connections.
3. Each child will increasingly recognize unfairness, have language to describe unfairness, and understand that unfairness hurts.
4. Each child will demonstrate empowerment and the skills to act, with others or alone, against prejudice and/or discriminatory actions.
   (pp. 4–5)

Another approach to early education came from the Southern Poverty Law Center (SPLC) in Alabama, where curricula and experiences from real early childhood centers and classrooms were collected in book form for teacher use (Southern Poverty Law Center, 1991). The purpose of each story in the book is to demonstrate that "children can learn to care about every other person's feelings, beliefs and welfare" with the long-term goal of making society "a kinder place" (Paley, 1991, p. i). More recently, the SPLC's website has developed online teaching materials, targeting the early childhood years specifically, under the title "Starting Small" (www.tolerance.org).

Children's participation in the creation of a classroom "embryonic society" (Montessori, 1949) or even in a more limited list of democracy-oriented activities is an example of constructivist early education as described by Piaget and Vygotsky (see Chapter 1). Promoting independence and thoughtful collaborations means allowing children to make occasional mistakes as they choose some of their own academic activities. When possible, children should be permitted to choose between working and playing alone or within groups. Most of all, the teacher needs to provide a secure, accepting atmosphere in which children are unafraid to make the choices that are provided them. Youngsters should be helped to observe more of the social/cultural world around them and to enter into its activities as they are ready. This does not mean that children should be pushed into growing up sooner than they are ready, but that they are offered the opportunity to be full participants in their school or center experience. In this way they will be taking the beginning steps toward full citizenship.

While this experiential approach to creating good citizens is totally appropriate throughout the early childhood years, it becomes increasingly desirable to provide children with more content knowledge in each of the social studies areas. In the following section on child development, we discuss the changes that take place in children's understandings that make such change possible.

## SOCIAL STUDIES AND CHILD DEVELOPMENT

In Chapter 1 we saw how young children's cognitive growth progresses through the pre-operational into the concrete operational stage. In the affective domain, children are also working through stages characterized by ego-centered concepts. To illustrate how development affects social studies education, we focus now on the emergence of spatial concepts, temporal concepts, racial awareness, and social awareness. Concepts such as these are at the heart of the social studies curriculum, and consequently, teachers must be sensitive to the ways these and similar concepts develop. Readers should keep in mind that these concepts are difficult even for some adults to grasp.

### Spatial Concepts

Young children learn first about maps by making them rather than by reading them (Seefeldt, Castle, & Falconer, 2010). When they create a primitive map of their school or trace from a map the route they take to get home each day, they are gaining a sense of belonging to their own community. As they get older and use maps to locate their community within state and country or study the migration patterns of their ancestors, they become aware that their immediate community is connected to a much larger world. This physical awareness is an important step in understanding the interconnectedness of the entire world community.

To a great extent, the reason children's early maps are primitive and the later ones are more complex and global is that children only gradually develop their spatial awareness. It is only from the adult viewpoint that visual space is logically and mathematically represented. Young children have much more subjective perceptions of space, and these begin when infants are just one or two months old and are discovering what their bodies can do in space (Seefeldt et al., 2010). Over the next few years, spatial relationships begin to be understood more widely as youngsters develop through the Piagetian sensorimotor and preoperational stages. Thus, the youngest children would begin drawing maps with their own personal relation to reality, perhaps with themselves pictured large in the middle. Eventually, skills would include the ability to draw maps that are representative of the actual environment and to infer information from being able to read maps.

### Temporal Concepts

Probably more important than geography to the development of good citizenship is the study of history. Learning about one's ancestors and the heritage they created gives a sense of continuity to citizenship. Understanding and avoiding the mistakes of the past while attempting to build on the positive is synonymous with good citizenship.

To even begin to understand history, however, requires a basic understanding of the passage of time. Very young children have little grasp of time and have difficulty sorting out yesterday from tomorrow, last night from this afternoon. As with the problem of spatial concepts, more research must yet be done before we can speak knowledgeably about each step of cognitive development. Piaget (1969) studied children's developing concepts of time and concluded that these moved from the simple and confused to the abstract.

One conceptual step children must take is to be able to separate time from space, and this is accomplished during the preoperational period. During the preoperational years, children learn the basics of sequencing but have difficulty differentiating between short and long segments of time. During the concrete operational years, children gradually develop the ability to understand long and short time spans as well as the complexity of simultaneous events. At about age five children begin to develop the adult sense of time, including using terms and concepts related to clock usage. The concept of a day seems to be understood first, then longer chunks of time such as a week, month, and year. The short time periods such as minutes and hours are understood next. At about age eight children can look at the future outside their everyday lives (Bauer, 1979; Seefeldt et al., 2010). Not until the upper elementary years, however, can children acquire a historical perspective of time.

### Racial Awareness

Children's understanding of racial characteristics as well as their attitudes toward their own and others' races has implications for several areas of the social studies: history, sociology, anthropology, international studies, current events, values development, and citizenship education. An important study in the 1970s (Katz, 1976) found the following sequence in the development from simple awareness to the appearance of attitude:

1. Observation of racial cues (simple awareness of physical differences; typically emerges at preschool age);
2. Formation of rudimentary concepts (awareness that people may label other races positively or negatively; may appear at preschool age);

3. Conceptual differentiation (children not only observe that others create positive or negative labels, but begin to use positive and negative labels themselves);
4. Recognition of the irrevocability of cues (understanding that racial identification never changes);
5. Consolidation of group concepts (ability to identify, label, and recognize members of a group; generally appears about kindergarten age);
6. Perceptual elaboration (children notice more clearly the differences between racial groups, while paying less attention to the differences within a single group; can appear at preschool through elementary ages);
7. Cognitive elaboration (complex racial attitudes begin to develop; what teachers and peers say is important in changing or maintaining attitudes);
8. Attitude crystallization/solidification (views on race and ethnicity become definite and hard to change; may appear at the end of the elementary years).

The fact that attitude crystallization may appear by the end of elementary school, and that differences between groups are emphasized as early as the preschool years, indicates the importance of helping children work through their understanding of race relationships. Teachers can and do have a big influence on children's development. Curriculum can be planned along the lines of the antibias curriculum and teaching tolerance ideas described earlier.

### Social Awareness

An important component of social studies learning pertains to lessons in democracy. At any level of education, but particularly in early childhood, this involves actual participation within the classroom or center. Piaget (1932/1965) has provided a helpful model that describes children's development along these lines.

Stage 1 (age: preprimary) was called "heteronomy" by Piaget. To be heteronomous is to be other-directed rather than self-directed. Positive behavior takes place because an authority figure decrees it, not because of an inner understanding of its benefits. Very young children will obey even when they do not understand. Discipline to them is arbitrary, meted out by authority figures in a nonlogical fashion. At this stage, it is generally impossible for a child to mentally step into another's shoes and discuss feelings.

Stage 2 (age: kindergarten-primary) Piaget called the "first transitional stage." It is the first step along the way to becoming truly autonomous in the early teen years. Children at this stage learn about the importance of rules, but they respond to them in a very literal sense. That is, a rule is viewed as a law that has been handed down by some authority figure: a parent, a teacher, even God. Thus, being right is critically important. It is especially important to young children that others obey the rules, while they themselves remain focused on their own self-interests. Is it any wonder that this is the exasperating age of the tattletale? On the positive side, children can be observed demonstrating the beginning of real cooperative work and play.

As children participate in an emerging classroom democracy, it is important for teachers to realize that their development from focus on self to understanding of others is a slow and often rough process. Nevertheless, very basic class meetings can begin even in preschool, and, if children are enabled to make at least a couple of their own rules, they are helped toward understanding that it is not only authority figures who have the power to do so.

## Diversity in Development

As applied to the social studies, diversity issues in both cognitive and social development are important, often becoming intertwined with each other. Historically, for example, the child with cognitive disabilities was seen as a menace, and institutions were developed to protect society from the child and the child from the cruel assaults of society (Hallahan & Kauffman, 1988). Terms such as *idiot, dunce,* and *imbecile* were used in part to ensure that such children were excluded from the privileges of normal, everyday social life (Heward, 2013). It was only in the 1960s and 1970s that lawsuits began to demand the inclusion of all children in public education.

Today, the idea that began as *mainstreaming,* and now is generally referred to as *inclusion,* is common in American education, particularly in the early years. When children of a wide array of abilities spend their days together, they gain a much more realistic view of society and its demands. Given an accepting and encouraging teacher who fosters an accepting and caring classroom, children learn firsthand what it means to treat others without prejudice and biases. In short, they gain real-life lessons in positive citizenship.

Creating a developmentally appropriate and successful society within the early childhood classroom can have long-term effects. Thus, adults who work with young children have a special responsibility to ensure that every single child is permitted to interact with others to the greatest extent possible. Coaching activities can foster increased development. For example, one approach to coaching young children with special needs involves the use of puppets, often found to be "effective tools for presenting activities that are engaging, interesting, and developmentally appropriate for the wide range of abilities of young children in early childhood settings" (Salmon et al., 2013, p. 510). Puppets of various sorts, such as glove, stick, or finger puppets, can be adapted for children with special needs. They can then be used to enhance social and emotional skills through such teacher-led activities as Simon Says, or teacher-and-puppet modeling of appropriate behaviors. Alternatively, children can learn to be leaders, using puppets as their confidence providing mouthpieces. Appropriate leadership activities might include announcing calendar information, reporting on the weather, and other daily routines.

We have discussed the current understanding of children's development related to space, time, racial characteristics, and social skills, as well as the implications of developmental diversity. In each case, as in all aspects of stage development, there is a movement over the years from self-absorption to interest in and understanding of others. Because the child's environment can have a major influence on attitudes and understandings, the teacher's role becomes an especially important one.

## INCORPORATING SOCIAL STUDIES INTO DAILY ROUTINES

Because the social life of the early childhood classroom should be aimed toward the development of a community with democratic characteristics, informal social studies learning can easily become a part of the daily routine. As one writer has stated, "Effective teachers know, as they teach children to read, write, compute, and problem solve, that they also must

- assist children in social/emotional growth,
- emphasize holidays that have community meaning,

- seek an anti-bias approach to values,
- collaborate with families, and
- foster the development of integrity in individuals and groups of children." (Mindes, 2005, p. 7)

There are many activities that can easily be incorporated into the regular curriculum. Some examples that early childhood teachers have found successful include the following experiences:

- *Classroom helper charts*, as described in the math chapter, are common, but we believe that further community building is provided when children are permitted to suggest the needed jobs. The younger the children are the more they may need adult support to help them add to the suggestions. Examples of jobs might include: line leader, line ender, office messenger, weather checker, pet feeder, plant waterer, and paper passers. Try to have a job for each child.
- In the science chapter we suggested a *weather chart*. To extend this daily routine into the social studies, have children compare and contrast weather in other locales

**Figure 9.1** The principal is being interviewed by these budding journalists for inclusion in the "Our School Helpers" section of the book about their school.

such as places their relatives live or, in the primary grades, cities, states, or countries they are studying.

- *The Book of Our School* can begin fairly shortly into the new school year. Discuss with students "words of wisdom" they might like to share with others about what makes their class and school a happy, safe community of learners. Depending on the age of the children, this book might evolve into a many-chaptered book with titles such as "How to Make Friends," "Things We Can Do at Recess," "Our Classroom Rules," "Our School Helpers," or "A Map of Our School." The book could also be written and illustrated by slightly older children to pass down to younger ones, or to children who will next move up to their grade. Keep the book as a manual in the classroom and read from it frequently, perhaps on a daily basis, adding pages and chapters throughout the year.
- Increase children's awareness of other cultures and languages by introducing languages that are reflective of their heritages and/or languages that you know. A simple way to do this is to incorporate "good morning" from other languages into morning roll call and "good afternoon" after lunch and "goodbye" at the end of the day. When possible, involve immigrant or multilingual parents in such classroom activities.

In the next section, we see how a social studies project can emerge from children's interests, the ways in which developmental similarities and differences are easily handled in such an undertaking, and the automatic integration that takes place when children are permitted to focus intensively on their own line of study.

## A CHILD-INITIATED INQUIRY EXPERIENCE

The children in Pam's class developed their interest in building an airplane after they found out that she is a pilot. The project they created grew so involved, complex, and exciting that Pam eventually published an article about it (Morehouse, 1995). Not all child-initiated inquiry projects will be this extensive, but we include it here because it was so meaningful for the children and because it demonstrates how several academic subjects can be incorporated within one social studies-oriented project. See how many you can identify.

*After thorough student-initiated research on airplanes—including a field research trip to our local airport and airport control tower—my kindergarteners and first graders decided to hire a local building contractor to help build their classroom plane according to their exact specifications. Of course they had no cash to pay him but instead enticed him with worms from the classroom vermiculture (they had learned he was a fisherman). The contract they developed with the builder is shown in Figure 9.2.*

*The children helped build the plywood, four-seater, child-sized airplane as they were able. They participated in sandpapering, creating the instrument panel complete with a "real airplane" yoke, and painting. It was determined that this was to be a VFR (visual flight rated) plane, leading to a need for clouds to look at. Before creating these, the children researched weather and cloud formations, and only then did they hang clouds from the ceiling to view as they flew.*

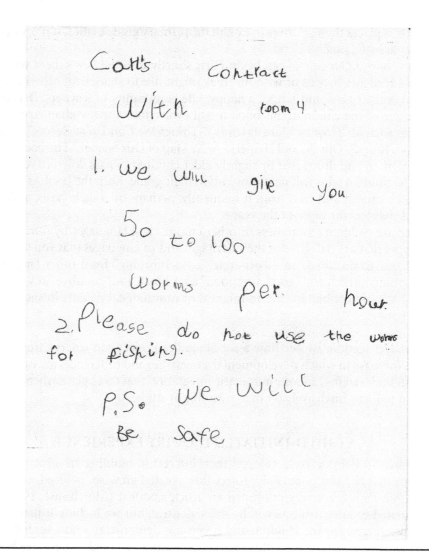

Cat's Contract

with room 4

1. we will give you 50 to 100 worms per hour.

2. Please do not use the worms for fishing.

P.S. we will be safe

**Figure 9.2** The young entrepreneurs drove a hard bargain with the building contractor they hired to help build their airplane.

*The next requirement, the children said, was a proper place to board the plane. A check-in table was set up, and the students decided that passengers and their luggage were to be weighed on a floor scale and the weight calculated so as not to exceed the plane's weight and balance criteria. Tickets were designed and printed and ticket prices decided.*

*But then another question arose: Where should this plane fly? Hoping to integrate the curriculum still further and continue to build on student interest, I asked the children to think overnight about where they would like to go. My own overnight assignment was to check with my Grade 4 teaching colleague to see if and how she could adapt her schedule to allow some of her students to aid my youngsters with their research.*

**Figure 9.3** Democratic teamwork was required to make the plane flight-worthy.

*The next day, the children came to school brimming with ideas of "fly to" places. Partners were chosen. After lengthy dialogue, each pair settled on a destination to research. Choices included Canada, China, Egypt, Florida, India, Mexico, New Mexico, and Saginaw. While I always try to focus the studies of young children on firsthand experiences, it was, of course, impossible to actually visit all these sites. However, students had family members, friends, and local travel agencies to use as resources, along with access to books, websites, and the assistance of their fourth-grade friends. Questions the children researched included weather, holidays, housing, clothing, games children played, pets that might be available, and what schools looked like. As the students found out answers to their questions, they compared and contrasted the information on graphs and charts. They made colorful trifold travel brochures. Large posters for each destination were created and placed on an easel in front of the airplane to remind the pilots and passengers where the airplane was flying. Finally, the class set up a travel agency and stocked it with the materials they had made.*

*And so, at last, the blue and red, high-wing, four-seat, plywood airplane was finally finished and practically begging the children to step inside and take off. For many months afterward, the airplane and its derivative activities provided rich role-play and learning experiences. The students reinforced their new understandings of other lands and people by sharing their expertise with any guests to the classroom. And, the little red airplane, powered by imagination, had places to fly.*

**Figure 9.4** Flight #4 leaving for Hawaii.

## THE SOCIAL STUDIES CURRICULUM

The most recent standards for social studies teaching and learning were established by the National Council for the Social Studies (NCSS) in 2010 and are focused on prekindergarten through Grade 12. According to the NCSS, the core aim of the social studies, for all ages including the youngest, is to educate students for civic competence, to help them be "active and engaged participants in public life . . . students who are committed to the ideas and values of democracy" (National Council for the Social Studies, 2010, p. 9). Using this civic mission as the basis for standards creation, the NCSS has divided the learning standards into 10 themes. These themes, which are listed here, are created as "a way of categorizing knowledge about the human experience, and they constitute the organizing strands that should thread through a social studies program" (p. 3):

- Culture;
- Time, Continuity, and Change;

- People, Places, and Environments;
- Individual Development and Identity;
- Individuals, Groups, and Institutions;
- Power, Authority, and Governance;
- Production, Distribution, and Consumption;
- Science, Technology, and Society;
- Global Connections;
- Civic Ideals and Practices.

The NCSS notes the importance of understanding that these themes are interrelated and that they come from all the social science disciplines. Many learning experiences in a single one of the themes will incorporate more than one social science at a time, and a learning experience from one social science might well include two or more themes.

### Social Studies Themes for the Early Grades

The NCSS explanation of each theme is divided into four sections: *Questions for Exploration, Knowledge, Processes,* and *Products,* which cover preschool through 12th grade. NCSS provides a wealth of ideas for application of the four sections to the 10 themes, far more than could be included in this textbook. Thus, only a selection of examples that are most applicable from preschool through the primary grades are included. At the conclusion of each theme and its four NCSS sections, real-life examples of teaching suggestions are added.

### Culture

The study of culture includes learning about one's own social group as well as others near and far. As young children learn about the traditions, institutions, and values that constitute their society's way of life, they begin to learn more about themselves as individuals and about their similarities and differences with the rest of the world. In addition to social studies, other subjects such as language arts, mathematics, science, music, and art can provide appropriate learning opportunities (National Council for the Social Studies, 2010).

### Questions for Exploration
- What is culture?
- How are groups of people alike and different?

### Knowledge
Learners will understand:

- Culture refers to the behaviors, beliefs, values, traditions, institutions, and ways of living together of a group of people
- Concepts such as similarities and differences.

### Processes
Learners will be able to:

- Ask and find answers to questions in the context of their school and community
- Explore similarities and differences in the ways various cultural groups meet their needs.

## Products

Learners demonstrate understanding by experiences such as:

- Interviewing and reporting on observations
- Developing a description of a subculture to which they belong and have access to such as friends, school, or neighborhood
- Creating illustrations that describe what they have learned about their chosen subculture
- Role-playing what they have learned about their subculture.

## Examples of Teaching Suggestions

Suzanne found that her second graders, who came from several different countries, were puzzled as to why there were words between their languages that had similar meanings and sounded somewhat the same. She then created role-playing situations in which the children "traveled" from one group to the other, trying to understand each other's languages but changing the words to fit better into their own languages (Krogh, 1990).

### *Time, Continuity, and Change*

Young children are just beginning to understand the passage of time and the changes that can go with it. They will be laying the early foundation for a real understanding of history, a subject that is developmentally appropriate to introduce in the middle grades (National Council for the Social Studies, 2010). One way to engage young children in learning the content associated with this standard is through stories about the past. As they learn about events and developments told in story format, youngsters begin to understand differing points of view, learn about basic ethical and moral issues, and realize that multiple sources of information may present multiple versions of truth.

## Questions for Exploration
- What happened in the past?
- How do we know about the past?
- How was life in the past similar to and different from life today?

## Knowledge
Learners will understand:

- The study of the past is the story of communities, nations, and the world
- Concepts such as: past, present, future, similarity, difference, and change
- That we can learn about the past by means of stories, biographies, and interviews.

## Processes
Learners will be able to:

- Ask and find answers to questions in school and community contexts
- Use a variety of sources to answer questions about the past
- Identify examples of both continuity and changes, as depicted in stories and photographs.

## Products
Learners demonstrate understanding by:

- Drawing illustrations to show their interpretations of multiple accounts
- Using artifacts in discussions and reports
- Enacting role-plays about past events.

## Examples of Teaching Suggestions
Carol Seefeldt (2005) suggests a number of useful activities: reading books that include passage of time themes; using hourglasses and kitchen timers when completing tasks; listing things they can do toward the end of the year compared to the beginning; talking about what was learned during a project and what might be learned in the future; and using family photos to demonstrate changes over time.

### *People, Places, and Environments*
The study of people, places, and environments helps children understand the relationship between human beings and the physical world. Such study begins with personal experiences in neighborhood, town, state, and possibly more distant sites. It includes learning to make and read maps and to use globes. Understanding of and concern for the use and misuse of the environment is part of this study as well.

## Questions for Exploration
- What questions are important to ask about places on Earth?
- Where am I?
- Why do people move?
- What are the physical and human characteristics of place?
- What are similarities and differences between places near and far?
- How do people change the environment, and how does the environment influence human activity?
- How do simple geographic skills and tools help humans understand spatial relationships?

## Knowledge
Learners will understand:

- Concepts such as location, direction, distance, and scale
- Factors influencing human settlement such as availability of land, water, and places to live
- Physical changes such as seasons, climate, and weather, and their effects on plants and animals
- Tools such as maps and globes and the ways they aid in investigating relationships among people, places, and environments.

## Processes
Learners will be able to:

- Ask and find answers to geographic questions
- Investigate relationships among people, places, and environments through the use of atlases, maps, and globes
- Gather and interpret information to inform their study about both past and present.

## Products
Learners demonstrate understanding by:

- Creating illustrations and composing answers
- Constructing a map of school or community that demonstrates an understanding of relative locations, direction, boundaries, and significant physical features
- Presenting an oral report that corresponds to a picture that shows land use locally.

## Examples of Teaching Suggestions
Understanding maps in all their abstract complexity is the work of several years over the course of elementary school. One kindergarten teacher walked her class around the school building having the children note the varying shapes of its structure then make a group drawing of it. Back inside, they walked the halls, noting the various rooms and placing them appropriately inside the building's walls. The final result was, perhaps, some distance from accurate, but the class proudly placed it on a wall by the door, using their map whenever they took "trips" to the world outside their classroom.

### *Individuals, Groups, and Institutions*
"Institutions are the formal and informal political, economic, and social organizations that help us carry out, organize, and manage our daily affairs" (National Council for the Social Studies, 2010, p. 18). Young children should learn about the ways institutions affect their lives, even including the ways in which institutions' goals and activities can conflict with each other. Children also benefit from learning how institutions are created and organized to meet changing group and individual needs.

## Questions for Exploration
- To what groups do I belong?
- How do the groups to which I belong influence me, and how do I influence them?
- What are similarities and differences among individuals and groups?

## Knowledge
Learners will understand:

- Concepts such as community, culture, role, competition, cooperation, rules
- Characteristics that distinguish individuals
- That individuals, groups, and institutions share common elements and also have unique characteristics.

## Processes
Learners will be able to:

- Ask and find answers to their questions
- Describe interactions between and among individuals, groups, and institutions.

## Products
Learners demonstrate understanding by:

- Creating illustrations of ways in which school and family influence how people live their lives
- Making a collage of work roles in the community.

**Examples of Teaching Suggestions**

The school and community contain organizations that are beneficial to young children and a study of these can bring a heightened awareness of the contributions they make. At the end of this chapter are suggestions for just such a study under the title *Preprimary Experiences: Helping the Community Helpers*. As the title indicates, the focus of this study is two-way, helping children increase their awareness of the care that adults have for them as well as for the ways they can contribute to the community.

### Power, Authority, and Governance

This theme addresses the foundations of political thought and the structures of power. Young children, who are developmentally drawn to issues surrounding fairness, can learn fair ways to engage in rights and responsibilities. They can, as well, learn firsthand about various government systems and appropriate ways to resolve conflicts.

**Questions for Exploration**
- What are power and authority?
- How is power gained?
- What are the rights and responsibilities of people in a group and those in authority?
- What is government?

**Knowledge**

Learners will understand:

- Rules and laws can help keep order and protect individual rights
- Fundamental values of democracy: the common good, liberty, justice, equality, and individual dignity.

**Processes**

Learners will be able to:

- Examine issues involving rights and responsibilities
- Examine issues involving unity and diversity
- Analyze conditions and actions related to conflict and cooperation.

**Products**

Learners demonstrate understanding by:

- Preparing a list of rules to support a just classroom
- Sharing possible solutions to school problems that would require working with people in positions of authority.

**Examples of Teaching Suggestions**

Anna's kindergarten class had elected Mitchell as class "leader." His job included helping the teacher gather the children at the end of recess, leading discussions during circle time, and substituting for various jobs when those responsible were absent. One day the children came back from recess, most of them very upset because Mitchell had decided that it was his responsibility to determine who should go down the slide first, forced people into line in the order he liked best, and made sure that his best friends went first. "That's not what a good leader does!" they declared. Anna led a discussion in which the class revisited the qualities they had decided would make a good leader. During the discussion she learned that Mitchell had overstepped his job description and the class decided to do something about it. They demanded, and got, a recall election—although they hadn't known that such a thing existed. In the days to come, however, the students decided that every child should have a turn to be class leader and added that to their chart of classroom jobs.

As might be expected, Mitchell was upset and Anna spent time helping him understand how his behavior affected others and suggested some steps he could take to restore friendships. After this experience, the class as a whole understood better the ways in which power and authority could work successfully for the whole classroom community (Krogh & Groark, 2013).

### Production, Distribution, and Consumption

A major learning experience for young children is to be able to separate needs from wants. Economic decision making can be difficult at any age, but in the early years the problem is exacerbated by a very incomplete understanding of what different denominations of money are worth, of the relationship between working at a job and receiving pay for it, and of the seeming ability to simply plug a number into an ATM machine to receive whatever amount of money would be useful. Basic approaches to understanding these concepts and the interactions between them are the focus of early education.

### Questions for Exploration
- What questions are important to ask about wants, needs, goods, and services?
- Why can't people have everything that they want?
- How are goods made, delivered, and used?

### Knowledge
Learners will understand:

- The difference between needs and wants
- The characteristics and functions of money and its uses
- How people deal with scarcity of resources.

### Processes
Learners will be able to:

- Analyze the differences between wants and needs
- Evaluate how the decisions that people make are influenced by their different options.

### Products
Learners demonstrate understanding by:

- Participating in a simulated classroom economic system
- Developing a visual that illustrates strategies for distributing scarce resources in the classroom or school.

**Examples of Teaching Suggestions**
One way that teachers can help children stand up to the persistent voices of consumerism is to supply basic building materials such as large appliance cartons and varieties of blocks, and then let the children create their own activity centers. Playing store, with each child receiving equal amounts of "money" to be budgeted, helps foster economic understanding. The items to be sold might be, for example, art objects created in a center that has been supplied with donated materials and paper left over and saved from other projects. The metamorphosis of a cardboard box into an activity center has the potential to engage children in inquiry-based learning topics that lead to the natural integration of subjects and encourage the application of basic skills.

*Science, Technology, and Society*
Advances in science and technology, coupled with their influences on society, create a complex field of study. Young children can study the basic technologies that surround them in their daily lives such as telephones, televisions, cars and other modes of transport, and air conditioning and heating.

**Questions for Exploration**
- What do we mean by science and technology?
- What are wants or needs to which science and technology have been applied?
- What are examples of science and technology that have impacted individuals and society?

**Knowledge**
Learners will understand:

- Science involves the study of the natural world, and technology refers to the tools we use to accomplish tasks
- How society often turns to science and technology to solve problems.

**Processes**
Learners will be able to:

- Use diverse types of media technology to research and share information
- Identify examples of science and technology in daily life.

**Products**
Learners demonstrate understanding by:

- Researching and presenting a project that shows the influence of technology on the school or local community
- Using diverse media to show a pictorial timeline that demonstrates the development of a scientific idea over time.

**Examples of Teaching Suggestions**
Applying knowledge of technology to social issues begins with an awareness of what technology actually is, particularly as applied to young children's lives. The technology

that surrounds them includes not only televisions and computers but pencils and crayons, toilets and sinks, light bulbs, and ovens. For learning experiences, the youngest children might consider what their lives would be like if there were no writing or drawing tools, finally ending up with a writing-in-the-dirt activity. Older students can graph the amount of time spent watching television and consider alternative activities for themselves or activities children in earlier days would have used to fill their time.

## Global Connections

Today's young children travel to more parts of the globe than did previous generations. In addition, so do many of the adults in their lives, who return with interesting stories to tell. Exposure to media on a daily basis, for many or most, means that the entire wide world needs explaining to youngsters whose developmental stages are still focused on themselves. The topic of global connections is, therefore, important for teachers to consider.

### Questions for Exploration
- How are people, places, and environments connected around the globe?
- What are examples of global connections in our families and communities?

### Knowledge
Learners will understand:

- Global connections affect daily life for individuals and those around them
- All cultures have similar needs, but meet those needs in different ways.

### Processes
Learners will be able to:

- Identify examples of global connections in their community and region;
- Use maps to look for global patterns;
- Describe examples in which language, art, and music can facilitate global understanding.

### Examples of Teaching Suggestions
One of the best ways for young children to make connections globally is to meet new friends through the use of email and Skype. A teacher from Georgia, who currently teaches second grade in Seoul, South Korea, teamed with a teacher in her old school to create email/Skype friendships between their two classes. Both groups of students were a bit nervous at first about not speaking each other's language, but their teachers helped them, sometimes through songs found in both cultures and sometimes by teaching each other the names of common school objects that could be seen on line. Common greetings also became familiar and comfortable to use. The children now have high hopes of actually meeting each other one day.

## Civic Ideals and Practices

Because the central purpose of social studies is education for citizenship, this might be considered the grand finale of the NCSS themes. Identifying, and doing something about, the gaps between ideals and practices is a focus of children's civics learning. Helping to set classroom rules and expectations, and learning how to balance the interests of individuals and the group are useful experiences.

## Questions for Exploration
- What are civic ideals?
- What are civic practices?
- How can we apply civic ideals and practices at home and at school?

## Knowledge
Learners will understand:

- Concepts and ideals such as fairness, the common good, respect for rules, rights, and responsibilities
- How people can live and act together as participants in a democracy.

## Processes
Learners will be able to:

- Ask and find answers to questions about how to improve life in the school and community
- Identify and exercise the rights and responsibilities of citizens.

## Products
Learners demonstrate understanding by:

- Participating in civic discussion and action about a school issue
- Drawing illustrations of examples of civic participation.

## Examples of Teaching Suggestions
From the earliest years, there are daily opportunities for children to learn about the rights and responsibilities of citizens in their own schools and centers. For example, daily care of the classroom, including putting toys away after playing with them or helping another child clean up a spill, should be introduced by the teacher from the very beginning. Feedback from the teacher during circle time can include the benefit to the common good of such behavior, and children can share their thanks for someone who helped in a difficult situation.

As children become accustomed to caring for one another in their classroom, they can begin to look outward to the rest of the school, the community, and even the world. Teachers need to be aware that such looking outward may have unexpected consequences if children's development is not taken into account. Two kindergarten boys gave up desserts for two weeks and, with the help of their parents, calculated the savings in order to send the money to an African country where they had heard children were starving. Several weeks later, the boys were confused when news stories reported on continued famine. "But we sent the money!" they exclaimed to their teacher. On the other hand, a second grader in a small-town K–12 school single-handedly organized a drive to collect food and money for another war-torn country. His teacher and parents helped him understand that his admirable undertaking would help some, but not all, children, and he happily went forward with his plan, having a more mature understanding of what was at stake.

## THE IMPORTANCE OF PLAY

In this chapter, the importance of play has been demonstrated in several instances, most notably in the many activities shared by the Native Americans at Trudi's school and in the experiences related to Pam's class and its airplane project. In the first case, children learned about Indian culture through playful participation in beadwork, games, songs, dances, and stories. In the second case, Pam's students used the airplane as a dramatic play center, where they learned about flight technology, interesting facts about other countries, and the skills needed to run a travel agency.

Dramatic play centers offer many opportunities to engage children in social studies learning. Olivia Saracho (2012, p. 122), referencing the active learning philosophy of John Dewey, says that, "The real world can be recreated through learning centers that offer children many opportunities to learn social studies and real world concepts." She suggests dramatic play centers that can be kept up for a long period of time as well as others that would be more temporary. Those that might be of long-term interest could include: grocery store, restaurant, rocket ship, pirate ship, office, or post office.

Ideas for more temporary centers could include a collection of packing crates, each one containing materials and props for limited time use. The collection of these "prop boxes" can be expanded to "respond to the children's emerging interests" particularly after "a shared experience or a field trip" (Saracho, 2012, p. 129). Choices might be those already listed above, or such sites as card shop, beauty or barbershop, hardware store, gasoline station, toy shop, flower shop, office, or bank. As much as possible, the contents of the prop boxes should be real items from the real world rather than children's plastic imitations.

## TECHNOLOGY AND EARLY CHILDHOOD SOCIAL STUDIES

Early childhood teacher Vivian Vasquez (Vasquez & Feldermen, 2013) reports on class projects that demonstrate how the increasing availability of computer technology over time has made collaborative social activism ever more possible for classes of young children.

In the first example, which took place in the mid-1990s, Vasquez read her three to five year olds fiction and nonfiction stories about endangered species, particularly those in rainforests. Within a short period of time, the class wanted to do something to help prevent the demise of rainforests and their animals. Class discussions led to the creation of "travel trunks," simple cardboard boxes containing information and artifacts to share with other children. Technology entered the picture as fax machines alerted other classes and schools of the trunks' arrivals, as home computers could make printouts of stories and pictures, and as the Internet could be used to communicate with a few of the other classes that had Internet access. Vasquez points out that, "At the time of this project, technology was very limited. . . . Today, so much more could be done with access to high-speed Internet and the use of social networking tools for making information rapidly accessible to a broader audience" (p. 33). She uses as examples a Voice Thread or podcasting.

As an example of what more can be done with current technology, even by very young children, Vasquez cites the more recent instance of a group of pre-K youngsters in Georgia. These four year olds observed with growing frustration the increasing pollution of the river near their playground. As a way to learn more about pollution and what they might do about it, the class turned to the Internet. Here, they learned that much of the water use in their city came from toilet flushing and that this was a potential source of pollution. It was also on the Internet that the teacher and children learned of an easily created device for toilet flushing using less water. Following online instructions, they were able to make these from empty plastic readymade-icing containers that could be filled with rocks. These young social activists collaborated on using the Internet as a "tool for change" and to work toward "a more sustainable community" (p. 34).

## ASSESSMENT AND EVALUATION

In her suggestions for working with the NCSS standards, Carol Seefeldt (2005) listed four ways that teachers can assess social studies learning: observe, interview, assign a task to perform, and analyze children's work. These and others follow. If review would be helpful, they are all described more fully in Chapter 3.

### Observation

- As children explore the earth's surface, learn about maps, investigate their neighborhoods, and interview interesting people, note their vocabulary. Is it expanding? Are there terms you need to introduce? Do the youngsters understand the words they are using?
- As children solve problems related to riding, walking, running, and building, observe their increasing skills. What seems to motivate them working alone or together? Consider possible scaffolding interventions.
- Notice children's outside play with maps—how they use rocks, drawings in the dirt using sticks, and so on, to create maps.

### Interview

- Ask individual children to name different surfaces of the earth and other social studies vocabulary. Note the results on their individual records for further interactions.
- As you interview, also note how accurate the children's understandings are.

### Assign a Task to Perform

- Ask children to draw a map of their play yard.
- Provide children with your own hand-drawn map of the play yard or nearby site. See if they can find landmarks you have included.

### Analyze Children's Work

- Note children's drawings of themselves at various times throughout the school year. See if they increase in their use of details, realism, and completeness.
- Examine spontaneous drawings of maps and analyze in the same ways.

## PREPRIMARY EXPERIENCES TO ENCOURAGE DEMOCRACY: CITIZENS OF THE CLASSROOM

If teachers want young children to begin learning the lessons of citizenship, and if they believe that children learn best by being active social scientists rather than passive recipients of information, then children must be given some firsthand experiences in democracy. This section offers helpful ideas that have been successfully introduced to even the youngest students.

A good place to begin is to consider the roles of teachers. In a democratically oriented classroom, teachers embrace:

- *A teaching style that is facilitative rather than directive:* If teachers simply tell children what to do, they will never learn to make decisions, and decision making is what democracy is all about.
- *Teacher modeling of appropriate behavior:* If teachers treat others (children, teachers, parents, principal) in a democratic fashion, the children will usually imitate their behavior.
- *Teacher trust:* Teachers must trust children to help care for the environment, to direct at least some of their own learning, to make some of their own rules, and to accept the consequences.
- *Teacher acceptance of the children's mistakes:* Democracy, even at the adult level, is always an experiment, a society in transition. Mistakes must be allowed.
- *Treating children with dignity:* This means practicing the Golden Rule. Unless teachers want to be treated condescendingly, talked down to, or disciplined imperiously, they should not do the same to their children.

The following experiences might be considered a yearlong unit. It is important that young children be introduced to them over time as they gain the necessary skills. It is equally important that children earn the right to freedom, democracy, and independence. To help them achieve each of these, teachers should introduce them gradually and in steps rather than all at once. Figure 9.5 displays the web for these preprimary activities.

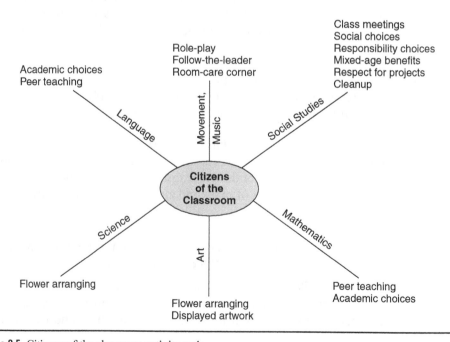

**Figure 9.5** Citizens of the classroom activity web.

### Care of the Environment

A concerned citizen is one who is aware of the environment and works to keep it healthy. Very young children can develop environmental awareness in their own classroom.

### Room-Care Corner

Have materials available for cleaning and polishing every surface possible. Nontoxic materials include hand lotion for wood polish and a tiny bit of vinegar in a large amount of water for glass or metal cleaning spray. Have a bag handy for dirty rags. A laundry tub can be used for washing the rags. Each of these cleanup activities can have its own box or basket with a descriptive label on the container and a matching one at its place on the shelf.

### Flower Arranging

Have available assorted garden flowers and greens and junior baby food jars to use as vases. Have children arrange, add water, and place where they desire to enhance the room's beauty.

### Cleanup

When introducing any new material, demonstrate specifically where it should be put. Stress the idea that putting materials away is simply the closing step of any activity, whether done alone or in a group.

### Follow the Leader

Using recorded music, lead the class on tiptoe or walk through the room—in and out of the furniture and around whatever materials are out. There is one rule: Don't touch anything. Conclude by pointing out the need to move carefully through the classroom at all times to avoid damaging property or disrupting activities. This game should be played the very first week of school, and every day for a few minutes. Soon, children will begin to move gracefully through the room on their own, taking care not to damage objects in their way.

### Displayed Artwork

If children want to leave their work at school, let them choose where they would like to hang it, when feasible. Their choices may not be the same as an adult's, but the children will enjoy the beauty they have created themselves.

### Care of One Another

A responsible citizen is one who cares about others and helps them when they are in need, or can determine when to help them help themselves. Awareness of others is a major step out of egocentrism and toward responsible citizenship.

### Respect for Others' Activities

After playing follow the leader, communicate daily the need to walk around, not over, each other's project, blocks, or toys. Say out loud, "I'm walking around your castle, Ricardo, so I won't hurt it."

### Peer Teaching

Make a personal chart of at least one thing each child has superior ability in. (Everybody has something.) Make sure all children have an opportunity to teach something to someone else. When children come to you for help in almost anything, try to find a child who can help instead. Encourage children to ask each other for help.

## Mixed-Age Benefits

If there is more than one age in the class, take advantage of it. Give children increasing responsibility for each other as they get older, and lead younger children to expect and ask for help from the more mature.

## Role-Play

When particular conflicts or irritations with each other are not quickly solved, try creating a story line that is similar to the classroom problem but removed sufficiently to avoid embarrassment. One good choice is to make the characters woodland animals dealing with a disagreement. Provide the actors with the situation, and then let them act out the plot, creating their own resolution to the situation. Finally, interview each character about the way things turned out and how they feel about it. The next time the conflict arises in the classroom, you can refer back to the role-play as a springboard to discussion.

## Making Choices and Decisions

While any society imposes some restrictions, a democracy has the fewest. Competent citizens know how to make knowledgeable and thoughtful choices, but this takes practice and it is never too early to start. Begin by offering the very youngest just two choices. Over time expand so that finally you can say, "What would you like to do this morning?" and the children will not feel overwhelmed.

## Academic Choices

When possible, give children limited choices. "Would you like to do this math game first and then go out and play, or would you like to play a short time before doing the math?" Another option is, "Would you like to play this math game or the one on the shelf?"

## Responsibility Choices

If there is work to be done, and it is not clearly one person's responsibility, give choices such as, "Would you like to help put blocks away or clean up the housekeeping corner?"

## Social Choices

Young children need to be given the choice of working and playing alone or with other children. They should also be allowed to choose between finishing what they are doing and joining the larger group for another activity. (Too often in our pressured schools children aren't given time to feel the satisfaction of finishing a task or enjoyable activity.) Try giving the occasional holdout the opportunity to work alone provided she or he does not disturb the rest of the class. If the whole-group activity is attractive enough, the child will either soon join everyone else or will continue working on the preferred project while watching (or singing or reciting) what the class is doing.

## Class Meetings

"Town meetings" in all their varieties are more successful when the participants have had practice in the appropriate skills. In preschool these meetings should be short, purposeful, and usually teacher-directed. The following guidelines are appropriate:

- With children participating, set up at the very beginning only two or three rules pertaining to taking turns, listening courteously, and so on.

- If all the meetings have the same general purpose, follow a set pattern or sequence of events.
- When a child behaves in a way that is against the rules, try simply repeating the rule or, better, ask the child to repeat the rule out loud.
- If the above steps are followed in a structured manner, children will soon begin to mimic the teacher's role. Children of kindergarten age may then be able to run their meeting without adult help. Rehearse the rituals with them first, and in the beginning choose the most mature to run the meetings. Try "working" a short distance away in case the need for help arises.

## PRIMARY EXPERIENCES: HELPING THE COMMUNITY HELPERS

Traditionally, children have studied their community during the primary years, usually in the first and second grades. Developmentally, this is an appropriate step out from the self-focus of the earlier years, and there are so many facets to learning about the community that it is a natural choice for applying the concepts of an integrated curriculum.

It is important for children to learn who in the community is there to help them. In the unit presented here, one addition to the traditional topic has been made. Because education for citizenship means encouraging children toward independence and self-confidence, it seems a bit shortsighted to study only the helpfulness of the helpers. Rather, it is important to find ways, even minor ways, that children can help the helpers.

In this unit, the community starts within the school and home and works outward. It can be taught in its entirety, or a few helpers may be chosen from the larger list. Since the list given here is designed to be representative, not exhaustive, others can certainly be added. Many of the activities are integrated with the rest of the curriculum (Figure 9.6). Each activity begins with a few suggested questions to get the class thinking about the designated helper. Children should be encouraged to add others of their own.

### *Helpers and Related Activities*
#### *School Custodian*

##### *Questions*

- How does the custodian help our classroom? The school?
- How can we assist the custodian to make his or her work easier?
- What tools does the custodian use? Which are adaptable to us?

##### *Experiences*

- *Custodian's talk:* Invite the custodian to class to demonstrate tools, describe his or her responsibilities, and suggest ways children can help.
- *Daily cleanup:* Incorporate custodian's suggestions into daily cleanup routine.
- *School tour:* Tour school to identify results of custodian's work and places class could volunteer to help.

#### *Parent Responsible for Primary Housekeeping Responsibilities*
##### *Questions*

- What jobs must be done to keep the home functioning smoothly?
- Which jobs are essential on a regular basis and which are done only occasionally?

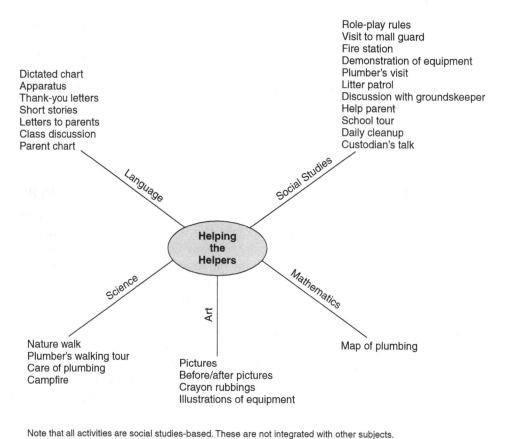

Role-play rules
Visit to mall guard
Fire station
Demonstration of equipment
Plumber's visit
Litter patrol
Discussion with groundskeeper
Help parent
School tour
Daily cleanup
Custodian's talk

Dictated chart
Apparatus
Thank-you letters
Short stories
Letters to parents
Class discussion
Parent chart

Language

Social Studies

Helping the Helpers

Science

Art

Mathematics

Nature walk
Plumber's walking tour
Care of plumbing
Campfire

Pictures
Before/after pictures
Crayon rubbings
Illustrations of equipment

Map of plumbing

Note that all activities are social studies-based. These are not integrated with other subjects.

**Figure 9.6** Helping the helpers activity web.

- What happens if the jobs are not done?
- Which jobs affect us (the children) directly?
- What jobs can we safely help with?

## Experiences

- *Parent chart:* Have a visit from a parent. List on a chart the jobs that need doing in the home. Discuss ways these are best done and ways children could help.
- *Class discussion:* Back at school, discuss the relevance of the trip to our own lives.
  - What new ways can we help in our own homes?
  - What will happen if the jobs we've helped with aren't done?
- *Letters to parents:* Children write letters to their own parents volunteering specific help with something they haven't done before at home and/or asking for suggestions for ways they can help.
- *Pictures:* Illustrate our experiences at the house.
- *Short stories:* Write short stories to accompany the pictures.
- *Class discussion:* In a class discussion, compare upkeep requirements of school to home. Consider new cleanup and care assignments.

*Groundskeeper at Public Park*

## Questions

- How does caring for the outdoors differ from caring for the school?
- How does the groundskeeper help maintain the natural environment? The playground area? The more formal gardens?
- How can children best help keep the park clean and useful?

## Experiences

- *Nature walk:* Go on a nature walk that includes identification of natural elements and human-made intrusions.
- *Discussion with groundskeeper:* Discuss with groundskeeper his or her responsibilities and ways children can help.
- *Litter patrol:* Hold a litter patrol as a class project.
  - *Before/after pictures:* Draw before and after pictures of litter patrol
  - *Crayon rubbings:* Make crayon rubbings of leaves and of paper-type litter.
- *Thank-you letters:* Write a thank-you letter to the groundskeeper that includes ways the class intends to help.

*Plumber*

## Questions

- For which repairs is a plumber responsible?
- What are the basic workings of a plumbing system?
- What are the necessary tools and how are they used?
- What are some ways we can help the plumber?

## Experiences

- *Plumber's visit:* Invite a plumber to visit either the school or a home of one of the children.
- *Plumber's walking tour:* Take a walking tour and have plumber point out pipes and outlets.
- *Demonstration of equipment:* Demonstrate the tools and give children an opportunity to try some out.
- *Care of plumbing:* Ask plumber to discuss proper care of plumbing apparatus including problems caused by introduction of foreign objects.
- *Apparatus:* Using a resource book such as *What Makes It Go, Work and Fly?* make models of plumbing apparatus from materials on hand.
- *Map of plumbing:* Create a map of the school (or student's house), and draw in the plumbing operation.
- *Thank-you letters:* Write a thank-you letter to plumber that includes awareness of ways in which children can help.

*Firefighter*

## Questions

- What different functions does the fire department carry out?

- What are the tools and equipment necessary for each function?
- In what ways can we help the fire department?

### Experiences

- *Campfire:* In an outdoor, sandy area of the building, demonstrate the way fire spreads easily from paper to leaves to sticks. Discuss: What would happen if sand did not surround this? If we were to blow on it or a strong wind came up? Why must we be extremely careful around fires? And not start them ourselves? How do we call for help if we see a fire?
- *Fire station:* Make a visit to a fire station.
- *Demonstration of equipment:* Thoroughly inspect each type of vehicle to see how its equipment works.
- *Class discussion:* Discuss with a firefighter, or representative, ways we can help prevent fires. Review the procedures for calling for help.
- *Thank-you letters:* Write a thank-you letter that includes a list of ways we can help.
- *Illustrations of equipment:* Make illustrations of equipment and written descriptions of their function.

## Mall Guard

### Questions

- How does the guard help us if we are lost or frightened?
- How do we locate a guard? Who else can help us in an emergency?
- What can we do to make the guard's job easier?

### Experiences

- *Visit to mall guard:* Visit a guard in the office at a mall. Actually walk through the steps to take if you are lost.
- *Role-play rules:* Role-play safety rules to follow at a mall, such as staying with parents or others in charge.
- *Dictated chart:* Have the class dictate the suggestions for items above and write them on a chart.

### Inquiry Projects That Might Emerge From These Experiences

As young learners engage in the various social studies experiences listed in this chapter, they might become sufficiently interested in one or more aspects of an activity to justify a child-designed project based on inquiry. When considering a topic for an in-depth, inquiry-based study that will be conducted by children, a discerning teacher is alert to the criteria that make a topic worthy of study.

Will the study of the topic:

- Build on what children already know?
- Offer hands-on relevance to the children?
- Encourage application of social and academic skills?
- Integrate subjects by interconnecting and weaving them, with the goal of furthering student understanding of the topic?
- Support transference of knowledge to future learning?

With these criteria in mind, we offer the following possibilities of topics that might develop into child-centered, inquiry-based learning projects. Each suggested topic area would be appropriate for preprimary as well as primary students, as each age of young learners will not only bring their own level of understanding to the proposed topics but also carry out investigations as developmentally appropriate to their skill level.

- A tool used by an adult worker might pique the students' interest. For example, an in-depth study of brooms might reveal the great variety of brooms, how brooms are made, brooms and sweeping implements of various cultures, as well as the evolution of such implements. Children might experiment with making their own brooms.
- Specialized clothing worn by adult workers could launch in-depth studies on hats, gloves, or boots. For example, an inquiry-based study on hats might show the different materials from which hats are made as well as how they are made, why workers tend to wear certain hats, work hats from various cultures, and protective hats that children wear.
- Flower arranging might lead to an inquiry project on how plants and flowers grow or perhaps develop into explorations of the various tools and equipment florists, gardeners, and farmers use to help them grow.

Remember: A wide variety of topics worthy of in-depth study present themselves when teachers are keenly aware of their students' interests. When turned into a topic of inquiry-based study, these interests can be used to sensibly and meaningfully integrate the curriculum.

## THE POWER OF INQUIRY LEARNING THROUGH INTEGRATION

Theory, research, and practice all indicate that social studies for young children will be most effective if based on, but not confined to, their immediate lives. Yet, in today's world of omnipresent media exposure with its resulting influences from across the globe, it is not possible to follow a pattern of social studies that begins with "all about me," moves on to "the community," and finally "the world." However, this spiral model can still provide the frame of reference for young children, who are, after all, "all about me." When they learn about what is happening around the world, for example, the relationship of events to themselves can be emphasized.

It is important, also, that teaching methodologies do not require young children to simply be recipients of preordained facts but, instead, permit them to be social investigators themselves—geographers, historians, economists, and anthropologists. This has been the call from social studies experts since the early days of the 20th century when Lucy Sprague Mitchell wrote her seminal book, *Young Geographers* (1934). When "young geographers" inquire about their world, they learn what maps are and how to create them, they map territories both familiar and new, and they investigate creatures—human and otherwise—who inhabit the terrain. It is as if they are explorers discovering new lands for the first time, a far more effective way to scaffold their understanding than having them simply hear or read about maps and new lands.

Woven together and applied to the early years, the various social sciences, when integrated with other subjects, can be adapted in such a way that the long-range goal will be to help create effective citizens. In our culture, this means creating citizens who will feel at home in the very demanding society called a democracy.

## TO DISCUSS

1. In a small group of colleagues list social studies subjects you feel less prepared to teach. Discuss what could, or should, be done to make you more knowledgeable in order to teach young children.
2. Make a list of all subjects included in the social studies. Then, consider how experiences in each might help in the education of young children for citizenship in today's democratic society. Introducing democracy into the classroom will be slightly different for different ages of children. Make a group chart that reserves a space for each age group and/or grade. Then discuss age-appropriate ways that children can take on more responsibilities of democratic citizenship.

## TO DO

1. If you are a teacher or if you are student teaching, look at your lesson plans for the current week. List as many places as you can find that would benefit from the addition of a social studies learning. Try to follow through on at least two of them.
2. Observe your own class or one you work with. List ways in which a more democratic atmosphere could be created. Try one or two of these ways on a temporary basis, with teacher permission if appropriate. If the children are old enough, poll them for their responses to the change. Take notes that include successes and difficulties. Discuss these with other classmates or teachers.

## NOTE

* Terms to describe the descendants of the earliest North Americans vary, the descendants themselves often disagreeing about the best choice. Generally accepted terms include American Indians, Native Americans, Indians, native people, or indigenous people (Nieto & Bode, 2012).

## REFERENCES

Bauer, D. (1979). As children see it. In Yamamoto, K., (Ed.), *Children in time and space*. New York, NY: Teachers College Press.

Derman-Sparks, L. (1989). *Anti-bias curriculum: Tools for empowering young children*. Washington, DC: NAEYC.

Derman-Sparks, L. & Edwards, J. (2010). *Anti-bias curriculum for young children and ourselves*. Washington, DC: NAEYC.

Goldberg, S. (2010). Preface. *National curriculum standards for social studies*. Silver Spring, MD: National Council for the Social Studies.

Hallahan, D. & Kauffman, J. (1988). *Exceptional children: Introduction to special education* (4th ed.). Englewood Cliffs, NJ: Prentice-Hall.

Herczog, M. (2010). Using the NCSS national curriculum standards for social studies: A framework for teaching, learning, and assessment to meet state social studies standards. *Social Education*, 74 (4), 217–222.

Heward, W. (2013). *Exceptional children: An introduction to special education* (10th ed.). Boston, MA: Pearson.

Katz, P. (1976). The acquisition of racial attitudes in children. In *Towards the elimination of racism*. New York, NY: Pergamon.

Krogh, S. (1990). Studying the Romans and their language: Second graders create their own curriculum. *International Schools Journal*, 20, 17–25.

Krogh, S. & Groark, C. (2013). *A bridge to the classroom and early care: A capstone*. San Diego, CA: Bridgestone Education.

Mindes, G. (2005). Social studies in today's early childhood curricula. *Beyond the Journal: Young Children on the Web*, September, 1–8.

Mitchell, L. (1934). *Young geographers*. New York, NY: Bank Street College of Education.

Montessori, M. (1969/1949). *The absorbent mind*. Kal, India: Kalakshetra Publications.

Morehouse, P. (1995). The building of an airplane (with a little help from friends). *Educational Leadership*, 52 (8), 56–57.

National Council for the Social Studies. (1989). Social studies for early childhood and elementary school children: Preparing for the 21st century. *Social Education*, 53 (1), 14–23.

National Council for the Social Studies. (1994). *Curriculum standards for social studies: Expectations of excellence*. Washington, DC: NCSS.

National Council for the Social Studies (2010). *National curriculum standards for social studies: A framework for teaching, learning, and assessment*. Atlanta, GA: NCSS Publications.

Nieto, S. & Bode, P. (2012). *Affirming diversity: The sociopolitical context of multicultural education*. Boston, MA: Pearson.

Pagano, A. (Ed.). (1978). Social studies in early childhood: An interactionist point of view. *NCSS Bulletin 58*. Washington, DC: NCSS.

Paley, V. (1991). Foreword. In *Starting small: Teaching tolerance in preschool and the early grades*. Montgomery, AL: Southern Poverty Law Center.

Pascopella, A. (2005). Staying alive: Social studies in elementary schools. *Social Studies and the Young Learner*, 17 (3), 30–32.

Piaget, J. (1965/1932). *The moral judgment of the child*. London, UK: K. Paul, Trench, Trubner.

Piaget, J. (1969). *The child's conception of time*. London, UK: Routledge & Kegan Paul.

Salmon, M., McConnell, S., Sainato, K., & Morrison, R. (2013). Using puppets in the early childhood classroom. In Heward, W. (Ed.), *Exceptional children: An introduction to special education* (10th ed.). Boston, MA: Pearson.

Saracho, O. (2012). *An integrated play-based curriculum for young children*. New York, NY: Routledge.

Seefeldt, C. (2005). *How to work with standards in the early childhood classroom*. New York, NY: Teachers College Press.

Seefeldt, C., Castle, S., & Falconer, R. (2010). *Social studies for the preschool/primary child* (8th ed.). Boston, MA: Merrill.

Southern Poverty Law Center (SPLC). (1991). *Teaching tolerance project*. Montgomery, AL: SPLC.

Vasquez, V. & Felderman, C. (2013). *Technology and critical literacy in early childhood*. New York, NY: Routledge.

# 10

## MUSIC, DRAMATIC PLAY, AND DRAMA

*All children are musical and their musical development is largely dependent*
*on the musical environment they are provided from infancy.*
—Susan H. Kenney

*Role-playing is an activity within which the child becomes oriented towards*
*the most universal, the most fundamental meanings of human activity.*
—Daniil Borisovich El'Konin

After reading this chapter you should be able to:

- Explain the importance of including music, dramatic play, and drama in the early childhood classroom;
- Describe some historical background and models for teaching;
- Share ideas that integrate these subjects with one another and with other areas of the curriculum;
- Explain how music, dramatic play, and drama can be incorporated into inquiry learning.

Music and dramatic play are typically found in early childhood centers, preschools, and kindergartens. In the primary grades, however, as school becomes viewed as a more serious undertaking, both music and dramatic play begin to disappear. Music is often relegated to formal theatrical experiences, and informal dramatic play is often only seen during outside recess. In recent years, even the recesses themselves have begun to disappear.

In this chapter, we incorporate music with both dramatic play and the more formal theatre-style production in our discussion because, in some respects, they can all be regarded as part of a continuum of development. In other words, the very natural role-play that emerges in the early years can be expanded and directed toward more mature experiences. At the same time, providing older children with opportunities to continue informal role-play experiences remains important. Music, dramatic play, and drama foster children's intellectual, social, and emotional growth. When combined with movement, as they often are, motor development is fostered as well. Providing appropriate experiences to encourage creativity in music and dramatic play in a crowded curriculum can be a challenge for teachers, but it can be possible when these, as well as the other arts, are integrated into academic subjects. To demonstrate, we begin with a second-grade experience. Note how Suzanne, the teacher in this case, found that what she did with the children actually took no extra time from the curricular demands of the day.

## THE CREATION OF A PRIMARY GRADE MUSICAL PLAY

Suzanne was presented with an opportunity to use music and drama to deal with classroom conflicts when one of her second graders suggested that such an approach might be helpful. His idea, to help address the classroom conflicts, was to make up a play, complete with songs. Perhaps, he thought, the class might want to perform the play for other classes or maybe even for their parents. Most of the other children agreed, and the entire class made suggestions for plot and characters based on their own problems getting along with one another. As the discussion proceeded, Suzanne thought that this would be an excellent opportunity for the children to try some creative writing, but they rejected the idea. Possibly because most of the children were English language learners, they preferred to "commission" their teacher to do the actual writing, based on the student-supplied rough outline of the story. The class decided that Suzanne would write a first draft and then submit it for full-class approval. Because she wanted this to be their play and not hers, Suzanne readily agreed to the children's model of what the creative process should look like.

The resulting musical play, titled *The Friendly Forest*, included a group of animals living in a magical place where everyone was a friend to everyone else, even to animals they might ordinarily choose as their lunch. A human, named Mr. Mean, suddenly intrudes on the idyllic setting, trying many tricks to alter the friendly atmosphere, and, for the first time, the animals become suspicious of and accusatory toward one another. As the plot progresses, the animals learn to overcome their distrust of each other and reject Mr. Mean's attempts at disharmony. Eventually, all ends happily. The animals even choose to reject the notion of getting even with Mr. Mean in favor of converting him to their friendly way of living.

Is there time for such a musical diversion in a primary-grade classroom when there are so many expectations to be met? To Suzanne's way of thinking, the time spent on the play probably took no longer than would have been required to use more usual classroom management and discipline techniques for dealing with the group's developing disharmony. While the children learned the play, and for many weeks afterward, all that was necessary when arguments and heated conflicts erupted was to say something like, "Has Mr. Mean come back? Is that who I'm hearing?" and a Friendly Forest mood would return. Parents and other adults even noted the amiable tone that resonated outside of the classroom.

In addition, there was meaningful coverage of several curricular areas during this time. Here are some examples.

### Language

This was a play to be read, memorized, and presented. Children learning English found that singing some parts was easier than speaking. The play also helped English language learners memorize grammar patterns and potentially generalize them to other situations in the learning environment.

### Art

The scenery was simple but quite charming. It consisted of just a couple large trees that the children designed, cut out, and painted. Student-made costumes depicting each character were made of poster board, fastened together, painted front and back, and designed to go over the young actors' and actresses' heads.

### Social Studies

The theme of the play was friendship, conflict resolution, and cooperation. The production of the play, including role assignment decisions, required the kind of cooperation and friendship espoused by the plot. Because the play's theme was a part of the children's real lives, this was done with occasional difficulty, but a satisfying end product was obtained.

### Music

The play's theme song was the traditional "The More We Get Together (the happier we'll be)." In addition, Suzanne relied on melodies from other typical children's songs and then altered the words, with the children's help, to fit the plot.

### Drama

Through kindergarten and even first grade, it is generally more appropriate to provide children with dramatic play opportunities, in which they act out stories using their own individual creativity. By second grade, however, the more mature structure of a real play can be quite enticing and seemed to be so for this class. This kind of developmental difference will be discussed later in this chapter.

### Math

The play itself did not offer obvious mathematics opportunities. However, Suzanne created math story problems based on the characters and scenery of the play. Children could solve the problems on their own, but they were also encouraged to work in pairs or small groups, reinforcing the values of cooperation and group harmony advocated by the play.

## WHY MUSIC, DRAMATIC PLAY, AND DRAMA MATTER: A BRIEF HISTORY

### Why Music

The importance of music in our lives is affirmed by its designation as one of the seven intelligences proposed by Howard Gardner (1983). Further, music is likely to be part of our lives, from early childhood through old age. Today's society, according to one writer,

assumes certain musical behavior from all of us throughout our adult lives. We are expected to dance at weddings, cheer at sporting events while clapping hands in time with the crowd, sing "Happy Birthday" to friends and relatives, or share a lullaby with an infant . . . the success of our musical experiences may depend on the musical nurturing we received during our preschool years. (Feierabend, 1991, p. 75)

"Musical nurturing" in the early years and beyond has been done for a variety of purposes, which have changed over the decades and centuries as the needs and interests of society and culture have changed. Today, we see it as a way for children to express creativity, engage in performance, learn about other cultures as well as their own, push the limits of their potential, and even demonstrate in-school capabilities that they can't show otherwise due to developmental delays or lack of English. Looking back over time, however, we see that most of these benefits were historically not a consideration.

The Pilgrims and the Puritans brought with them an enjoyment for music, primarily devoted to religious purposes. A hundred years after their arrival however, Cotton Mather, a socially and politically influential Puritan minister, used his rigid religious views to bring such enjoyment to a close. By this time, music had become largely secularized and included dancing, a development he decried (Keene, 1982). Due, in part, to Mather's influence, singing schools now focused on teaching young and old how to sing psalms more effectively. Throughout the 18th century these schools retained their popularity, providing a major source of music training for everyone.

As towns and cities flourished, music education continued to grow in importance. For example, in 18th-century Philadelphia there were fashionable boarding schools that educated "young ladies" in dancing, singing, and the playing of instruments. By the next century, some attempts were made to introduce music into the public schools, but there were critics and the going was rocky.

Nevertheless, throughout the 19th century, schools did begin to incorporate music, and a philosophical argument began that sounds much like the arguments that accompany the philosophies of reading. Should children learn many songs just for enjoyment and then, much later, learn the mechanics of reading the notes and other symbols? Or should they first learn the tools and how to use them before learning to sing? The arguments on both sides continue today. By 1864, the first series of singing books for younger schoolchildren had been published and several others followed soon after.

The 20th century brought first the mechanical player piano and then the phonograph into the schools, thus making music appreciation possible as a course of study. Younger children were given little instruction in what they were listening to and were simply left to be entertained. In 1920, however, the book *Music Appreciation for Little Children* was published by Victor Co. to give teachers direction in helping small children learn to experience and to love music. The book's philosophy clearly was on the side of those who present music first for enjoyment and later for skills learning: "Children should hear music long before they are asked to master the symbols of the printed form, the rules of grammar of its language, or the techniques of its performance" (quoted in Keene, 1982, p. 257).

This argument was echoed by Carl Orff in Germany in the middle years of the century. He felt that too many young children learned to play instruments without ever having experienced music. The system of music education he developed was imported to this country and continues to influence the music education of young children (Saracho, 2012).

Rhythm was Orff's starting point, and it grew out of children's speech patterns: "For the child, as for primitive man, speaking and singing, music and movement cannot be isolated" (Keene, 1982, p. 343). Percussion instruments were to be used along with body movements. Children worked in groups and were introduced to basic instruments such as drums, cymbals, and water-filled musical glasses. Orff himself composed melodies largely to traditional nursery rhymes and songs. Creativity was an important part of music education, and children were expected to integrate their music making with poetry movement, playing, and dancing—all part of children's natural activities.

From Hungary came another imported method for teaching music to young children. Zoltán Kodály (Koh-dye) held many beliefs that were similar to Orff's, but he was influenced more strongly by his country's highly academic, structured educational system. Rather than beginning children's training with Orff's playful music experiences, Kodály preferred to start their education with national folk songs. He was inspired to do this after hearing student teachers in a university preparing songs to teach to their elementary children. He considered their selections insipid and shallow and determined that instead children should be exposed to their rich national heritage. When his method was introduced in the United States, he suggested that the 40,000 folk songs available in the Library of Congress would be a generous source.

Hungarian children begin their music training in preschool, and Kodály believed that their best curriculum would be movement and singing games. As soon as children were ready, reading and writing of musical notation should be introduced. The method, although structured, is simplified in its presentation and uses role-play, pictures, and body movements.

Although both Kodály and Orff sought to make use of the natural development and interests of small children, they approached training in opposite directions. Orff argued for much experience with music before symbols were introduced; Kodály felt that even very young children could learn notation if taught properly (Saracho, 2012). In theory and in practice, both methods have much to recommend them, and the two are sufficiently compatible that ideas from both could be used in one classroom. Books devoted to the two systems are usually available from music curriculum offices and can be adapted for use by regular classroom teachers.

A third approach to young children's music emerged at the turn of the 20th century, was ignored for a while, and has regained a small amount of popularity. It was begun in Switzerland by Émile Jaques-Dalcroze and demonstrates, perhaps best of all the approaches, the efficacy of integrating movement and music. He was in agreement with his countryman from the century before, Heinrich Pestalozzi, that music's power to evoke feelings made it a desirable course of study for young children. And he agreed with Pestalozzi that the "purpose of education was to foster the harmonious development of moral, physical, and mental capability" (Brown, 1987, p. 89). Dalcroze, in applying this philosophy to music for the young, stressed the importance of integrating music with rhythm and body movement, thus focusing on educating the whole person.

The Dalcroze eurythmics (Greek for "good rhythm") begins in preschool with relaxed listening, the playing of singing games, and acting out the musical accompaniments of stories. As children get older, they coordinate body movement, ear training, and improvisation at the piano. The Dalcroze philosophy is that there is a "coordination of brain, nerves, and muscles when the child responds with physical actions to musical stimuli.

This then creates a greater depth of feeling and sensitivity to music" (Bayless & Ramsey, 1978, p. 171).

A final approach to teaching music to young children comes from Japan. Shinichi Suzuki, son of Japan's first violin factory owner, developed a system he called *talent education*. Its philosophy was that very young children could learn music in the same way they learn their mother tongue: by observation, imitation, repetition, and increasing intellectual awareness (Mark & Gary, 1999). Americans first became aware of Suzuki's method in the late 1950s when a film was made of 750 Japanese children playing a Bach concerto on small-scale violins. It soon became known that Japanese four and five year olds were able to play with great skill while American children generally didn't begin learning violin until the end of elementary school. Since that time, occasional public schools have adopted the Suzuki method, but it is more readily seen in private schools or specific Suzuki music schools. As applied to early childhood education, it may be worthwhile to reflect on the fact that very young children are capable of making music at a much higher level than typically thought possible, particularly if it is presented to them in the same natural way they learn language.

### Why Dramatic Play and Drama

Although drama, unlike music, has not been designated a specific intelligence, it does call upon most of the intelligences proposed by Howard Gardner's theory (1991). Whether children are engaged in informal dramatic play or presenting more formally to an audience, they draw on such intelligences as interpersonal (negotiating with others such considerations as plot and staging or reaching out to an audience), intrapersonal (thinking about their own roles), kinesthetic (block building, dancing, or other role-play related activities), spatial (creating scenery, planning stage sets, or presenting a play to an audience), and language (almost always required to keep the plot moving, whether created for the occasion or memorized more formally). In addition, drama experiences can also foster the musical intelligence, as part of a structured theatrical presentation or during informal dramatic play such as when a child plays the role of a mother singing to her baby.

For some historical perspective, we can turn to a discussion of medieval children and their choices of games and toys. In a work designed to belie the misconception that there was no such thing as childhood in those days, Nicholas Orme (2001) has the reader consider a complex painting by Pieter Bruegel from 1559. Titled "Children's Games," the painting depicts about 200 children playing more than 75 games. Close inspection of the painting reveals that many of these consist of boys and girls engaging in dramatic play, imitating the lives of the older generation. Upon reflection, it might be assumed that young children have always engaged in such imitation, and here is one of the first major depictions of such natural behavior. There was not yet, however, an understanding that dramatic play should be part of the education of young children.

When, in the mid-19th century, Friedrich Froebel created the kindergarten, he determined that he should harness this natural activity, calling play the work of the young child (Brosterman, 1997). Yet, free, dramatic play was not on the list of activities he created or sanctioned for his classrooms. Rather, most of them were adult interpretations of what were perceived to be enjoyable activities for the three to five year olds the kindergarten served.

In the United States, the early 20th century brought a child study movement that redefined play so that it was more open and free. With the advent of John Dewey's work at about the same time, dramatic play in early childhood education made its formal, documented appearance. Materials in dramatic play centers typically reflected home and community life. In recent years however, with the fixation on goals and evaluation, many centers and classrooms have forsaken the need to provide dramatic play areas. Such loss has been decried by those writing about the early Dewey laboratory school (Tanner, 1997). Schools for young children today

> are missing the opportunities presented by young children's natural interests in the basic activities of the home that involve food, clothing, and shelter. The idea that these activities and interests are actually the roots from which organized knowledge can grow has simply become lost. To be sure, children's dramatic play is seen by many teachers as a means of language development or a way of teaching science concepts, but Dewey's conception concerned the curriculum in its totality. (p. 28)

As Tanner wrote, acknowledgment of the importance of dramatic play for young children is no longer as prevalent as it once was, although it can still be found in some kindergartens and most preschools. Early childhood theorists, philosophers, and researchers continue to find the many benefits of including dramatic play in early

**Figure 10.1** By engaging in dramatic play in the hospital they constructed, after doing inquiry-based research on hospital rooms, these youngsters are applying many curricular skills.

childhood education. As one researcher has said, children's "sociodramatic play is a powerful, collaborative learning opportunity that may influence their social competence, language development, cognitive development, and creative fluency. When young children engage in sociodramatic play, they participate in oral playwriting. They serve as audience, voice, and oral co-editors of one another" (Fromberg, 2002, p. 35). So powerful and age appropriate is dramatic play for young children, according to this well-regarded early childhood specialist, that it should continue through the primary grades as well. This is a view that is not widely accepted today and seldom seen in American elementary schools. Instead, current education systems focus on meeting standards in the primary grades, and dramatic play generally disappears, replaced, if at all, by formal theatrical performances at designated holidays or seasonal festivities.

## MUSIC, DRAMATIC PLAY, DRAMA, AND CHILD DEVELOPMENT

Again, this chapter separates the two subjects for the purpose of explanation. In this case, it is because developmental differences at different ages lead to varying implications for teaching. Although physical development is discussed in other chapters, it will be referred to here as well, because rhythm and movement are such an important part of our understanding and enjoyment of music.

### *Music and Child Development*
#### *Infants Through Age Two*

Between three and six months of age, infants try out many movements and sounds. When either one is reinforced by some result, such as a crib mobile wiggling or an adult imitating the infant's vocalizations, the baby will repeat the movement or sound over and over. This kind of repeated response to environmental stimuli was called *circular* by Piaget.

At about six months, babies begin using somewhat rhythmic whole-body movements in response to music. In the ensuing months they will learn to clap, point, move backward, crawl, slither, roll, push, and pull—all important movements for responding to music.

Learning to walk, sometimes after the first birthday, offers vast freedom to infants. By 18 months they will bounce to music or to their own inner sense of rhythm. They enjoy being rocked and sung to, bounced in rhythm on an adult knee, or swung in the air to music and rhymes. Some children are able to sing parts of songs. When creating their own movement, they enjoy making plenty of racket using their enthusiastic physical energy.

The developing capabilities and enjoyment of infants come in response to the environment, a fact with important implications. If the environment is rich, so will be the infant's responses.

Those who care for infants can enhance the atmosphere with plenty of talking, singing, and rhythmic activities appropriate to their ages. Mobiles in the crib, wind chimes in the window, playing musical instruments for the child to listen to—all provide possibilities for growth.

### The Two Year Old

The abilities of walking and talking as well as better overall body control make new activities possible and old activities more skillfully done. For example, we can still expect children to prefer banging pots and pans to create wonderful (to them!) noises. Now, however, they may pick and choose which pots they prefer. Still, there are limitations in that they may choose two pot lids as cymbals because they are the same size, not because they are auditorily preferable. At this age, their visual discrimination is ahead of their ability to make choices in sound.

Musical commercials on TV or radio, or various melodies on electronic devices, now catch their attention and they will sing snatches of a song. A few children can sing whole songs, sometimes while rocking a doll. There are spontaneous songs, too, usually growing out of motor activities. These often use the minor third (as in "Rain, Rain Go Away").

Two year olds still prefer solitary and sometimes parallel play, so they should not be forced into group situations for movement activities. Because two year olds also crave independence, they are happiest when adult direction leads to independent capabilities. Since their attention shifts quickly from one thing to another it is a good idea to alternate active with more sedentary activities. Most of all, two year olds need happy reinforcement of their attempts at improving their skills: running faster, walking up and down stairs, climbing around and over things, and moving to rhythmic beats.

### The Three Year Old

Most children's speech is now fairly fluent, making it more possible for them to sing lyrics and recite very short poems. In addition, galloping, jumping, running, and walking are now done with such ease that three year olds can keep fairly good time to music. Most can even stamp their feet while clapping their hands at the same time. This is a good time to introduce rhythm and melody instruments as well as singing games. Children may fall a little behind with the words or the movements, but they enjoy trying.

### The Four Year Old

Children of this age are able to classify and to order sounds, and they can organize them to express a story. Because they are beginning to remember sequences, they can make use of them in songs, memorizing or inventing their own. Nonsense words and silly plots or phrasing are entertaining to four year olds in songs just as they are in stories.

### The Five Year Old

Cognitively, five year olds can combine simple ideas into more complex ones and apply them to new situations, thus making them capable of more complex musical experiences. Because children are now more capable of cooperative play, they can also cooperate to create or reproduce musical events.

Musically, children can respond more accurately to rhythm. They can repeat musical and rhythmic patterns. They can begin to sort out the multiple musical sounds of a band or an orchestra. Many can sing back a musical pattern, on key and in rhythm.

Although four year olds can begin to participate in group songs, it is the five year olds who can really produce. Providing them with opportunities to explore movement and song is important. They can differentiate between types of instruments and their functions, including making decisions about what instruments might best accompany recorded musical pieces.

### The Six, Seven, and Eight Year Old

Changing social interests, including more focus on the importance of peers, means that children are developing an interest in activities that require teams and groups. The significance for musical experiences is that more complex interactions and projects are now enjoyed. Planning performances together is more important than individual effort or impositions from above.

Concerning children's abilities to produce musical pitch, carry a melody, and perform metrical tasks, the most important influence appears to be experience and contact. Some first graders can do all these things well, and others take a number of years, although researchers do not yet know why. But one thing seems certain: The children who have more contact with musical experiences become more capable sooner.

As primary-grade children attain the Piagetian concrete operational stage, they become capable of new and more complex musical experiences. For example, children who can perform concrete operational tasks involving number can also combine musical sounds in their memories. By third grade, children are competent in reading and notating music, but they often prefer to fall back on the rote learning they have done in all their previous years. Third graders are also able to sing simple two-part songs and in rounds if they have had sufficient training.

Children make great strides in their music capabilities during the early years. Although rather specific ages were given in this section for the development of skills and capabilities, remember that individual children develop on different schedules. Use the age divisions as guidelines only.

### Dramatic Play, Drama, and Child Development

This section traces the progress from egocentric role-play to capabilities in public performance. Important to such development is an increasing ability to mentally step into another's shoes, to understand that others have feelings and interests that may not be the same as our own. Chapter 1 deals with this ability in more depth, but here the topic is referred to as it specifically applies to dramatic play and drama.

### Infants and Toddlers

Anyone observing infants can see that acting skills are already developing. For example, early dramatic play is demonstrated by one year olds who sit in a bathtub pretending to drink from a plastic cup or who grab someone's coat to make believe it is a security blanket, curling up as if for a nap and giggling all the while.

The pretend play of two year olds expands on such activities, when toddlers imitate life as they see it. They develop memories of family events and rituals and combine them for dramatic play activities. For example, two-year-old Decker owned several plastic vehicles large enough to sit in and "drive." A particularly observant child, he had mastered the art of parallel parking as well as his mother's typical follow-up sequence that included rolling the windows up, turning off the engine, opening the door, carefully placing shopping bags on the curb, making sure keys were in hand, closing the door, and yelling, "I home!" For all these actions, the single real object was the car itself.

During infancy and toddlerhood, youngsters are egocentric in the Piagetian sense, first developing an awareness and understanding of themselves, only gradually learning to look outward. Thus, one year olds role-play personally meaningful activities, while two year olds begin to mimic family events and rituals but make them their own.

### Preschoolers and Kindergarten Children

Between the ages of three and five, children gradually begin to understand that others have feelings too, but for a long time assume that those feelings are identical, or at least similar, to their own. Their understanding of self relates primarily to physically observable traits and relationships: hair color, height, siblings, pets, and location of home, for example.

Dramatic play reflects this development. Preschoolers enjoy dressing up together and pretending to do what older siblings and adults do, but they frequently engage in an early form of social interaction called *parallel play*. Here is an example of an overheard conversation in the dramatic play area where two three-year-old girls are dressed, more or less, as adult ladies. One of them is pushing a baby carriage with a doll inside, while the other holds a cooking pot in her hand.

**Child 1:**  I'm taking the baby for a walk, okay?
**Child 2:**  Dinner is at six o'clock. We're eating pasketti.
**Child 1:**  We'll be back for a nap.
**Child 2:**  I think we'll have salad too. But no tomatoes. I hate tomatoes.

From an adult perspective, the children are playing side by side, but barely playing *together,* although the children would no doubt argue otherwise. Still, we can observe the beginnings of true theatre as costumes and props are selected, and the actors delve into the realities of their roles as they see them. There is as yet, however, no sense of or need for an audience.

This begins to change in kindergarten, although attempts at formal stage productions with outsiders, such as parents, in attendance may well lead to some form of chaos. Most teachers who have tried such performances frequently do so because of administrative or parental pressure. It is likely that many teachers would recommend that, when possible, dramatic play experiences be left to children's enjoyment within the classroom and without formal production expectations. We have found that an in-classroom audience consisting of family members and student-familiar school personnel provides a satisfying spectator base as young learners share their researched findings from inquiry-based learning projects, or perform informal, child-initiated and produced, performances. Figure 10.2 displays an invitation to such a performance.

When creating dramatic play areas, it is important to take into account differences across cultures. Since these centers are typically focused on reflecting the real world, teachers need to understand what their children's real worlds are. For example, one school had children from a variety of Asian countries. One day, the kindergarten teacher took a good hard look at the clothing she had furnished for dress-up and realized that it consisted only of very Westernized items, while her children's mothers regularly showed up in their national dress. She then substituted yards and yards of variously colored sheer

**Figure 10.2** This informal, in-classroom winter festival was planned and performed by the students, with teacher assistance as asked for by the children.

fabrics, which the children immediately began to drape around themselves according to what their parents wore.

*Primary Grades*

In the first and second grades, teachers can expect children to begin understanding what it is like to be in someone else's shoes—to take someone else's perspective. In addition, by second grade most youngsters have developed an interest in learning what is "right." That is, they want to know how to draw pictures that mimic reality, read words correctly, spell with accuracy rather than inventively, and so on. When this development takes place, it is time to introduce the idea of performance of memorized scripts, poetry, or music. Typically, children feel most comfortable if the audience is other classes or parents and familiar school personnel. Exceptionally confident and outgoing children may be ready for more public performances, particularly if their classmates are on stage with them. Many times, the classroom itself, with ingenuity on the part of the teacher and students, can be rearranged as the stage for performances, with extra chairs brought in

**Figure 10.3** Anthony very capably and assuredly announces each performance at room 4's informal Winter Festival.

**Figure 10.4** The Five Little Snowmen get ready for their performance.

for the audience. This provides an intimate, comfortable, less-intimidating setting than the more formal auditorium stage.

Despite the increasing maturity of primary-age children, it is important to remember that they still need opportunities to engage in self-directed dramatic play. Recess should not be denied them, because it is typically there that they take the opportunity to engage in various sorts of imaginative play, even at times basing such play on their academic experiences, particularly social studies.

### Diversity in Development

Music, dramatic play, and drama can provide many rewarding experiences for children with developmental delays and disabilities and for those just learning English. Children with cognitive impairments, who find academic requirements frustrating, often find relief in the opportunities that music and dramatic play can provide. Youngsters with visual impairments many times find music a joy. Even those with hearing difficulties can often respond to rhythm. English language learners should find support in the slower pronunciation requirements of singing and in the smaller language requirements that usually accompany a dramatic play situation, since actions can so often be used to express thoughts and ideas. For language learners in the primary grades, structured play parts and recitations provide gateways to increased linguistic competence.

Some young children show an early talent for music or acting, and they should be given the freedom needed to develop those talents, without the pressures of large audiences and structured training. It is tempting to permit the more openly talented children to take starring roles, but there are many introverted, budding young actors and actresses just waiting for an opportunity to shine on stage as well.

## INCORPORATING MUSIC, DRAMATIC PLAY, AND DRAMA IN DAILY ROUTINES

Making music and role-play experiences an integral part of classroom life creates a positive atmosphere that can go a long way toward fostering children's love of learning and being in school or center. Integrating these experiences into the fabric of the day takes virtually no extra time, thus making possible an increased curriculum in the expressive arts even when there seems to be no room for it. Some ideas to try:

- Quietly play high-quality music as background to work, and even play, times. Whether your choices are jazz, classical, or other, avoid vocal music during important work periods so that the music is not distracting. At the end of work time, you might turn the music up for a brief discussion of it. If you repeat selections, children can remember what they hear, and they can identify the music.
- When it is time for a rest period, play quiet, soothing music to settle everyone down. Teachers have been observed who actually play march music during rest time and wonder why the children won't calm down.
- When the class becomes overly noisy, avoid the all-too-common flashing of lights and stern teacher voice. Instead, try singing very quietly, "Can you hear me?" The children respond, using the same melody, "I can hear you." Then, make a brief statement—spoken or sung—that corrects the behavior. Using such call-and-response melody keeps the atmosphere pleasant and conducive to more learning than does a sternly managerial approach.

- When you are working with a small group and need quiet for the entire class, your entire group can sing, "We can hear you" (do-re-mi-do.) It is almost guaranteed that a new level of quiet will ensue immediately.
- When calling children individually to line up or come to a group, sing their names. They can respond with any designated choice. Alternatively, whole groups can be called using singing, "Are you wearing blue?" Children can respond, "I am wearing blue," using the same melody.
- Another choice for lining up or moving from one site to another is to have them dance there, with or without music. In this case, rules of appropriate behavior should be established in advance.
- Acting like animals or characters from favorite stories can work for lining up and moving as well. Again, proper behaviors should be established in advance.

## A CHILD-INITIATED INQUIRY EXPERIENCE

*Although Leslie was familiar with inquiry learning projects, it would not have occurred to her that her young learners would want to explore musical concepts in this fashion. Her four and five year olds, however, harbored no such limitations. It started because their admiration for Raul's ability to pick out tunes on the classroom piano began to develop into something akin to jealousy. During what was typically a brief class meeting, two of the children said that they wanted to learn how to do what Raul could do. Leslie wasn't sure how to make this happen, but before she knew it, the conversation took a different turn. The class decided instead that they wanted to learn how the piano made its noise. The conversation about pianos continued animatedly, when, somewhat timidly, Evan raised his hand and quietly shared, "My dad makes violins." A hush fell over the class and one girl ventured, "How does he do that?" Another child queried, "What's a violin anyway?" Immediately the conversation turned to violins.*

*Leslie knew she had the ingredients to make violins a topic of an inquiry-based learning project. Those necessary ingredients included: student interest and curiosity, relevance for meaningful learning, first-hand resources (Evan's dad and instruments), an opportunity to weave academic and social skills, and a topic that would support future transference of knowledge.*

*The next day the children discovered an old guitar that Leslie had placed next to the piano. "Look," the first child to spy it declared, "Evan brought one of his Dad's violins." "Huh uh," reported expert Evan, "that's not a violin. That's a guitar. It's like a violin, but it's not one." Leslie knew this was a perfect time to enter into the discussion. She wrote down statements from children to help define what a violin was. Statements included: "They're breakable." "Kids and dads can play them." "I don't really think I ever heard one." "You use a stick on them." Leslie then explained to the group that, yes, the instrument she had brought to school was indeed a guitar, an old guitar that the children could pick up and strum, even though it didn't stay tuned very well. But the children were determined to learn more about violins.*

*As the attention of the students was still fully engaged, Leslie made a decision to ask them what they might want to know or what they wondered about violins. The violin wonders included: "What do they look like?" "How do they make their noise?" "How can you play them with a stick?" "Can I pick one up?"*

With the help of Evan's dad, who graciously took time to come to school with violins in various stages of completion, and the middle school orchestra teacher, who lent two violins to the class, Leslie's eager inquirers found out more information than they believed was possible. They discovered important details about violins, including how they were made, what sounds they produced, what they smelled like, and how much they weighed. The budding musicians were delighted as they very maturely and responsibly plucked the violin strings, and compared and contrasted the violins to the old guitar.

The students' enthusiasm for musical instruments did not stop at the violins. Leslie, with the help of other parents and the orchestra teacher, was able to introduce the young learners to a variety of musical instruments. The old upright classroom piano became a primary source of knowledge as the children carefully groped around inside, observing how it produced its sound. Raul was no longer a source of envy; he became an expert that the children now turned to as they sought greater knowledge about pianos.

But this was not enough; the young investigators were determined to make instruments of their own. The children were ingenious in their use of cylinder tubes to make percussion instruments, assorted small boxes with various seeds and beans to create maraca-like instruments, and boxes with rubber bands to mimic guitars and violins. In addition, they invented songs to play for one another, never minding their less-than-realistic instruments. As the year progressed, the children eventually lost interest in making instruments and spent their time observing and mimicking Raul at the piano. Now, they exhibited no envy but tackled their own efforts with self-confidence.

## THE MUSIC AND DRAMA CURRICULUM

### The Music Curriculum

The MENC: National Association for Music Education (previously known simply as the MENC or Music Educators National Conference) has developed national standards according to children's age groups, two of which apply to the concerns of this text. For the youngest children, ages 2–4, the MENC's beliefs concerning musical learning include:

- All children have musical potential.
- Children bring their own unique interests and abilities to the music learning environment.
- Very young children are capable of developing critical thinking skills through musical ideas.
- Children come to early childhood music experiences from diverse backgrounds.
- Children should experience exemplary musical sounds, activities, and materials.
- Children should not be encumbered with the need to meet performance goals.
- Children's play is their work.
- Children learn best in pleasant physical and social environments.
- Diverse learning environments are needed to serve the developmental needs of many individual children.
- Children need effective adult models. (MENC, n.d., p. 1)

It is apparent that the MENC has high expectations for even very young children, in addition to expectations for teachers that include a playful approach and the use of high quality experiences and materials. There are just four content standards for the youngest children, and they apply to children who have developed through the toddler years and now reached age four. Table 10.1 presents a condensed version of the full list.

The MENC content standards for school-age children are longer and more complex, but again we have condensed them in Table 10.2. For access to the full set of standards, see the MENC entry in the references at the end of the chapter.

### The Dramatic Play and Drama Curriculum

No organization provides curriculum standards for dramatic play. Much of the time, simply supplying materials and opportunities will allow children's creativity to emerge. Perhaps surprisingly though, many young children need to be taught dramatic play skills. Since the 1960s, when Sarah Smilansky (1968; Smilansky & Sheftaya, 1990) first researched the dramatic play of children with difficult lives of poverty, it has been known that pretend experiences do not come naturally to all children. The technique that has been found to work is to provide the typical dramatic play center and plenty of free time to use it. The teacher then observes for a while until stepping in seems appropriate. She or he then takes a minor role in the drama, making a suggestion or two to help move the "plot" along. When things are progressing more satisfactorily, the teacher finds a plot-related reason to move back out and leave things to the children.

Although there are no formal standards for dramatic play, the following section provides standards related to drama. Once these standards have been covered, we will put music and drama together to see how these subjects are related to the other expressive arts.

The drama standards reflect the position of the American Alliance for Theatre & Education, as published by the Consortium of National Arts Education Association

**Table 10.1** MENC Content and Achievement Standards for Age Four Plus

| Content Standards | Related Achievement Standards |
| --- | --- |
| 1. Singing and playing instruments | Children:<br>a. Use their voices expressively as they speak, chant, and sing<br>b. Experiment with a variety of instruments and other sound sources. |
| 2. Creating music | Children:<br>a. Improvise songs to accompany their play activities<br>b. Improvise instrumental accompaniments<br>c. Create short pieces of music. |
| 3. Responding to music | Children:<br>a. Identify the sources of a wide variety of sounds<br>b. Respond through movement to various kinds of music<br>c. Participate freely in music activities. |
| 4. Understanding music | Children:<br>a. Use their own vocabulary and standard music vocabulary to describe voices, instruments, music notation, and music of various genres, styles, and periods from diverse cultures<br>b. Demonstrate an awareness of music as a part of daily life. |

**Table 10.2** MENC Content and Achievement Standards for K–4

| Content Standards | Related Achievement Standards |
| --- | --- |
| 1. Singing | Students:<br>a. Sing independently, on pitch and in rhythm<br>b. Sing expressively<br>c. Sing from memory a varied repertoire of songs representing genres and styles from diverse cultures. |
| 2. Performing on instruments | Students:<br>a. Perform easy rhythmic, melodic, and chordal patterns on classroom instruments<br>b. Perform expressively a varied repertoire of music representing diverse genres and styles<br>c. Echo short rhythms and melodic patterns. |
| 3. Improvising | Students:<br>a. Improvise "answers in the same style to given rhythmic and melodic phrases<br>b. Improvise short songs and instrumental pieces, using a variety of sound sources. |
| 4. Composing and arranging | Students:<br>a. Create and arrange music to accompany readings or dramatizations<br>b. Use a variety of sound sources when composing. |
| 5. Reading and notating music | Students:<br>a. Use a system (that is, syllables, numbers, or letters) to read simple pitch notation in the treble clef in major keys. |
| 6. Listening to, analyzing, and describing music | Students:<br>a. Identify simple music forms when presented aurally<br>b. Identify the sounds of a variety of instruments, including many orchestra and band instruments and instruments from various cultures. |
| 7. Evaluating music and music performance | Students:<br>a. Explain, using appropriate music terminology, their personal preferences for specific musical works and styles. |
| 8. Understanding relationships between music, the other arts, and disciplines outside the arts | Students:<br>a. Identify ways in which the principles and subject matter of other disciplines taught in the school are interrelated with those of music. |
| 9. Understanding music in relation to history and culture | Students:<br>a. Describe in simple terms how elements of music are used in music examples from various cultures of the world<br>b. Demonstrate audience behavior appropriate for the context and style of music performed. |

in 1994. The Alliance defines "theatre" as "the imagined and enacted world of human beings" and a major way that young children learn about life: "about actions and consequences, about customs and beliefs, about others and themselves." The Alliance points out that the many ways in which children of preschool age live a life of pretend mean that "children arrive at school with rudimentary skills as playwrights, actors, designers, directors, and audience members." From kindergarten and beyond, it is expected that teachers will "create a seamless transition from the natural skills of pretend play to the study of theatre." This should be done by scaffolding children's experiences in such a way that they continue to develop their independent approach to drama (p. 30). Table 10.3 presents the content and achievement standards in condensed form.

### Applying the Standards

To see how the music standards can be incorporated in an early childhood classroom, we suggest you return to Leslie's inquiry project (p. 276) and determine which standards for four year olds apply. Music standards also apply to Suzanne's Friendly Forest experience (p. 263) as do several of the theatre standards. Try applying these as well.

If what is known about child development is matched with the benefits of dramatic play, and what the standards say about music and drama, a list of appropriate activities emerges. Here are some ideas to try.

**Table 10.3** National Content and Achievement Standards for Theatre Education, K–4

| Content Standards | Related Achievement Standards |
| --- | --- |
| 1. Script writing | Children:<br>a. Collaborate to select interrelated characters, environments, and situations for classroom dramatizations<br>b. Improvise dialogue to tell stories and formalize improvisations by writing or recording the dialogue. |
| 2. Acting | Children:<br>a. Assume roles that exhibit concentration and contribute to the action of classroom dramatizations based on personal experience and heritage, imagination, literature, and history. |
| 3. Designing and arranging environments | Children:<br>a. Collaborate to establish playing spaces for classroom dramatizations and to select and safely organize available materials that suggest scenery, properties, lighting, sound, costumes, and makeup. |
| 4. Directing | Children:<br>a. Collaboratively plan and prepare improvisations and demonstrate various ways of staging classroom dramatizations. |

### Preschool and Kindergarten Activities

- Create an out-of-the-way corner where you keep a collection of different items that can make sound (small blocks, bells, spoons, pot lids, and so on).
- Do informal singing all day long (see suggestions in section "Incorporating Music, Dramatic Play, and Drama into Daily Routines").
- Perform songs with plenty of freely interpreted action.
- Provide rhythm instruments (with something for each child).
- Offer music for listening that reflects a variety of cultures, with strong rhythms and variations in mood.

- Repeat experiences in listening, playing, and singing, offering the same music.
- Do mirror images: To recorded music, children move rhythmically while imitating various characters, animals, and so on.
- March from one type of activity to another with appropriate musical background and while taking on the movements of various story, or other, characters.
- After hearing a story about particular animals, ask children to move to music as the animals might.

### Kindergarten and Primary Activities

- Provide a device for playing recorded music for children to use on their own (headsets can take care of noise problems).
- Offer a few rhythm instruments near the music device for free choice accompaniment.
- Discuss recorded music after several listening experiences (focus on mood, pitch, rhythms, and so on).
- Invite visitors who can play and describe instruments; follow up listening experiences to identify instruments in music; choose instruments from a variety of cultures and countries.
- Develop a repertoire of favorite songs to use during field research trips, during cleanup, and so on.
- Dramatize favorite stories using in-class materials inventively as props; children create, choose dialogue, and act with as little teacher scaffolding as possible.
- Expand children's collection of songs, and include those with multiple verses.
- Have children make up new words to old favorite songs.
- Teach simple rounds.
- Dramatize songs or have children write plays that incorporate favorite songs.
- Continue to listen to recorded music and learn about new instruments from many cultures.
- Learn folk dances of this and other countries, including some simple square dancing.
- Sing while moving in different ways: walking, marching, hopping, skipping, and so on.
- Dramatize favorite stories and perform for other classes as desired; incorporate music where appropriate.

## THE IMPORTANCE OF PLAY

Those who have set standards for music and drama are well aware of the benefits of play. As the MENC states, echoing Froebel's words from more than a century past, "Children's play is their work" (MENC, n.d. p. 1). The position of the American Alliance for Theatre & Education is that the pretend play of early childhood prepares youngsters for almost every task and job associated with drama (Consortium of National Arts Education, 1994). It is, perhaps, the playful nature of music, dramatic play, and drama experiences that make them so generally popular for children. Skills are certainly included, and the knowledgeable teacher provides scaffolding as necessary but knows that it is equally important to step out of the way and let the children take over when possible.

**Figure 10.5** A cardboard box can be used in many ways for dramatic play in a classroom steeped in inquiry learning.

## TECHNOLOGY AND EARLY CHILDHOOD MUSIC, DRAMATIC PLAY, AND DRAMA

If a recording device is available, either teacher or children can choose to record dramatic or musical events; such events do not have to be formal ones. It should be noted that even some older preschoolers can learn to use this technology, thus providing them with an additional learning experience. Recordings can be made of children's singing and instrumental experiences, again without the necessity of a formal performance and with the possibility that the children themselves can learn the technology. Today's technological advances allow students to integrate music and drama with the other curricular subjects more easily, thus respecting learners' multiple learning styles. Such integration can also lead to the production of stunning and creative works of dramatic and musical art, which can be saved for years to come. Teachers are encouraged to investigate continually emerging software that can support early composition, listening, and performing skills. With modern technology, the possible ways to share performances, instantaneously or otherwise, are endless.

## ASSESSMENT AND EVALUATION

As the MENC points out, young children "understand much more about music than they can verbalize" and, in addition, there is a "very wide range of individual developmental differences displayed by young children" (MENC, n.d., p. 2). These situations lead to assessments that rely on observational techniques. Thus, the MENC suggests that the following approaches to assessment of young children's knowledge, skills, and dispositions might include:

- Checklists or anecdotal records that describe verbal and nonverbal behavior. These can be useful in determining children's language learning, social interactions and skills, and self-confidence.
- Systematic observation of a more formal nature that includes such things as time on task, repeated behaviors (positive and negative), and participation tendencies.
- Rating scales that provide information about accuracy, originality, or degree of involvement and interest.

When Smilansky (1968) engaged in her research into assisting children with dramatic play, she developed a system for viewing and assessing it that other researchers and teachers have continued to find valuable. Here is a modified overview taken from writings on play (Van Hoorn et al., 1999, pp. 274–275).

1. *Observe children's role-play:* Beginning level—children imitate one or two aspects of their familiar worlds. Advanced level—children expand concepts to include outside world.
2. *Observe children's use of props:* Beginning level—children physically use real objects. Advanced level—children can pretend any object or motion is a prop.
3. *Observe children's make-believe:* Beginning level—children imitate simple, familiar actions. Advanced level—actions are part of a make-believe plot.
4. *Observe length of time children play:* Beginning level—involvement is fleeting. Advanced level—children are involved for more than 10 minutes.
5. *Observe degree of interaction with others:* Beginning level—solitary play. Advanced level—children act cooperatively with others.
6. *Observe verbal communication:* Beginning level—talk centers on use of toys and objects. Advanced level—talk is more about the play theme.

## PREPRIMARY EXPERIENCES CELEBRATING MUSIC AND DRAMATIC PLAY THROUGHOUT THE CURRICULUM

If music and dramatic play are used throughout the day as part of the usual classroom routines (see pp. 275–6 for ideas), it is difficult to avoid integrating them into the entire curriculum. Songs and singing games that provide opportunities to act out the plots while including math concepts are common in the preschool years. From "The Ants Go Marching One by One" to "Six Little Ducks," there are plenty of opportunities for young children to learn counting skills, to understand time through repetitions and verses, and to gain knowledge of space when acting out the plots and sequences.

Language is integrated with music and dramatic play the instant that words are involved. Learning verses to songs adds richness to a child's language growth. For example, repetition of a grammatically correct phrase, in the context of a song, can encourage correct usage at other times.

Art integrates with dramatic play when sets and costumes are designed and created. Learning songs appropriate to the theme of current interest can enhance social studies, and the diversity of cultures becomes wonderfully vivid through music and drama. Preschool children love to portray animals and, in doing so, can come to see and feel how the animals really move while suitable background music reinforces animal cadences.

The ideas that follow can be expanded on indefinitely. The alert teacher seeks ways throughout the day to enjoy music and dramatic play on the children's own terms and to integrate them into appropriate areas of the curriculum. By so doing, the school experience becomes both memorable and joyous. The following suggestions are made for including music and dramatic play in some typical preschool curriculum topics. Figure 10.6 shows a curriculum web for preprimary music and dramatic play activities.

### Language Activities

#### New Props

Collect a wide assortment of props for the dramatic play area. Include some that are unfamiliar. Children can learn the specific names for props and discuss the use of props for pretend as well as their traditional use in the world outside of the imaginative classroom.

#### Songs for Stories

Have individual children create snippets of songs that illustrate a repeated set of words from a familiar story. Have the whole class use these during the reading or telling of the story. For example, from "The Gingerbread Man," a song can be made to accompany just the last part of his chant: ". . . and I can run away from you, I can, I can!"

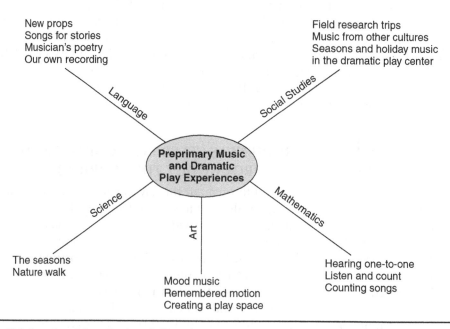

**Figure 10.6** A music and dramatic play activities web.

### Musician's Poetry

Choose music that suits the mood of a favorite poem; then read it to children as they listen. Repeat the music, and have children create movements that help tell the story while you read the poem again.

### Our Own Recording

As children learn songs and poems, record them. Place in the classroom listening center. Even very young children can learn to turn a recording device on and off themselves so that they can play "their" music and poems and sing or dance as they like.

## Mathematics Activities

### Hearing One-to-One

Play a brief rhythmic pattern on a drum, and count each beat clearly. Have children repeat by pounding on the floor and counting. They can also step or march in time. (It is good at first to make the beats an even rhythm.) Follow up with simple march music for a more complex music and rhythm experience. To this can be added role-play ideas with children marching as different characters in their stories might.

### Listen and Count

For this activity you will need a musical instrument—piano, guitar, xylophone, set of bells, and so on. Have children count to three out loud. Then, have them count silently as you play three different pitches on the same instrument you have chosen. Next, have the children sing "one, two, three" as you play the melody again. Once they are comfortable with that sequence, play the instrument again, this time adding a fourth note. Introduce the number four and continue as above. As children are able, add more numbers, extending the pattern.

### Counting Songs

We have already mentioned "The Ants Go Marching" and "Six Little Ducks," both familiar songs in preschools. Others include "Five Little Monkeys (jumping on the bed)" or "Five Little Speckled Frogs." If these are unfamiliar, or to learn new choices, take time to leaf through available music books or go online for more songs that include counting.

## Science Activities

### The Seasons

As the seasons change, children can act out what is happening. Some can be falling leaves while others are the wind gently pushing them to the ground. Everyone can be snow—first falling, then spreading over the ground, and finally melting. There can even be a truck coming through spattering mud. In the spring, new leaves grow, flowers come up, and rain falls gently. Using recorded background music will enrich the mood. Before kindergarten it is preferable to concentrate only on the season at hand.

### Nature Walk

Take a walk in the nearest woods or natural setting. Take time to observe everything around. While there, children replicate the scene they observe, each of them taking on the role of a tree, squirrel, vine, so on. When they return to the classroom, they can reenact their experience, this time creating pretend characters and plot to match.

## Social Studies Activities

### Field Research Trips

Before taking any of their investigative learning out into the non-school world, have children role-play the jobs of people they will meet as well as their own roles while they are there. After the trip has been completed, replay the roles and have the children reflect on their changed perceptions. Both before and after the trip, supply the dramatic play center with related materials.

### Music From Other Cultures

Even in a school or center that appears to be monocultural, there will be different family traditions. Invite parents to share their songs and other music, or perhaps a dance that has special meaning. These activities can be combined with the following two activities for a more complete experience.

### Seasonal and Holiday Music

During free-play and work times, play traditional and folk songs as background music. Through repeated listening experiences and informal singing by the teacher, children will pick up the melodies and words of seasonal songs that otherwise might be too difficult for them. Of course, songs about friendship and love are not only meaningful in February, but are pertinent all year long.

### In the Dramatic Play Center

As children learn about one another's cultures, outfit the center with clothes and artifacts that are applicable. Ask parents for appropriate donations and possibly a visit to explain what they have brought. If they are willing, they can even be asked to take a minor role in a play experience.

## Art Activities

### Mood Music

Have children listen to music and then choose one crayon or marker. While they continue to listen, have them draw the way the music makes them feel. For older children, play a contrasting piece of music and repeat it. Then have children dance as the two contrasting pieces are played once again. Do not expect all children to interpret the moods of the music as you would, or to choose colors that you would opt for. (There are some children who think that black is truly joyful.)

### Remembered Motion

Have children move to recorded music, portraying characters or animals or simply dancing. Then, while the music plays again, have them draw their experience. They should draw what they felt, not what they saw. (There may be swirls to represent turns and pounded dots for marching.)

### Creating a Play Space

Collect one or two discarded refrigerator or stove boxes from an appliance store. Discuss with children the dramatic play possibilities for the boxes. Cut doors, windows, and so on as the children direct (a knife with a serrated edge will work best). Then, let the children decorate with paints as they see fit, followed by time for dramatic play.

## PRIMARY EXPERIENCES THAT CONTINUE TO PROVIDE
## JOY THROUGH MUSIC AND DRAMA

In the primary grades, children still enjoy participating in many of the preceding preprimary activities. But now, aided by their abilities to read and write, young learners can expand on these activities to give each one a more mature and personalized look, all the while incorporating their budding academic skills.

### *Primary Students Have the Skills Now to:*

- Write simple songs to include words they know. For example, in the song "Oh, a hunting we will go" students can write their own rhyming words in the blanks. "We'll catch a little _____ and put him in a _____, and then we'll let him go."
- Record information gathered on sound-seeking nature walks and write experience stories upon returning to class.
- Partner with a buddy to record drum beats into an addition problem: 4 beats + 5 beats = 9 beats.

**Figure 10.7** A small, portable puppet stage provides a perfect showcase for puppets to act out child-created stories and plays.

- Tally slowly given drum beats by groups of five.
- Write sentences describing moods they feel when listening to various music selections. "When I hear _____, I feel _____."
- Develop and write simple story plots for the classroom's puppets to act out.
- Act out a favorite story from a classroom reading book; paraphrase the plot.
- Sing a poem that is being read to a made-up or familiar tune.

### Inquiry Projects That Might Emerge From These Activities

As children engage in music and drama experiences, they might well find themselves sufficiently intrigued by one or more aspects of an activity to warrant a child-designed project based on inquiry. When considering a topic for an in-depth, inquiry-based study that will be conducted by children, a wise teacher is mindful of the criteria that make a topic worthy of study.

Will the study of the topic:

- Build on what children already know?
- Offer hands-on relevance to the children?
- Encourage application of social and academic skills?
- Interconnect (weave) or integrate curricular subjects with the goal of furthering student understanding of the topic?
- Support transference of knowledge to future learning?

With these criteria in mind, we offer the following possibilities for inquiry-based learning projects, stemming from children's exposure to music, drama, and dramatic play. Each suggested topic area might well be appropriate for preprimary as well as primary aged students, because young learners at each age will not only bring their own level of understanding to the proposed topics, but will also carry out investigations as developmentally appropriate to their skill level.

- Exposure to a variety of instruments may pique young investigators' curiosity to study one or more instruments in greater detail to find out how the instrument was made, what it is made of, what countries have similar instruments, and so on.
- A fascination with dramatic props may instigate an in-depth study of a particular item of clothing—for instance, hats. The vast variety of hats could be explored to include their production, their composition, and cultural varieties.
- An investigation of a formal stage, either in the center or school or at a nearby high school auditorium or theatre, would help to alleviate apprehensions surrounding stage performance as well as provide fascinating backstage information.
- An unusual song from another country may well trigger the students' curiosity to learn more about the country and its inhabitants.

Through experience, we have found that when the interest and enthusiasm of young learners is attentively watched, a wide variety of topics worthy of investigation present themselves. Teachers must be aware of such areas, as these interests, when turned into a topic of inquiry-based study, can be used to logically and meaningfully integrate the curriculum. In this way, music, dramatic play, and drama can remain part of the learning of young children, even in times of more narrowly focused pressures.

# THE POWER OF INQUIRY LEARNING THROUGH INTEGRATION

Music, dramatic play, and drama assume important supporting roles in a child-centered environment that stars integrated and inquiry-based learning. These arts provide venues for young learners to display creative self-expression and to communicate and cooperate as they apply academic skills. Integrating these modes of creativity throughout the school day sets a pleasurable stage that helps children to gain confidence to pursue and participate in opportunities that may let hidden talents shine. Children can use music and drama to give voice and action to their culture, their feelings, and their academic understandings. A well-crafted song or dramatic experience can be a powerful, personal, and pleasing influence in the lives of young learners as well as of adults.

Appropriate curriculum for music and drama is, to a great extent, all about inquiry. As children explore musical sounds and rhythms—when they find answers to questions they pose about various instruments, including their own voices—they are engaging in inquiry learning. When young learners investigate topics such as drums or dances, their queries will take them on journeys through geography and cultures as they meaningfully apply their academic skills.

Young learners can use music and drama as an engaging means in which to share knowledge they have gained through an in-depth study of a topic—mimicking the ways animals move in accompaniment with the sounds they make; demonstrating caterpillar to butterfly stages; acting out researched weather phenomena. Perhaps the culminating experience of an inquiry-based project, similar to the building of an airplane featured in the in-depth study described in Chapter 9, results in a dramatic play prop to be used throughout the year.

Whatever the outcome, when music, drama, and dramatic play have roles when integrating the curriculum through inquiry learning, the pathways children take as they investigate and discover can lead to new heights of creativity.

## TO DISCUSS

1. Consider and discuss ways in which music, dramatic play, and drama can be made a part of academic experiences. If you have opportunities to observe children learning in academic situations, think about ways these subjects could be incorporated into them. If you observe teachers doing just this, and are reading this textbook as part of a course, share with your class what you have observed.
2. Discuss the difficulties you observe in your own state or district in incorporating music and dramatic play into the curriculum. List every possible barrier, then brainstorm ways to surmount as many as possible.
3. Brainstorm a potential list of topics, stemming from music, dramatic play, and drama, which could possibly be used for an in-depth, inquiry-learning project. For each potential project, discuss ways academic subjects might be integrated.

## TO DO

1. Observe children in a dramatic play center, then ask if you might join. Take a small role and, when appropriate, suggest a new direction for the plot. Observe what happens next, removing yourself when it seems right. Write down the experience for sharing with your class or with other teachers.

2. If you are teaching, make a list of activities you expect to do on your next day in the classroom. Plan as many ways as possible to include music and pretend play as a part of them. Carry through on as many of these as feasible. Write a journal entry when you are finished to share with others.

3. If you are teaching reading, plan at least one activity for your next story. Children might dramatize the whole story. Or they could act out a new ending. Or you could ask them to demonstrate the feelings of individual characters at turns in the plot.

4. Sing old favorite songs with children. Note which one seems the most familiar and easily sung. Try making up new words to the melody that are related to something happening in the classroom and/or to the children.

5. Expand your own experience: Attend a concert or play, choosing a type of music with which you are unfamiliar or a kind of drama or comedy you think you probably do not like. Write a journal entry describing your response, perhaps waiting a day before doing so.

## REFERENCES

Bayless, K. & Ramsey, M. (1978). *Music: A way of life for the young child.* St. Louis, MO: Mosby.

Brosterman, N. (1997). *Inventing kindergarten.* New York, NY: Harry N. Abrams.

Brown, A. (1987). Approaches to teaching classroom music for children. In Peery, J. et al. (Eds.), *Music and child development* (pp. 184–193). New York, NY: Springer-Verlag.

Consortium of National Arts Education Association. (1994). *National standards for arts education: What every young American should know and be able to do in the arts.* Reston, VA: Music Educators National Conference.

Feierabend, J. (1991). Music in early childhood. In Overby, L. (Ed.), *Early childhood creative arts.* Reston, VA: American Alliance for Health, Physical Education, Recreation, and Dance.

Fromberg, D. (2002). *Play and meaning in early childhood education.* Boston, MA: Allyn and Bacon.

Gardner, H. (1983). *Frames of mind.* New York, NY: Basic Books.

Gardner, H. (1991). *The unschooled mind: How children think and how schools should teach.* New York, NY: Basic Books.

Keene, J. (1982). *A history of music education in the United States.* Hanover, NH: University Press of New England.

Mark, M. & Gary, C. (1999). *A history of American music education.* Reston, VA: Music Educators National Conference.

MENC. (n.d.). *The school music program: A new vision. The K-12 national standards, pre-k standards, and what they mean to music educators.* Retrieved from www.menc.org/publication/books/prek12st.html.

Orme, N. (2001). *Medieval children.* New Haven, CT: Yale University Press.

Saracho, O. (2012). *An integrated play-based curriculum for young children.* New York, NY: Routledge.

Smilansky, S. (1968). *The effects of socio-dramatic play on disadvantaged preschool children.* New York, NY: John Wiley.

Smilanksy, S. & Sheftaya, L. (1990). *Facilitating play: A medium for promoting cognitive, socio-emotional, and academic development.* Gaithersburg, MD: Psychosocial and Educational Publications.

Tanner, L. (1997). *Dewey's laboratory school: Lessons for today.* New York, NY: Teachers College Press.

Van Hoorn, J., Scales, B., Nourot, P., & Alward, K. (1999). *Play at the center of the curriculum.* Upper Saddle River, NJ: Merrill.

# 11

## ART

*. . . drawing is a natural human response. Our brain is . . . programmed to draw. What if this skill were nourished and nurtured for all children? What if it had value as a way to communicate as speech does? What if it were stimulated, rewarded, practiced, trained, and educated? What would happen in the brains of human beings so nurtured and so educated?*

—Geraldine Schwartz

After reading this chapter you should be able to:

- Explain the stages of child development in art;
- Describe how art can be used in everyday routines;
- Describe how essential art goals can be applied to foster artistic development;
- Explain how essential art goals can be integrated into an inquiry-based learning project;
- List ways to incorporate art into other subjects as part of an integrated curriculum.

One warm but misty day, a four-year-old boy sat on a large rock next to his father, quietly watching the surf of the ocean pound the shore. Suddenly he sucked in his breath and exclaimed, "Oh, look at the beauty!" Half an hour later the child sat at the little table in his bedroom, swirling gray and blue crayons around on a piece of paper, all the while saying, "Pssh, pssh," in an apparent imitation of the sea. Not long after that, the paper lay awkwardly bent on the floor between a few toys that were now of more interest.

This brief experience demonstrates several attributes of children's approaches to art. An adult might have been inspired by the beauty to create a picture, too. But the child entered into the endeavor with his voice and body, becoming the ocean himself. What was produced on paper was secondary to the process of creation. Once he had relived the experience, the little boy had no more need of the paper, and it lay on the floor, crumpled and forgotten. Perhaps most important, the child's experience was a very natural one, moving from his seaside exclamation to the role-play on paper in one unself-conscious flow.

It is this very naturalness that makes art with young children such a rewarding experience. Children are appreciative and accepting of beauty, and they love being a part of its expression. When their home and school experiences support this attitude, children can take a very positive first step in a lifelong love of the visual beauty that is called *art*.

The importance of art across history—to countless cultures and to life itself—is hard to overstate. It is often the artwork of a culture that is most remembered centuries later, so it is important to consider what our culture's art is saying to coming generations. How this statement applies to our own culture at this time in history will be an integral part of this chapter. In addition, we will look at the influence of another country (Italy) on early childhood art teaching in our contemporary American preschools and primary classrooms.

## ART AND THE FIELD TRIP

Before beginning our discussion of art and the young child, we'll observe an art lesson in action. The class is a third grade, and art is used here as a follow-up activity to an experience that was part of the science curriculum.

*The children had just returned from a morning at the zoo, where they had been observing characteristics of mammals. Now they were taking grapefruit-size chunks of malleable pottery clay from a large box and working with them individually at their desks.*

*As they settled down, their teacher, Steve James said, "Close your eyes and imagine the mammal you've chosen to sculpt. Can you see it?" Some of the children could and some couldn't, so they all closed their eyes again. Steve went on, "Think about your animal in the position you want it to be. Close your eyes and let it move slowly so that it's sitting or lying or standing—just as it will be when you make it. Don't open your eyes until you can remember everything you need. When you know you can see your animal, start sculpting it. Whenever you can't see it right, just close your eyes again until you can."*

*At first the room was almost silent as the children began manipulating the clay. Soon, however, the sound of pounding, rolling, and intermittent animated chatter filled the room. Occasionally a child sat in total silence, eyes closed, concentrating. This was followed almost immediately by more pounding, rolling, and chatter.*

*Steve walked throughout the room, talking informally with the children, reviewing their knowledge of mammalian characteristics. "Now, be sure you don't forget to give these animals feathers."*

*"Feathers?!" several children answered, laughing.*

*"Mr. James," one girl said, "you're always kidding us. You mean fur."*

*"Oh, yes," he answered as if just remembering, "it's fur." The children continued as before until one boy declared, "But I can't figure out how to make the fur!" Immediately, another boy who had been working steadily and quietly answered, "Look, you can do this." He displayed a partly completed grizzly bear with scratched-in lines along its back. "See? I did it with this broken pencil." Several children looked on with interest and soon a number of old pencils had taken on a new use.*

*As Steve moved throughout the room, observing and offering help, he noted that some children had broken the clay into small pieces and were putting it together bit by bit. Others had retained the original chunk and were pulling, squeezing, and molding. He knew that some of the clay animals made by the first group of children might not be able to be fired successfully but made a decision not to correct their method at this time. They were involved, happy, and working in creative ways, and that, he decided, was more important this time.*

*Then Steve introduced a science-related idea again. "Wings!" he said suddenly. "You've all forgotten the wings."*

*"Wings!" the entire class shouted, several children adding, "Mammals don't fly."*

*"Are you absolutely positive?" Steve asked.*

*"Positive," a couple answered. Others looked uncertain.*

*"Well," Steve mused, "what about the bat that was in my garage last night?" Suddenly the children recalled what he had told them earlier about that, and one girl ventured, "Well, most of them can't fly."*

*"You're right," Steve agreed and smiled. The children all smiled back, knowing that in this class it was okay to be wrong sometimes.*

Steve's lesson was used to reinforce the children's science experience at the zoo. His informal and lighthearted discussion with them as they worked provided a review of biological details, which were then expressed in the sculpted products. Of course, he could have tested the children on their knowledge of mammals more formally. However, not only would the atmosphere have been more tense, but the learning would not have been as concrete, as visual, or as enthusiastic—and probably not as permanent.

There are many opportunities throughout the day and the curriculum for incorporating art. As in Steve's experience, art can be used for reinforcement of any academic learning or for informal testing. In writing experiences, art can be used to illustrate, once something is dictated or written; or when used first, art can also be used to provide inspiration for a story. Art can decorate any paper of which a child is proud. Art in any form can be used to calm an upset child. Figures 11.3 and 11.4 (pp. 308 and 309) demonstrate how art can reflect students' prior knowledge of an inquiry-based learning topic.

## WHY ART MATTERS: A BRIEF HISTORY

In a position paper titled "Art: Essential for Early Learning," the Early Childhood issues group of the National Art Education Association (ECAE) laid out its beliefs about why art matters. Choosing to speak on behalf of the entire Consortium of National Arts Education Associations (NAEA), the ECAE expanded its position to include, not only the visual arts, but all the arts. You will read more about this important umbrella organization in the upcoming Curriculum section. "The arts are essential to early learning," the ECAE stated, adding that "Our beliefs are based on our understanding of research and theories of child development and the arts" (ECAE, n.d., p. 1). The ECAE's core values and beliefs related to the importance of art for young children include:

- The arts support multiple ways of knowing and learning that are inherent in the unique nature of each child.
- The arts empower children to communicate, represent, and express their thoughts, feelings, and perceptions.
- The arts offer opportunities to develop creativity, imagination, and flexible thinking.
- Every child has a right to his or her cultural heritage. The arts can enrich a young child's understanding of diverse cultures.

**Figure 11.1** When children work together, as they are working here on an art project, they begin to understand an interdependent society.

### Preparing for Democracy in a Culturally Diverse Society

Further sections of the ECAE position statement address the benefits of linking schools and communities. When Steve's class took their trip to the zoo, they were getting better acquainted not only with the mammals they went to study but also with a community resource. The entirety of their experience—the trip to the zoo, the clay work later—would long be remembered by most of them. As third graders they were old enough to see the zoo as a useful and interesting part of the community, and this learning could be solidified and expanded through the art experience.

Art, in fact, can be used in many ways to help children understand their society better. Renowned art educator June McFee (1917–2008) wrote eloquently on the place that art has in the preservation of our society, its democratic basis, and the environment in which we live. In her classic book *Preparation for Art* (1970), she argued that teachers need to do better in teaching children that part of their responsibility as citizens is to help maintain the visual attractiveness of the environment. Among other things, children need to "be able to see what is going on in the visual environment . . . to understand that appearance is related to use . . . and . . . to understand how changes affect the quality of the environment they all share" (p. 340).

In later years, McFee (1998, p. 63) pointed out that, years ago she and some of her art education colleagues had been "calling for recognition of cultural diversity in art and among students," and that, by the 1990s, the diversity among people in this country had become far greater. Thus, teachers must recognize that diversity in the United States includes an infusion of people from more places around the world. " . . . [T]he so-called dominant culture is no longer dominant, and the question of whose art to teach becomes paramount" (p. 64).

McFee's observations of increasing demographic diversity from the late 1990s have become even truer in recent years. For example, the U.S. Census Bureau has estimated that, by 2050, Whites would represent 50.1% of the total population as compared to 69.4% in 2000 (Nieto & Bode, 2012). Thus, McFee's hopes for art education that is culturally relevant to every child are as important today as they were then. Historically speaking, the recognition of diversity within schools and across the curriculum, including within art education, is relatively recent. Today there is an understanding that teachers should learn more about the backgrounds and interests of their children's families and that this, in turn, can lead to a richer art curriculum and expand children's knowledge of the world. One kindergarten teacher, for example, was perplexed when a child recently arrived from Myanmar (Burma) consistently colored in human faces so that they emerged in bright blue, green, or even purple. She wisely chose to say nothing but to study more about the child's home culture, and eventually learned that his family's religious beliefs precluded realistic portrayals of the human figure. Such sensitivity to the culture of immigrants has not always been a part of our country's history, and we can appreciate, even celebrate, this change.

The implications for teachers, even early childhood teachers, point to the necessity of learning about the cultures of their children's families, including the artwork and approaches to participation in art that inform their lives. Study Table 11.1 to understand more of McFee's thinking on ways to involve even very young children in art experiences that will foster their successful entry into a multicultural democracy.

### Increasing Cognitive Perception

Art can be regarded as an important influence on the cognitive development of young children. It has long been understood that, until about the age of 10, there is a strong relationship between art ability and intellectual ability (Althouse, Johnson, & Mitchell, 2003; Winner & Hetland, 2000). Further, it is now generally agreed that all school subjects, including art, have both cognitive and affective components, although art is often taught as if it were just about feeling and emotions, and not about ideas (Efland, 2002, 2004).

**Table 11.1** Art Education in a Democracy

| Assumptions About People in a Democracy | Related Art Experiences |
| --- | --- |
| People have infinite value. | Give children an opportunity to develop their unique potential through creativity. |
| People need and have capacity for freedom of choice. | Give children independent decision making through art activities. |
| People have equal rights with others to develop their potential. | Flexibility of results in art activities helps provide equality of opportunity. |
| People have the capacity for self-government. | Children learn to evaluate their own work as well as others'. |
| People have the capacity to work with others as equals. | Group-planned art projects help children understand an interdependent society. |
| People are able to use reason. | Art processes necessitate anticipation of new outcomes. |

*Source*: Adapted from McFee, J. (1970). *Preparation for art*. Belmont, CA: Wadsworth, p. 345–346.

When young children draw, even in the early scribbling stages, they often combine what they are feeling with the symbolizing of an event. The drawing becomes a concrete, visible reminder of the event as well as a way to clarify and organize it cognitively. This is especially important for very little children when their verbal abilities are limited; their expression through art provides a kind of shorthand to describe feelings, visual memories, and actions. This use of art as a concrete cognitive experience could certainly be observed in the seaside experience of the four-year-old boy described at the beginning of the chapter. It also helps unite various areas of the early childhood curriculum. And art can help make any subject more concrete as seen, for example, in the science-related activities in Steve's class.

## Providing Creativity

The importance of learning about democracy and of art as a contributor to creativity in the classroom cannot be underestimated. Creativity is an essential ingredient needed by people living in democracies where they must rely on their own resources, both for survival and for "the pursuit of happiness." Creativity is a critical element in the design of new goods and services that form the basis of a capitalist economy. When education focuses primarily on the basics at the expense of creative experiences, a lifelong pattern of non-creativity may begin, which could deter children from eventually participating in their society to the fullest.

In recent years, art educators have become increasingly concerned about just this happening as the requirements of the federal No Child Left Behind and Race to the Top laws are instituted. Noting the many hours that teachers must devote to preparing children for standardized tests, one observer has commented that, "In elementary schools, test-preparation and test-taking may well exceed the 26 hours typically devoted to visual arts instruction in a year" (Chapman, 2005, p. 13).

In a discussion of the importance of creativity in art development, Judith Burton points to four specific cognitive abilities that underlie much research in creativity: "elaboration, originality, fluency, and resistance to closure" (2001, p. 38). *Elaboration* includes entertaining "different possibilities on an idea, problem, or experience." *Originality* builds on taking these possibilities and thinking of them in new ways . . . "making the familiar strange, and vice versa." *Fluency* means "the ability to make ideas flow, to move them forward, to sift out and interweave ideas and responses into new entities." And *resistance to closure* "implies the ability to keep an open and independent mind . . ." (p. 39). Important to an early childhood educator is the research finding that elaboration, originality, fluency, and resistance to closure are all "strongly represented among young people who have been exposed to arts education for considerable periods of their education" (p. 39). In other words, teachers can make an important difference in children's creativity and artistic development.

## Giving Aesthetic Enjoyment

In addition to the other benefits of artistic experience, there are psychological benefits. To be able to appreciate and enjoy an aesthetic creative experience, or the result of another's, adds richness to life.

In its *National Standards for Arts Education*, the Consortium of National Arts Education Associations emphasizes the importance of the visual arts for young children:

[They] exhibit a sense of joy and excitement as they make and share their art work with others . . . They learn to coordinate their hands and minds in explorations of the visual world . . . Their natural inquisitiveness is promoted, and they learn the value of perseverance . . . Through these efforts, students begin to understand the meaning and impact of the visual world in which they live. (1994, p. 33)

## ART AND CHILD DEVELOPMENT

From the early years of the 20th century, art educators and researchers attempted to identify stages in children's art development. Two leaders in this movement were Victor Lowenfeld and Rita Kellogg who defined developmental stages in terms of moving from scribbles to realistic representations (Kellogg, 1970; Lowenfeld & Brittain, 1982). The psychological orientation was the Freudian view that creativity is a reflection of the repressed subconscious, with works of art "the result of the mind's own activity, the wellspring of creativity" (Efland, 2002, p. 50).

After some decades of widespread acceptance, these theories came under deeper scrutiny when critics began to speak of the ways in which the theories ignored differences in cultures as well as the ways in which children might be more influenced by the artistic needs of the moment than by a theoretical stage of development. For example, one pointed criticism has been that, while artists and art educators regularly celebrate and defend abstract, nonrepresentational art, children's development is seen to become mature when highly representational and realistic products appear. Nevertheless, it is apparent that children's abilities develop from scribbling and clay mashing to ever more sophisticated abilities to show detail, as they grow older. As Judith Burton, whose views on creativity were quoted earlier, observed, ". . . one of the great strengths of Lowenfeld's contribution is to a vision of continuous artistic development originating in infancy and projecting forward into adolescence" (Burton, 2001, p. 36). In that appreciative spirit, and knowing that such structure can provide helpful guidance, developmental stages as based on the combined work of Lowenfeld and Kellogg are described as follows.

### Infancy to Two Years

Infant observations of the world begin to move toward more active involvement at the end of the first year. Simply holding a writing or drawing instrument becomes a fascinating challenge. Learning that such instruments make marks on paper or other surfaces is an amazement. Marks are made for the simple pleasure of seeing them appear, thus defining the first steps in creating visual art, generally perceived as scribbles. As toddlers approach their second birthday, scribbles take on patterns, but these appear as a coincidence rather than as part of planned pictures.

### Two to Four Years

Not long before or after their second birthday, toddlers are able to identify parts of the body and draw symbols that represent them: a single mark for the head, two for the feet, and so on. Now, basic forms and shapes appear, some of them universal symbols seen around the world: mandalas, suns, ladders, spirals, wavy lines, and rainbows. It is possible to consider these design elements as the precursor of writing. Children may see that a design they have made looks like a familiar object and they will identify it as such. Toward age five, the order is reversed as youngsters begin to engage in attempts at representation, naming their intended picture before drawing it. Pictured objects all face forward and float in space rather than being found anchored to a base.

### Four to Seven Years

By kindergarten, objects in drawings are more likely to stand on a base and may face in varying directions. For the first time, humans wear clothing. Pictures now may tell stories or illustrate stories that have been dictated or written. As children move into the primary grades, they become comfortable with their methods of representation and drop the openness and experimentation of earlier years.

### Creativity and Artistic Development

The four qualities just discussed have traditionally been associated with creativity in general. Here, they are applied specifically to the visual arts. For many decades, the observation that children tend to lose, rather than develop, creativity in the elementary school years has been debated. Parents, educators, and outside observers alike have noted the often extreme, even flamboyant, creativity of very young children and the equally extreme deadening of this creativity once they have entered school. Is this loss due to some sort of natural development? Are the schools themselves, with their structure and rigor, to blame? While some research appears to have answered the first question affirmatively, it might be argued that many children's school experiences certainly contribute to the change.

The very natural development of creativity follows what has been likened to a U-curve, as those who begin as creative preschoolers, lose their creativity in the elementary years, and then regain it later on. The development of people who begin childhood as enthusiastic creative artists, but never return to an interest in artistic production, might be described as an L-shape (Kindler & Darras, 1997). Preschool children use their art experiences to explore the materials and make products that express ideas and feelings more often than they mimic visual reality. These products are often compared in their expressive quality to the work of adult artists: "The symbols employed have universal appeal and they are often organized into balanced or unified compositions" (p. 48).

Sometime in the primary years, such visual creativity goes into decline. Now, children have entered into a literal time of life in which they become more aware of what things really "should" look like and they become disappointed by their incapacity to make their artwork express what they see. In addition, they are developmentally interested in what is right and wrong in many facets of life, and this may apply to their art experiences as well. The power of the school to squelch creativity has been described by some as pertaining to the focus on learning symbol systems related to literacy and mathematics. That is, children "now want their drawings to accomplish what words and numbers can do: to more precisely describe . . . They want their drawings to tell the real story and enumerate the correct number of details. Their literal bent lowers their tolerance for the abstract" (Davis, 1997, p. 51). Primary aged students' perseverance to show detailed likeness is evident when they are engrossed in producing a realistic observational drawing as part of an inquiry-based learning project.

It is during the primary years that children begin to recognize the creativity in others' art. Their own art compositions may lack unity, balance, or creativity, but they can successfully point out these qualities elsewhere. Whether children re-enter a period of creativity in adolescence, thus climbing back up the right side of the "U," or lose interest in art production entirely, thus tapering off into an "L," will be determined by their artistic persistence. How much of children's choice in this matter is determined by their earlier learning experiences has not been determined. In the following story, you can see how Suzanne's experience when teaching art to second graders demonstrates the challenges and enjoyment of helping children of that age move through the bottom of the "U" and prepare for later escape from the "L."

### Second Graders Demonstrate Developmental Theories

In the late 1980s, Suzanne taught second grade for a year in an international school in Barcelona, Spain. The previous year, her then first graders had been obsessed with mermaids and mermen, incorporating them in much of their artwork, even when totally inappropriate, and fantasy games on the playground often centered on this theme. By second grade, however, the children had become equally obsessed with capturing the reality of the physical world around them. They spent hours, for example, trying to draw exact replicas of biological models—hands, ears, hearts, and so on—borrowed from the high school science classes. The school's art teacher capitalized on this new interest by introducing them to a large and complex painting by Diego Velazquez that hangs in Madrid's Prado Museum. An almost photographically realistic portrayal of royal life in the 17th century, *Las Meninas* inspired many hours of enthusiastic imitation on the part of the second graders. The resulting group painting was so stunning that it almost became the opening scene of a movie!

The art teacher then introduced the cubist work of Pablo Picasso and, once again, the children tried diligently to make their work look like his, but their enthusiasm was far less than it had been for Velazquez. The previous year they had willingly and with great interest learned about abstract art, but now they wanted reality. Suzanne and the art teacher were not, however, about to give up, particularly since they had a plan. Their plan was to take the children to the Picasso Museum downtown where they would see the cubist version of *Las Meninas* that Picasso had painted in the 1950s, along with a large number of smaller studies that had preceded the full painting. Although not told in advance of Picasso's derivative painting, once at the museum the children immediately understood what Picasso had intended and they spent an entire morning drawing their own mini-Picassos, even briefly lobbying to skip lunch.

By the next week, however, they requested, even demanded, a return to reality. For the rest of the school year, all artwork by second graders ignored abstraction in favor of relentless attempts at reality (Krogh & Magana, 1988). It should be added that, just as researchers have observed children ignoring a supposed stage in development in favor of the artistic needs of the moment, Suzanne noticed that the first grade mer-people would reappear on occasion. For example, several girls once found it advantageous to add mermaids to a lake that was part of a clay social studies project on Africa.

### Diversity in Development

Many teachers, including your authors, find that art is a great equalizer for children concerned about their capabilities as compared to those of other children. These teachers present materials and curriculum in such a way as to ensure success and self-confidence for everyone. As one art educator has described this situation, art experiences provide "a comfort zone where students get their first bit of confidence at school, a place where there is no pressure, where all students can be on equal footing" (Eubanks, 2002, p. 44).

**Figure 11.2** This tenacious first grader is determined to cut on his own using specially designed scissors.

The most obvious challenge for teachers of this subject is to choose positive experiences for children with visual impairments. Although such youngsters lack one avenue to artistic skills, there are others that can provide the enjoyment they deserve. For these children, materials that develop tactile knowledge, such as clay, play dough, collage materials, and plasticene, help to foster appropriate learning while encouraging self-expression.

Children with cognitive delays are well served by art experiences that require less in the way of academic skill. Their development follows the sequences of typically developing children, but is slower. They benefit from careful, direct, systematic instructions, including step-by-step demonstrations. Expressing themselves with artistic materials that include paint, markers, crayons, clay, and play dough can be especially rewarding because complex thought processes are not required.

Physical impairments must be dealt with on an individual basis, with every child's needs analyzed and solved the best way possible. In recent years, an increasing number of tools have been created to meet an ever-widening array of challenges, and teachers should most often be able to find implements that meet their children's needs. However, this is not always the case and some ingenuity may be called for. For example, Pam once had a wheelchair-bound first grader whose manual abilities made it impossible for him to cut with the standard primary scissors. His ever vigilant and supportive peers gladly helped him when needed, but this tenacious first grader was determined to cut on his own. Finding no commercially made scissors that would work, Pam enlisted her inventive, resourceful father-in-law who devised a motorized cutting device that allowed the child to safely fulfill most of his desired cutting needs.

Art is an especially strong counterbalance to trauma, fears, and illness. Children with emotional disabilities often find release in art activities. Psychologists have long used children's pictures for analysis, even when the children can't express their concerns verbally. Months after the events of September 11, 2001, Suzanne observed second graders illustrating Roald Dahl's *James and the Giant Peach* by substituting the World Trade Towers for the Empire State Building, with airplanes, rather than a peach, flying in. Yet, when the children talked about the book and their illustrations, not one shared what he or she had substituted. Perhaps, Suzanne thought, just engaging in the drawing was sufficient for their needs at that moment.

Another strength of art is that it can provide confidence building for children just learning English. One teacher has said that, "I think art is important because it is a universal language. Like a smile, like a painting, like a piece of pottery, it's something that everyone can understand. You don't have to have language to communicate an idea in art" (Eubanks, 2002, p. 45). Agreeing that art experiences provide a helpful means of communication for English language learners (ELLs), Olivia Saracho states that "Art experiences reinforce the ELL's language concepts and develop their visual symbolism." Further, "Art experiences encourage ELLs to discuss their artistic projects. Positive questions and encouragement about the projects can assist ELLs to be comfortable when sharing their projects" (2012, p. 327).

Giftedness in art presents a special challenge for teachers. It is tempting to "ooh" and "aah" over a precociously painted picture or clay model, but their creators should have the same freedom to experiment and create that the other children do without the pressure that comes from too much attention. Further, the less gifted should not be deprived of their joy in artistic production. In one multi-age class, an especially advanced three year old drew a profile of her teacher's head, complete with earring and correct hairstyle. Her five year old, and not as talented, sister was in the same class and, unfortunately, overheard the teacher's exclamations of surprise and delight. Hearing this one time too many, the older child burst into tears. While this was an extreme case, it is instructive to consider that similar situations might silently arise in any class where such obvious, and no doubt unintentional, comparisons are made. Asking each child what he or she wants to communicate about a piece of art, including what went well, or other personal comments, lets the child evaluate his or her individual expression and performance free of comparisons. The teacher can then make suggestions based on the child's analysis and level of understanding.

## INCORPORATING ART IN DAILY ROUTINES

If we regard the aesthetics of the classroom as both a manifestation of art and as necessary for the ongoing well-being of the class, we can easily see how incorporating art in daily routines is a natural consideration. For example:

- The attractiveness of the classroom is enhanced by a collection of potted plants, chosen for their varying leaf colors, shapes, and blooming schedules. As the children care for the plants, some may sense and remark on the diversity in beauty while others will more likely do so with some teacher assistance.

- A "unique and wonderful area" made from a low table, draped with attractive fabric, or even a child-level set of shelves, is a showcase for interesting objects and can be a source of delight. Suggestions for display objects include shell collections, cut flowers in small vases, or rocks of varying sizes and textures. These will need dusting and straightening as well as occasional replacing as part of classroom routine. As children engage in such routine care, they take ownership of the classroom's distinctive objets d'art. In addition, they can be encouraged to bring in small, unique, and wonderful items to add to the showcase.
- A large part of early childhood art is based on creative experiences with found objects. After a storm, particularly a windy one, cleanup may be necessary in the play areas. Or you may have outdoor cleanup as a part of your regular schedule. Rather than throwing away branches and other interesting items, bring them indoors for various art projects.
- If your classroom has a large whiteboard, bulletin board, or empty wall, donate a portion of it to the children to decorate as they see fit to beautify the area. This might even be designated a "task" with different pairs of children assigned each day.

In the following vignette you will see how simple queries, based on the curiosity of children, initiated an engaging inquiry-based learning project centering on an artist's coveted tool—a pencil.

## A CHILD-INITIATED INQUIRY EXPERIENCE

*An unusual, oddly shaped pencil lying on the teacher's desk caught the eye of a girl walking by. "Mrs. Morehouse, how did this pencil get so squished?" the student asked.*

*Pam explained that the pencil belonged to a carpenter who was helping her do some remodeling on her house. "Yeah, but why does he have a flatty pencil?" another boy persisted.*

*Instead of telling her students the answer, Pam responded with a question. "Why do you think he would want to have a flat pencil instead of a round pencil like we use?" Student answers included: The pencil would fit in his pocket better, he could stack them up if he wanted to, it might not cost as much money to make pencils this way, this kind of pencil might last longer. One girl proclaimed, "It probably wouldn't roll off of his table."*

*Instead of reading a story during the next 15 minutes before recess, Pam chose to continue this discussion with the children. She quickly hung a piece of tag board on the wall and continued, "You seem very interested in this pencil, and you have wise thoughts about why this pencil might be flat. Hmmm, what else do you know about pencils? Please tell me your thoughts, and I will write them on this chart."*

*The "What We Know about Pencils" chart was quickly filled with many astute observations including: Pencils come in different shapes, some pencils have erasers on them, some pencils have colored stuff to write with on the inside of them, not all pencils are made of wood, pencils have numbers on them, pencils have to be sharpened. Some pencils don't have to be sharpened, some artists use pencils.*

*Too soon it was time for recess. With the students gone, Pam made a quick mental note of the academic skills that might be applied if this high-interest topic of pencils were to be continued, and she decided that, yes—this was a topic that was worthy of in-depth study.*

*When the young questioners returned to class, they found their containers of pencils removed from the tables. Pam asked them to use crayons to make a "memory drawing" of a pencil (without looking at a pencil), and to write a short story about a fond memory they had about the pencil they drew. Pam was a scribe for the kindergarteners who needed help writing a story. (Note: Memory drawings and stories are typically used as a step in the beginning stage of an inquiry-based learning project. They help not only to personalize the topic of study but also to show degrees of understanding of the topic.)*

*Before the children departed school that day, they were instructed to think of things that they would like to find out about pencils—things that they wondered about concerning pencils.*

*The following school day the children noticed containers of colored pencils placed on their tables in addition to their regular pencil containers, and each of these new containers also held two carpenter pencils and one "very cool" twist-up pencil that didn't require sharpening.*

*Throughout the school day, the students shared and used these writing implements. Toward the end of the day, the class met and, with Pam again being the scribe, constructed a "What We Want to Find Out about Pencils" chart. Some of the deep wonders included: How do they make the fillings of pencils different colors? Why do pencils have different numbers on them? How do they make pencils? Who invented pencils? How long do pencils last? Why do artists like to use pencils?*

*Pam knew that the enthusiasm of her students and the quality of the questions they posed were two of the necessary ingredients to successfully weave many subject areas together. As the students sought to answer their questions, they used books and did research on the computer. Experiments were set up to see how long certain pencils would last. Pencils were sorted and classified in many ways. Detailed observational drawings were made of pencils and compared to the memory drawings. Child-illustrated word lists of pencil adjectives and pencil verbs were hung around the room. The students constructed charts to display their newly acquired knowledge of pencils. A parent who worked in a stationery supply store came to the classroom, and the students eagerly asked her questions. And when a grandfather, an amateur artist who drew with pencil and charcoal, visited the classroom, the young artists were eager to learn his artistic secrets.*

*When the young investigators tried to make pencils on their own they failed, but they were not daunted as their attempts led them to create other writing tools. Ingenious writing implements were made in many ways including Q-Tip-stuffed straws, foil-wrapped string, and tied-together broom straws. These writing tools soon became the implements of a classroom of very creative artists.*

*The artwork that was produced by these kindergarten and first-grade artists was proudly displayed around the school with each artist's name signed with a "flatty" pencil.*

## THE ART CURRICULUM

### NAEA's Six Essential Goals

As described in Chapter 10, the Consortium of National Arts Education Associations collaborated on a 1994 position statement related to "what every young American should know and be able to do" in dance, music, theater, and the visual arts. The resulting document provides guidance to arts educators to this day. As one part of this effort, the National Art Education Association (NAEA) listed six "Essentials of a Quality School Art Program (Consortium of National Arts Education Associations, 1994). These six essential goals will provide the basis of our discussion of the visual arts curriculum for young children. The views of the NAEA are clearly supportive of the goals set forth earlier in this chapter: preparing for democracy in a diverse society, increasing cognitive perception, providing creativity, giving aesthetic enjoyment, and supporting the development of all children.

---

> Goal 1: A quality art program should provide children with an ability to "have intense involvement in and response to personal visual experiences" (p. 6).

---

As we describe the goals we will also return to Steve's classroom and post-zoo art experience. It will be possible to see that one experience can demonstrate how the goals for a quality art program can be met within the framework of an integrated curriculum.

These experiences may be either the enjoyment of the art created by others or the creation of one's own work. In either case, for very young children an intense involvement is a supremely natural state; thus, a primary target of the curriculum is an atmosphere that fosters it.

### Involvement With Others' Art

Look carefully at classrooms for young children. How many of them have artwork posted at heights of 5, 6, or even 8 feet above the floor? Try squatting down to the children's level. How does the artwork look to them? Will they even pay attention to it? Before posting anything on walls, it is a good idea to try seeing it through the eyes of children. Above their eye level, broad expanses of color and design are appropriate, but not detailed work that asks for two-way communication.

If mobiles or other pieces of art are hung from the ceilings, it makes good sense to have them low enough that children can see them well. This poses something of a hazard for the teacher moving about the room, but it is a small price to pay for the children's involvement.

It is good to note how long pieces of artwork have been placed in their current positions. Long enough to fray at the edges, fade, or even rip? If a picture is a sentimental favorite and no replacement is available, there is an excuse to leave it up. Otherwise, it is probably time for a replacement. At the same time, artwork should be left up long enough that children grow familiar with it, and this is particularly true with the youngest children, who enjoy the stability of the familiar.

### Involvement With One's Own Art

For small children, involvement can mean experiments in modes of touching, in the sounds made by some media as they are used, or in their smells. An occasional child is offended by the smell of tempera, disgusted with the feel of finger paint, or intimidated by the muscular effort required of clay or play dough. It is important to be sensitive to children's responses and not to assume that every one of them will react positively to everything we introduce.

### Steve's Classroom

In Steve's class, each child was intensely involved in one way or another. This was natural as the art experience grew from another involving experience: the field trip to the zoo. The quietness as each child began sculpting and the subsequent excited sharing were manifestations of the class's involvement.

Goal 2: A quality art program gives children opportunities to "perceive and understand visual relationships in the environment," that is, to help children become "visually literate" and even "make informed visual judgments" (p. 6).

Children can learn to observe classic art prints with a knowledgeable eye. As children look at professional art, they can discuss the use of color, the comparative sizes of objects, and so on. Older children can learn such things as the concept of making objects smaller to give them distance.

Children in the preschool years who are primarily interested in process will not be able to critique artwork. But even kindergarteners can begin to look more critically at what they and others have created and, when asked, can share ideas for improvement.

### Steve's Classroom

In Steve's third-grade class, one boy offered guidance for the others as he shared his solution to the problem of representing grizzly bear fur. It is important that the children with problems were quite open about their inability to create what they needed and that the solution was taken in stride without any need for external reinforcement, reward, or critical acclaim.

Goal 3: A quality art program lets children "think, feel, and act creatively with visual art materials" giving them the same opportunity a professional artist has to transform materials "into a whole work of art" (p. 6).

When children are viewed as young artists, a new emphasis on quality materials and programs must follow. Respect for children as artists suggests that materials be of high quality, unstructured enough to inspire creativity, and basic and simple enough to give children confidence as they work. A list of materials for the early years might include:

Washable markers;
Tempera paints;
Brushes of high quality and varying sizes;
Round tipped safety scissors;
Crayons of varying sizes;
Watercolors;
Finger paint;
Chalk;
Collage materials, including fabric, of varying textures and variety;
Play dough (note the recipe for play dough on p. 52);
Assorted scraps of wood for sculptures (with nontoxic wood glue);
Picture-filled magazines to tear or cut up;
Newsprint, manila, and white drawing paper.

### Steve's Classroom

The material in Steve's class was clay that could be fired, a professional medium. At the same time, he was accepting of children whose methodology was such that firing would be impossible. He made this decision based on his observation of the children's involvement. At a later date he would probably give a demonstration of technique before the children became so deeply interested in other aspects of the project.

---

Goal 4: A quality art program provides opportunity for each child to "increase manipulative and organizational skills in art performance appropriate to his abilities. The development of skills is an important outcome for every student" (p. 7).

---

The position of the NAEA is that skills are attained only through much practice. "Through using materials one does increase manipulative and organizational skills; it is the chance to work with art materials and to think that allows one to begin to THINK, FEEL, ACT CREATIVELY WITH VISUAL MATERIALS" (Consortium of National Arts Education Associations, 1994, p. 7). (The emphatic capital letters are the NAEA's.) It would seem that the once-a-week art specialist, no matter how talented, will not provide children with the practice they need to become skillful. While we often provide preschool children with plenty of art materials, we more frequently neglect them in the primary years. Just having these materials available for children to use at odd moments during the day not only will provide practice in skills but also can go far toward making the most of the time that is available. Children should be permitted to use art materials between work assignments, after tasks are completed, and so on. More important, art should be integrated into other areas of the curriculum on a regular basis.

Children also need some instruction in method, especially when being introduced to a new medium or when learning to make new applications with a familiar material. It is during these times that a sensitive teacher can pick up reluctance on the part of some children to deal with some media.

### Steve's Classroom

We can see that Steve expressed the NAEA's intent that children learn skills through practice. No doubt he uses art in other curricular activities as well.

---

Goal 5: A quality art program should help children "acquire a knowledge of man's visual art heritage . . . Youngsters can begin to see connections between what has happened in the arts, ways in which different people have lived, and what they are trying to make and do in their own lives" (p. 7).

---

It is never too early to start. One teacher of three and four year olds hung inexpensive museum prints of works by the French impressionists throughout her classroom. The four year olds seemed interested in learning what techniques the artists used to achieve different results, and the teacher found herself giving them suggestions. Soon two or three of the older children were actually trying to imitate the pointillists. They could be heard in one corner of the room gently beating the points of their colored markers against the paper as they chanted, "Dot, dot, dot . . . " Although these children were too young for a class field trip to a museum, they were already responding to museum art in a very positive way.

> Goal 6: The quality art program should assist the child in using "art knowledge and skills in his personal and community life. As students grow they must begin to assume responsibility for their own actions, personally and publicly" (p. 7).

The key phrase regarding adult expectations of children assuming responsibility is "as students grow." Nevertheless, even preschool children are not too young to transfer their school learning to a sense of aesthetics in the home and community. There is a story that Maria Montessori liked to tell about the children in her school who took their newly acquired aesthetic sense home with them. She had encouraged the children to beautify the classroom in various ways, including the use of little pots of flowers throughout. Before long she observed that the apartments surrounding the school were displaying pots of flowers in their windows and learned that parents had put them there at the encouragement of their children.

Most children are at least minimally aware of the natural beauty around them and, with the teacher's encouragement, can become more conscious not only of beauty but of everyone's responsibility in its upkeep and longevity.

### *Steve's Classroom*

We can see that in just one art activity, four of the six criteria for a quality art program have been met. Further, art can be used to enhance and build on the learning from another curricular area—in this case, science.

### *Using Art as the Basis of Developmentally Appropriate Curriculum*

From a very early age, as we have seen, children use various art media to communicate feelings and ideas. During this preliterate stage of their lives, art processes do for them what writing systems cannot: provide a means of communication, both within themselves and with others. The wide array of possibilities for self-expression through art has been referred to as an important part of "the hundred languages of children." As such, expression through art has, for many years, laid the foundation of early education in the now-famed schools of Reggio Emilia, Italy, where a founding father, Loris Malaguzzi, first coined the "hundred languages" phrase to describe the many ways preliterate children have to communicate (Edwards, Gandini, & Forman, 1993). You have read about Reggio Emilia in previous chapters, and their schools provide inspiration for ideas throughout this text. It is, perhaps, the art program, however, that has most influenced early education in the United States.

In Reggio Emilia schools, a central feature of each building and curriculum is an *atelier*, or art studio, complete with an *atelierista*, or art teacher. Children engage in cross-curricular, inquiry learning that includes art-related expression. The suggestions at the end of this chapter are intended to model this approach. Most notable to American

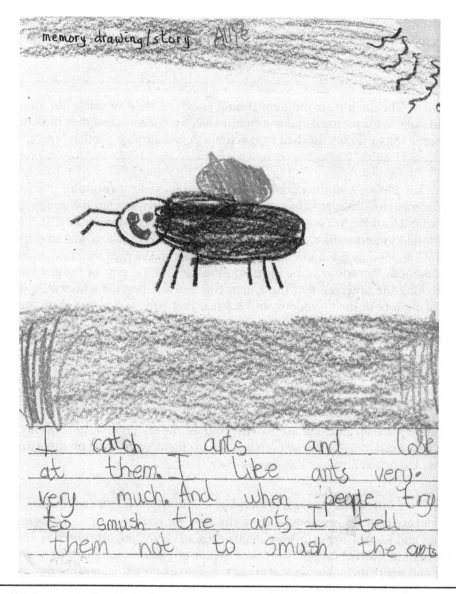

**Figure 11.3** A memory drawing adds detail to a child's written or dictated memory story.

educators is the fact that this work is taken quite seriously by the teachers as well as by the children, and it is incorporated into both short- and long-term learning. One observer of the Reggio schools, Lilian Katz, has suggested that an important lesson for American teachers to learn from them is that

Preprimary school children can communicate their ideas, feelings, understandings, imaginings, and observations through visual representation much earlier than most U.S. early childhood educators typically assume. The representations the children create with such impressive skill can serve as a basis for hypotheses, discussions and arguments, often leading to further observations and fresh representations. (1993, p. 25)

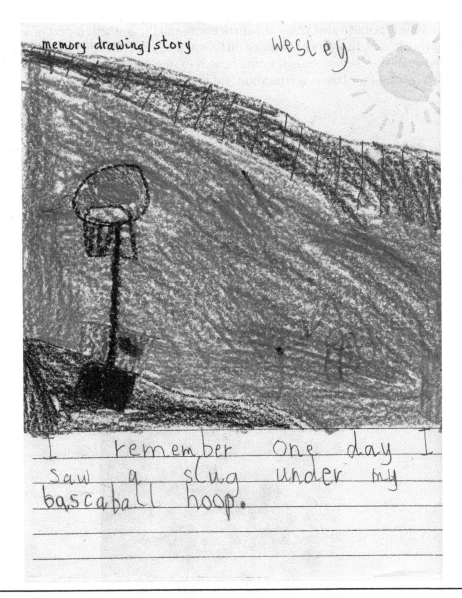

memory drawing/story

Wesley

I remember one day I saw a slug under my bascaball hoop.

**Figure 11.4** An in-depth study of slugs elicited this memory drawing.

U.S. educators concerned with early art education have, in recent years, learned from and been inspired by the Reggio Emilia approach. For example, three art educators (Althouse, Johnson, & Mitchell, 2003) were impressed by the fact that "In the Reggio Emilia approach, the arts are integrated into the school program as problem-solving activities, rather than as discrete subjects or disciplines taught for their own sake . . ." (p. 9). Others have observed that "the children's artwork is displayed with all the attention and care given to the work of professional artists. Mobiles hang from the ceiling, translucent works are attached to glass, some works are framed on a wall-mounted light box, and many sculptures are neatly arranged on shelves. The effect is delightful" (Isenberg & Jalongo, 2006, p. 88). In other words, in Reggio Emilia schools, art processes are used as languages for communication; artwork by even very young children is respected and taken seriously;

art as a subject is integrated across the curriculum; and the aesthetic aspect of art is never lost but celebrated. In an era of focusing on tests as a way of evaluating children's progress and the quality of their schools, it would be well to stop and consider the possibility that art is truly one of the basics in education and life.

## THE IMPORTANCE OF PLAY

The creativity associated with art experiences has been an emphasis of this chapter. Promoting creativity in center or classroom requires providing children with freedom to express themselves with as few restrictions as possible. The respect and seriousness that Reggio Emilia schools give to children's art is in no way diminished by permitting freedom as well. In fact, the opposite can be argued if, by providing freedom, teachers can be seen as regarding children to be capable of such self-management.

Freedom is the foundation on which artistic play is built. A number of other qualities are inherent as well, as summarized by Olivia Saracho (2012, pp. 308–309):

**Figure 11.5** Making a gingerbread house requires the incorporation of many skills. Family and friends enjoyed working with the students during this festive event.

A play experience is intrinsically motivated (doing for the sake of doing), freely chosen, pleasurable, spontaneous, flexible, and actively engaged both physically and psychologically, which are the characteristics of artistic play. Children's art has a fresh, spontaneous, and flexible quality.

Allowing free play through art experiences can foster growth in all areas of development. For example, children mixing colors of paint enjoy the beauty of what they are creating, thus engaging in an emotionally satisfying experience. In addition, the knowledge they gain from the results of mixing provides cognitive growth that can be relied on in future similar situations. A group of children building a clay structure require cooperation for success, thus encouraging social development. Clay activities are also a good source of physical experience, both large and small motor. Play through art offers young children a multitude of benefits. To quote Saracho again, "Art also supports children's play as they learn to cooperate, to share, to delay gratification of their impulses, and to imagine themselves assuming other people's roles" (2012, p. 309).

## TECHNOLOGY AND EARLY CHILDHOOD ART

In 2012, the National Association for the Education of Young Children (NAEYC), in conjunction with the Fred Rogers Center for Early Learning and Children's Media, issued a position statement addressing technology and interactive media in early childhood programs. Referring to the use of digital materials across the full curriculum, the organizations' position is that "Teachers must take the time to evaluate and select technology and media for the classroom, carefully observe children's use of the materials to identify opportunities and problems, and then make appropriate adaptations" (NAEYC, 2012, p. 6). As applied to art education, their position is that careful choice of technological tools can provide extended learning, but should not be the center of it. "For example, drawing on a touch screen can add to children's graphic representational experiences; manipulating colorful acetate shapes on a light table allows children to explore color and shape." However, "These opportunities should not replace paints, markers, crayons, and other graphic art materials but should provide additional options for self-expression" (p. 8).

## ASSESSMENT AND EVALUATION

Although there are accepted national standards, art education has not, traditionally, placed an emphasis on assessment. In the 1920s, there emerged a period of assessing children's artistic aptitude or intelligence through analysis of children's drawing. In the 1940s and 1950s there was a movement toward assessment, but it was squelched by the growing emphasis on child-centered and self-expressive art education. In more recent years, educational organizations, including those focused on art education, have explored developmentally appropriate methods of assessment. For the most part, these have centered on the "alternative" or "authentic" approaches discussed in this text's Chapter 3. In its most recent position statements on the subject, the National Association for the Education of Young Children (NAEYC) has taken this approach, suggesting that teachers talk with children about their art and then "have children revisit projects and media, giving them opportunities to revise and expand their ideas and refine their skills" (Copple & Bredekamp, 2009, p. 245). As discussed earlier in this chapter, informal assessment by children with the assistance of their teacher can be appropriate and helpful. Particularly as they near kindergarten age and older, they are able to discuss their intentions and their possible solutions. Helpful, too, is experience assessing the intentions and solutions of professional artists, as these can influence the work of the children.

## PREPRIMARY EXPERIENCES FOR INTEGRATING ART

Young children are generally drawn to art materials if they are made available. This is particularly true if their teacher has provided age-appropriate supplies—along with modeling of their usage as needed—and varies supplies over time. With appropriate materials and an atmosphere of respect and acceptance, experiences using similar materials and related to a single event can be quite different for different children. For example, upon return from a trip to the zoo, a child who is capable of representational attempts may use crayons to draw the family of chimpanzees she observed. Another who has not moved beyond scribbling may represent the chimpanzees by enthusiastically brushing brown all over a large paper on the easel.

This is one of art's strengths as a vehicle for communication: Children at varying skill levels are all able to feel the satisfaction of expressing themselves, perhaps to share with others or simply to talk to themselves. Because children in the early years may be at such widely varying levels of ability, it is a good idea to provide materials and activities that lend themselves to everything from scribbling to representation. The artistic activities described in the next part of this book can be flexibly adapted to please any ability level likely to be found in the preprimary years.

Activities have also been chosen for their potential for curriculum integration as well as a maximum of creativity. They are grouped by separate artistic skill areas. Figure 11.6 provides a look at art across the preprimary curriculum.

### Painting Activities

Easels may be a convenience, but they are not a necessity. Tabletops, outdoor floors, or any other washable surface may be used. Adding soap flakes to tempera paint will make it easier to clean up.

Generally, an easel or painting "station" will be used by more than one child during the day. Teacher demonstrations of the painting process are essential to keep the painting area freshly usable for everyone. For example, it is helpful to show children how to wipe excess paint off the brush and to avoid painting over colors while they are still wet. For children this age, putting one brush in each container of paint is most likely to keep things less messy. However, if children are to use only one brush in several containers of paint, be sure to carefully demonstrate how to clean the brush each time. It is important to keep in mind that, for preprimary children, each of these procedures provides a learning experience that presents some difficulty, both physically and cognitively. Thus, patience with youngsters' awkwardness will be important.

### Language

Young children like to work side by side, although they cannot be expected to cooperate on a mural based on a specific theme. On a large sheet of butcher paper, let children work alone or in small groups to make a mural by adding whatever they find beautiful. Use the mural as a background for dictated mural stories, announcements of upcoming events, and other visual displays.

## Social Studies

As a break from the usual rectangular sheets of paper, supply the paint center with precut thematic holiday shapes: hearts for Valentine's Day, shamrocks for St. Patrick's Day, and so on will provide recognition of the holiday without resorting to stereotyped patterned "art." If specific colors are associated with the holiday, they can be provided in the paint jars while others are temporarily removed. Make sure to include associations from holidays of various cultures that may be represented in the class.

## Mathematics

Again, cut the painting papers, this time into geometric shapes. Informally discuss the name of the shape as children paint or as you help remove the paper when they are done. Do not confine shapes to the customary square-circle-triangle triad. Children are equally capable of saying and seeing rhombus, trapezoid, and parallelogram.

## Science

Supply only the three primary colors. Challenge children to invent as many colors and shades as possible. Discuss with them the varying ways different children achieved their results.

Match paint colors to your nature observations. Watch for the arrival of different kinds of birds, and discuss the nature colors that can be seen in them. Note the varying colors of leaves on the trees. Supply paint and let children mix it to get the right shades. This in itself is one activity for preschoolers. Have children pair a swatch of paint on one side of the paper with an artifact of nature on the other.

## Music

Painting to mood music is usually interesting and pleasant for children. Use the opportunity to introduce the sound of new instruments and compositions. In one sitting you might want to choose just one mood or, perhaps, two contrasting moods. If the latter, be sure that the differences are starkly obvious. For example, a country music choice offers quite a contrast with something classical. Or, within one genre, the same thing can be achieved; perhaps two people, one male and one female, singing the same tune. Provide a variety of colors, but do not expect children to choose the same colors for the same moods that an adult would. Black may very well make a child happy.

## Woodworking Activities

Check local lumberyards and factories for scraps. Leave no source unchecked; one teacher relied for years on a mousetrap factory.

Even the youngest children enjoy hammering but, of course, some supervision is required. Using very lightweight wood, it is possible to create assorted sculptures and other objects with wood glue. Joining two or three pieces of wood together may be all the sculpting the smallest children need. Youngsters can experiment using sandpaper with varying grit, thus easily solving the problem of wood that may be too rough.

## Language

When interesting things are happening in the woodworking corner, the experience can be enhanced by woodworking stories dictated to the teacher. Have children describe what they have made and attach these descriptions to the object. Or have children describe the steps they took and follow up with a story focusing on sequential events.

## Mathematics

This subject is virtually unavoidable in woodworking. For any project children under-take, some form of woodworking measurement is necessary, whether formal or primi-tive. Even the experimental gluing and hammering by the youngest children will produce an expanded knowledge of spatial relationships. Older children can learn to choose one piece of wood as a measuring rod and compare it against other pieces of wood. Or some other object in the classroom, such as a pencil, can be used as a unit of measure when choosing pieces of wood of the right size.

## Science

Observing which objects float and which do not is a popular activity in preschool. In the wood box, provide pieces of varying density and size. In a nearby tub of water have children experiment and hypothesize about what will float and why. They might also nail or glue two or three pieces of wood together in varying configurations to see what will float. Some children will see these floating sculptures as "boats," a good springboard for discussion as to what real shipbuilders must look for in their designs.

## Clay Activities

Homemade or commercial play dough and hand-dug or purchased clay all provide chil-dren with a unique sensory experience. Some children really get into it—literally and figuratively—thumping, rolling, squashing, and manipulating. Others are more reti-cent and want to work only with their fingertips. This latter group can be encouraged to participate more fully by suggesting to them that this time, just for a minute, they try pushing down with the side of the hand. Next time introduce something else that can manipulate the clay: the elbow, palm, or knuckle, for example.

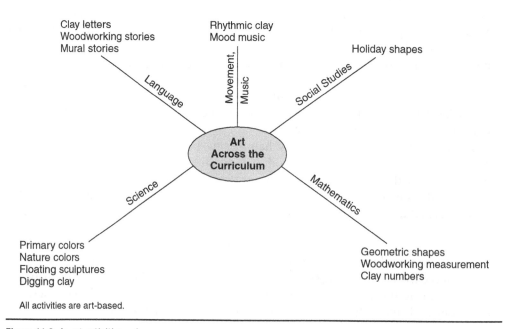

All activities are art-based.

**Figure 11.6** An art activities web.

*Language and Mathematics*

A number of four year olds and an occasional three year old will be interested in the formation of numbers and letters although their dexterity is not yet developed enough to write with pencil and paper. Clay offers a large-motor outlet for their budding interest. Begin with the clay letters of their names or the clay numbers that are their ages or some other symbol of real interest to them. Usually children will make any of these by rolling out snake shapes and then manipulating them into the proper shapes.

*Science*

Having children dig their own clay (if available) gives them a heightened understanding of what a source of supply really is. Comparing the texture and malleability of clay with other substances such as sand and dirt gives practice in classification as well as an increased understanding of the positive elements of clay as an art medium.

*Music*

On a day when energy needs an outlet, pounding clay to the rhythm of favorite music is a satisfying learning experience. Try using those that have strong rhythms. Singing very rhythmic songs is also fun to do but is more of a conscious effort and may detract from involvement with the art experience.

## PRIMARY EXPERIENCES FOR INTEGRATING ART

Primary-age children enjoy many of the same art endeavors as do their preprimary counterparts. Most adults, if they were asked, would probably admit that they also enjoy the artistic release afforded by engaging in preprimary-type art activities. And, as with other the other arts of movement, music, and drama, it is the maturity and academic understanding that learners bring to their productions that personalizes each endeavor.

It is with this in mind that we, rather than present individual art activities for the primary learner at this time, choose to have you take a glimpse into a first grade class to see an inquiry-based learning project unfold to focus on art. As you read through this project, note the variety of art experiences the learners generated through their in-depth study of fast food restaurants even before they arrived at their artistic finale.

The Room 4 Restaurant experiences a bustling business. It was constructed in the classroom over a period of three weeks and reflects the young learners' newly acquired knowledge gained from field research trips to the local drive-in and a Dairy Queen. During class "workshop" time the first grade students eagerly frequent the restaurant either as customers or as workers. The food and beverage choices are extensive; the most expensive, but very realistic looking, paper and play dough salad is a bargain at $1.00. Complex wood and cardboard machines help prepare and dispense the food items. After clocking in, the workers don their handmade and decorated cloth aprons, and are courteous as they hand out artistically decorated menus, take down orders, and fix and serve the food. Young patrons are appreciative and leave positive written comments on the restaurant's feedback cards.

During class discussion a few weeks after the grand opening of the classroom restaurant, a boy commented on some "very silly" pictures that he had seen on the walls of a unique local restaurant. This, of course, reminded other children that they, too, had seen pictures in restaurants and sometimes things even hung from the ceilings or displayed on shelves. The teacher took the liberty of leading the discussion toward artwork that included sculpture. "Well, maybe we should put up some art in our restaurant," Kaydie suggested. All of the children agreed it would be a very realistic and much needed touch to add artwork to their Room 4 Restaurant.

With the aid of parent volunteers, who energetically tackled the task of becoming "art experts," the children studied, at their level of understanding and over a period of time, works by Picasso, Audubon, Seurat, Monet, Pollock, and others, and brief biographies of these artists. Various media were used as the students did their own artwork in the style of the artists they studied. Three-dimensional artwork was also introduced. All children had a chance to display, on a rotating basis, their own artwork on the walls, ceiling, or shelves of the Room 4 Restaurant. Each creation was labeled with a title and had a brief description written, or scribed by an adult, about its style. The Room 4 Restaurant was now as authentic and aesthetically appealing as could be.

### Inquiry Projects That Might Emerge From These Activities

As children engage in art experiences, they might well find themselves sufficiently intrigued by one or more aspects of an activity to warrant a child-designed project based on inquiry. We remind our readers that, when considering a topic for an in-depth, inquiry-based study that will be conducted by children, a wise teacher is mindful of the criteria that make a topic worthy of study.

Will the study of the topic:

- Build on what children already know?
- Offer hands-on relevance to the children?
- Encourage application of social and academic skills?
- Interconnect (weave) or integrate curricular subjects with the goal of furthering student understanding of the topic?
- Support transference of knowledge to future learning?

With these criteria in mind, we offer the following possibilities for inquiry-based learning projects, stemming from children's exposure to art and artistic endeavors. Each suggested topic area would be appropriate for preprimary as well as primary students, as each age of young learners will not only bring their own level of understanding to the proposed topics but also carry out investigations as is developmentally appropriate to their skill level.

- A certain material used in artistic endeavors may draw children's interest. In-depth research on how paint is made, where clay comes from, or how paper is produced could culminate in children manufacturing their own materials.
- Implements used by artists have excellent potential for in-depth inquiry as children explore different varieties and construction of brushes, or discover tools that sculptors use. Tools used by artists through the ages and by various cultures, depending on their hands-on accessibility, might also prove to be an engaging topic of further inquiry.
- An item of art—a vividly glazed ceramic bowl, for instance—may well pique young learners' curiosity sufficiently to encourage investigation of other types of bowls from different countries and cultures, including how they are made, what they are made of, and how they are used.

Through experience, we have found that when the interest and enthusiasm of young learners are attentively observed, a wide variety of worthy topics present themselves. Teachers must be aware of such areas of interest, as these interests, when turned into a topic of inquiry-based study, can be used to logically and meaningfully integrate the curriculum.

## THE POWER OF INQUIRY LEARNING THROUGH INTEGRATION

Art for young children has always been about aesthetic enjoyment, but it can be about so much more. Cognitive development and art abilities bear a strong relationship in young children. Art provides an important communication vehicle for the preliterate, no matter what their age. It offers a major way of expressing creativity. Perhaps surprisingly, and as we showed earlier in the writing of June McFee, art education for young children can even promote the growth and understanding of democracy.

Most important to the theme of this text, art can be the driving force at the center of an integrated, inquiry-based curriculum. Young learners use their artistic skills as they draw lifelike observational drawings, as they record data in descriptive pictures, and as they recreate in child-like fashion with paint, paper, and cardboard, everything they remember from a field research trip. The catalysts of wonder, which start inquiry projects, may center on any aspect of art or the products made by artistic endeavors. And the spell of learning through inquiry is evident as young learners explore, experiment, and invent using artistic media to make creations that are distinctively their own.

Art readily weaves and interconnects other subjects. Whether it is the illustration in a written or scribed story, a loving message in a card, depictions of data obtained on a field research trip, or an artistic rendering of a new academic understanding, art is at the heart of integration. Today, just as it has for centuries, art communicates and integrates not only academic knowledge, but emotional understandings as well.

## TO DISCUSS

1. Talk with class members or colleagues about the varying cultures found in your classroom or center. In what ways do you see the children's backgrounds reflected in their teacher's art projects? Are there others you might suggest?
2. Do you think that, since there are art standards, assessments should be developed based on them? Discuss why or why not.
3. Look online for suggested art activities for younger children. Discuss with others some examples of those you consider appropriate based on the NAEA's standards and those that are not.
4. Review what you know about what constitutes a topic worthy of inquiry-based, investigative learning. Based on this knowledge, what topics, other than those suggested in this chapter, might emerge from young learners' artistic endeavors? Explain how each topic might integrate the curricular subjects.

## TO DO

1. Once you have determined what online art lessons are appropriate (see Item 3 above), choose one or two to teach to children. Reflect on whether the lessons were, in fact, appropriate.

2. Observe children of different ages as they are involved in art activities. What developmental differences do you see?
3. Refer back to the Room 4 Restaurant inquiry-based learning project. Write down all the art activities that were apparent from the description of the project. Use your imagination and describe other ways, not stated in the vignette, that art may have been, or could have been, integrated as the students constructed the restaurant.
4. The renowned artist, Pablo Picasso once said, "Every child is an artist. The problem is how to remain an artist once we grow up." If you are uncomfortable as an artist, try challenging yourself to be one although you are grown up. If you are fearful about teaching art because you haven't expanded your talent since you were in elementary school, take an art class, even a brief one. Feel free to share your fears with the instructor right at the beginning; most will be supportive and positive and happy that you are there. If you are already comfortable with art, expand your skills with a new medium, even if you only have time for a brief effort.

# REFERENCES

Althouse, R., Johnson, M., & Mitchell, S. (2003). *The colors of learning: Integrating the visual arts into the early childhood curriculum.* New York, NY: Teachers College Press.

Burton, J. (2001). Lowenfeld: An(other) look. *Art Education,* 54 (6), 33–42.

Chapman, L. (2005). No child left behind in art? *Art Education,* 58 (1), 6–15.

Consortium of National Arts Education Associations. (1994). *National standards for arts education.* Reston, VA: The National Art Education Association.

Copple, C. & Bredekamp, S. (2009). *Developmentally appropriate practice in early childhood programs serving children from birth through age 8.* Washington, DC: NAEYC.

Davis, J. (1997). The "U" and the wheel of "C". In Kindler, A. (Ed.), *Child development in art.* Reston, VA: National Art Education Association.

ECAE. (n.d.). *Art: Essential for early learning.* Retrieved from www.arteducators.org.

Edwards, C., Gandini, L., & Forman, G. (1993). *The hundred languages of children.* Norwood, NJ: Ablex Publishing Corporation.

Efland, A. (2002). *Art and cognition.* New York, NY: Teachers College Press.

Efland, A. (2004). The arts and the creation of mind: Eisner's contributions to the arts in education. *The Journal of Aesthetic Education,* 38 (4), 71–80.

Eubanks, P. (2002). How art specialists adapt curriculum for ESOL students. *Art Education,* 55 (2), 40–45.

Katz, L. (1993). What can we learn from Reggio Emilia? In Edwards, C., Gandini, L., & Forman, G. (Eds.), *The hundred languages of children.* Norwood, NJ: Ablex.

Kellogg, R. (1970). *Analyzing children's art.* Palo Alto, CA: National Press Books.

Kindler, A. & Darras, B. (1997). Map of artistic development. In Kindler, A. (Ed.), *Child development in art.* Reston, VA: National Art Education Association.

Krogh, S. & Magana, D. (1988). The eyes and hands of second graders: From Velazquez to Picasso. *NewsLinks,* 8 (3), 1, 6.

Lowenfeld, V. & Brittain, W. (1982). *Creative and mental growth.* New York, NY: Macmillan.

McFee, J. (1970). *Preparation for art.* Belmont, CA: Wadsworth.

McFee, J. (1998). *Cultural diversity and the structure and practice of art education.* Reston, VA: National Art Education Association.

NAEYC. (2012). *Technology and interactive media as tools in early childhood programs serving children from birth through age 8.* Retrieved from www.naeyc.org/files/naeyc/file/positions/PS_technology_WEB2.pdf.

Nieto, S. & Bode, P. (2012). *Affirming diversity: The sociopolitical context of multicultural education* (5th ed.). Boston, MA: Pearson.

Saracho, O. (2012). *An integrated play-based curriculum for young children.* New York, NY: Routledge.

Winner, E. & Hetland, L. (2000). The arts and academic achievement: What the evidence shows. *Journal of Aesthetic Education,* 34 (3–4), 300–306.

# 12

## MOVEMENT AND PHYSICAL EDUCATION

*Movement is as necessary to mental and physical development as food.*
—Grace Nash

After reading this chapter you should be able to:

- Explain why movement and physical education are vitally important to the development of young children;
- Describe the physical development stages of young children;
- Demonstrate ways that movement can be incorporated into classroom life all day long;
- Describe how movement can actually be the central theme of integration and inquiry.

The quotation that begins this chapter might be seen as an overstatement, but we would argue that it is only marginally so. From life in the womb and on through infancy, children learn about their world specifically through their physical interaction with it. With entry into preschool, physicality remains critical to learning, even when such things as symbol systems for reading and mathematics are first introduced. The primary grades are a time when children are moving into what Piaget termed "concrete operations," a more sophisticated time of development. Yet, the very concreteness that is essential for real understanding of the world indicates a need for children to be physically interactive with their learning materials.

Despite the importance of physical activity to all areas of development, our entire nation has, in recent decades, moved away from recognizing this fact in favor of sedentary, indoor activities, even for the youngest children who need activity the most. Here are some findings that should give all educators reason to reverse this trend:

- Physically active children have a greater chance at lifetime health.
- This may be the first generation ever in which parents outlive their children.

- The childhood obesity rate in the United States has almost tripled in the last 20 years, so that now 12.5 million children (17%) between the ages of two and 19 are clinically obese.
- Lack of physical activity can lead to less healthy bones, muscles, and joints; increased fat and reduced muscle; high blood pressure; depression and anxiety; and less capacity for learning. (CDC, 2013; Sanders, 2005)

These findings indicate that it is imperative that teachers find time to incorporate movement throughout the day. The teacher of young children who continually seeks ways to provide outlets for movement and who has a good understanding of appropriate physical education activities for each age will, no doubt, foster a wide variety of developmental pathways for his or her youngsters. Important, too, is being an active role model. "Teachers who display physical vitality, take pride in being active, participate in activities with students, and are fit, positively influence youngsters to maintain an active lifestyle" (Corbin & Pangrazi, 2004, p. 18).

In this chapter, as in the others devoted to curriculum, the ideas for you to try are based on research and position statements from the appropriate curricular organizations. In addition, we share some of what we have learned through our own experiences. We begin with a preschool observation that helped Suzanne learn how to teach and manage a movement experience, even before she studied early childhood education.

## SUZANNE LEARNS TO TEACH MOVEMENT WITHOUT CHAOS

Many years ago, I used to strap my son Peter on the back of my bike and set off to his Montessori school a couple miles from our Washington, DC, apartment. After dropping him off, I would window-shop on my way home, and I soon discovered an intriguing viewing opportunity somewhere between the small Safeway and a dress shop. A sign over the large window invited passers-by to stay and observe the preschool class inside for as long as they liked, and I found myself drawn to the interesting activities going on.

One day in particular stands out to me, because in just 10 minutes of viewing, my approach to the teaching and management of movement activities changed forever. At the time, I had experience teaching second and third grade but had never been really involved in early childhood education. Here, step-by-step, is what I observed:

- With the children seated in a circle, the teacher brought in a stack of newspapers, giving each child a single two-page sheet.
- Holding a sheet of paper to her ear, the teacher crumpled the paper and suggested the children do the same and listen to the sound.
- She then continued with other suggestions that became more and more active, until the children were moving all around the room, newspapers seeming to fly everywhere. Chaos appeared imminent.
- Then, however, the teacher briefly disappeared, returning with a very large plastic trashcan, which she placed in the center of the room. "Oh! Look what I can do!" she exclaimed, wadding her paper into a ball and throwing it sideways over her head into the trashcan. Immediately, the children imitated her movements, then noticed that their teacher had twirled around and now sat cross-legged on the floor. They did likewise, forming their usual circle.

- In the absolute silence that followed, the teacher began to debrief the experience in a subdued voice while the children listened intently . . . and a bit breathlessly.

Here are the lessons I learned that day . . . the approaches to teaching and management that were new to me:

- Young children will learn new movements with almost no verbalizing or explanation on the teacher's part. Nothing but a few words and some modeling will be needed.
- A movement activity just prior to a sedentary experience helps ensure attention during the latter.
- Any movement activity that finishes with a return to a state of quiet is one that successfully incorporates management without the necessity of discipline.
- If the teacher incorporates clean-up into the activity itself, then clean-up is automatic and requires absolutely no instruction or nagging on the part of the teacher.

About a year after this experience, I enrolled in a Montessori training course. During a lecture on management, I was reminded of the newspaper lesson when our trainer stated, "I don't care if the children are climbing the walls—so long as you know how to get them off the walls!" I had already learned one way to do just that and the "newspaper teacher's" approach has never failed me.

## WHY MOVEMENT AND PHYSICAL EDUCATION MATTER: A BRIEF HISTORY

Let us begin with definitions appropriate to early education. *Movement* opportunities for young children include creative movement activities and dance. For preschool children, these experiences are most often free-form and unstructured, focused more on the process of learning how their bodies work and move than on products suitable for public display. *Physical education* incorporates movement activities but also adds more structured approaches and incorporates activities specific to fitness, games with rules, and sports skills. It has been said that, "Learning to move and learning through movement are the broad-based aims of all quality physical education programs" (Gallahue & Donnelly, 2003, p. 10). Applying this statement specifically to early childhood education, we can say that "learning to move" is critical for development from infancy onward and that "learning through movement" is important to an inquiry-based, integrated curriculum for young children. In the following sections, we will focus more fully on the developmental implications of learning to move and on the multitude of opportunities to incorporate movement into all areas of the curriculum.

Here, we look further at this broad-based view that is both new and very old. Bits and pieces of it have been present in educational philosophy for many centuries. In one way or another, movement education has usually been incorporated into the school day since ancient times. For example, the early Greeks and Romans incorporated play into their education for young children, and before them the Egyptians trained young boys in tumbling, dancing, tug-of-war, ball games, juggling, wrestling, swimming, and more.

Later, in the European Middle Ages, physical education was decried as being too focused on physical life, rather than the spiritual, and this potential evil was removed from the curriculum in cathedral schools. Boys in the royal court schools, however, learned to swim and dive, use various bows, joust, wrestle, and fence—all activities that would be useful when they were later admitted to knighthood.

The Renaissance brought a return of the attitudes of the Greeks and Romans, and physical education again had wide acceptance. Nevertheless, this acceptance was primarily practiced in the upper classes, and the poorer children suffered ill health and had little time for physical play. Thus, as the American continent was first colonized, "a combination of hard physical labor and puritanical fervor left little inclination for play among early settlers" (Shephard, 1982, p. 15).

By 1852, however, some schools in the Boston area began incorporating gymnastics, and St. Louis and Cincinnati soon followed suit. By 1866, California was requiring physical education in all its schools. The first public playground appeared in Boston in 1885, and four years later the same city required gymnastics in the schools. The primary purpose was to provide children with a break from study. In fact, the gymnastics could be done right in the classroom between heavy study sessions. At the turn of the 20th century, John Dewey introduced games and dancing as part of young children's physical education into the University of Chicago Laboratory School but, for the most part, schools did not change from formalized gymnastics programs until after World War I.

Physical education finally came into its own as an important subject for schoolchildren after World War II, a period notable for the emergence of "movement education" as an appropriate approach for younger children. Begun in Germany with the work of Rudolf Laban, expanded in England, and then imported by the United States, movement education takes a different approach to what is expected of children when they are educated physically. The traditional teaching of progressive skills, the same skills to all children in a group whether they are ready or not, is rejected. In its place, children's physical and emotional development are enhanced by using games, gymnastics, and dance in a less competitive and more creative way.

The several goals of this type of program are quite different from those traditionally associated with physical education, particularly in the primary grades. Even though preschools have traditionally focused less on performance and competition and more on creativity and games, the goals of post-World War II movement education became broader still (Kirchner, 1978, p. 4):

- Children will become physically fit and skillful in a variety of situations.
- Children will understand the principles of movement and become aware of what their bodies can do.
- Self-discipline and self-reliance are encouraged.
- There are opportunities for self-expression and creativity.
- Children develop confidence in meeting physical challenges.
- Cooperation and sensitivity to others are encouraged.

In recent years, not only do the goals of movement education continue to prove their validity, but research has demonstrated that when learners have opportunities for physical movement, such movement can lead to higher academic scores (Mears, 2003). Younger children, in particular, learn most effectively through increased movement. Despite these findings, the attitude persists that movement education is an unnecessary frill. The adults responsible for children's education have often felt that there is so much pressure to teach academics, coupled with the need for their classes to measure up to current academic standards, that there is simply no time for movement in the school day.

Today, as many children have fewer natural opportunities to learn to move and to learn through movement, it becomes more necessary for their teachers to provide school- or center-based experiences that will foster their development. The next section explores the topic of physical development based on the overview in Chapter 1 and includes examples of real-life experiences.

## MOVEMENT, PHYSICAL EDUCATION, AND CHILD DEVELOPMENT

Children of all ages need plenty of time devoted to both informal physical activity such as recess and more structured physical education. Since the fundamental movement phase lasts from about age two to age seven, it will be the most important one for early childhood teachers to consider. However, primary grade teachers can expect to see the beginnings of the sports-related movement phase with many or most of their children, and will need to make curricular adjustments based on their careful observations. Descriptions of children's development in the upcoming sections are from Corbin and Pangrazi (2004); Gabbard (1995); Gallahue and Donnelly (2003); Holt/Hale and Parker (2000); and Kun (2005).

### The Fundamental Movement Phase

The *fundamental movement phase* comprises ages two to about seven or eight. Children in this phase attain increasingly complex use of their bodies, yet their skills remain basic. In other words, the skills are not yet ready to be completely integrated into the complex maneuvers required of true sports or choreographed dances. During this phase, children attain greater and greater control of their bodies, making it possible to move in more accurate rhythm while performing progressively more complex movements. By the end of this phase, the beginnings of sport and true dance are possible.

Teachers need to be aware of the cognitive and social/emotional development that accompanies each of the movement phases, so that appropriate teaching decisions can be made. For example, at age five, many children are physically ready to take on the challenge of team sports, but socially are not sufficiently mature. Here is an example of the disaster a lack of awareness can lead to:

Christian was a well-regarded high school soccer player who needed to fulfill a community service requirement. He chose to coach a team of kindergarten children and to referee at their first game. After a few practices, during which the children's greatest love was running up and down the field and occasionally kicking the ball in the general direction of the goal, the day of the tournament arrived. The children were excited to put on their new "costumes" and got ready to face the team they had never before seen, all dressed as they were, but in different colors.

But then reality hit and it became apparent to all that there would be winners and losers and that whistles would be blown to indicate "bad" moves. Although Christian's team won, by the end of the game a few of his children and virtually all children on the losing team were in tears, and vowed never to participate in such a horrible activity again.

Christian agreed with the children. He demanded that, in the future, the soccer league would let "all my babies" win, and, having observed the emotional wreckage of the tournament game, the soccer league board agreed. From then on, children less than seven engaged in games that subjected them only to the joy of running, kicking, and playing together.

Later, the cognitive ability to coordinate the movements of soccer along with the knowledge of boundary lines, the need to kick into the net, and so on would develop along with the social/emotional ability to deal with the disappointments of losing or letting down one's team members.

If you observe children in the Fundamental Movement Phase, you can expect to see the following at each age.

### The Two Year Old

Children at this age run, gallop, walk on tiptoe, and jump rhythmically. They can walk up and down stairs, at first with both feet on a step, then later just one. They enjoy rolling balls and can throw overhand as well as kick from a standing position. Arms are used for balance and to keep rhythm, and hand clapping is rhythmic. The rhythm of older two year olds is more competent, and they become more interested in imitating the rhythms of others.

Children at this age are more self-sufficient; thus, lack of adult attention may not be as devastating as it can be for younger infants. Nevertheless, if a child is to learn to throw a ball, for example, then someone must be around to demonstrate and help.

Because two year olds still prefer solitary and sometimes parallel play they should not be forced into group situations for movement activities. At this age children also crave independence, so they are happiest when adult direction leads to independent capabilities. Since their attention shifts quickly from one thing to another, it is a good idea to alternate active with more sedentary activities. Most of all, two year olds need happy reinforcement of their attempts at improving their skills: running faster, walking up and down stairs, climbing around and over things, and moving to rhythmic beats.

### The Three Year Old

Now children walk in a way that looks much more adult. They swing their arms, rather than using them for balance, and the rhythm is right.

Now that their coordination and rhythm are improved, simple, imaginative dramatic play becomes attractive. They are likely to introduce some variety into their body movements and to experiment with their use of space. A lot of energy goes into movement, and children may occasionally lose control and fall (but at least it's not too far to the ground)! The ability to ride tricycles gives much more mobility, and no preschool can possess too many of life's first vehicles.

General movement capabilities increase for the three year olds. They can walk forward and backward on a straight line, walk up and down stairs with more ease, jump off the bottom step or two, run with a more even stride, balance for a moment on one foot, and maybe even hop a bit. They can now kick a ball while running, and some children can bounce it fairly well.

For some children there can be a temporary relapse before they turn four. There may be days when everything goes well and others when they seek the reassurance of an adult hand going up or down stairs or when they cannot get the beloved trike to do what it ought to. This appears to happen during growth spurts, when the body seems to need to adjust to new changes. However, three year olds are making great strides in coordination.

### The Four Year Old

At this age, children are agile, energetic, and more active than when they were younger. They run up and down stairs, can throw a ball overhand, and are learning to skip. Jumping is great fun as they learn to do it from a running position. These children will climb as high as they can on playground equipment or trees, and then they sometimes cannot get back down again. Stunts and tricks are popular activities. They can march in time, and some can hop on one foot. They are beginning to like to do things in groups, such as singing, but most times they like to do things their own way without too many interfering directions.

The implications for working with four year olds include being sure that there is plenty of space and time for energetic movement experiences. There should be climbing equipment and supervisors to be sure all goes well. This is a good time for dramatic play; acting out stories in free interpretation, possibly with song, is excellent also.

### The Five Year Old

At five, children offer a respite from the energetic year before. Refining and consolidating already acquired abilities is more the keynote than is exploration and expansion. A good sense of balance is pretty well established by now, and fine motor development is improved. For most children, but not all, handedness is established. Children can walk the balance beam, execute simple dance steps and, in general, control bodily activity more smoothly. Hopping and skipping are now no problem, and skipping rope is an attainable challenge for many. Some children can hit a swinging ball, play two-handed catch, and bounce the ball repeatedly, but none of these skills is at a mature level. Body rhythm is confident and natural, and both body awareness and body image are increasing. At five, children no longer have the all-out constant physical exuberance of four year olds, so a balance between active and more passive activities is a good idea once again.

### The Six, Seven, and Eight Year Old

By the time children enter first grade, they are also entering an important new stage in their development. Although there are change and progress between the ages of six and eight, the course is more steady and unvaried than it was in previous years. Thus, we can cluster several ages together in one group.

After the "breather" that the five year olds provide, the six year olds demonstrate again what energy and activity young children are capable of. By now, if all has gone well, children have, at the least, a simple mastery of the fundamental motor skills. You will recall from Chapter 1 that these are the skills necessary for future use in sports and recreational activities. They include those we have discussed: running, jumping, hopping, skipping, galloping, balancing, climbing, and throwing; bouncing, catching, kicking, and hitting a ball. These fundamental skills are important enough to children that teachers need to observe them knowledgeably and support children's progress in refining them. By elementary school, physical education teachers become a part of children's lives, but unless you are in the rare school district that provides a class every day, you will find yourself supervising much of the children's outdoor activity. At such times it would be a good idea to observe these skills and provide help—or seek it from physical education professionals—when it is needed. Children who become competent in the fundamental skills will feel much more competent as they begin new sports. And that is true all the way through life. Following are some ideas of what to observe:

- Running: First graders can run in much the same fashion as adults; all the coordination elements are present. They are not as fast, for speed comes over the next three years with growth and practice. First and second grades are generally a time of great increase in speed, both for fast dashes and for longer runs. Boys tend to be just slightly faster than girls.
- Hopping, galloping, and skipping: In this instance it is girls who outperform boys, usually acquiring all three skills a little earlier. It is in first grade that skipping is usually mastered, although girls may be more graceful and boys may weigh more and be flat-footed.
- Jumping: Before children enter first grade, their jumping interests focus more on jumping down rather than up, over, or far. In the primary grades, children begin to learn about long jumps and high jumps in their physical education classes, and a different interest grows. As they enter school, girls have a slight edge over boys in how far they can jump, but boys then improve more rapidly and by the end of third grade have become more adept at jumping than girls.
- Throwing: Between the ages of seven and 11, children increase their throwing distances by 100%. However, boys outdistance girls markedly at all ages.
- Kicking: Again, boys perform better at all ages, both in velocity and distance. For both sexes there is great improvement between the first and third grades.
- Balance: There are four interrelated types of balance: postural balance (walking and sitting upright), static balance (keeping a position without moving), dynamic balance (controlling posture while moving through space), and gymnastic balance (needed for stunts and complex movement combinations). Studies of children working on balance beams (dynamic balance) showed great improvement between first and third grades, with boys and girls almost identical in their abilities. Various apparatuses have been used to measure static balance, and curiously, children improved through age seven, tapered off at age eight, then increased performance again at age nine. Coming into first grade, boys were less capable than girls but were then able to catch up.

### The Sports-Related Movement Phase

At about age seven, the onset of the Sports-Related Movement Phase finds children ready to coordinate their emerging general physical skills with the specific skills needed for participation in sports or movement activities such as dance. Since this phase extends through the high school years, teachers of young children should expect to observe only beginning capabilities.

Again, it is important to keep in mind the cognitive and social/emotional development of children this age when choosing appropriate movement activities and sports. To demonstrate, here is an example of the capabilities of second graders:

In the beginning of the school year, Ms. Frances observed that her rising seven year olds were not yet emotionally capable of dealing with winners and losers in physical education activities. After one or two attempts, she and the physical education teacher gave up in the face of the children's anger, disappointment, and occasional tears.

One day in May, however, the children on their own determined that there should be winners and losers in the relay races they were about to begin. Ms. Frances agreed that they could try this, although she observed that a few of the children looked dubious, even fearful. After much energetic discussion of start and finish lines, appropriate places to tag at the far end, what constituted real running, walking, and hopping, and the need for a referee, the races began. At the end of a half hour, very few actual relay races had been attempted, but the children seemed greatly satisfied that they had moved to a higher level of sports experience. (The few children who had looked dubious continued to do so.)

As the children returned to their classroom, Ms. Frances suddenly recalled reading that Piaget (1932) had witnessed exactly the same thing as young boys spent an entire recess planning for a snowball fight that never happened. They, too, had appeared to feel quite satisfied despite the lack of an actual game.

### Diversity in Development

Although growth and development charts can provide generalized explanations of physical development and movement skills, it still remains true that there can be wide divergences between children of a single age within one classroom. For example, asking a group of four year olds to repeat rhythmic patterns by beating their hands on their knees can lead to any number of responses, some of them right on beat, others partially or totally out of sync.

In addition, in many classrooms are children with diagnosed physical disabilities that make keeping up with the various activities difficult or impossible. For this group, as well as for everyone else, an activity-based approach to instruction can prove beneficial. *Activity-based instruction* (ABI) was developed in the 1980s and early 1990s by Diane Bricker at the University of Oregon (Pretti-Frontczak & Bricker, 2004). ABI is based on the idea that neither the teacher-directed intervention model traditionally favored by special educators, nor the child-directed approach favored by most other early childhood educators, is sufficient. Although the traditional model does give the teacher control over the class along with targeted goals and objectives for the children, it does not provide children with the possibility of creativity or initiative taking. And, although the child-directed model corrects for these failings, it leaves little room for goals and objectives. As applied to movement and physical education, the second approach may well not provide needed practice or feedback for those who need the extra attention.

Combining the best of each model, ABI suggests to teachers that they act as mediators, modifying the environment as necessary to make children comfortable in their surroundings. "In essence, the teacher actually helps the child practice individual objectives, but it is the child who directs the teacher when, where, how, and how long to work on a particular objective . . . While the children get to choose where they go and what they play with, the teacher has specific goals and objectives in mind for each child" (Block & Davis, 1996, p. 234).

Applying ABI principles to movement education includes making objectives and activities meaningful to children. Daily routines are a good place to start. It may well be that, for some youngsters, just participating in the daily routines that involve physical activity will be a challenge. Such activities as walking into the room, using body management to take off a jacket, using upper body strength to pick up objects at centers, or sitting in a chair may be sufficiently difficult as to require goal setting on the part of the teacher and child. These are all activities important to children's daily lives and to their feelings of belonging to the group.

Teachers often find themselves concerned, nervous, and even fearful about teaching children with physical disabilities. If ABI, with its combination of teacher direction and child freedom is utilized, however, adaptations and adjustments provide much needed help. In addition, there are some easily instituted solutions to some of the most common fears that teachers have (these are adapted from suggestions by Huettig, Simbeck, & Cravens, 2003):

- **Fear 1: I don't have enough help.**

  **Solutions:**
  - Design a peer buddy program in which children take turns helping as needed and appropriate.
  - Make use of parent volunteers or "between duty" school workers.
  - Make sure, as a teacher, that you provide feedback to all students, while keeping an extra eye on children with special needs.

- **Fear 2: I'm afraid I can't communicate successfully.**

  **Solutions:**
  - Use simple gestures with thumbs up, down, and neutral—effective in communicating with all children.
  - Use exaggerated facial expressions to convey basic emotions.
  - Use music (or perhaps a whistle, outside) to start and stop activities.

- **Fear 3: I'm worried about keeping children safe.**

  **Solutions:**
  - Establish an emergency procedure at the beginning of the school year. (You should do this at any rate, even if there are no children with disabilities.)
  - Consult with parents, district adapted physical educator or special educator, physician, university adapted physical educators, and websites to get ideas for your specific children.
  - Keep a cell phone or walkie-talkie with you outside.
  - Create a few rules focused on safety and review them frequently.
  - Observe children at all times and stop unsafe practices immediately.
  - Before taking children outside, make a quick check of the play area to be sure no potential hazards have appeared.

It is important for teachers to understand young children's physical development when choosing appropriate activities for them. Each age offers its own level of capabilities that inform teachers' choices. Nevertheless, as demonstrated in the experiences of Ms. Frances and Christian, it is equally important to be aware of the other areas of development as well, because movement activities foster children's development in social, emotional, and cognitive areas as well as the physical. Adjustments may need to be made to take into consideration the special needs of some children.

## INCORPORATING MOVEMENT INTO DAILY ROUTINES

Movement activities can be incorporated throughout the day from the very first moment children arrive in the classroom until they leave some hours later. Here are examples to try:

- Place a balance beam in an area of the room that would not cause a two-way traffic problem. Incorporate its use as children move from one activity to another.
- Begin a recess session by taking a run around the edge of the playground; all children are cheered for their efforts, not for their ability to come in first.
- During transitions, play music that contains a variety of moods and permit the children to dance from one activity to the next.
- Have children move from one activity to the next by mimicking various animals (choosing them yourself based on the level of noise and motion you are willing to accept).
- Offer youngsters an opportunity to "get their wiggles out" by standing up and stretching, swaying, and reaching, while incorporating a variety of movements.

## A CHILD-INITIATED INQUIRY EXPERIENCE

*Not often did snow fall in the town where Mrs. Morehouse taught first grade. So on the day that it fell like huge, magic sparkles from the sky, all eyes in the classroom, young and old alike, were focused on the transformations taking place outside. The whirling and twirling snowflakes beckoned the children to do the same. Mrs. Morehouse, perhaps also caught up in the silent music that came from outside, realized this was an opportune time to integrate movement, based on wonder, into the day. And so, the children observed the movement of the flurrying snowflakes for a few more minutes, then began to move like snowflakes themselves, quietly and gently spinning around the furniture in the classroom. Suddenly, the outside wind picked up, the snowflakes outside whirled out of control, and the young "snowflakes" inside did the same. The classroom turned into a blizzard of out-of-control energy.*

*Mrs. Morehouse chose to move from her planned teaching path that morning and decided instead to use this relatively seldom weather gift to the students' and her advantage. She sensed that the snow would probably be gone by the afternoon so there was really no reason to steer the young learners toward an in-depth inquiry-learning based project on snow. The use of movement to capture the snowy moment, as well as the students' energy, however, had good potential.*

*Because the students had become accustomed to working cooperatively together and enjoyed the dynamics of working on group projects, the young collaborators already had an idea in mind before meeting together on the work rug area. They would become snowflake dancers! But, wait, some of the children had seen icicles form, fall, and crash off the edges of roofs. Therefore, icicle dancers were also needed. And indeed, as the snow quickly turned into rain, rain dancers were also in demand.*

*And so, the 23 first graders, in democratic fashion, divided into four dance troupes: two groups of snowflake dancers, one raindrop dance group, and one dancing icicle group (consisting of all males). All during the day, as the children found time, they would meet in their groups and practice the less-than-intricate dance moves they created. It soon became apparent that music and costumes would add sensory appeal to each dance. So, with the teacher's assistance, each group chose accompanying music. Each group also drew a sketch of a simple costume that was then made from school materials of foil, crepe paper, and butcher paper. Silver glitter added a sparkly, albeit messy, touch.*

*The diversity of weather phenomena was well captured and depicted when the dancers performed in front of the class. It was a performance, the teacher knew, that family members would cherish. And so, at the teacher's suggestion, each child wrote and illustrated a short letter to invite any and all family members, including adult friends, to come and see the short performance.*

*It was a packed house in the classroom's makeshift auditorium on the day of the performance. And, as the snow dancers spun and bowed, the raindrops pranced and plopped, and the icicles stomped and crashed, moisture was seen glistening in the eyes of some of the spectators.*

## THE MOVEMENT AND PHYSICAL EDUCATION CURRICULUM

As explained in Chapters 10 and 11, the Consortium of National Arts Education Associations collaborated on standards in their fields (Consortium of National Arts Education Associations, 1994). As applied to movement education, there are three "nested" organizations that can provide us with direction on how best to create and deliver movement curriculum to young children. The umbrella organization is the American Alliance for Health, Physical Education, Recreation and Dance (AAHPERD). Within AAHPERD can be found the National Association for Sport and Physical Education (NASPE), and within NASPE is the Council on Physical Education for Children (COPEC). It is members of COPEC who have developed position statements concerning appropriate practices in movement and physical education programs for younger children, one for ages three to five (Holt/Hale & Parker, 2000) and one for elementary school (Rampmeyer, 2000). Because the approaches to each age group differ somewhat, we have divided them accordingly.

### Quality Movement Programs for Children Ages Three to Five

The appropriate approach to early movement education according to COPEC is to focus on the fundamental motor skills, on concepts of movement, and on the joy that comes from moving (Rampmeyer, 2000). Underlying this philosophy are five premises that teachers need to understand, agree to, and develop:

1. *Teachers of young children are guides and facilitators.* COPEC emphasizes how important it is for teachers to be fit, set an example of joy in movement, and model at least some of the activities their youngsters participate in. In addition, careful observation leads to appropriate activities for follow-up and optimum development.
2. *Children should engage in movement programs designed for their developmental levels.* Child-movement specialists generally take the position that development is age related, not age determined. In other words, while there are general expectations for what preschoolers and kindergarteners should be able to do, teachers need to understand that each child develops at his or her own rate and with different levels of interest and ability. In addition, it is important to remember the developmental differences between these younger children and those in the primary grades.

3. *Young children learn through interaction with their environment.* The fact that youngsters learn through interaction with the people, objects, and surrounding atmosphere (both physical and social-emotional) should provide some direction for teachers developing curriculum. Everything needed for movement experiences is right within reach.

4. *Young children learn and develop in an integrated fashion.* COPEC reminds us that all elements of development—motor, cognitive, emotional, and social—are inter-related, and that teachers should remember this when creating activities. Such interrelationships will only increase in importance as children develop their skills and begin to learn cooperation and teamwork necessary to group sports and dance.

5. *Planned movement experiences enhance play experiences.* Adults often assume that all children play naturally and competently, but this is not always the case. Many years of research inform us that, depending in part on their living environments and life experiences, children exhibit a wide variety of play capabilities. Providing movement experiences in the classroom setting enriches the experience and imagi-nations of all children.

Based on these five premises, COPEC (Rampmeyer, 2000) takes the position that teachers' practices can be either appropriate or inappropriate. Here is a selection to reflect upon.

1. Appropriate practice: "The curriculum includes a balance of skills and concepts designed to enhance the motor, cognitive, emotional, and social development of every child." Inappropriate practice: "Teachers plan the movement curriculum around personal interests, preferences, and background . . ." (p. 4).

2. Appropriate practice: "Teachers design movement activities for the total develop-ment of children. The unique role of movement programs, which allow children to learn to move while also moving to learn, is recognized and explored." Inappropri-ate practice: "Teachers view movement programs as separate from other areas of instruction. They are felt to be a means of 'burning excess energy'" (p. 5).

3. Appropriate practice: "Teachers employ both direct and indirect teaching methods." Inappropriate practice: "Teachers implement highly structured, teacher-directed lessons most of the time" (p. 5).

4. Appropriate practice: "Teachers use authentic assessment based on the scientific knowledge of children's developmental characteristics and ongoing observations of students in activities." Inappropriate practice: "Teachers assess children solely on the basis of test scores, such as motor skills tests, norm referenced tests, and stan-dardized fitness tests. Teachers use tests to merely audit performance rather than improve it" (p. 6).

More recently, NASPE created a task force of early childhood experts for the purpose of creating guidelines for infants, toddlers, and preschoolers (Kun, 2005). Their conclu-sion was that infants should not have their movement restricted for prolonged periods of time and that daily physical activities are important; that toddlers should accumulate at least 30 minutes a day of structured physical activity; and that preschoolers should accumulate at least 60 minutes of structured physical activity. Toddlers and preschoolers should accumulate at least 60 minutes, and up to several hours, of unstructured physical activity and should not be sedentary for more than 60 minutes at a time unless they are sleeping.

Putting into effect the COPEC premises and positions on appropriate practice should lead to activities that will enhance young children's development and enjoyment of movement. Here are some time tested and well-regarded suggestions:

- Active games that require simple counting or chanting;
- Simple rhythms and marching;
- Very basic yoga movements;
- Freeform dancing to a variety of music types;
- Climbing and jumping from and over sturdy boxes and building blocks;
- Throwing and catching slow-moving objects; rolling them if children express major nervousness;
- Simple singing games;
- Noncompetitive games;
- Movement games that require quick stops, starts, and changes of direction;
- Jumping through simple grids, leading to hopscotch when children are able.

### Quality Movement Programs for Children in the Primary Grades

Taking a slightly different approach to defining quality programs for children at the end of the fundamental movement stage and the onset of sports-related skills, COPEC begins with NASPE's list of program outcomes for school-age children (Holt/Hale & Parker, 2000, p. 2). The outcome, they state, of a program that is developmentally and instructionally appropriate is a physically educated person who:

- Demonstrates competency in many movement forms and proficiency in a few movement forms;
- Applies movement concepts and principles to the learning and development of motor skills;
- Exhibits a physically active lifestyle;
- Achieves and maintains a health-enhancing level of physical fitness;
- Demonstrates responsible personal and social behavior in physical activity settings;
- Demonstrates understanding and respect for differences among people in physical activity settings;
- Understands that physical activity provides opportunities for enjoyment, challenge, self-expression, and social interaction.

Because these attributes define long-term goals for children in elementary school programs, teachers of children in the primary grades should regard them as inspirational goals, rather than expecting youngsters to achieve such levels. For the primary years, COPEC suggests another set of five premises that should prove helpful in curriculum creation (Holt/Hale & Parker, 2000):

1. *The ultimate purpose of any physical education program is to guide children into being physically active for a lifetime.* Because we live in a world of rapid change, it is possible that today's young children will find that the physical activities they now engage in will be quite different when they get older. Therefore, it is the job of their teachers

to help youngsters develop the basic movement skills appropriate to their age, thus facilitating later adaptation.

2. *Children should engage in physical activity appropriately designed for their developmental levels.* COPEC reminds us that young children are not miniature adults or even sixth graders, that physical activity and sports that are appropriate for older children and adults must be altered or avoided. This is important if we hope and expect that what we do with young children will become the basis of a lifetime of activity.

3. *Recess and physical education are important, but different, parts of the school program.* This is a highly important distinction, one that teachers tend to ignore, forget, or misunderstand. *Recess* involves free play, which can lead to creativity, informal social interactions that promote friendship and cooperation, appropriate competition, conflict resolution, and decision making. In addition, recess provides children with an opportunity for physical activity, certain to promote more openness to learning once it is over. *Physical education*, on the other hand, is a planned instructional program (note the word *education* in the term). It should be regarded as an essential component of the school curriculum, dedicated to increasing "the physical competence, health-related fitness, and self-responsibility that facilitates enjoyment of physical activity for all students" (p. 3).

4. *Physical activity and physical education are not the same.* Here, again, is a distinction for teachers to remember. Simply stated, "physical activity is the subject matter of physical education" (p. 3). Teachers need to be sure that physical education time isn't taken up with equipment removal and return, team selection, standing in line, and so forth. When that happens, the subject matter has been lost from the experience.

5. *Physical education and athletic programs are different.* Athletic programs are designed for children with special talents or interests. Teachers need to keep athletic programs out of the school curriculum, focusing instead on creating experiences designed for every child in the class. While this particular premise most often needs to be a reminder for teachers in the upper elementary grades and beyond, it can occasionally be an issue even in the early years.

Now, we can apply the premises and position statements to consider some physical education and movement experiences for the primary grades:

- Organized practice in skills: throwing, catching, dance moves, and so on;
- Rules and playing fair during games, with beginning steps toward competitive experiences and sportsmanship;
- Teaching of safety and good judgment;
- Challenging movement problems, with adjustments made for individual capabilities: tumbling, apparatus work, complex dance moves;
- Simple folk dances;
- Avoidance of highly organized ball games that demand quickness and accuracy;
- Ball bouncing and dribbling skills to rhythm.

To summarize, the lists of activities we have provided should be regarded as some that might be added to readers' original ideas. Major considerations in planning should include avoiding competitive games until most of the children begin to request them or seem to be ready (remember Christian and Ms. Frances!); providing sufficient activity throughout the day with attention given to the NASPE guidelines regarding time; including skills practice to make children comfortable, but not requiring them for extended periods of time; and, most of all, making sure that children understand and feel that physical experiences are positive and joyful. And don't forget to model what you want your children to do and be!

## THE IMPORTANCE OF PLAY

Throughout much of the early childhood curriculum, movement can be a source of beneficial play experiences. During language and math for example, children can build letters and numbers with their bodies, relying on their personal creativity—either individually or in groups—to create replicas of what they see in books, online, or on paper. Music experiences can include playing with movement as children spin, dance, or march. As teachers take children outdoors to investigate nature, movement can be used to dramatize the experiences they predict they will have.

Physical education classes for young children are devoted to movement, sometimes through directed drills, but more often through play. In the preschool years, such play is informal and freeform; in the primary grades, rules with winners and losers are introduced. Developmentally appropriate play experiences help children grow, not only in their physical abilities, but also in their social, affective, and cognitive domains. As NAEYC points out, play gives children "opportunities to develop physical competence and enjoyment of the outdoors, understand and make sense of their world, interact with others, express and control emotions, develop their symbolic and problem-solving abilities, and practice emerging skills (Copple & Bredekamp, 2009, p. 14).

One form of active play that has become controversial in recent years is so-called *rough and tumble play*. In toddlers, this generally takes form as chasing or spinning around. Preschoolers begin to wrestle and chase each other with more one-on-one interaction. Primary grade children are the biggest fans of rough and tumble play, with boys preferring wrestling and holding each other down, and girls primarily chasing. It is, as would be expected, the wrestling that has become controversial as adults have become more concerned about negative physical or social results. Yet, rough and tumble play helps children understand the physical limits of their strength, the placement of their bodies in space, and the social consequences of their choice of actions.

Frances Carlson (2009), who has argued for permitting rough and tumble play, maintains that it is "essential for children's development and learning." Adult concerns, she says, can be addressed by helping them understand the difference between active "big body" play and real fighting. When children are playing, they often smile and even laugh; when they fight, there are frowns and even tears. Children who are playing participate willingly, remaining as long as they are enjoying themselves; when the activity is aggressive, one child is usually dominating.

Carlson suggests that adults help children before they engage in this kind of play by creating safety rules such as no kicking, tagging with open hands only, no choking, and keeping hands away from hair and heads. Finally, "Smiles stop—play stops" (p. 72).

# TECHNOLOGY AND EARLY CHILDHOOD MOVEMENT AND PHYSICAL EDUCATION

One education writer (Castelli, 2005) suggests that teachers ask themselves three basic questions when considering the integration of technology into movement education: "(a) Will the technology improve my efficiency as a teacher? (b) Will the technology foster learning in the students? And (c) Does the technology accomplish something that could not be accomplished previously without it?" (p. 6). These are excellent questions to ask when incorporating technology into any teaching experience.

Budding athletes can use a video device to observe their performance for the purpose of improving skills or for assessment of performance. The early childhood educator might consider using video to make youngsters more aware of what happens when they and others move or to observe the modeling of movement by more expert performers. With the relative simplicity of today's video devices children may well be able to take recordings of one another. And a video camera is also the perfect tool for recording performances that were planned and presented by young learners, so they can view the fruits of their labors from another perspective.

Technology can be used to motivate people to exercise—adults as well as children. Pedometers that can measure walkers' speed, distance, and stride length may enthrall youngsters. There are numerous interactive video games that encourage running, jumping, and stretching, with specific games geared toward young movers. In addition, there are exercise games that do not require a video monitor or computer screen. If it is possible to use movement and exercise technology in the classroom, teachers may well find enjoyable benefit in participating along with their students.

# ASSESSMENT AND EVALUATION

Appropriate assessment of young children, according to the National Association for Sport and Physical Education (NASPE), is focused primarily on teacher observation with occasional forays into written products and, by the primary grades, peer observation. Examples suggested by NASPE (1995) include:

- Preschool/kindergarten observation: The teacher or aide observes children at play during recess and periodically records their choices of high, medium, and low intensity activities, as well as no appreciable activity (standing around). This provides the teacher with a more accurate understanding of each child's level of activity choices than do informally created opinions.
- Kindergarten observation: Children perform a "dance of locomotors" requiring them to move through space in various creative patterns as announced by the teacher. The teacher uses a checklist focusing on, for example, the ability to define and stay in a personal space, moving with an awareness and consideration for others, and identification and demonstration of a variety of locomotor skills.
- First grade weekly or monthly list: Youngsters keep a simple track of what activities they did and when. On blank weekly (or monthly) gridded pages students write (or draw) an activity (or activities) they did during each day. The more advanced students may choose to keep track of the amount of time they spent on each activity as well.

- Second grade written product: Children keep journals in which they record their physical skill goals, interests, accomplishments, and activities . . . both personally chosen and designated by the physical education teacher. They might draw pictures of themselves engaged in their activities, and then circle the body parts (muscles) used in each of them.

From infancy onward, young children learn best about their world when they are permitted plentiful opportunities to engage in movement, both informal and more structured. Teachers have an opportunity and a responsibility to ensure that sufficient movement opportunities are provided and to incorporate movement into daily routines as well as integrate it into specific academic subjects. Movement activities should not be regarded simply as ways to burn off energy, get out wiggles, or keep children happy . . . although these are certainly positive side effects. Movement is much too important a part of children's learning and growth to keep it marginalized; we need to resolve to keep it at the center of life.

## PREPRIMARY ACTIVITIES CELEBRATING MOVEMENT THROUGHOUT THE CURRICULUM

When teachers of small children have movement uppermost in their minds, opportunities can arise spontaneously as observation informs them that the time is appropriate, perhaps even necessary. In addition, planned movement activities can add richness to the rest of the curriculum. In this section we present some ideas that teachers have successfully used. Figure 12.1 (p. 339) shows a curriculum web with preprimary movement activities.

### Language Experiences

#### What I Did This Weekend

Have children share what they did over the weekend while you record the information on a flip chart (see Chapter 6 for more information on the value of this to literacy learning). Then, call out each activity and have the entire class "do" or act out what various children reported.

#### Describing Words (Adjectives)

Make a list of words that describe objects or people. Use words you hear from the children as well as others you would like to introduce to them. Ask children to act them out individually or in groups. Some suggestions are *slippery, sticky, hungry, frightened, fidgety, happy.*

#### Letters in the Air

Ask children to "paint" letters in the air using their fingers, toes, knees, elbows, and heads.

#### Making Stories Come Alive I

When you tell or read a story, take time to let the children act out the plot. If the activities take place at truly appropriate times, they will enhance, rather than interrupt, the flow of the story.

### Making Stories Come Alive II

Choose books or stories that lend themselves to dancelike movements. Nature books with pictures of many kinds of animals are notable for what they might inspire. As children observe a picture and learn about the animal's life, have them move as the animal would in various activities of its life.

## Mathematics Experiences

### Making Shapes

Suggest a familiar geometric shape and ask children to make it any way they choose with their bodies. The shapes can be carried on the wind and then fall to the ground.

### Short and Tall

Have children imitate animals that are short and those that are tall. Older children can make this a guessing game as the others try to guess what animals they are.

### Being Numbers

Have children use their bodies, or any part of their bodies, to create numbers. Challenging them to move their numbers through space adds a further dimension. Keeping their shapes, they can become kites as you direct them to float through space, move with bigger and smaller winds, and then gently fall to the ground as the wind ceases blowing.

### Shape Doors

Use large cardboard boxes for children to crawl in and out of. In the sides, cut holes of varying geometric shapes to be used as doors. Outline the shapes with a bright, wide line of tempera paint. Let children move boxes around and play with them as they like. Use the shape names informally, as you converse with the children during their play. As in the Making Shapes activity, it is good to introduce shapes beyond the usual basic ones.

## Science Experiences

### The Weather

Use recorded music that evokes images of weather and let children move as they interpret it. Choices of music can be made that coincide with the current weather, or if a particular type of weather has been absent for a noticeably long time, it can be remembered through music and movement. (One good source is Grofé's *Grand Canyon Suite*.)

### Growing Plants

Before planting seeds, have children describe through movement what will happen to them over time. Explain that the actual process will take much longer. Each day, role-play the process as it has been achieved so far.

### Animal Comparisons

Do this after learning the characteristics of several animals. Ask children to name an animal that moves very slowly; then have everyone demonstrate the movement. Continue with quick movements—pouncing, slithering, crawling, swimming, climbing, and so on. Be sure to increase vocabulary by using the different verbs.

## Social Studies Experiences

### Community Helpers

Young children often study about the service providers in their community. Both before and after a field research trip or guest visit, have the children act out what the service provider might do during the day. Ask if they can explain the differences in their actions after knowing more about the career of their guest.

### Class Rules

Children are more likely to obey rules when they have created them themselves. And children are more likely to understand the rules if they have acted them out. As children create rules, present hypothetical situations; then, give them the opportunity to act out following the rules in the situations.

### Safety Rules

Safety rules are particularly appropriate when introducing rules for playing on outdoor equipment. Ask children to tell a rule they know for playing on the equipment. Then, have children describe through movement what might happen if they disobey the rule. Follow up with a description through movement of what will happen if they obey the rule. (Always end on a positive note.)

### Classroom Courtesy

At the beginning of the school year or anytime that manners and consideration for one another are lagging, role-play correct behavior. There is usually no need to lecture or to discuss recent bad behavior; role-playing the correct behavior and praising it will change things around.

## Art Experiences

### Learning to Sculpt

When children begin to work with clay, take the opportunity to role-play what happens when we sculpt. Divide children into pairs, one the sculptor (a good word to learn) and one the clay. The sculptor moves one body part at a time until the "finished product" is achieved. Children can share their shapes with others if they like, then reverse roles.

### Shadow Shapes

Early in the morning while shadows are long, take children outside to a large, preferably concrete area. Challenge them to make long and short shadows as well as curved, twisted, narrow, and wide ones, and so on. If you are against the side of a building, experiment with making the shapes go up and down the wall.

### Move and Paint

Outside, place cans of water and paintbrushes of varying sizes. Place a recorded music device nearby and select rhythmic music. Permit children to paint anything they choose, their only instruction being to listen to the music as they do so, painting in the way the music makes them feel.

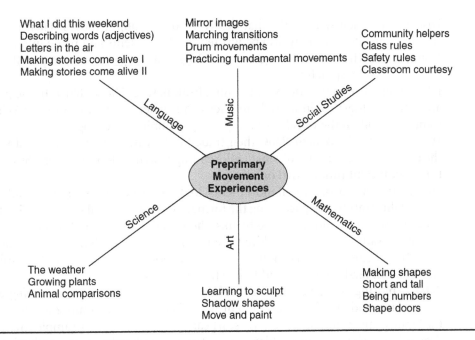

**Figure 12.1** A movement activities web.

*Music Experiences*

*Mirror Images*

To recorded music, move rhythmically while children imitate; children can be leaders as they gain confidence.

*Marching Transitions*

As children move from one type of activity to another, play music with a marching tempo.

*Drum Movements*

Play the drum(s) in varying rhythms and have children move as they feel inspired.

*Practicing Fundamental Movements*

Using piano or recorded music, instruct children to hop, skip, gallop, jump, and walk.

## PRIMARY EXPERIENCES CELEBRATING MOVEMENT THROUGHOUT THE CURRICULUM

The joy of experiencing movement need not stop at school, nor end when one reaches adulthood. As learners acquire skill and sophistication, so will their maturation be reflected in their movement endeavors. Movement activities in the primary grades gain an added dimension when young learners add their reading and writing skills.

Primary students have the skills to:

- Read a verb from a class brainstormed, written, and student-illustrated "Verb Chart." Have the whole class act out each verb when it is read.

- Discuss, and then write verbs that describe how an object moves. Then move as the verbs dictate. This may also be written out by students and made into a book. Examples of what students might write: Dogs can _____ (run, jump, roll). Kids can _____ (skip, spin, hop).
- Fill in a sentence frame adding something from nature. The sentence-frame papers are gathered together in a book and acted out when read. For example: When I went on a walk in the woods I saw a _____ (rabbit, snake, dog).
- Write a simple *Movement Book*, then trade books with others to read and follow the directions. (Examples of what children might write: Hop two times. Sway four times. Skip eight times. Twirl one time.)
- Discuss the variety of animal movements. Make a class book, with each child writing and illustrating one page using the format of: I can _____ like a _____. Students copy the sentence and fill in the blanks, then draw a corresponding animal illustration. (Examples of what children might write: I can hop like a rabbit. I can fly like a bird. I can waddle like a duck.) When the book is completed and assembled, children can read each page and follow the movements.
- After exploring movement using brightly colored scarves, write a *Moving Scarf Book*. Have students describe different ways their scarves can move as they fill in the blank of the frame sentence: My scarf can _____ (Examples that children might write to fill in the blank: go fast, make circles, do zigzags, make shapes). When the book is completed, read it aloud as the children make their scarves mimic the actions.
- After a discussion of opposites, explore opposites of motion such as sit/stand, fast/slow, run/walk, up/down. Make class or individual student books depicting these opposites. Act out the opposites, as they are read, when the books are completed.

### *Inquiry Projects That Might Emerge From Preprimary and Primary Experiences*

As children engage in movement experiences, they might well find themselves sufficiently intrigued by one or more aspects of an activity to warrant a child-designed project based on inquiry. As we have emphasized before, when considering a topic for an in-depth study an astute teacher keeps in mind if the study of the topic:

- Builds on what children already know;
- Offers hands-on relevance to the children;
- Encourages application of social and academic skills;
- Integrates subjects by interconnecting and weaving them, with the goal of furthering student understanding of the topic;
- Supports transference of knowledge to future learning.

With these criteria in mind, we offer the following possibilities for inquiry-based learning projects, stemming from children's participation in movement activities. Each suggested topic area would be appropriate for preprimary as well as primary students, as each age of young learners will not only bring their own level of understanding to the proposed topics, but also carry out investigations as is developmentally appropriate to their skill level.

- An item used to enhance a movement activity may draw children's interest sufficiently enough to launch an inquiry study. A study of scarves, for instance, may reveal how scarves are made, where they come from, and other countries that have scarves, as well as present a vast array of scarves for comparing and contrasting. The vast variety of balls might also pique youngsters' interest.
- Awareness of the amazing ways bodies move may trigger a curiosity of a certain part of the body, for instance, the foot. This might lead to a study that includes research on the feet of other animals.
- Movement as it is used in dance has potential to steer young investigators to research dances popular in other countries, or specific costumes worn for dance.
- A more abstract topic, difficult however for the younger learners, might evolve from observing movement in nature, which could lead to research on wind. Movement over time lends itself to plant research.

## THE POWER OF INQUIRY LEARNING THROUGH INTEGRATION

Curriculum integration is important enough to the physical education community that one professional journal, *Teaching Elementary Physical Education*, published an ongoing series of articles, some research-based, devoted to the topic. Here are some observations, opinions, and findings as they relate to younger children:

- Incorporating academic conceptual learning into physical education can "provide a means for students to understand how movement and physical activity can be integrated into their lives beyond motor skills learning" (Ayers & Wilmoth, 2003, p. 11).
- Through movement, children are able "to immerse themselves physically, emotionally, and intellectually in activities that apply developmentally appropriate concepts. Foremost, they experience knowledge through kinaesthetic awareness that enables a broader understanding of interconnected subject matter" (Kalyn, 2005, p. 32).
- Using an "interdisciplinary approach . . . provides visual, auditory, and kinesthetic learners an appropriate avenue for learning" (Carpenter & Stevens-Smith, 2003, p. 37).
- "Movement is a way for children to come to a deeper understanding of important topics and vocabulary; that is, movement is a way for children to become more 'literate' about the world" (Rovegno, 2003, p. 24).

The significance of movement and being active can be highlighted even more when components of movement are used as topics of in-depth studies and thusly used to integrate the curriculum. Consider the curricular subjects the topic of "running" could integrate as young inquirers ask and seek answers to questions such as: How fast can kids run? What do special running shoes look like? What happens to your body when you run? Why is it good for people to run? Do lots of people run? How far can people run? What animals run and why? And so on.

When the interest and enthusiasm of young learners are attentively observed, a wide variety of worthy topics present themselves. And a thought-provoking topic, when used as a focus of inquiry-based study, can logically and meaningfully integrate the curriculum.

## TO DISCUSS

1. Reflect on your physical education experiences when you were in the primary grades. Discuss what you remember these experiences entailing. Which were your favorite activities? Why? Which were your least favorite activities? Why?
2. Using your reflections from Item 1, discuss what you would have done, with the knowledge you gained from reading this chapter, to change or modify the "least favorite" activities.
3. Based on your knowledge of what constitutes a topic worthy of inquiry-based, investigative learning, what topics, other those suggested in this chapter, might emerge from young learners' participation in movement activities?
4. With a partner, discuss the pros and cons of supporting rough and tumble play. Reflect on memories—good and bad—you and your partner have of such type of playing when you were young children.

## TO DO

1. Create a collection of movement activities that apply to the various curricular subjects. We recommend an index box with file cards. Put just one idea on each card and file them according to curriculum subject. This provides you with a quick reference guide when you need an on-the-spot idea in addition to giving you planning inspiration. Keeping the ideas filed electronically is excellent for long-term storage, but may not always work as quickly as needed in an on-the-spot situation.
2. If you are teaching reading, plan at least one movement activity for your next story. Children might dramatize the whole story. Or they could act out a new ending. Or you could ask them to demonstrate the feelings of individual characters at turns in the plot.
3. Observe children of different ages as they are involved in movement activities. What developmental differences do you see?
4. Choose a topic worthy of study that might evolve from movement activities. Write down possible ways that the subjects of art, math, reading, writing, social studies, and science might be integrated through the study of the topic.

## REFERENCES

Ayers, S. & Wilmoth, C. (2003). Integrating scientific subdisciplinary concepts into physical education. *Teaching Elementary Physical Education*, 14 (4), 10–12.

Block, M. & Davis, T. (1996). An activity-based approach to physical education for preschool children with disabilities. *Physical Activity Quarterly*, 13, 230–246.

Carlson, F. (2009). Rough and tumble play 101. *Exchange*, July/August, 70–73.

Carpenter, A. & Stevens-Smith, D. (2003). Locomotor skills skip to a new level. *Teaching Elementary Physical Education*, 14 (1), 37–39.

Castelli, D. (2005). Technology integration: Virtually possible. *Teaching Elementary Physical Education*, 16 (5), 6–7.

CDC. (2013). *Childhood obesity rates*. Retrieved from www.cdc.gov/obesity/data/index/html.

Consortium of National Arts Education Association. (1994). *National standards for arts education: What every young American should know and be able to do in the arts*. Reston, VA: Music Educators National Conference.

Copple, C. & Bredekamp, S. (2009). *Developmentally appropriate practice in early childhood programs serving children from birth through age 8*. Washington, DC: NAEYC.

Corbin, C. & Pangrazi, R. (2004). *Physical activity for children: A statement of guidelines for children ages 5–12*. Reston, VA: National Association for Sport and Physical Education.

Gabbard, C. (1995). P. E. for preschoolers: The right way. *Principal*, May, 21–24.

Gallahue, D. & Donnelly, F. (2003). *Developmental physical education for all children.* Champaign, IL: Human Kinetics.

Holt/Hale, S. & Parker, M. (2000). *Appropriate practices for elementary school physical education.* Reston, VA: National Association for Sport and Physical Education.

Huettig, C., Simbeck, C., & Cravens, S. (2003). Addressing fears associated with teaching ALL our children. *Teaching Elementary Physical Education,* 14 (3), 7–12.

Kalyn, B. (2005). Integration. *Teaching Elementary Physical Education,* 16 (5), 31–36.

Kirchner, G. (1978). *Introduction to movement education.* Dubuque, IA: W.C. Brown.

Kun, P. (2005). *NASPE releases first ever physical activity guidelines for infants & toddlers.* Retrieved from www.aahperd.org/naspe/template.cfm?template=toddlers.html.

Mears, B. (2003). The ABCs of effective reading integration. *Teaching Elementary Physical Education,* 14 (5), 36–39.

National Association for Sport & Physical Education. (1995). *Moving into the future: National physical education standards: A guide to content and assessment.* Boston, MA: McGraw-Hill.

Piaget, J. (1965/1932). *The moral judgment of the child.* New York, NY: The Free Press.

Pretti-Frontczak, K. & Bricker, D. (2004). *An activity-based approach to early intervention.* Baltimore, MD: Brookes.

Rampmeyer, K. (2000). *Appropriate practices in movement programs for young children ages 3–5.* Reston, VA: National Association for Sport and Physical Education.

Rovegno, I. (2003). Children's literature and dance. *Teaching Elementary Physical Education,* 14 (4), 24–29.

Sanders, S. (2005). *The issues: Physically active for life.* Retrieved from www.pbs.org/teachersource/prek2/issues/703issue.shtm.

Shephard, R. (1982). *Physical activity and growth.* Chicago, IL: Year Book Medical Publishers.

# Part Three
## Concluding Thoughts

For this final part, we ask you to think with us about the philosophical underpinnings of a book that is subtitled "inquiry learning through integration."

We have chosen three themes to focus on, all of them related to fostering the development of young children with a view to their future lives as citizens in a rapidly changing world. *Tolerance* is more than just enduring, or putting up with, those who are different. It includes having a fair and objective attitude toward, as well as a goal of understanding, those whose opinions, practices, race, ethnicity, nationality, religious beliefs, and so on are unlike those in our own experience. *Social justice* follows naturally and logically from an attitude of tolerance. It enters our lives as a concept when, as preschoolers, we begin

to worry about what is fair and not fair in our lives as students. It continues and expands in our adult lives when the news bombards us with social issues or we experience them in our own lives. *Sustainability* has been a critical issue for our world's survival for a long time but has only come to mainstream consciousness in recent years. Now we realize the very health and survival of our planet are at stake. It is the young children we teach who will ultimately be responsible for the world's survival, and so we must address sustainability issues now.

Part Three consists of just one chapter, but we hope that it is one to which you will devote much thought. Tolerance, social justice, and sustainability are not subjects for any current high stakes test, but the stakes related to our achievement of them could not be higher. For us, these are the prime reasons for advocating that young children be taught in ways that will prepare them for the world they are inheriting.

# 13

## THE "WHY" OF INQUIRY LEARNING
## AND CURRICULUM INTEGRATION

*"And what is as important as knowledge?" asked the mind.*
*"Caring and seeing with the heart," answered the soul.*
—*Flavia Weedn*

*The highest result of education is tolerance.*
—*Helen Keller*

Why take time to build on the curiosity of young learners? Why teach children how to seek answers to their questions? Why bother to look for ways to integrate the curriculum in meaningful and relevant fashion? Why go to great lengths to enable young learners to work cooperatively, self-direct, and self-manage? Why encourage students to become independent and interdependent thinkers and doers? These questions may remind one of the seemingly incessant "why?" questions which flow from the mouths of our youngest learners, but your authors have asked themselves these same questions. Therefore, this chapter serves to remind us "why."

### INTEGRATING TOLERANCE AND SOCIAL JUSTICE

It is certainly undeniable that acquisition of knowledge and application of skills are worthy and necessary goals of educational systems. Mindful teachers capitalize on transfer of knowledge, relevance of material being taught, and meaningful engagement in order to strengthen their students' dispositions to be eager and continual learners. The development of socially competent citizens is also a desired end product of educational systems. The seeds to be inquisitive, fruitful, responsible learners are planted in the minds of youngsters at an early age and grow through their childhood experiences. As is to be expected, the caliber of educational experiences either nourishes or stifles the growing seedlings. But there is more.

Other seeds equally important to, if not more important than, academic learning are planted in learners' minds in early childhood as well. These other seeds, depending on how they are planted and how they are cultivated, will grow to foster tolerance, social justice, and peace. However, lack of attention and negligent tending allow these seeds to develop as invasive weeds, which spread bigotry, injustice, and hatred.

The young learners of today are charged with an enormous responsibility. They will be future stewards of their community, their nation, and their world. Yes, competency in academic and social arenas is crucial, but first and foremost, teachers should be concerned with the *kind* of people their students are becoming. They should be concerned with the kind of adult citizens produced that will be using those early-attained academic and social skills. What is planted and nurtured in children's minds in their early educational experiences is significant indeed when educators are confronted with such critical questions as:

- Will our young learners grow up to be citizens who blindly follow group consensus, or will they cherish independent thought and critical thinking?
- Will they, as adults, have the skills necessary to listen to, as well as collaborate with, other autonomous and analytical thinkers?
- Will our young learners grow up to be empathic citizens who have the courage to speak out and use their gift of inquiry to seek, and continue to seek, answers to questions in order to discover cures for diseases and solutions to issues such as global warming and global peace?

Just as an inquiry-based, integrated curriculum helps to weave inquiry and observation through subjects, so too must education for tolerance and social justice be woven into the learning tapestry. Children must be urged to question injustices as they seek to learn more about themselves, their peers, and the world around them. Young learners must be taught and encouraged to be critical observers and empathic thinkers as they strive to make sense of their environment. Tolerance and social justice are integral to human rights, and it is the weaving of tolerance and social justice throughout all that transpires in the school setting that helps to prepare our young learners to assume their roles as passionate and compassionate citizens.

If children are to embrace and practice tolerance, then educators must model by example as well as teach their youthful charges what tolerance toward others looks like, sounds like, and feels like. In addition, teachers must reflect on any biases or stereotypes they, themselves, may have. Such reflection may illuminate the reasons why a certain child seems to "push the teacher's buttons" or is deemed difficult to teach. Teachers must not only examine their own biases, they must work to overcome them.

The ability to think deeply about issues such as tolerance and social justice, as well as the ability and courage to act on our beliefs, develops over time and reflects our stage of life as well as life experience and education. At this point, you might wish to return to Chapter 9 and review what Piaget (1932) had to say about heteronomous (other-directed) young children and how they gradually develop a sense of autonomy (self-direction). How well and how quickly children do this can be influenced by our approaches to teaching. If our classrooms are democratic with plenty of opportunities for inquiry learning, development toward autonomy should take place for each child at optimum pace. If, instead, we insist on using an authoritarian approach to our teaching methods and children's social interactions, this development will ordinarily be slowed, perhaps irreparably.

In the 1960s and 1970s, much research was done that validated and expanded on those studies of Piaget's that led to his theory about how autonomy develops. Both children and adults were study subjects and, from this research, not only was a better understanding of development reached, but a realization as well that inquiry learning and democratic environments could make an important difference (Damon, 1977; Hersh, Paolitto, & Reimer, 1979; Kohlberg, 1971; Krogh, 1981; Selman, 1980).

The studies from this time provided a rich and complex source of knowledge about development. Following is a brief summary of these studies' findings that should prove useful as you determine how best to foster the growth of your young learners and reflect on your own values.

## HOW THINKING ABOUT SOCIAL ISSUES DEVELOPS

### How Children in Preschool and Kindergarten Think

Heteronomous children, being other-directed, look to authority figures to guide them. They will turn first to adults, but can also be drawn to those who are simply bigger or somewhat older, or are perceived to be more physically attractive. When very young children are left alone, the authority figures no longer matter and they will do as they please, actually justifying any misbehavior on the basis of that absence.

Heteronomous children, being egocentric, view everything from their own point of view and believe that others share this view. A child may convince himself that it was okay to hit another child because the victim actually wanted to be hit. Another may believe that she doesn't need to share the toys she likes because she needs them and others just don't.

Because very young children are authority-oriented and egocentric does not in any way mean that they are defective small adults. It is true that for many centuries people believed this and punished accordingly, but the 20th century research provided new explanations. Teachers can certainly expect behavior that reflects tolerance and social justice, but their children's explanations for such behavior will be based on their own developmental understandings, not on adult value statements.

### How Children in Kindergarten and the Primary Grades Think

It is typically in kindergarten, or possibly just prior, that children become fixated on fairness. For many five year olds, fairness may be the single most important social issue of their school day. Everybody receiving exactly the same treatment or quantity of a treat is, for a period, the single definition of that fairness. Later, as maturity and experiences enrich their lives, children begin to understand that there are times when one person or group might be more deserving than another, perhaps because of need or meritorious behavior. Coupled with this new maturity is the first understanding of what rules are about, why they are necessary, and that it makes sense for children as well as authority figures to create and revise them. Youngsters can become as fixated by rules as by fairness. It is then that they turn to tattling, a situation that can be extremely trying for teachers, particularly when children are obviously more interested in others obeying rules than in their own behavior. Helping children understand the difference between self-interested tattling and reporting social injustices is an important task for teachers, and one that is generally successful only when the children have matured sufficiently to understand the difference on their own, or without much adult help.

As children enter first grade, they may still be focused on perfect balance as fairness and on the importance of others obeying the rules, or they may be taking the next step away from heteronomy and toward autonomy. This involves stepping into others' shoes and understanding that they may have different but legitimate ideas. Eventually, it can also include the understanding that others' ideas, if they incorporate intolerance or injustice, may well not be legitimate, even if held by authorities or other admired people. When children achieve this level of maturity, they are ready for class discussions about difficult issues and experiences. By third grade, most children can, with practice, generally be expected to understand tolerance and social justice as adults would understand them, although related, of course, to issues pertaining to their own interests.

### How Adults Think

It is important, first of all, that we have some patience with ourselves. Daily life gives us many opportunities to revert to the ways we thought in preschool or the primary grades, because we don't simply drop off our earlier ways of thinking but expand and improve upon them. Here is an example of what this means: It is very adult thinking to suggest that you follow the speed limit because it is for the safety of the others in your car and of those on the road around you. It is much more childishly egocentric and authority-oriented to do so simply because you know where the patrol car will be hiding. Yet, both kinds of reasoning are understandable and familiar to us.

When it comes to such values as tolerance and social justice, we may understand them in a mature way, realizing that human beings deserve such treatment. Yet, there may be other times when we simply wish to avoid censure for being politically incorrect. It is our work as adults to help ourselves grow out of the latter point of view and understand, and act upon, the former. And it is our work as teachers to help young children do the same. Heteronomous children may not understand the phrase *political correctness*, but they certainly get the concept when they behave well to please the teacher, while having little understanding of a philosophy of tolerance or social justice. When teachers create classroom environments that incorporate democratic elements, expectations of fair treatment for all, and self-management coupled with care for others, young children will respond first to the pleasantness of such an environment and eventually begin to understand *why* it feels so right. Then their progress will truly have been fostered by the actions and attitudes of their teachers. The next two sections provide qualities and behaviors you might expect to observe, or that are worthy of achieving, on the road to true tolerance and social justice.

## TOLERANCE

Tolerance must be visible. The following descriptions of the attributes of tolerance are appropriate goals for young children, achievable as they develop the capacity and understanding for them:

### Open-Mindedness
- Children look beyond social, economical, and cultural differences, focusing instead on positive similarities.
- Young learners know the dangers of stereotyping and the benefits of not having preconceived biases.
- New ideas generated by children, as well as adults, are encouraged.

- Children are shown how to observe and take action from points of view other than their own.
- Students all feel seen, heard, and valued by their school peers as well as by their teachers.
- Youngsters are secure in their own identity, which allows them to be better equipped to reach out to others with different cultural and social identities.
- Opportunities are provided for children to genuinely get to know each other as they work and play.
- Newcomers to the class feel welcome and quickly establish a sense of belonging.
- The teacher reaches out warmly and sincerely to every child in the learning environment, from the greeting each child receives upon entering the room to the goodbye at the end of the day.

### Respect for All People Regardless of Their Abilities, Beliefs, Culture, Race, Socioeconomic Level, or Gender

- The learning setting's physical environment is adapted, as needed, to facilitate learning and social interaction for all members of the class.
- Visuals, including reading materials and learning activities, depict different races and cultures, physically challenged individuals, and a variety of family models.
- There is a variety of multicultural toys, materials, and activities.
- Activities and materials are not gender specific nor are emotions stereotyped as being male or female. Examples of inappropriateness include: "Girls don't play with trucks." "Boys don't cry."
- Children's curiosity about race and ethnicity, physical differences, and proclivities is encouraged and having a diverse variety of people in the world is cause for rejoicing.
- Put-downs are not tolerated. There is an awareness of inadvertent put-downs such as: "This is easy so you can do it in no time." "Surely, you all know this story."
- Children, as well as teachers, fight against the "just like me" bias—the tendency to favor those who are similar to us.

### Listening to and Seeking Understanding of Others' Opinions

- The conviction is reinforced that everyone has valid and worthy opinions, and that opinions are needed in a democratically inspired classroom.
- Children are encouraged to share ideas in spoken, written, and pictorial forms.
- Time is provided for all students to be heard.
- Patience and guidance are provided as young learners strive to make themselves understood by others. After sharing an experience or idea, a child is encouraged to ask his or her peers: "Any questions or comments?" (The teacher is always ready to pose a question, should no one else be so inclined.)
- Ample time is provided for children to plan and work together on small and large group projects.

### Courage to Speak Out Against Hate and Injustice

- Adults respond immediately to any disrespect, degrading language, or incivility in the learning setting.
- A clear message is sent by the teacher stating, "I will not allow ridicule in our classroom."

- Children feel safe to question what they see or hear if it seems unjust.
- Learners feel empowered to speak up if they feel they, or their classmates, have been targets of an injustice. The difference between this and tattling is part of the learning process.
- Peaceful means for resolving disagreements and conflicts are taught and practiced.
- Students know how to separate an undesirable deed or behavior from the doer, "I like you. I don't like what you did (are doing)."
- Young learners feel confident that they can and will make a positive difference.

## SOCIAL JUSTICE

Tolerance will survive and thrive in environments that support and apply social justice. Young learners will eventually grow to be cognizant of fairness and equality and act appropriately. If we want our children to venerate social justice then we must make it a practice in our centers and classrooms.

As educators, it is not enough just to espouse the principles of social justice. These principles must be consciously taught and reinforced. The classroom should be a model of participatory democracy, established with the knowledge that the teacher has done, and will continue to do, all in his or her power to ensure that all participants are safe and empowered to make their voices heard. This is the secure, nonjudgmental groundwork that must be laid before young investigators can voice their queries and collaborate with peers to seek answers using integrated knowledge.

If children are to support and promote social justice and democratic principles, they must be afforded avenues and opportunities in the school setting to learn, practice, and be committed to the responsibility of such principles. Young learners must have opportunities to make choices, pose questions, seek answers, and be accountable. Social justice and democracy must become a part of everyday classroom life.

Principles of social justice and participatory democracy are evident in learning environments that teach and expect children to care for and respect themselves, each other, their classroom and school, their community, and their world. Evidence of ways in which young children learn to put social justice principles into practice include:

For *themselves*, children will:
- Become responsible for their own words and actions as well as their personal being and belongings;
- Take time to deliberate on their words and actions;
- Make and fulfill academic and social choices;
- Have courage to speak up and take a stand;
- Be morally responsible even when someone is not watching;
- Understand they are an integral part of their learning community.

For *each other*, children will:
- Understand the need to take turns and comprehend why one doesn't always get his or her way;
- Value collaboration to solve problems;
- Cooperate rather than compete;
- Work harmoniously and encourage success for all;

- Know each can count on the other to offer help when needed;
- Demonstrate compassion.

For *their classroom and school*, children will:
- Determine rules together and work to abide by the rules;
- Assume responsibility to help the classroom run democratically;
- Be stewards of the learning environments.

For *their community and world*, children will:
- Develop behaviors to help safeguard our natural resources and promote sustainability;
- Participate in environmentally friendly practices such as recycling, re-using, reclaiming, and nonlittering;
- Value research, experimentation, and observation.

The principles of social justice reach out to embrace environmental justice as well. If young learners are going to be charged, when they get older, with the care of their community and be held responsible for their impact on the world, then conscious thought must be given as to how they can be prepared in their younger years for that weighty task. Children are not too young to notice the effort, or the lack of effort, that adults give toward the care and sustainability of the environment. The future generation of world caretakers needs to be shown how to develop behaviors that help to safeguard natural resources and promote sustainability.

## DEMONSTRATING SUSTAINABILITY

When children form a connectedness with their environment, whether it be walking through the woods in a nearby park, observing water burbling in a stream, listening to the birds chirping in the distance, or using a magnifying glass to scrutinize a bug, they begin to develop an appreciation of and respect for the beauty of the world and the marvels it contains. Positive, hands-on interactions with nature such as climbing a tree, digging a hole, feeding the birds, or planting a garden, further present nature as a source of wonder and awe, worthy of being sustained. Walks and experiences in the out-of-doors, however, may also show youngsters the negative impact that people, both big and small, have on the environment as children observe signs of litter, pollution, and waste. It is through such experiences, good and bad, that youngsters cultivate a need to protect and take care of their environment.

Although younger children may not be old enough yet to understand why concern and care for the environment are important, they are old enough to begin forming habits that are environmentally healthy. Environmentally conscious adults can comment, when children see litter, human-damaged flora and fauna, or unwise uses of the environment, that such careless acts are not healthy for the earth or the living things in it.

Demonstrations of respect toward nature, care of the environment, and practices of sustainability are much more effective than just dialogue around such issues. Even young learners can become aware of environmentally friendly actions, actions that include their participation, when they follow the modeling of adults and are encouraged to:

- Turn lights off when they aren't needed;
- Be aware of using only the water necessary to perform tasks;

- Put litter in appropriate containers;
- Recycle materials such as newsprint, metal, plastic, glass;
- Reclaim and reuse materials to make new, imaginative creations;
- Take care of toys and other belongings, and when possible, allow items to be repaired rather than throwing them away to be replaced with new ones;
- Reuse toys by trading them with other children.

The modeling and teaching that young learners receive concerning sustainability will help them prepare for the best possible future as they make conscious decisions about caring for the environment and conserving nature's resources. Children must be taught, through action, that sustainability is a key element in relationships with nature, just as sustainability is a valuable component in relationships with each other.

## IT TAKES TIME

Just as the use of inquiry and integration to enable children to grasp relevance in learning takes time, so does it also take time to address moments of intolerance and social injustice and to guide youngsters to develop healthy habits of sustainability.

It takes time to discuss an unfairness that happened at recess time, or to interrupt a lesson because an incivility needed attending to. It takes time to teach young learners how to be self-directive. Some teachers lament that teaching principles of tolerance and social justice takes time away from their academic responsibilities. Some educators also complain that they don't have time to listen to and weave young learners' questions and observations into the curriculum. In a world filled with threats of environmental devastation and global violence, learning to be conscientious citizens who will build caring, sustainable communities should not be considered a waste of time.

If educators have opened young learners' minds to gain knowledge through inquiry and curiosity; have allowed children to apply their understandings in meaningful, productive, and relevant ways; and have reinforced the need to work and play cooperatively, compassionately, and tolerantly, then educators have given students a most cherished gift indeed.

The creation, presentation, and unwrapping of this gift takes time. It also takes effort and devotion on the part of the teacher to help develop citizens who possess intelligence, tolerance, and integrity. As Aristotle said, "The habits we form from childhood make no small difference, but rather they make all the difference."

## TO DISCUSS AND TO DO: PERPETUAL QUESTIONS

In previous chapters, we have included topics for class discussion as well as topics on which to take action, and it is appropriate that the topics offered in this chapter be used for those purposes as well. However, as a befitting culmination to a textbook in which inquiry and integration are revered, your authors pose two questions worthy of pondering, with that pondering calling for action as well. We have great hopes that you will not deliberate and act on these questions only for a class period, or merely for a few hours, days, or months. These parting two questions deserve a lifetime of contemplation and discourse with the perpetual goal of attentive and knowledgeable action. Please remember Mahatma Gandhi's words—"You must be the change you want to see in the world"—as you address the following.

1. In addition to basic academic skills, what do we want our children to learn, not only to survive but also to thrive in the world?
2. What do we want our children to learn to help the world not only survive, but also to thrive?

## REFERENCES

Damon, W. (1977). *The social world of the child.* San Francisco, CA: Jossey-Bass.

Hersh, R., Paolitto, D., & Reimer, J. (1979). *Promoting moral growth: From Piaget to Kohlberg.* New York, NY: Longman.

Kohlberg, L. (1971). Stages of moral development as a basis for moral education. In Beck, C., Crittenden, B., & Sullivan, E. (Eds.), *Moral education.* New York, NY: Newman Press.

Krogh, S. (1981). Moral beginnings: The just community in Montessori preschools. *Journal of Moral Education,* 11 (1), 41–46.

Piaget, J. (1965/1932). *The moral judgment of the child.* New York, NY: The Free Press.

Selman, R. (1980). *The growth of interpersonal understanding: Developmental and clinical analyses.* New York, NY: Academic Press.

# INDEX